Oracle:
A Database
Developer's Guide

2ND EDITION

ISBN 0-13-841420-3

9 780138 414207

90000

Oracle:
A Database
Developer's Guide

2ND EDITION

Ulka Rodgers

YOURDON PRESS
Prentice Hall Building
Upper Saddle River, NJ 07458
www.phptr.com

Editorial/production supervision: *Kathleen M. Caren*
Cover design director: *Jerry Votta*
Cover designer: *DesignSource*
Manufacturing manager: *Alexis R. Heydt*
Marketing manager: *Dan Rush*
Acquisitions editor: *Jeffrey M. Pepper*
Editorial assistants: *Bart Blanken, Linda Ramagnano*

©1999 by Prentice Hall PTR
Prentice-Hall, Inc.
A Simon & Schuster Company
Upper Saddle River, NJ 07458

Prentice Hall books are widely used by corporations and government agencies
for training, marketing, and resale.

The publisher offers discounts on this book when ordered in bulk quantities.
For more information, contact: Corporate Sales Department, Phone: 800-382-3419;
Fax: 201-236-7141; E-mail: corpsales@prenhall.com; or write: Prentice Hall PTR,
Corp. Sales Dept., One Lake Street, Upper Saddle River, NJ 07458.

Printed in the United States of America
10 9 8 7 6 5 4 3 2

ISBN   0-13-841420-3

Prentice-Hall International (UK) Limited, *London*
Prentice-Hall of Australia Pty. Limited, *Sydney*
Prentice-Hall Canada Inc., *Toronto*
Prentice-Hall Hispanoamericana, S.A., *Mexico*
Prentice-Hall of India Private Limited, *New Delhi*
Prentice-Hall of Japan, Inc., *Tokyo*
Simon & Schuster Asia Pte. Ltd., *Singapore*
Editora Prentice-Hall do Brasil, Ltda., *Rio de Janeiro*

Table of Contents

Preface

This book was originally published in 1991. The preface then suggested that you should not believe in the sales hype about relational technology. Today, the sales hype is about objects and the Internet technology. Do you still believe the latest sales hype that this technology will solve your application problems? If you do, or have learned differently from experience, then this book is for you. Development tools are still oversold in the effect they will have on application backlogs. The pace of technology—and the ever increasing sophisticated demands of users—has just one net effect: frustrated information systems managers, overworked programmers, and disappointed end users. This book is about the right way to develop quality applications regardless of the changes in technology.

There are many reasons why the sales hype does not pan out in practice. It only describes the achievements of organizations that already have significant expertise in using the tools and techniques. If you are just beginning, you have to master the initial learning curve before you are able to accomplish similar results. You also need to establish an environment that nurtures quality development practices. We will discuss how the organization's maturity affects the development practices and what you can do improve it.

As a consultant, I help many organizations manage their systems development efforts: from strategic planning, application requirements definition, development and implementation. This book discusses many of my experiences—you are likely to face similar challenges. The topics should be of interest to

- **Information officers**, who are looking for tools and techniques for effective information planning.

- **Managers**, who need techniques to manage user expectations throughout the development effort on the one hand and on the other hand they must improve the quality of systems developed.

- **Analysts and designers**, who face the challenges of enterprise wide systems and require tools and techniques to support their activities.

- **Developers**, who need tips on using Oracle's fourth-generation tools.

- **End users**, who need to be involved in the development effort.

Oracle's products cover the gamut of database and related technologies. It has products that support all phases of software development in addition to its core database management product. Its analysis and design tools support many techniques using object modeling, entity-relationship models, function hierarchies and process flow models. The tools then proceed to support code generation for systems derived from these models. This book provides the methodology you need to make effectively use these tools to develop maintainable systems. This book is organized into four parts:

Part 1: Managing the Implementation

This part covers management issues such as the skills you need to foster in your organization, and how to rise above the fire-fighting chaos prevalent in many IT organizations. We cover techniques for gathering requirements for supporting the business and how the Oracle Oracle Designer tools support these models. We discuss project approaches—RAD or waterfall, and the conditions under which they are appropriate.

Part 2: Designing Oracle Applications

This section takes you through the transformation from business orientated models to systems oriented models. We describe the challenges of this transformation and the compromises that might be needed during the process. We also discuss peripheral issues such as database administration and how the development and production environments differ. Our design addresses both the development and target production environments. We also define the architectural issues involved in designing for roaming, Internet-based, and data warehouse environments.

Part 3: Developing Oracle Applications

This part is the nitty gritty issues of developing in the database environment. We explore some of the features of Oracle's GUI tools. We also discuss how the Oracle Designer generators make use of these features when generating code. This section is aimed at the development of serious operational systems.

Part 4: Data Warehouse, Distributed Systems, and the World Wide Web

These technologies are part of the normal environment, although not yet common for our daily operational systems. We discuss how to model and manage historical data in a data warehouse. In particular we describe how to address the challenges of consolidating data from disparate legacy systems. There are many issues raised by the need to support global operations with multiple physical systems locations. We address these in the distributed systems issues and the use of the world wide web environments.

I have learned a lot since the first publishing of this book. The funny thing is that I have not *unlearned* anything. I have incorporated many of the techniques I have learned into this book. Also included are some related approaches from the respected leaders of our industry that complement the methods outlined here. They help put the various models in context. They also help you understand the level of success you can expect based on the capabilities and maturity of your own organization.

This book includes tips and techniques I gained on a variety of projects. Although too many to identify individually, I am grateful to the initiator of each of those projects for the opportunities to practice my ideas and theories. I am also grateful to the many people involved in hours of discussions on the pros and cons of alternative approaches. Thank you, friends and colleagues.

My particular thanks go to my partner in life and business, Paul. The tremendous effort involved in writing this book would not have been possible without his playing Mr. Mom on weekends. Writing technical matter while reciting Dr. Seuss stories to my daughters is a whole another experience—probably one not to be repeated.

Finally, thanks to the publishers and staff at Prentice-Hall, in particular, Jeffrey Pepper and Kathleen Caren for jump-starting my stalled project. Thanks also to the production staff. This book would not be possible without their efforts.

Introduction

Oracle was founded in 1978 as a relational DBMS (database management system) vendor. The company has its headquarters in Redwood Shores, California, in the United States of America Oracle products run on most hardware platforms. In fact, portability of the products, and applications developed with them, is one of the main reasons for their popularity.

Although its core product is a DBMS, the company has a diversified product line including software engineering tools, packaged applications such as financials, manufacturing, and human resources-based on the DBMS, and services such as systems integration. Its products support the latest technologies such as multimedia, object database management, and network computers. Its stated objective is to be a global solutions vendor in the twenty-first century.

In this chapter, we examine the issues faced by the information industry and how Oracle's products address them. These issues include building applications faster, the increasing sophistication of users' demands, and improved understanding of the role of information systems. We introduce issues of managing application development, the primary focus of this book. In particular, this chapter covers the following:

- Buzzwords like "productivity" and "application backlogs" are common. What are the real issues that raise these discussions?

- Technological silver bullets promise to solve many of these difficulties. But, can they deliver on their promise?

- What makes an application successful? Does using the latest development technology really suffice?

- Where do Oracle's offerings fit in these myriad promises?

1.1 The Productivity Challenge

Computers have come a long way from their number-crunching predecessors. Today, we use computers to store and manage information, not just perform calculations faster. Information may be text, numbers, graphics, video, sound, and in fact, anything that can be transformed into a digital storage form.

Our management information systems (MIS) departments have kept pace with such advances. Information systems today manage not only the company's numerical financial data, but also textual market and technical research data; they track prospects and clients; and they even send anniversary cards to employees. These systems support national and international exchange of this information—not as printed paper reports, but electronically over networks and phone lines.

Technology advances have changed the expectations of those people who already use computers in their daily work and new users who now can use them for the first time. New technology leads these people, the clients of MIS departments, to ask for applications to support their job functions in new and different ways. Their requests are fast and frequent—and getting faster. Unfortunately, MIS groups have limited resources. These resources may be hardware, software, or development staff. Lead times to acquire new resources are, relatively speaking, long. The hardest to acquire are experienced development staff who can understand and use new technology.

In the meantime, applications already developed do not stand still. Changing business needs require changes to these applications—and, of course, staff to make these changes. The volume of existing applications is directly proportional to this maintenance effort. And you cannot ignore it—these applications are the life and blood of your business. They form a large proportion of the predictable, and therefore budgeted, work effort of today's MIS departments.

Just to keep life interesting, technology changes too while all of these other activities are going on. The advent of the World Wide Web has radically changed the business environment. To remain competitive, businesses must provide services via the Internet and an intranet. Hardware manufacturers release new products, which means your applications have to be converted to work on the new machines. Software manufacturers, not to be outdone, also release new versions of their products. Of course, your applications must change to take advantage of the new and wonderful features offered by these new versions. This vicious cycle is illustrated in Figure 1-1. All in all, it is difficult to see how MIS departments ever find time to work on new applications.

So, requests for new applications pile up—euphemistically called *application backlogs*. The relative cost of development staff to the cost of hardware and software is far higher than in the early days of data processing. The only way out of this cycle is to get the same number of staff to do more work. MIS departments look for ways to improve the amount of work each staff member can do, that is, to improve their productivity.

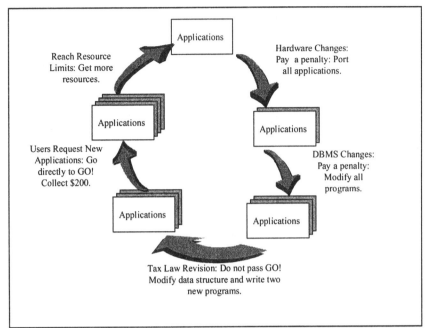

Figure 1-1: The MIS Dilemma

There are three areas where we could improve development productivity: by developing new applications faster than is possible with traditional programming tools, by reducing the effort required to incorporate changes in existing applications, and by reducing the effort required to administer applications in production. These are the three areas addressed by modern development techniques.

1.2 Another Silver Bullet?!

Each new technology heralds the end of application backlogs. In the 1970's, structured programming methodologies claimed to improve programmer productivity—and they did. In the 1980's, relational DBMS's together with their fourth-generation development tools, claimed to improve the productivity of your development staff—and they did. In the 1990's, client-server and object-oriented technologies claimed more improvements—only to be overshadowed by the Internet/intranet interfaces of the 2000s. No doubt, they have many success stories to recount. You may have some bitter experiences to relate. However, you also may have had some successes. Let us examine the contexts in which you can expect success and poor results.

First, you cannot move all of your applications to use a new environment overnight. In fact, you probably don't use RDBMSs yet for all your applications. The typical approach to introducing a new technology is to develop a few new applications. GUI tools supplied with DBMS products allow you to prototype user requirements in fairly short order and then turn them into production systems. Thus, you shorten the time

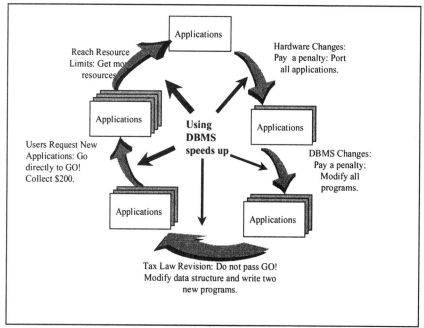

Figure 1-2: Tools Impact on MIS

from receiving a user request to delivering an application into production. You also require fewer developers to complete the implementation.

Unfortunately, client-server DBMSs and their GUI tools require rather more machine resources than do their finely tuned terminal-oriented and third-generation counterparts. Client workstations run out of resources quickly and you usually have to upgrade client hardware earlier than anticipated. Thus, the cost of running your applications in production increases significantly. This cost overshadows the success of producing the requested application in a timely manner.

Applications developed using GUI tools require a little less effort to enhance than do their third-generation counterparts. Thus, you shorten the time-frame to modify programs and changes in business requirements have less impact on your ability to change applications. However, you do not realize this benefit until much later in the life of an application. By that time, the productivity improvement is an accepted part of development. Changes to the data structures, however, are a different story. GUI tools offer no help in modifying the underlying data structures. Instead, changes to data structures often mean more extensive changes to the code.

Object-oriented methods promise to isolate the impact of structural changes to a few objects. Since each object is made up of data structures *and* methods for manipulating the data, structural changes can be hidden from the major portion of the application. Thus, it should be easy to identify the objects responsible for the data and modify them without affecting other objects. In practice, achieving this level of isolation requires tremendous architectural skill in designing the objects. Objects can be reused

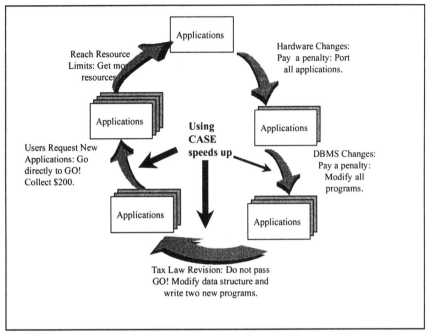

Figure 1-3: CASE Impact on MIS

in further development—another means of improving productivity. However, to achieve effective reusability of objects requires engineering of more than one or two applications. You may only realize the benefits of reusability after several development projects.

When you upgrade hardware, older applications still require a significant effort to port to the new environment. In addition, you might have to delay installing the new hardware until your DBMS vendor makes their products available on the new hardware. So, if you have already reached the limits of your hardware, you will have to delay upgrades even longer. Figure 1-2 illustrates the proportion of impact that a DBMS and object-oriented development may have on the MIS cycle.

If you use a highly portable DBMS product, the changes to your programs due to hardware changes are few. DBMS products usually buffer you from hardware-specific dependencies. Thus, the effort required to change hardware is smaller, even if you have to delay installation of the new hardware. The total time-frame is probably shorter than if you were converting third-generation language programs and file structures.

New technology and fancy tools do not make you immune from poor design of data and applications. They merely shorten the time for implementing an application, whether well-designed or not. Thus, an application built in a short time-frame can still fail to meet user expectations—leading to a bitter implementation experience. In the next section, we examine the criteria that make for a successful application.

Changes in business requirements can require significant redesign of database structures. These changes have a cascading effect on your programs, whether or not developed using client-server GUI tools. Although a DBMS allows you to make changes to data structures more easily, it does not protect your programs from the effects of poor database design. The impact of poor design is the same whether you use relational or object DBMSs. Technology is no silver bullet against poor analysis. This scenario is where computer-aided software engineering (CASE) tools claim to improve productivity.

The methodical and rigorous regime imposed by CASE tools and associated methodologies helps you to identify areas prone to changes. However, considerable talent is necessary to identify such areas clearly. Drawing diagrams using CASE tools does not magically highlight them. The correct use of CASE is to help your talented analysts discover potential changes prior to their occurrence. Figure 1-3 illustrates the areas of the development cycle impacted by the use of CASE.

Thus, CASE tools used by talented and experienced staff are invaluable aids to designing flexible data structures and applications. Object or relational DBMSs provide scant help in this area. Even the models developed with CASE tools may not suffice in handling massive reengineering caused by mergers and acquisitions, although they will provide significant groundwork.

1.3 Successful Information Systems

Experience shows that a well-developed application is not sufficient for success. There are many other factors that make your applications successful. One of the primary factors is understanding the role of the application in achieving business objectives. Another factor is gaining users as champions of the application rather than passively accepting your offering.

This area has been largely ignored until recent years. Development methodologies and CASE tools help in addressing some of these areas. Realize, though, that these techniques merely aid you in discovering the requirements—their use does not guarantee an understanding of users' requirements. The characteristics of successful applications are

- They are driven by end users, not just accepted by them. The difference between these two scenarios is one of subtle perception. User-driven does not mean that users dictate the entire design including the technical trade-offs that need to be determined throughout. Instead, they believe that it is their application— not one forced on them by MIS. In other words, they have taken ownership of the application. Experienced analysts can subtly direct users to make suitable choices in the design, rather than dictating these choices.

- They are sponsored by managers with responsibility for meeting business objectives, not dictated by MIS staff. This is another facet of users taking ownership of an application. Although MIS staff may proactively suggest applications which help support a business function, the business managers must be responsible for initiating their development. Typically, this scenario also means funding the application. After all, is there a better way of making managers responsible for an application's success than to put their money where their mouths are?

- They support the achievement of business plans and objectives. A terrific application which is easy to use and developed with the latest and greatest technology will not be successful if it does not support a genuine need. For example, a market research database for a company that manufactures only space shuttle parts is useless.

- They are flexible enough to require minimum changes as the business needs change. This is usually due to a good design which implements more than a specific solution to a specific need. The analysts must anticipate the types of changes likely over a period of time and mold the application so that they are adaptable to these changes.

- They are actually used by their target users—not just shelved as an interesting experiment in development. In fact, successful applications are those which clearly meet users' expectations and serve their needs.

Notice that most of the characteristics of successful applications revolve around user perceptions and expectations. This is a hard lesson to learn when developing applications. Whiz-bang features and elegant coding might make a good application, but not necessarily a successful one.

This area is where CASE methodologies and tools assist the MIS staff. They provide direction in how to guide user expectations such that they closely match the application direction. In addition, they provide techniques which help analysts understand what the user needs, as opposed to what they ask for. The effect of clear communication with users and clear expectations helps make an application successful. A good understanding of actual user needs improves productivity in application development by eliminating false starts and misunderstanding.

1.4 Where Does Oracle Fit?

Oracle seems to have recognized that a DBMS is not sufficient. Although, the DBMS is Oracle's core product, the product line has diversified into related GUI and multimedia tools, CASE tools, OLAP tools, Object-oriented development tools, World Wide Web application tools, and off-the-shelf application packages. Figure 1-4 illustrates some of the core products. These products usually require the DBMS as the base. Off-the-shelf packages include products for financial accounting, managing human resources, manufacturing, project tracking, and so on. These products use Oracle as the DBMS and other tools for their application interface.

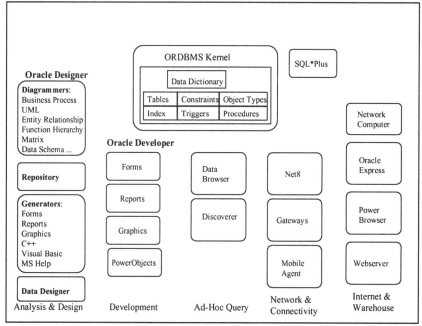

Figure 1-4: Some Oracle Tools

1.4.1 Development Tools

This set consists of GUI utilities grouped under the name Oracle Developer, which is used for building complex business applications. This set consists of Oracle Forms for building interactive forms-based programs, Oracle Reports for reports, and Oracle Graphics for business-oriented graphical presentation of data. In addition, an integral part of the database is SQL*Plus, an extended implementation of the standard SQL language for querying the database, and PL/SQL which contains procedural extensions for batch processing. PL/SQL is also used for programming complex business rules into the Oracle Developer components.

1.4.2 CASE Tools

This set is grouped under the name Oracle Designer. Its components encompass utilities to support development from analysis through implementation. Central to this set is a repository which contains meta data about your applications. All Oracle Designer components share a common repository. The analysis components consist of diagramming tools for developing business process diagrams, object diagrams in UML notation, entity relationship diagrams, function hierarchy diagrams, and data flow diagrams. To transition from analysis to design, there are two wizards: one to transform the logical entity relationship definition or object type model into a physical Oracle schema, and another to transform logical functions into implementation modules. The detail design environment, called the Design Editor, consists of a data schema diagram, module data diagram, module network diagram, and a logic editor.

Implementation utilities included in the Design Editor consist of a number of code generators. The server generator generates SQL for database objects and also for stored procedures and triggers. The code generators include a Oracle Forms program generator, Oracle Reports program generator, a Visual Basic code generator, and a Webserver PL/SQL generator for execution by the Oracle Webserver product to dynamically create HTML page definitions. The MS Help generator generates files for use by the Microsoft Windows help system.

1.4.3 Ad-Hoc Query Tools

This set consists of tools that are so-called end user tools: Data Browser and Discoverer/2000 to name two. Your users still need to understand the structure of the data in the database before they can effectively use these tools in their work. These tools let you visually select the tables and columns to include in a report. They provide a query by example interface to permit the specification of query criteria. They can also use database constraint definitions to automatically determine how to join tables. However, the user still needs to know which tables to choose to get the data they want. Meaningful table and column names help—but, fully normalized databases are not always easy to navigate for novice users. You can use database facilities like *views* to present more intuitive data structures. Keep this in mind—definition of these views is as much a part of your database design and development process as programming forms.

Some people might suggest letting users use SQL. I still do not believe that SQL is suitable language for end users who have little technical background, and even less knowledge of the data structures of their database.

1.4.4 Warehouse and Data Mart Tools

This set contains Oracle Express, a tool integrated with the Oracle DBMS product after its acquisition. Express is a multi-dimensional database with associated data loading tools. You can load summarized and aggregated data into the Express data server or keep it in the Oracle database instance. The Express product contains a meta data repository that defines the source and transformation of the data.

Oracle also provides a Data Mart suite of products. This is really a set of Oracle products packaged together to provide the tools needed to develop and deploy a data mart. It contains portions of the designer repository, the database kernel, and query tools. Over time, other useful products may be added to this suite.

1.4.5 Object-Oriented Development Tools

This set contains Oracle PowerObjects which is a GUI point-and-click interface for developing object-oriented applications. The Oracle Developer toolset also provides object-oriented programming facilities such as the ability to define classes of objects, subclasses, and inheritance. These tools work with the relational and object-oriented facilities of Oracle8. We will discuss many of these database features and development tools later.

1.4.6 Internet Tools

This set includes Oracle's Webserver product with its support for data-centric applications written in PL/SQL, Java, and other common Web development languages. In addition, you can deploy Oracle's Oracle Developer-based applications on the web by using the *application server* product. This product executes the Oracle Developer forms executables in the server while the user interface portion is handled by a Java applet running in the client browser. This allows you to take advantage of the thin client used in the web environment without major redevelopment of your software.

1.4.7 Network and Connectivity Tools

This set is based on Net8. Previously known as SQL*Net, this product comes in many flavors, each appropriate to the underlying network protocol. For example, there is SQL*Net TCP/IP which is suitable for use on networks running this protocol, SQL*Net DECnet, SQL*Net SPX/IPX, and so on. You must already have the appropriate network protocol installed to use these products. Net8 is a necessary ingredient of client-server processing, with the front-end tools running on a machine different from the Oracle DBMS instance. It is also essential for implementing distributed databases, whether with snapshots or with replicated data.

Oracle also supports connections to non-Oracle databases. These tools are collectively called gateways, with different flavors for each of the other products supported. They allow you to share data and run Oracle applications against non-Oracle products. For example, there is a gateway for DB2. Oracle also supports ODBC access; so Oracle's development tools can transparently access any database that provides access via this de-facto standard interface. There are usually limitations-based on the capabilities of the other product, however.

1.5 Expectations and Infrastructure

Using Oracle tools does not mean you automatically develop successful applications. Only your methods for analyzing requirements and managing user expectations can achieve that. The user interface presented by most Oracle tools requires a lot of user training. You can control how much training is necessary by setting company standards and conforming to the style guides of your Windows interface. All of these standards imply significant developer training. So, be ready to persuade developers and users that faster delivery of applications is worth a little extra training time.

This book focuses primarily on the tools useful for application development, from strategic planning of information systems through implementation of finished applications. I add tips from my own experience on related issues like management.

This book addresses the growing areas of data warehouses and Internet and intranet applications in Part 4. Each of these areas has concerns different from those of typical operational applications. We will examine when these technologies are relevant to your business and how to make strategic plans to utilize them. In addition, we will discuss the in-depth details of implementing such applications in an Oracle environment.

This book also covers issues relating to developing distributed systems. This topic is of emerging interest as many organizations discover the power of small machines relative to their cost. We examine the differences between cooperative processing in a three-tier architecture versus distributed databases, with pros and cons of each. In addition, we examine the types of information analysts must gather to develop cooperative or distributed applications. In this context, we discuss Oracle facilities like snapshots, replication server, and their configuration in scenarios appropriate to the business.

Part

1

Managing Implementation

"We don't have time for a methodology! It takes too long and our backlogs are growing too fast."

"Since GUI client-server tools allow us to build applications very quickly, why do we need CASE tools? We can change the database and the programs as the users require."

"We will use object-oriented development on our projects and create reusable components or buy component libraries. Why do we need CASE tools?"

Is this your reaction too? Try answering the following questions before you dismiss this part of the book.

1. Do you find that users change their requirements frequently, sometimes even before you finish their first request?

2. Do you spend a lot of time gathering more detail from users on each of their requirements?

3. You have a user representative who knows the business to help with requirements definition. But when you implement the application, do many users complain that it does not do what they need?

If you answered "Yes" to any of these questions, you really ought to read the chapters in this part of the book. You may discover some of the root causes of your difficulties. If you have tried unsuccessfully to use methodologies, look again—development using GUI tools is different from traditional programming projects.

Management Strategies

Information is power in a business: information about your competition, your company's financial well-being, the demographics of your markets, the list goes on. A business can be wildly successful if IS adequately support the business strategies, regardless of the nature of the business. The IS (IS) group organizes such information and makes it accessible to the company. Successful IS support business strategies.

There are many client-server tools available, but they are only as good as the use to which they are put. Success requires a methodology that utilizes these tools to build useful systems. In this chapter, we discuss some of the key tools and techniques used in establishing an IS strategy. We will also introduce methodologies that combine object-oriented techniques and traditional analysis techniques, such as

- How to tie IS to business strategies to help make the business successful. Models are a key ingredient in this link. Information systems are a critical success factor of the new products and services for many companies.

- Roles and responsibilities which help you to gain management and user commitment and manage the quality of your IS. Setting clear tasks and deliverables for your staff and users helps manage the project.

- Budgetary issues, including some methods for justifying the cost of IS.

- A review of techniques, their deliverables, and their role in systems development using an extended Zachman Framework. This is a high-level review only intended for use by managers.

- Approaches for moving IS from their current environment to a new environment which uses Oracle's technology.

2.1 The Preparation

As we mentioned, information systems are successful only if they help a business become successful. So, we need to know what will make our business successful. These criteria are the realm of company managers: the chief executive officer, the chief operating officer or the president. Of course, I am not suggesting that you take the company officer's chair. However, you should maintain open channels of communication with them. They should communicate to you the directions of their business plan, short- and long-term. In turn, you should provide input to them on how IS present (or planned) make one strategy more feasible than another. One of your primary goals, as a manager of IS, is to establish an organization so that such communication becomes possible. Section 2.3 Roles and Responsibilities addresses organizational issues in more depth.

As an example, suppose your company plans to grow sales by 25% this year. To achieve this growth, management plans to penetrate a new market which was identified by the marketing department. A data warehouse that maintains customer purchasing history would be invaluable in researching the new market and extracting initial prospects.

Can you just ask about the company's business plan? Unless the company's officers also read this chapter, the answer is probably no—they will likely be alarmed about your understanding of your role. First, you need to educate them. You need to describe your plan to implement IS most suitable for the company. By the way, this education process is the first step in winning their commitment to your plans!

What should you include in your discussions with company officers? Here is a typical checklist:

- A definition of the business mission, that is, a statement of what service your company provides.
- A list of short-term and long-term business objectives. Examples of short-term business objectives are "To increase sales by 25% over the previous year" or "To reduce costs by 10% over previous year's costs". A long-term objective is "To become the largest supplier of widgets." You may even find some of the long-term objectives described in the company's annual report if your company is publicly traded.
- Critical success factors for the business to achieve these objectives. Critical success factors are conditions, events, or equipment without which an objective cannot be achieved. For example, a critical success factor to increase sales might be skilled sales staff.
- Priorities of these objectives from the view of the business. For example, increasing sales might have a higher priority than reducing costs for a start-up business.

- Projected value to the business of achieving these objectives, that is, the benefits expected whether in revenue increase, reputation enhancement, or some other improvement.

- A statement of the IS mission.

- A list of short-term and long-term IS objectives and how they correspond to the business objectives.

- An assessment of which of these objectives are satisfied by current systems.

- A road map of how you plan to convert, enhance, or build new systems to meet your objectives.

Seems like a chicken and egg situation, right? You need to know the business plan before formulating your IS plan. Yet you cannot quiz company officers about it. Here is one way around this dilemma. Build a draft plan-based on your understanding of your company. Use the draft as the basis of a meeting with the company officers to verify and correct it. Your plan is not cast in concrete, however! You will need to revise it frequently, at least as often as the company revises its business plan. Be sure to publish it: It is a roadmap for business management as well as your subordinates in the IS group.

If it is all so easy, why doesn't every IS manager do such planning? There are a few practical difficulties. In small companies, a well-defined business plan is a rarity. So, you need to help company management refine it. Such refinement can be difficult if your company managers do not like to pin down specific objectives with hard numbers. Your efforts at planning systems are key to revealing the need for them. A management consultant specializing in your particular industry might help develop such a plan.

Large corporations suffer from a different issue. The business plan, developed by high-level executives, is common in large corporations. However, the plan is diluted over many departments and divisions, each of which is responsible for a small portion of the objectives only. In many such corporations, IS executives are closely involved in the business planning process. If your company is one of these, you have a head start. In other companies, you may work with only one division or department of the corporation. In such a case, start with the highest executives at the department or division level. Typically, such executives report directly to the CEO or COO, or are one level removed from them. Your success at this level may change the company's view of how IS contribute to the business.

Here are a few more notes for your benefit. The last three items in the preceding list are easier said than done. Listing IS objectives is easy, but describing how they mesh with business objectives is hard! Refine this list through a lot of interaction with company officers. Remember to use a draft plan in your meetings with them. It keeps your meetings focused. Corrections to the draft are also a satisfying deliverable of your meeting.

Functions \ Organizations	Sales	Purchasing	Inventory	Shipping	Receiving	Accounting	Personnel
Business Plan Priority							
Prepare and Mail Catalog							
Select New Products							
Search for Vendors							
Ship Products							

Figure 2-1: Application Priority Matrix

How do you assess whether existing systems meet any of your IS objectives? This is a tough problem. Vague statements of objectives will result in a vague assessment. You really need to know how the business works and what its needs are before making a precise assessment. One of the techniques for understanding the business operations is to build a model of your business. The assessment, then, compares each existing system to the model. We discuss some techniques for building a model in the next chapter.

Once you know what needs to be done to bring your IS up to snuff, you need to prioritize these tasks. Your priorities should match business plan priorities while accounting for dependencies between applications. For example, sales reporting functions require a sales order entry system first. Get input from your company officers for prioritizing your task list. Figure 2-1 illustrates a matrix for recording priorities. The relative priority of the different organizations, such as sales, human resources, and so on, is decided by the ultimate decision-maker, the management committee or COO. Relative priorities of different functions define the current focus of the company's business plan. Don't be surprised, therefore, if it changes as frequently as once or twice a year.

Notice how we interact frequently with the decision-makers. The key is to get them involved throughout the process. Ask for their input often, even if you shelve it sometimes. They need to take ownership of the applications if your requests for budgets are to be successful. Frequent interaction and a sense of ownership are necessary paving stones for a successful information system.

2.2 Why Model Your Business?

Modeling your business means defining the functions and data essential to running the business. Both management consultants and IS consultants use business models to understand what a business needs to do for its livelihood. The actual techniques for documenting a model vary depending on the methodology used and results intended. For example, a reengineering consultant may use a process model to help you streamline your organization structure. An IS consultant, on the other hand, may use it to identify areas where automation may be helpful. The next chapter will discuss the techniques that many methodologies use and that are supported by the Oracle Designer products. We will also examine some of the new techniques that you may want to use even if Oracle Designer does not support them at present.

The basic components of a model are organization, business processes, business rules, and data. There are additional nuances that elaborate on these basic components. For example, operational data is distinct from the history over time. Historical data must account for changes such as those in organization structure. You need to put the definition of these components into context. You establish the context by defining the business objectives, the short- and long-term goals, the critical success factors, and the business priorities. So, all of these context components form the strategy-level model of a business.

Are you wondering if you already know these components for your company? True, you know what they are overall, and possibly you have some detail on them. Unfortunately, they have probably changed somewhat since you were involved in them. Forms that were used a year ago may have been replaced, or new pieces of information added to them. Unless IS staff are constantly interacting with business staff, you may not be aware of what changes occurred or why they happened. Such changes are often a reason why applications requirement definitions should not depend on one or two users representing several dozens. Other reasons include differences in needs at each geographic location or department which is managed locally.

Ideally, every conscious change in the business should involve IS staff, so that you identify very early on corresponding changes to IS. Use the model to identify whether you already accommodate the changes in an existing application. If you need to enhance an application, use the model to assess the impact on other applications. Such assessment of existing applications is sometimes called portfolio analysis.

You need to position the IS group to get involved in the decision-making process which precedes changes. Early involvement means you can detect and implement systems enhancements in a timely manner. You can thus control the extent of the application backlog and prevent user complaints about too little, too late!

The model cannot, of course, determine how to achieve business objectives. The company's officers will develop creative solutions to do that. What you could offer, with the aid of the model and IS, is a test bed for their ideas. For example, if the company is considering a new product offering, use the model to determine the impact on each part of the company.

The model is not merely a representation of what information is available today and how it is used. Although many methodologies stop developing it at this point, use it to represent what could be available tomorrow and how new information could prove useful for company growth objectives. Don't wait until the company decides to enter a new market to determine that you need a new information system. Start your investigation as soon as someone suggests the idea. You can then participate in the business planning rather than passively waiting until users request a new system. With some experience in participation, get ready to try a more proactive role of suggesting new systems. Of course, by getting your users involved in developing the model, they probably will start coming up with their own ideas.

2.3 Roles and Responsibilities

The previous discussions probably implied that you have to build the model yourself. Relax! That is the purpose of the organization structure you put together. In this section, we will discuss the roles and responsibilities of your staff to support your endeavors effectively. Read this carefully if a DBMS or object-oriented environments are new to your organization. The roles and responsibilities are significantly different from those in a traditional environment.

Let us examine the functions that your organization needs to perform before we detail roles and responsibilities.

2.3.1 Building and Maintaining the Business Model

For your interactions with the company officers, you need capabilities to define and refine business models. These are typically provided by senior analysts trained in the techniques used for model definition. These analysts should also be able to compare existing systems with the model to pinpoint gaps and opportunities for new applications. You can also use the model to evaluate packaged products against your company's requirements.

The initial development of a model often requires skills which are of little use afterward. Unless you have sufficient similar work for these analysts, you should not hire specifically for the initial development. Consider using consultants over the short term. Involve your staff analysts throughout the initial model development so they gain intimate familiarity with the techniques. Maintenance of the model then becomes their job.

Analysts skilled in modeling a business are sometimes split between process analysts and data administrators. This structure is prevalent in large corporations that use traditional development methodologies. The work is divided by the type of modeling skill. However, there is more to the model than just process or data definition. The model also involves business rules, organization structures, and function-entity matrices which require cross-training in modeling skills. Firms that have embraced the object-oriented methodology now have a modeling group that consolidates process and data perspectives. But, you can consolidate and cross-train your analysts even if you retain traditional modeling methods.

These positions are very senior ones, since they cross all boundaries of functional areas, applications, products, and software. Key talents needed for these positions include excellent communication capabilities, ability to abstract from specifics, and the ability to see the big picture without getting bogged down in detail. These analysts will frequently interview high-level company executives and must be able to extract maximum information in short conversations.

As the IS manager, you need in-depth understanding of the business model. In most cases, you will need sufficient technical training to read diagrammatic models and express their descriptions in terms that company executives understand.

2.3.2 Defining the Architecture

The complex combination of products and technologies available today requires someone with a long-term vision of your IS and resources. Unplanned introduction of products and tools results in a spaghetti of applications which strain your support staff skills. One of my clients, a large corporation, once decided that their architectural goal was to be independent of tools vendors. So, they chose a different development tool for each project. Over a period of two years, they had a dozen applications in production requiring trained support staff in about six products including Oracle Developer, Powerbuilder, SQLWindows, Omnis7 and so on. Their developers were stretched thin trying to support these environments, resulting in poor-quality systems, which in turn increased the support activity. A strategy defined by a knowledgeable architect could have avoided such degradation.

A system architect uses broad vision and knowledge of technological advances in the industry to define an architectural strategy. Such a strategy includes hardware infrastructure, software product mix, development and testing tools, production support, and monitoring tools. The system architect should continuously revise the strategy-based on new technology while ensuring reasonable assimilation when new products are introduced into the organization. A good architect will plan the transition to new technology to make the best use of resources.

You will need to perform some additional tasks in an object-oriented development environment. The system architect should define a component reuse strategy with tools to facilitate reuse. Then you will need to establish and maintain a library of reusable components, whether developed in-house or purchased from a third-party. These components must undergo a stricter set of quality assurance checks since they will be core to many applications. Plan to put your best and most experienced staff in charge of developing these common components.

The architect should also understand business and competitive pressures. The burgeoning popularity of the World Wide Web, for example, has created significant pressure on corporations to establish a Web presence. A system architect would determine not only the appropriate tools, but also which information the company should present, and a progression plan from the initial applications.

2.3.3 Defining and Maintaining Application Databases

The business data model is related to physical database structures, but it is not the same thing. You need design staff with special skills to meet performance requirements and geographical distribution. In addition, knowledge of the specific product of choice, in our case Oracle, is a prerequisite. These functions are essential throughout the design and development of an application. They are typically performed by development DBAs (DBAs). Development DBAs are skilled in creating and updating schemas, loading and reloading test data, and so on.

After implementing applications, you will need to monitor database activities to tune database performance further. Other maintenance functions include planning and implementing upgrades to DBMS software, data conversion from old software to new versions, and so on. In organizations using multiple vendors' products, the DBA also oversees the downloading of data from one product's database to another or ensuring that gateway products install and operate correctly. A DBA in charge of a data warehouse will assume responsibility for the periodic data loads into the warehouse. Notice that production DBAs, who perform these tasks have different skills from development DBAs. Ask these personnel for their input in capacity planning for database and server hardware when designing the architecture of your application.

If your organization uses multiple DBMS products, you will need at least one DBA per product. This role is new in a DBMS environment. In a traditional environment, programmers designed files with no further monitoring required. Key skills for DBAs include the ability to understand the abstract business models and convert them into physical database definitions with appropriate performance trade-off decisions.

As a manager of IS, you need only a passing familiarity with the deliverables of this function. You will need an awareness of the trade-off decisions and their expected and actual impact. When multiple DBMS products are involved, consult your DBAs while you analyze the impact of a strategic change in the products used in the business.

2.3.4 Designing and Building Application Programs

This function was traditionally divided among separate design and programming groups. Some methodologies, embracing the rapid application development (RAD) principle, have combined it into a single group. So now, one person performs both design and development functions. The skills required, however, remain separate.

The design function derives module definitions from the business functions portion of the model. Interactive modules may be prototyped using appropriate GUI tools. The purpose of prototyping is typically to obtain detailed screen and report layouts and user interaction dialogs. Finalizing validation criteria that are not in the data model or business rules is also part of this function. Traditionally, specifications were passed on to programmers for actual coding and testing of programs. When your staff use tools such as the Oracle Designer generators, there is no clear distinction between design and programming tasks. In other tools, you may sometimes need the traditional separation of skills.

Analysts/programmers that perform this function need the ability to understand the business model and interpret it into its implementation equivalent. Knowledge of specific programming tools, client-server tools, object component and class libraries, and the like is essential. The function includes testing of the code together with other programs and making corrections or modifications-based on user input. Code optimized for performance is essential.

As an IS manager, you will find these personnel invaluable in assessing the specific impact of change. They can also support you in estimating the effort of building new applications. You need only superficial knowledge of the development tools. Accept advice from programmers on the limitations of tools so that you do not promise anything that you cannot deliver.

2.3.5 Assuring the Quality of Application Development

Many IS organizations ignore this function with detrimental effects. Others expect designers and programmers to monitor quality in an ad-hoc fashion. However, this function is more than reviewing programs after they are developed.

The Software Engineering Institute (SEI) at Carnegie Mellon defines a progressive measure of organization maturity-based on software quality practices. The five maturity levels, as described by Watts Humphrey, are

1. **Initial:** At this level, your development process is unorganized. You may plan projects but may not meet the plans. You may have difficulty controlling the quality of the end result and the results are not consistently predictable. Most organizations operate at this level.

2. **Repeatable:** At this level, organizations use rigorous project management methods to monitor their tasks and progress. Through this tracking history, they become aware of the characteristics of successful projects. In some cases, they are able to reproduce these successes in similar projects. An independent quality assurance group exists at this level to monitor all planning, implementation, and verification tasks.

3. **Defined:** In addition to a rigorous project management method, organizations at this level also establish a complete development methodology which is *actually* used even during a crisis. Change management, testing, and reviews are all part of this methodology. A process group, dedicated to continually improving the development

process, exists at this level. These are foundations for major and continuing progress.

4. **Managed:** Process measurement is a key ingredient at this level. Without an accurate quantification of costs and benefits of every process, an informed assessment against historical experience is not possible. The quality assurance group uses such assessments to track progress against a quality plan. For example, the cost and yield of error detection and correction processes can be used to determine processes that improve quality of the end product. Very few organizations achieve this level of maturity. Those organizations that do have an almost effortless transition to the next level, because the improvements to make are obvious.

5. **Optimizing:** Although this level is described separately, much optimizing occurs in the earlier levels also. The major shift in this level is in optimizing across all processes. For example, you can reduce errors detected during testing through structured inspections in earlier analysis and design tasks.

At each level, your organization gains better control over the software process to obtain quality improvements. Your goal in the culminating level, Optimizing, is defect prevention rather than just correction.

In my experience, no silver bullet technology is effective if your organization is at the first level of maturity. However, these are the very targets for the marketing media. Such organizations are too prone to revert to crisis fire-fighting methods at the smallest sign of a fire. We, the information technology people, have a lot to learn from the various quality programs employed by the manufacturing industry.

The earliest maturity level for successful implementation of a development methodology and CASE tools is when transitioning to the Defined level. So your target is to improve your organization to at least this level of maturity. This constraint applies to both traditional and object-oriented methods. If you subscribe to an object-oriented method, realize that you need to achieve at least the Managed level to achieve effective reusability. This may be the reason why object reuse has achieved spotty effectiveness in organizations.

Here are some suggestions to get you started in your journey toward improving your organization's maturity level. Initially, you will need standards for a number of developmental items. Key items include conventions for naming tables, columns, and other database items; standards for screen and report layouts; and conventions for program names. You will need environments set up for individual development, team development, testing, and production. If you use multiple hardware platforms, these environments should enforce portability standards. You will also need source code control for tracking modifications to programs. Regression testing on modifications is almost as important as testing new code to maintain the credibility of your group.

All documentation, from the business model through to individual programs and the user guide, is subject to quality assurance checks. Consistency and clear communication are a must for maintaining a harmonious application development environment.

As an IS manager, you must be aware of and committed to quality assurance procedures. Pay close attention to the findings of quality assurance reviews to discover your top performers. Reward good work, and you will encourage others to improve their work.

2.3.6 Assuring the Quality of Data

Everyone knows that computer systems work on the garbage-in-garbage-out principle. Yet few organizations make an effort to administer the quality of data. We depend entirely on the validation capabilities of programs to maintain quality of data. Unfortunately, automated validation is only part of the story.

Data quality is critical for the successful implementation of a data warehouse. Good quality data makes data mapping into the warehouse more logical. Such data will require less scrubbing prior to loading into the warehouse and hence will result in a better quality warehouse.

There are many quality judgments that a program cannot possibly make. Consider, for example, a skill matrix that contains Joe's proficiency in the French language. Programs can validate only that Joe is a known employee and French is a valid language. But can they verify that Joe speaks French fluently? Such a judgment must be made by a human. When building applications, we often ignore issues of this type with detrimental effects. Poor-quality data renders an application useless.

What is really needed is a set of procedures which users follow prior to entering data requiring value judgments. Typically, designing good business rules will be key to obtaining good procedures. Ideally, business rules and their associated procedures should be designed by concerned company line managers in parallel with application design. If they take ownership of the application, they will be interested in designing such procedures and of course ensuring that they are executed. For example, language proficiency could be verified by Joe's supervisor initially during an interview or later during periodic performance appraisals. We will address these issues in more detail in Chapter 3.

You will need to lay the groundwork in encouraging company management to develop new procedures as new IS are designed. The key to the success of this difficult task is to get users to believe it is their system!

2.3.7 Managing the Development of an Application

This function is really rather different from managing a group of people. It is a key position when gaining control over your projects.

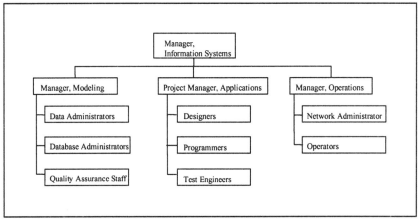

Figure 2-2: Hierarchy for Small Organizations

An application development manager develops schedules for a project, monitors costs and expenditures related to the project, monitors progress of projects, and works with users to coordinate schedules for implementation. In addition, this manager plans appropriate training schedules for staff, assigns tasks-based on the project schedule, and monitors their work. Typically, project management software is of great benefit in this function, especially if it speeds the frequent task of reporting status.

Development managers have a technical background which enables them to assess the impact of technical difficulties. They can also assess staff capabilities so that work is apportioned according to capabilities. A day-to-day involvement in the project ensures that they pay close attention to deliverables and time constraints.

These personnel are indispensable when developing your IS plan. Their status reports will keep you informed on the progress of every current project while you focus on future needs. But be sure to accept their estimates for effort, rather than dictating politically motivated deadlines that invalidate their efforts.

2.3.8 Managing and Operating Computer Systems

This function within your organization is necessary for smooth operation of your systems. It includes installation and maintenance of all hardware, communication networks, operating systems, and utility software. It is typically performed by computer operations staff whose role does not change significantly in a DBMS environment.

2.3.9 Typical Organization Structures

Notice that we did not define the number of people who might perform the functions just discussed. Obviously, the numbers depend on the size of your company and business. Small companies may have one person perform data administration as well as manage projects. Many combinations are possible depending on the skills of your staff, their career goals, and training. I leave the possibilities up to your creative imagination.

Figures 2-2 and 2-3 show typical hierarchies of organizations for small and large IS groups, respectively. Small groups typically mean that one person performs more than one function. Hence, small groups support fewer applications or use outside resources for new development. Larger groups need to be aware of communication difficulties within the group attributable to the large number of staff. Formal methodologies and recording tools foster better communication and offset the potential detrimental effects on productivity.

2.4 Obtaining Budgets

Once you have convinced company management that IS are an integral part of the business, getting budget approval becomes a lot easier. They will no longer view IS as a luxury, to be indulged using *spare* cash. However, you still need to justify expenditure on systems. For example, a company with $10 million revenue is not likely to spend $1 million on its IS, unless IS are its business. Here are some tips on how to justify your expenses for a new system.

Get the company into the habit of using annual budgets. This budget will cover your usual expenses of staff, current computer systems, maintenance on current software, and packages.

The next step is to get your company sold on your IS plan. This step is a little more difficult because first you need to invest some effort in doing a strategy study. If you plan to use outside consultants to help, you will need to obtain approval to spend the money. Even if you have the necessary skills among your staff, you have to dedicate their time to it. So, your best approach is to sell the company officers on the idea of a strategy study. We have already discussed why an IS strategy is important in earlier sections. Here is a summary of the arguments for your toolkit:

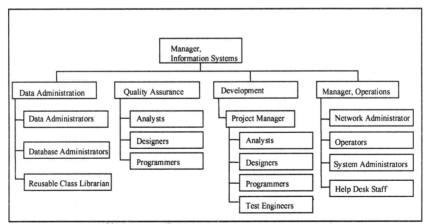

Figure 2-3: Hierarchy for Large Organizations

- Information is an asset to the business, but it is useful only if there are adequate systems to access it.

- Good IS support business functions and are an integral part of business planning.

- The priorities for IS development should match the business priorities for optimal effect.

- A strategy study focuses on outlining the business functions, business rules, and data to determine potential areas of automation.

- The IS strategy prioritizes potential areas of automation to match the business priorities.

- The strategy deliverables are essential for you to assess where existing systems leave gaps in support of the business.

Remember that a strategy study is only the first step in your plan. Armed with the strategy, you can attack the budgetary needs of further work.

The method for obtaining budgets is different for each company. In small companies, you need approval from only a few senior executives. In larger companies, user departments may fund IS development. In such cases, try to develop as many of your objectives as possible before you broach the subject. Typically, one or two examples of inadequate support of business functions is sufficient to spark the interest. Don't forget to emphasize how a structured strategic analysis uncovers more such areas and allows you to estimate their impact on the business.

In very large corporations, you will probably need to convince a committee about the viability of your approach. However, getting budget approval for strategy development is easier in the case of committees, because you can get them excited about the potential. The deliverables of a strategy study are valuable to them, whether or not they like your implementation plan. You will, however, need to educate individual committee members and get their input for your plan prior to presenting the final version.

Regardless of the size of your company, you have to present cost justification analysis before getting approval. Approach cost justification one phase at a time, starting with the strategic analysis phase. Then, go one step farther: Get the target user community excited about the approach so they volunteer cost justification information. Here are some of the items used in a cost-benefit analysis.

2.5 Typical Benefit Items

2.5.1 Cost Reduction—Labor

A new system might reduce labor costs in either the IS or the user organization. A system built with Oracle Designer tools and generators requires fewer programming staff to maintain and enhance programs than does one built with traditional third-generation technology. A system that has been enhanced repeatedly over several years gets harder to maintain as the cumulative changes affect its original design.

A new system might help eliminate inefficiencies in the operation of a department. For example, if fewer paper forms are necessary than in the old system, staff can be more productive. Less time is needed if the new system reduces rekeying of data from one system to another. For example, consider a new human resources system which shares employee salary data with the payroll portion of an accounting system. Human resources staff no longer need to print salary change reports from their system to pass to payroll staff for rekeying into their system. Such improvements are the foundation of BPR (BPR).

2.5.2 Cost Reduction—Timely Information

If a new system reduces the time delay between a user's request for information and its delivery, the information is more valuable. Suppose, for example, you plan to replace an aging batch reporting system by an online query system. The shipping department can be more responsive to customers on the phone with online queries than with outdated batch reports produced once a day. If, as a result of this new system, the order entry department can predict more accurately whether an item is back ordered, your company's service is greatly improved.

Such improvements can be quantified, although not easily. This is where aid from your users is invaluable. Try to determine the amount of time wasted in rekeying, or callback to customers. Then, calculate the dollar value of the delays. For example, if each customer phone call requires 10 minutes of research and a couple of callbacks, an order entry person can service one customer every 15 minutes. If this time were reduced to 5 minutes, the gain is two extra customers for each order entry person!

2.5.3 New Opportunities

The flexibility of the new system might provide new opportunities which the company does not consider today. Try, with help from your users, to quantify the benefit of such improvements. Ideally, such improvements are the result of a considered business plan.

2.5.4 Informed Control

A new system that includes flexible management reporting might provide better control. The benefit of this improvement is intangible, but obvious, to most managers.

2.5.5 Quicker Response to User Requests

If you are reducing the bureaucracy necessary in a centralized system by providing more local control, your users can list many benefits. Some of these benefits might be quantifiable as opportunities lost currently.

2.5.6 Presenting Your Analysis

There is a knack to presenting your cost-benefit analysis most effectively. For years, we simply presented the numbers in boring columns, page after page. Today, there are many presentation tools available to us. From small companies, where you present to only a couple of people, to large company committee presentations, a picture really is worth a thousand numbers.

Take the time to use graphing tools to prepare your presentation. A line graph showing the break-even point for cost recovery is more effective than the same figures presented in columns. A pie chart showing the cost of opportunities lost through an inadequate system is an excellent way to bring home the cost justification of the new system.

Once you win the company's trust for your approach, shelling out the dollars should be an easy decision!

2.6 Methods: Waterfall, RAD, or Object-oriented

The inexperienced manager, overwhelmed by the pressures of business, often asks *"Why do we need a development methodology? Why can't we just start programming and get all this work done?"* This kind of misguided attitude leads to the organization remaining at the lowest level of maturity. In fact, I have seen organizations struggle up to maturity level 3, Defined, only to suffer a management change and tumble back to the Initial maturity level.

A methodology is necessary to develop systems that meet business needs. Systems developers rarely know the intricacies of the business. Without user involvement, they may develop a technologically superior system—but one that is quite useless to serve the business need. Every methodology stresses user involvement and provides a template of how to develop systems together with users.

Object-oriented methodologies are one of the latest in vogue. You have probably also heard of RAD, or *rapid application development*, and *Waterfall* methodologies. There are two basic underlying styles of development, *stepwise* and *iterative*. The stepwise style recommends that you complete each step before moving on to the next step. The traditional life-cycle methodologies, commonly termed Waterfall methodologies, embody this principle. The iterative style suggests that you move through the development cycle for each system as fast as you can, but repeat the cycle several times. This style is often called the RAD style of development. Object-oriented methodologies usually embrace the iterative style of development.

Each development style has a set of suggested tools and techniques. You need to choose the tools and techniques that are appropriate to your project from the suggested set. In later chapters, we will describe several of these techniques.

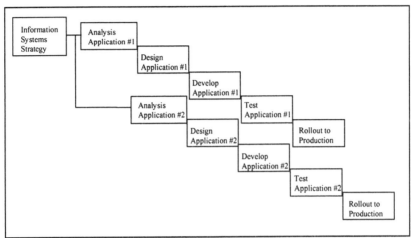

Figure 2-4: Waterfall Approach

Regardless of the methodology you choose, your project needs to perform the following activities: strategy, analysis, design, programming, testing, business process redesign, integration, user training, conversion, and implementation (or production). The order and frequency of these activities will differ in each methodology and its underlying style. For example, in a Waterfall-style methodology, you would complete analysis on the entire system before starting design, and complete design before starting programming. Figure 2-4 illustrates the phases and organization of a typical Waterfall methodology. In a RAD methodology, you would take a small portion of the system and perform all of the activities in a matter of weeks. In an object-oriented methodology, you might perform all of the activities on one component at a time. Figure 2-5 illustrates the organization of a typical object-oriented methodology.

There are many books written on development methodologies by industry experts such as James Martin, Edward Yourdon, Grady Booch, Ivar Jacobsen, Rumbaugh, and so on. There is a list of some of my favorites in the bibliography. Superficially, methodologies that embrace a particular style of development all follow a similar development life-cycle and suggested techniques. The techniques vary in flavor and depth-based on the methodology and the founder of the technique.

The driving principle underlying methodologies is to change information systems development from an art to an engineering discipline. In days gone by, engineers like Telford designed bridges on the back of an envelope. Today, there are methods for building short-span and long-span bridges that engineers all over the world follow. They can communicate with each other easily since they all follow similar standards. In the IS industry, we still design systems on the back of an envelope. We have recognized the benefits of a common language and standards. However, the frequent radical changes in our development tools, and more importantly the constant influx of uninitiated labor force, keep our methodologies from achieving the regularity found in engineering.

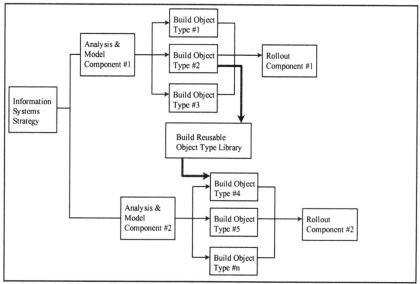

Figure 2-5: An Object-oriented Approach

The underlying principle in all engineered systems approaches is *divide and conquer.* The methdologies differ only in the techniques for dividing the scope and tools used to conquer each piece. In all cases, a strategy is a prerequisite to determining the scope of the divisions. You probably have firsthand experience in getting overwhelmed with enterprise-wide systems. Relax. Only the strategy phase need consider the entire company. Each subsequent phase divides the scope into manageable chunks such as just one functional area or a subject. The strategy deliverables help keep all of the latter separate portions linked. Without the big picture, you would have too many peripheral functions to cover each time you tackle an application area.

There are three basic ingredients to a business: organization structure, data, and processes. So, any business model must include a model of these ingredients. The techniques used to model them differ-based on the role in the business. For example, a business owner or a chief operating officer is interested in objectives and goals. These people will perceive the model as lists of the different aspects. A business analyst will conceive the model as an interrelated set of entities, functions, rules, and organizational units. A system developer will portray it as a set of data files or databases and programs. We can formalize these different views as a set of modeling techniques touted by consultants in their level of operation.

	Data (What)	Function (How)	Network (Where)	People (Who)	Time (When)	Motivation (Why)
Objectives / Scope	List of Things Important to the Enterprise	List of Processes the Enterprise Performs	List of Operating Locations	List of Organizational Units	List of Business Events / Cycles	List of Business Goals / Strategies
Business Model	Entity Relationship Diagram, Object Diagram	Business Process Flow, Interaction Diagram	Location, Process & Data Matrix, Distribution	Organization Chart, with Roles	Master Schedule, Event Response Matrix	Business Plan
Information System Model	Data Model Entity Relationship, Object Type Diagram	Data Flow Diagram (essential), UseCase	Distributed System Architecture (Instances and Replication)	Human Interface Architecture (Roles, Access)	Dependency Diagram, Entity Life History, Object State Model	Business Rules
Technology Model	Data Architecture Schema Diagram (Tables and Columns)	Structure Chart, Pseudo-Code	System Architecture (Hardware, Software Tools)	User Interface (How the System will Behave)	"Control flow" Diagram	Rule Enforcement Design
Detailed Representation	Data design (Denormalized), Physical Storage Design	Detailed Program Design	Network Architecture	Security Architecture (Who can see What?)	Interrupts and Machine Cycles	Rule Servers, Logic
Functioning System	(Working Systems)					

Figure 2-6: The Zachman Framework

Each of these perceived views has many dimensions. For example, an executive's perspective of organization includes not only organizations, data, and processes, but also geographical location of organizations, how these organizations interact, when they interact, and why they perform their processes. A system implementer is concerned with networks and business timing requirements as well as data storage and programs.

John Zachman has formalized these views and dimensions in his famous Zachman Framework. This framework represents the different views (as rows) and aspects (as columns) in a two-dimensional matrix. The cells of this matrix indicate the techniques commonly used to express the model at this view. Figure 2-6 illustrates the Zachman Framework modified to use the terminology and techniques described in this book

2.7 Business Process Reengineering

Business models serve many purposes other than determining the IS impact. During the process of building these models, inefficiencies in business procedures become apparent. By involving departmental managers in detecting inefficiencies, you become part of their planning process. Your objective is to get the departmental managers to detect and correct inefficiencies so that they own the ideas and the changes. Your role is to facilitate the process. Thus, you can establish the credibility of your modeling process by helping the company in ways other than IS.

Business Process Reengineering (BPR) is the buzzword, popularized by Michael Hammer, for a project that focuses on examining business processes. Its sole objective is to uncover inefficiencies and design ways of improving processes. It may make small changes or radical ones. The changes may involve procedural changes or technological changes. In all cases, it aims to redirect the way business is conducted to achieve radical improvements. You may have heard the saying, *"Revolutionize, not rationalize!"*

Any successful BPR project is sponsored from the top down, although smaller changes may be initiated at the middle or lower management level. Because BPR aims to achieve radical improvements, BPR projects span functional areas and usually result in reorganization of responsibilities. Changes implemented at lower management levels can only achieve incremental improvements because of the smaller span of control over processes. This goal is reflected in the typical mission stated for a BPR project. Here are some examples:

> *Radically improve customer service from initial contact to product implementation.*—This project resulted in reorganizing my client's company from a traditional function-based division to a customer-centered team structure. As a result, the customers dealt with a single, dedicated contact team regardless of where they were in the sales or implementation cycle, rather than being handed over from sales to accounting or technical support or service departments. The key to the radical improvement was a complete reorganization of the company—not just a superficial change that appointed a customer contact division that in turn dealt with the traditional departments, as implemented by some competitors. The superficial change simply increased overhead without improving the service.

> *Cradle to grave tracking of chemicals throughout the manufacturing process to monitor and improve environmental impact of the company's operation.* — This project was initiated in response to severely restricting environmental regulations. It resulted in a sophisticated discharge monitoring system for tracking actual pollution from all sources in the product manufacturing process. The data from these monitors was gathered and analyzed resulting in integrated controls built into the manufacturing information system. For example, it appeared that sources of the chemical ingredients caused variations in the

resultant pollutants and the company was able to select sources to purchase their materials appropriately.

Before you start BPR, you need to establish

- Which area of the business needs reengineering?
- What benefit can you expect? Cost reduction? Improved customer service?
- How to quantify the benefit?
- What is the competitive advantage of the reengineering?

These are the typical questions initiated in a strategy. However, you will need much more detail than a strategy study can provide. A strategy study will define the desired goals that a BPR project needs to achieve. However, it is up to the BPR project to determine how to meet those goals. A BPR project is generally conducted in several phases:

- **Analysis:** In this phase, the BPR approach examines the current processes to determine its shortcomings and to identify the opportunities for improvement. The team also proposes several solutions to management and obtains their commitment to implement one of them.

- **Development:** In this phase, the team acquires or develops any supporting technology and systems to the solution selected during analysis. This phase is often overlapped with the implementation phase.

- **Implementation:** This phase implements the new processes designed using the technology obtained in the development phase. Typical activities include establishing among the business employees staff quality circles, implementation teams, training sessions for systems and other technology, and measurement procedures to demonstrate improvements.

There are two basic approaches used during the analysis phase: benchmark and process costing. The benchmark approach is used in a competitive environment to compare the performance of your company against the "Best of Breed" businesses in your industry. The process costing approach is used when a benchmark cannot be performed or is not desired. For example, if your company is already among the best in the industry, a benchmark is not necessary. You need to look at other ways to improve your business processes.

The development phase consists of more traditional methods of publishing Requests for Information or proposals for the technology desired, evaluating the technology, and purchasing packaged software and customizing it or developing in-house software.

The implementation phase deals with getting business users to make the best use of the selected technology. It requires heavy involvement throughout the development phase to get their buy-in. This is one reason why this phase overlaps the development phase.

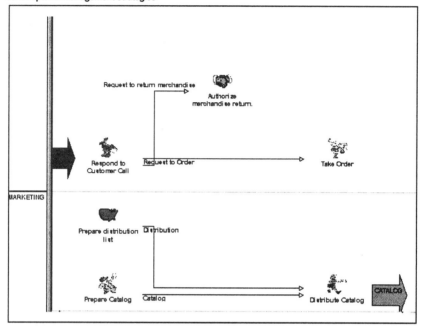

Figure: 2-7: A Business Process Diagram

An IS group should play a major role in all of these phases. The BPR analysis phase provides invaluable insight into the *why* and *how* of the systems developed or acquired in the development phase. Traditionally, the IS group's involvement was limited to only a portion of the BPR development phase. Continuous involvement of IT analysts and designers in the BPR analysis phase significantly improves the usability of the developed system.

Oracle Designer supports several of the activities in the BPR analysis phase. It provides a process modeler with sophisticated multimedia capabilities that may be useful during the BPR analysis and implementation phases. It can record details about functions that assist in process costing. It even includes reports that calculate process costs. Figure 2-7 illustrates the process model used during the BPR analysis phase of our case study.

When exploring alternative business processes, you might use Oracle Designer to design them and assign cost parameters to the new processes. The reports then indicate the cost for the new processes that you could then compare to the existing model. There are third-party products that provide the ability to simulate cycles of executing processes and provide cost information. These third-party products can be integrated with the Oracle Designer repository.

Notice that the BPR phases overlap with those of the systems development methodologies described earlier. Here, finally, is the reason why systems developers often misunderstood the intent of their system. We have traditionally paid little attention to how a particular system will fit into the business process, even though we spent great effort in training users in the changes to their daily work. We can all recount tales of how a completed system met what the users asked for but not what they needed. By involving ourselves in the BPR analysis, we gain an understanding of our users' needs beyond that obtained through our traditional systems-oriented analysis.

2.7.1 Implementing New Technology

Is dive in the deep end the only way to adopt a new technology in your organization? There are actually two aspects you need to consider: skill base and disruption to operations. Let us examine each of these aspects in the context of the two approaches discussed here. The new technology might be an object DBMS, development methodology, or implementation of a new business process.

I call the two approaches macro and micro. The macro approach is to start using the new technology for everything—no more use of older technology. Consider the example of adopting a methodology and CASE tools. You would start with a strategy phase, follow up with analysis for the highest-priority application as soon as you have staff available, and so on. No enhancements to older existing systems would be undertaken—only emergency fixes!

The micro approach is to try the new technology on a pilot project to gain experience first, then start applying it to other projects a little at a time. In our methodology example, you would start by using the methodology on just one small-sized project. Then, the veterans of this project would start one or two more projects with several other inexperienced staff, and so on.

Some of the pros and cons should be immediately obvious in each approach. It boils down to two questions: Can you train the majority of your staff together? And can the company survive with only emergency attention to existing systems while new systems are being built? Small companies gain significant benefits from using the macro approach. A consistent software development environment is achieved much more quickly than waiting to complete one project at a time. The macro approach is acceptable if company management already has the right attitude toward IS: They are an essential asset.

Large corporations, on the other hand, find the training requirements of the macro approach prohibitively expensive. Besides, getting approval for a complete revamp of all systems would be next to impossible. Building all their systems using one technology would be considered much too risky by their commonly used risk assessment programs.

There are technical reasons also for using one approach over the other. If you are less than confident of your chosen tools and techniques, use the micro approach to test them out. For example, if you are not sure if the Oracle GUI or Web tools are the best choice in your environment, use the micro approach. The macro approach is suitable for spreading the knowledge gained in a pilot to the remainder of the company.

A Case Study: Widgets, Inc.

Throughout this book, we will use examples based on a mythical company. The idea is for you to have a complete working example from beginning to end. Where applicable, we will use Oracle Designer terminology and techniques. In some cases, such as the priority matrix, I use my own conventions. Such facilities were not easily available in Oracle Designer tools at the time of writing.

Widgets, Inc. is a mail-order company-based in Timbuctoo, United States. Timbuctoo was chosen because of tax breaks offered by the township. Cheap labor is plentiful to staff their warehouse operations. It has also made special agreements for quick shipping anywhere in North America with a number of services including Airborne Express, United Parcel Service, and Federal Express.

Widgets' buyers purchase goods from many different manufacturers. The inventory boasts between 1500 and 2000 different products at any time. Every month, Widgets, Inc. publishes a catalog and mails it to consumers throughout the United States. Customers can order items using the order form included in the catalog or by phone. Widgets, Inc. staff pride themselves on shipping orders within 36 hours. Customers can pay either with a major credit card or by enclosing a check with their order. Alternatively, Widgets, Inc. will send an invoice when shipping the order if the customer is preferred club member.

Two years ago, Widgets, Inc. bought an accounting package that runs on a small multi-user UNIX system. It includes accounts payable, accounts receivable, payroll, and general ledger. Widgets, Inc. also has an order entry system which was custom built by its programmers in C. Unfortunately, the accounts receivable module cannot import data from the order entry system. The firm also has a PC-based mailing list which consists of 15 million names. This list is used to print labels for mailing catalogs. This list is something of a problem—Widgets, Inc. would like to add many more names, referred by existing customers, to this list. But, printing the current list of names already takes several days.

Management would like to increase sales with a three-pronged approach. The first approach is offering more targeted catalogs, for example, a tools catalog for customers who bought do-it-yourself products in the past. However, their only source of information on customer buying history is the order entry system. This system will require significant modifications to add customer history to the files. Reporting programs will take even longer. Order entry data is typically purged every month when the account books are closed.

The second approach is offering their products via the Internet. This approach should increase the market for Widgets by opening the international market. But management is skeptical—they have heard stories about Internet commerce being a money sink.

So, they would like to tread with caution into this untested field. Long-term, Widgets, Inc. would like to open a physical operation in Europe. This is planned for opening in about four years. Any systems built today should be usable in the European operations as well.

As part of a strategic business analysis, we collected some preliminary information from the company executives.

Widgets, Inc. Objectives

- To provide products to consumers by mail order

    To the largest number of consumers

    At the lowest possible cost

    With fastest delivery

    For a profit to the company

Business Priorities

- 100% growth in revenue within two years

    By targeted marketing of catalog items

    By opening an electronic storefront on the Internet

- Reduce operating costs within two years

    By improving order-to-shipping time to 24 hours

    By reducing warehouse time of products

    By reducing customer service costs

- Establish international presence in Europe within five years

    By offering products via the Internet.

    By opening or acquiring a physical operation in Europe

Critical Success Factors

- Easy access to customer data, including

    Product purchasing profiles and history

    Hobbies profile

    Payment history

- Integrated order entry, accounting, and shipping
- Impact of currency exchange rate fluctuations

Constraints

- Maintain current head count in all departments
- Budget limit of $2 million

Key Performance Indicators

- Revenue increase of 50% over previous year by end of this year
- Specialist catalog sales to be 20% of total revenue by year end
- Internet-based sales to be 10% of total revenue by year end
- Average order-to-shipping time of 24 hours by year end

Strategy Techniques

Having obtained an appreciation of the management issues, you are now ready to perform a strategy study. A strategy study encompasses all functional areas of the company. It culminates in a definition of application boundaries with a clear scope for leading into detailed analysis of individual applications. Which application to tackle first depends on the business priorities communicated by upper management.

This chapter will introduce some of the techniques used in a strategy study. Our aim in the strategy study is to discover opportunities for supporting business objectives through the use of information technology. These objectives may be to reduce costs, increase sales, improve productivity, or initiate a new line of business. The findings of our strategy study may range from redesigning specific business processes to redesigning information systems. The topics discussed in this chapter are

- How to conduct a strategy study to obtain the most information and help break business managers out of a set mold. A smaller scope study for an application uncovers the users' key expectations.

- Components of a strategy study, which you use and revise throughout the life of your company's information systems.

- Techniques used in modeling a business for strategic analysis including modeling business objects, processes, function hierarchies, entity relationship diagrams, business rules, and business organizations.

- Products to support diagramming and repository of model information. We will examine which of these techniques are supported by Oracle's Oracle Designer product. Look to third-party products to fill the gaps or map these models by extending the Oracle Designer repository.

3.1 Strategic Business Analysis Phase

Although our description here covers strategy at the corporate level, you may apply these techniques to conduct a strategy study for individual applications. Bear in mind that a strategy for an individual application attempts to set the scope of development. It targets areas that the application will support. So, its scope will ignore elements and processes that will not be automated. The corporate-level strategy, on the other hand, should cover all areas perhaps with less detail for each element. A strategy study at the corporate level should take at most several weeks to complete, assuming you have the stakeholders readily accessible. An application strategy should take much less time.

The approach used in the strategy phase is top-down. The aim is to develop a business model together with the executives of the company. The key to a successful strategy study is planning your work and working your plan. Throughout your study, it is important to maintain a high-level interest in the process from company management.

At the start, you need to establish the scope of your study. From our discussion in the previous chapter, the scope is the highest level within the company that sponsors your study. In small companies, the scope would be all of the business operations. In very large corporations with division-level sponsorship, your scope is the division functions.

3.2 Information Gathering

You need to gather specific information about your company's business before developing a strategy-level model. Here are a few ways to get started:

- Start with a generic template of the work performed by the business area addressed. Modify this template with your own knowledge and research about the company. Then, you can interview specific managers to refine the model. There are several sources of generic templates among the books listed in the bibliography.

- If you have a corporate data administration group that is the keeper of a strategic business model, you have a head start. In fact, you can recruit their aid to revise the strategic model for the changes in the business. If you don't have such a group, consider establishing one on completion of your strategy study.

- Build a model from scratch with your own knowledge of your company or similar businesses. A consultant with knowledge about the industry can be very helpful. However, involve your staff to get in-depth transfer of knowledge from the consultant. Make sure that you avoid modeling just the existing applications. These may no longer represent the way business is done. Again, you can refine the model through interviewing specific managers.

- The least recommended approach is to start by interviewing managers without preparing any models or researching the background. Most training courses appear to suggest this approach. However, observe the experts at work—you'll notice them applying prior knowledge to the task—in other words, experience from similar companies or similar businesses.

Compose your interview list with help from your executive sponsor. Try to cover as wide a variety of management as possible within your scope. Remember though, the time required for the study is directly proportional to the number of interviews—so don't go overboard. Interview at least one manager from each functional area to avoid incomplete information.

The basic work plan of a study is an iteration of interview, trial models, and feedback of your findings for verification. Before starting the interviews, a briefing session for all interviewees helps clarify your methods, their roles, and the goal of the study. After interviews and feedback sessions are completed, you will develop the strategic plan.

Throughout the interviewing tasks, you model specific information gathered from each interview. You might repeat business objects or functions found in more than one interview in various trial models. This is called *divergent modeling*. In *convergent modeling*, you consolidate repetitions and specifics into abstract, but more flexible, structures. You can converge models once you have sufficient information about a functional area, typically after completing all interviews for that area. The next chapter describes these techniques in detail. Convergent models are essential for a stable model on which to base your systems strategy.

Here we discuss three approaches to conducting interviews. You may use any combination of these approaches on a project. As a general rule, one-on-one interviews are easier with high-level executives, particularly because they are easier to fit in their busy schedules. The event matrix and UseCase techniques are appropriate for group interviews. However, make sure you have adequate facilitation support to control discussions in a constructive manner.

3.2.1 Interviewing Techniques

A common way to conduct interviews is one interviewee at a time. This seems a long-winded way compared to techniques such as the joint application development (JAD) method. However, your mission in a strategy study is fact-finding. You want to hear gripes from your interviewees. They would not be as free with their comments in the presence of their peers and superiors. JAD works well when you already know what needs to be done and you are deciding how to do it.

Don't conduct all of your interviews in a hurry. Allow time before each interview to prepare your questions. After each interview, take the time to organize your notes. Prepare a trial model after each interview, or refine previous models with the additional information gained. As you prepare trial models, you will find unexplored areas, or ambiguities. Use a subsequent interview to clarify them. If you do all your interviews before attempting a model, you will have to return many times to your interviewees for further questions. Since interviewees at this strategy stage are busy executives, they will not appreciate such a time-consuming process.

Here is a simple work plan. Try to arrange interviews so that you do no more than one per day. If an interview is in the afternoon, leave the next day free for organizing your notes and trial models. Typically, other people in your team may have trouble reading your notes. So, rewrite your notes into bulleted lists and organize them into logical groups after each interview. Documents on shared server drives are invaluable in making your notes accessible to others. Your trial models may be in the repository too, again shared and accessible by any members of your team.

Ideally, you should interview executives in a functional area (or business unit) together. Trying to overlap interviews across functional areas causes confusion. You might get a little overwhelmed with the amount of information supplied to you.

The purpose of an interview, in this phase, is to gather as much information as possible about what the company does. Make your questions as specific as you can to your interviewee's areas of responsibility. Prepare these questions in advance. If you are new to the business of your company, here are some common questions you might ask an executive:

- What are the mission and objectives of your group? How do you plan to achieve these objectives?

- What are the responsibilities and how are they allocated between members of your group?

- Could you give me an overview of a typical work cycle in your group? How long does it take? How often is the cycle repeated? How do you monitor progress?

- What information do you use to support this work? Where does it come from?

- Which other departments do you communicate with? About what? How often?

- What information does your staff provide you? How often?

- What information, if we could get it for you, could you use? What information would help you that you do not have today?

- How up-to-date does this information need to be?

These are not questions to be asked in parrot fashion! Add questions based on your knowledge of the business. Listen to the answers very closely. Find leads for further questions. Make sure you understand what is being said. Remember, though, you don't need detail—you need understanding! Interviews are very intense—you are trying to understand, in a short time, functions in which these executives have years of experience. In fact, I call these sessions a *crash course* in the business!

The hardest part of interviewing is to not let your misconceptions interfere, especially if your knowledge base is from another company. It often helps to have at least one other teammate with you on every interview. Then, one of you can conduct the interview and the other takes notes. Some people use cassettes to record interviews. This can inhibit your interviewee from being free and open about concerns. Besides, you still have to take notes—cassettes are a difficult medium when searching for specific information.

3.2.2 Group Sessions

One major challenge in conducting group sessions for information gathering is crowd control. Your interviewees have important information to impart but are used to one-on-one meetings. Start by laying down the rules for group interactions. Any book or training class in facilitation techniques covers them in detail. Here are some of the key points:

- Only one person can speak at a time.

- Facilitator notes differences of opinion and has complete authority to stop further discussion.

- Facilitator is not involved in the information gathering exercise during the session—that is, neutral facilitation and full concentration on facilitation is essential.

- Appropriate facilities are available: meeting room, projection equipment, flip charts, disabled telephones, and so on.

Another major challenge is scheduling the session. These busy executives usually have full calendars and coordinating schedules may be difficult. However, this is also a test of their commitment to your project. If you cannot get the right people together in a room, consider using one-on-one interviews regardless of the requirements of your methodology.

3.2.3 Event Matrix

I have found this technique useful in a group interview session. The approach assumes that every process in the business is a response to some event. Examples of events are: catalog mailing, customer contacts to order, customer contacts for information, end of accounting period, and so on. We gather information about business processes and rules by using a three-element matrix: event, organization or group, and response processes. Figure 3-1 illustrates a sample matrix.

You can get an active group session by preparing an initial matrix before the session. You can start with the events you know and add to them throughout the session. For each event, write in at least one business process performed by each involved organization in the corresponding cell. Whenever multiple business processes exist, use a sequence number to indicate the order in which they happen. You can even use

Organizations \\ Events	Sales	Shipping	Receiving
Customer call	•Determine requirement •Accept order •Verify payment •Authorize returns	•Ship order •Generate backorder	
Returned goods received		•Return to manufacturer	•Reconcile with order •Examine condition
Credit card transaction approved	•Authorize shipping of order		
Credit card transaction rejected	•Request alternate payment from customer		

Figure 3-1: Event Response Matrix

the group session to fill in the processes and order them. In every case, note the business policy and how the business processes implement the policy.

Clearly, you will need significant planning and preparation prior to the session. Plan to conduct several half-day sessions, of about half day, at least one session with each business area. Follow up with additional sessions that address specific gaps or require input from multiple organizations. The initial sessions should include policy-setting executives as well as senior or middle managers who have knowledge of actual operation.

3.2.4 UseCase Technique

This technique, popularized by Ivar Jacobsen, is part of his object-oriented methodology. It is very useful as an information gathering technique used in a setting with multiple interviewees. At the strategy-level, use it strictly for information gathering. If you try to use it as prescribed in Jacobsen's method, you might find yourself in the midst of detailed analysis. In particular, don't spend too much effort in making sure that each UseCase is completely defined—that is a task for detailed analysis. It is important, however, to identify as many UseCases as you can. They can be subdivided during your project planning task to define the scope if each project.

A UseCase is a set of related interactions with an *actor* about a particular business function. A particular actor is involved in many UseCases. By defining all UseCases

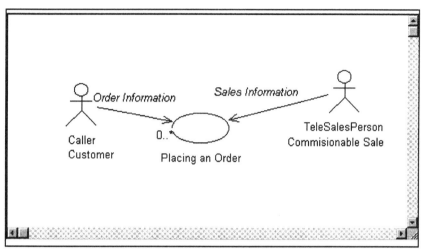

Figure 3-2: Strategy Level Sample UseCase

for all actors, we will have a complete set of business functions. Figure 3-2 illustrates an example of UseCases at the strategy-level. Detailed definition of each UseCase is more appropriate during the analysis for a specific application.

During this process, identify the objects that these actors manipulate as part of a UseCase. We will model these business objects at a high level as part of our strategy model as described in Section 3.5 Business Objects.

Before you identify UseCases, you need to define what exists outside the context, represented by *actors*, and the processes performed inside the context, the UseCases. The context in a strategy study is the entire company's business or the division for which you are conducting the study. The idea of a context is a little different from the original definition of UseCases—Jacobsen uses the term "*system*" instead. Restricting the context to a *system* is appropriate if our strategy study is for a specific application system.

You can conduct a facilitated session with several interviewees about a particular area of the business by introducing actors based on your background research. Then you initiate discussions with open-ended questions like:

- What are the major tasks for each actor?

- What outside business events does the actor react/respond to?

- What internal business events the actors need to be informed of or react/respond to?

- What are the activities performed in response to these events?

- What other processes follow on? Which actors do these processes interact with?

Notice that these questions are similar to those listed in Section 3.2.1

Interviewing Techniques, except that the terminology matches the UseCase technique. In very simple words, we are asking the interviewees: *What do you do?* From the responses to these questions, we can identify UseCases.

At the strategy level, you can use the technique to draw scenarios of specific subject areas without attempting to fully define each UseCase. These scenarios provide understanding of the business process and may indicate potential candidates for BPR. Remember to prepare template UseCases based on your experience prior to the session to make effective use of meeting time.

3.3 Components of a Business Model

In the previous chapter, we described the basic components of a business model. In this chapter we will examine each of these components in detail. All methodologies aim to capture the following essential elements:

- The *things* of the enterprise that are variously called internal entities, objects, data, or information. They may be represented by entity types, object types or classes.

- The *operations* on the things of the enterprise that are represented as methods, operations, messages, actions, or uses.

- The *people* of the enterprise who are represented as collaborators, actors, users, external entities, sources and sinks, or organizations.

- The *interactions* between people and things represented as business process flows, data flows, UseCases, or interaction diagrams.

- The *causes and constraints* on the interactions, commonly called business rules, policies, integrity rules, external events, or triggers. There are many notations and diagramming conventions to represent state transitions and timing diagrams, as well as for recording business rules.

We will describe some techniques for capturing each of these elements, graphically or otherwise. Differences between these are implied by programming languages which are of no concern at the strategy level. We will use the above terms interchangeably, although we will try to use consistent terminology throughout the book.

Remember that in these days of multinational corporations, it is not sufficient to model the organizations, business processes, and business objects. We need to also model the logistics, that is, the geographic distribution of functions and responsibilities; and the dynamics, that is, the events that trigger processes.

We will use several modeling techniques from the object-oriented world. Some of these techniques have proved to be very effective at the strategy level, while others are useful at the detailed analysis or design level. Oracle Designer does not yet support these models, but its repository allows us to record similar information. We will examine alternatives for representing this information in Oracle Designer.

3.4 Organization Model

The easiest model to compose is the organization structure. Most companies have a chart of their organization structure. If a formal chart does not exist, it is quite easy to construct one. Just quiz a long-time executive secretary or a peer who has been with the company for some time.

Notice that typical organization structures are hierarchical. However, follow the threads of responsibilities and you may find that reporting paths may be a matrix structure. In our model, we care more about functional responsibilities than formal titles and organization charts. But stick with the department or division names in common use, so that you can communicate the functional responsibilities via the process flow diagrams.

A business unit can be any division, department, or organization within the company. If your company has more than one geographic location, each location may be treated as a different unit. This way, you record volume and frequency information in the detailed analysis phase essential for analysis of distributed environments. More discussion on this topic is included in Chapter 14 Distributed Systems.

The repository object navigator is the one tool for recording the name and description of each business unit. You can also record organization properties via the property sheet in the process modeler. I suggest that you record the following in the text description:

- **Responsibilities of the unit**: For example, The sales department calls customers and takes orders. Be as concise as you can, you don't need to repeat all of the functions from the process model.

- **Current head of department**: Don't forget the date of this entry as the information gets out of date quickly.

- **Size**: The number of people within this group. For example, the sales group consists of two supervisors each supervising five salespeople.

- **Planned growth**: The plan for growth in staff, revenue, or some other appropriate measure, over some period of time. For example, the sales department expects to hire two more salespersons this year and targets a revenue of $20 million by the end of the next year. Last year's revenue was $10 million.

3.5 Business Objects

The object-oriented community has matured since the previous publication of this book. They have grown from focusing on the programming aspects of OO to applying OO concepts to analysis. My experience suggests that these concepts also apply to strategy studies. In fact, I find that OO modeling at the strategic level avoids many of the difficulties we faced when using entity relationship diagrams. My clients always had heated discussions about whether or not to normalize or to use many-to-many relationships at the strategy level.

The point at the strategy level is to model just enough to provide a basis for formulating an information technology strategy or to discover opportunities for BPR projects. These models may change significantly during analysis, perhaps with additional detail, or by restricting the scope of the analysis project to a particular subject area. In fact, I recommend that you maintain a strategy-level model of your business separate from the detailed analysis or implementation-level models. This model is the cornerstone for planning systems projects, setting project scope, and maintaining your focus on the business goals and objectives.

The Oracle Designer product set includes an object diagramming tool. However, you will need some training before you can be productive with it. In the meantime, you have two alternatives: use a third-party tool for strategy and load the information into Oracle Designer for individual projects, or use the entity relationship diagrammer together with function and usage definitions to capture the definitions of an object model. Section 3.8 Mapping Models into Oracle Designer describes one of the ways of mapping. In this book, I have used Rational Corporations' *Rational Rose* product to illustrate OO concepts.

3.5.1 What are Objects?

Objects are the *things* of the enterprise: customers, products, orders, and so on. They contain all of the information needed by the company to conduct business, together with the operations that could be performed on them. For example, a product can be manufactured or purchased. It can be stocked in inventory, ordered, sold, shipped, and so on. In object-oriented terminology, we might call these *things* object types or classes.

There are many conventions and notations in the object-oriented world to model objects: Booch, OMT. UML, and so on. Rather than introduce you to all of these notations, we will simply use the **Unified Modeling Language** (UML) notation popularized by the joined forces of Booch, Rumbaugh et al. Figure 3-3 illustrates this notation. You may browse through the references listed in the bibliography for more detail. We will use the terms "object type" and "class" interchangeably in this text. (Note: In conventional object-oriented terminology, the term "*object*" refers to an *instance* of an object. I prefer the term "*instance*" to avoid confusion between object and object type.)

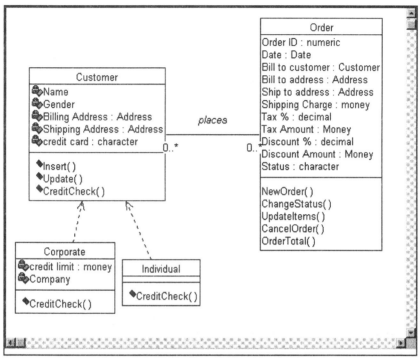

Figure 3-3: UML Class (Object Type) Diagram

Business objects are a higher-level representation than the entities described later in this chapter. They may decompose into several entities. Their definition includes attributes as well as the methods they present to the outside world. Objects can be categorized such that all subtypes of a supertype share certain characteristics, but may have additional characteristics of their own. Figure 3-3 also illustrates the customer supertype with its subtypes, *corporate* and *individual* customers, with the shared attributes and methods listed in the supertype and subtype specific attributes and methods listed in the appropriate box. Here are brief definitions of some of the key terms in the object-oriented world:

Class or Object Type: These terms refer to the set of objects that have the same characteristics and can perform the same operations. An object is an instance of an object type. For example, *Publication* may be an object type and this book, *Oracle: A Database Developer's Guide,* may be an object of that class.

Sub Class or Subtype: These terms refer to the subset of objects within a class that have some characteristics that are different from those in another sub class. For example, *Book* and *Magazine* are sub classes or subtypes of the class *Publication*.

Operations or Methods: Methods are operations that an object type can perform to deliver a result. The internal structures and procedures used by the object to execute the method are hidden from the interface.

Inheritance: This term refers to the fact that subtypes inherit the characteristics of their supertype. A subtype may inherit attributes as well as methods. For example, the *Book* and *Magazine* subtypes may inherit the attributes *Publisher* and *Publication Date* from the supertype *Publication*.

Polymorphism: This capability allows separate subtypes of a supertype to provide the same interface, even though internally they use different structures, parameters, or procedures to implement it. For example, a subtype may override the inherited method with its own if it has different internal procedures, provided that the external interface remains the same. In our example in Figure 3-3, the *CreditCheck* method for a *corporate* customer may be different from that for an *individual* customer.

Encapsulation: This term refers to the fact that object types present only their external interface. Internal structures and procedures used to present this interface are hidden from other object types.

Association: Objects are related to each other. For example, an order is for one or more products. Associations are usually represented as lines between object types in the diagram. The notation and types of associations vary widely between the different OO methodologies. For example, the Booch notation includes a subtype relationship called an *is-a* association. The Coad/Yourdon notation calls the subtype relationship *generalization/specialization*. Most notations include relationship cardinality, that is, one-to-one, one-to-many, and many-to-many. They also include optionality at each end of the relationship though notations are different. Some OO methodologies add another type of association, called an *aggregation* to describe a master/detail relationship.

This is not an exhaustive glossary of OO terms, but it gives you sufficient basics to understand the discussions in this book.

3.5.2 Finding and Modeling Objects

Many methodologies have elaborate descriptions about how to find objects. They describe taking interview notes and locating the nouns. Then you need to determine if the noun represents an object type, an instance, or an attribute of an object type. This approach works if you have very little knowledge of your company's business. Chances are, however, that you know more than you realize. Here are a couple of alternate approaches that capitalize on your knowledge and save valuable interview time.

At a very high level, certain objects exist in every company. The differences are in the specifics. For example, every company has customers, products, and vendors. However, the source of the product may be different—a retail company might simply purchase its products from vendors. A manufacturing company, on the other hand, makes its own products and consequently requires objects such as work orders, equipment, and so on. The type of product also makes a difference: *chemicals* have different attributes from *apparel*. These are obvious differences that you can model long before your first interview. So, I would suggest you start with a model from your own knowledge of the company. Then, flesh out the specifics through interviews.

Another approach is to start with a generic template for the subject area. These templates show excerpts of models that you can copy and refine. Most such templates have a narrow focus but provide a good start to your modeling process. It is rare to find a published template for a specific industry. Unfortunately, there are not many templates that provide strategy-level models. Feel free to peruse the books listed in the bibliography. However, these books have one of two drawbacks: they may use entity relationship diagrams not object models, or they may contain patterns at the programming level not at the strategy level. Regardless, they are good sources for ideas.

Stay focused on the strategy-level model. You need not define every attribute, subtype, and method of every object type. It is a fine balance between capturing the peculiarities of your company's business and getting bogged down in detail. Only experience can provide the guidance in controlling scope creep. Keep in mind that it is more important to formulate a strategy than to get every modeling detail accurate. The objective is reversed during a project-specific analysis where accuracy can save much rework and delay.

3.6 Business Process Flow

This modeling technique allows us to represent interactions between the things, the operations, and the people of the enterprise. Object-oriented techniques use interaction diagrams instead of process flows. I prefer business process flows because they capture human interactions and physical flows like movement of material as well as object interaction.

An alternate technique is UseCases, described earlier in Section 0. You can use the business process modeling technique during a facilitated session with multiple interviewees also. However, it is harder to keep interviewees focused on describing the processes without reference to current technology and politics. The UseCase technique provides a better approach to keeping the session focused.

The business process flow model is critical to communicating with executives as well as for discovering opportunities for improving a business' cost and service structure. These models are used by management consultants to demonstrate inefficiencies in particular processes. In times of recession, potential improvements may be presented in the guise of cost reduction. In times of a booming economy, you may look for service improvements that gain competitive advantage or provide an opportunity for new lines of business. Figure 3-4 illustrates a sample process flow. Process flows consist of the following components:

- Business process, usually denoted by a box.

- Event, usually denoted by an arrow.

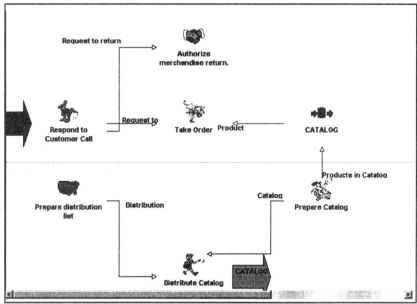

Figure 3-4: Process Flow with Business Objects

- Collaborators, actors, or specific role within an organization, usually denoted by stick figures or a drawing.

- Organizations, usually denoted by a meaningful icon.

- Business objects, denoted by boxes containing lists of attributes and/or methods.

How many processes should you depict in a single process flow diagram? Some practitioners recommend an arbitrary number like 7 ± 2 processes which is related to the span of human comprehension. Others recommend all processes in one giant, and incomprehensible, diagram.

My suggestion is that you illustrate one full process cycle in the process flow. For example, in a sales division model, you should use one diagram to illustrate the cycle beginning from the initial contact with the customer through the completion of an order, either through completed shipment or cancellation. Although this approach means each process flow diagram has quite a few processes, there are other benefits. You will notice when you are delving into too much detail—the number of processes in the diagram will get unmanageable. These process cycles will provide business management an appreciation of the complexities involved and opportunities for change. BPR tackles entire process cycles to get the desired radical improvement, not small portions of the cycle.

In the process cycle, you will also notice the groups of processes that comprise useful implementation units. These units are potential candidates for projects. You may also notice dependencies between these units. Use these dependencies to determine phased implementations in large projects.

The key to a good business model is to map everything that a business needs to do, whether or not it relates to a data processing function. This allows us to put data processing functions in perspective with other workings of the business. Don't decide at this point whether some process can be or currently is automated. Also, don't leave out of the model processes that you think are not IS functions. In fact, your model of business processes should not depend on any technology, data processing or otherwise.

Avoid describing processes in terms of mechanisms, because mechanisms depend on technology that changes frequently. A mechanism is a *means* by which a task is done. Mechanisms can be difficult to detect, sometimes, as they are deeply ingrained in our day-to-day life. For example, a check is simply an authorization for the bank to pay a certain amount of money—it is a mechanism for the authorization. Therefore, a process description of "Send a paycheck to employee" depends on a mechanism. Today, electronic funds transfers commonly replace checks. So a better way to describe this process would be "Pay employee." Then, this function includes payment by cash, checks, electronic funds transfer, or some other means not yet dreamed of.

Notice how removing mechanisms or implied technologies from a process description helps make the wording simple and clear. A clear, unambiguous statement of business processes helps everyone understand the model. Beware also of using grand-sounding, long words. If you can use a simple word, do so—you will avoid long explanations to your users. A classic book about clear writing style, *The Elements of Style*, by William Strunk, Jr., and E. B. White, is an invaluable aid to any analyst.

There is a drawback to removing mechanisms from your process descriptions. Your descriptions might become too abstract for users. In such cases, add the current method as an example in the process description. Thus, our example description becomes "Pay employee," that is, "send a paycheck."

At the strategy level, you need not dot every *i* and cross every *t*. Focus on modeling the broad overview of the business cycles. Don't let your project get bogged down in detail or you'll spend too long on the strategy study, resulting in lost credibility. Once you have determined the scope of individual projects, you can concentrate on detailed analysis which should capture the minutiae.

There is more to a process flow diagram than the pretty pictures. You need the metrics associated with each process for several evaluating activities. Some useful metrics are:

- Frequency.

- Time required to complete process.

- Capacity constraints, if any.

- Costs for overhead, labor, and materials.

At the strategy level, you may gather gross figures for these processes. These gross numbers should be sufficient to discover potential improvement areas and justify a project to corporate management. For example, the delay in communicating an order to the warehouse could account for a significant portion of the time required to ship it. An information system that supports integrated access by the two operations offers an opportunity for radical improvements.

I am often asked what the difference is between a method and a business process. A business process shows interaction between people. A method defines a service that an object can provide. It indicates the event to which the method responds, but not who initiates the event or how the event occurs. It also isolates any sequence of interaction between objects. The object runtime model assumes that any object that can respond to the event can do so independently of other objects. This model is somewhat reminiscent of the assumptions of *processors* in the essential data flow models.

Oracle Designer provides a process modeler containing all of the components described earlier: process, event, collaborator, object, and organization. In addition, you can specify many multimedia options: images, video clips, sound, and so on. These options, together with process timing information, provide the basis for *animation* of the business process flow. You can thus provide a graphic demonstration of the flow to business executives—one way to capture their attention and obtain meaningful feedback on your model.

Don't confuse *animation* with *simulation* of a business process flow. Animation simply plays out the flow, enhanced by multimedia effects, using sequencing and time information. Simulation, on the other hand, calculates volumes, costs, and other metrics as it runs through each step. These metrics are the basis for benchmarking or BPR activities. There are some third-party products available with simulation capabilities which can exchange data with the Oracle Designer repository. Oracle Designer itself provides only a few static reports on these metrics.

3.7 Modeling the Dynamics

The model of business processes and objects is not static. Objects interact with processes and each other to achieve some higher purpose—for example, to complete a particular business process. Understanding these interactions is essential to compose an information systems strategy that melds with the business cycles and its changing environment. There are several aspects of interaction:

- Events.

- Object states and transitions.

- Business rules.

We will examine ways of modeling these interactions individually. However, keep in mind that all of these integrate with the process and object models. They simply express the different columns in the Zachman Framework described in Chapter 2.

3.7.1 Events

Business events are events to which a business must respond. For example, a business must react to a customer calling to place an order. In our process model, events trigger one or more business processes. Any process which is not triggered by an event or another process indicates missing information or a redundant function. Business functions, in turn, can result in an event. For example, an event *"Applicant resume received"* may trigger two processes *"Maintain applicant information"* and *"Screen applicant"*. The process *"Screen applicant"* might, in turn, result in an event *"Candidate found."* In Oracle Designer we define trigger events and other functions triggered are items we define for each process in the process modeler or as the event element in the repository object navigator.

This example illustrates two types of events: *time* events and *change* events. Change events may have an external source to the model, as is the case with *"Applicant resume received"*, or an internal source, as is the case with *"Candidate found."* Time events occur usually in an artificial environment, such as cycles of a payroll, regulatory reporting, or accounting period. Change events indicate an update to some data, an object, or an attribute. Another type of event is a *system* event, where the completion of one process triggers the start of one or more other processes.

The repository object navigator lets us define quite a lot of detail about an event. We can define the condition which causes the event and other details appropriate to the type of event. These details are essential for detailed analysis, but not essential at the strategy level.

Defining an event and determining which processes it triggers is a good check for completeness. It helps in detecting missing or overlooked functions. It also has other benefits. You can use events to follow the execution of processes to understand a business cycle. An equivalent check in the object-oriented techniques would be an interaction model covering a complete cycle.

3.7.2 Object States and Transitions

Many earlier methods ignored the effect of state transitions on business models. The assumption was that only real-time or embedded systems needed to model object states. Only the entity life history technique made much use of states. Object-oriented methodologies have dispelled this myth.

Most business objects carry their status as part of their encapsulated information. For example, an order may be *created*, obtained *credit card approval*, *shipped*, *back-ordered*, and so on. The methods offered by the object usually effect a status change internal to the object. For example, the method *"Obtain Credit Card Approval"* for the object *order* will change its status to either *"Approved"* or *"Rejected."*

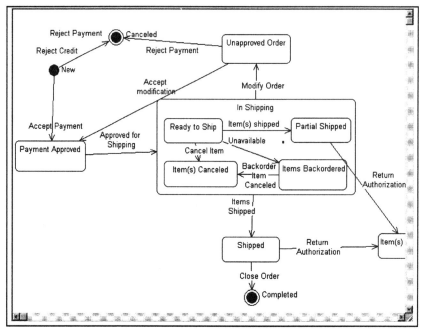

Figure 3-5: A State Transition Diagram

During a strategy study, we typically do not explore what's inside an object. We care only about the external interfaces it offers. However, many of our business processes react to specific states of an object. For example, if credit card payment is rejected, we must obtain an alternate form of payment from the customer. Our model would not be complete if it did not indicate that such a rejection may occur.

UML includes a state transition diagram to illustrate transitions between states of an object as illustrated in Figure 3-5. The boxes in this notation, Harel notation implemented by Rational Rose, represent states and arrows represent transitions. States can be nested within other states allowing us to show transitions to anyone of a group of states. Regardless of notation, these models indicate the following primary components:

- The state of the object, shown as a node in the model.

- A transition from one state to another, shown as an arrow.

- The method or process that caused the transition.

You may use these models to ensure completeness of your business model or to discover the missing processes or methods. State diagrams illustrate some of the business rules that govern transition between an object's states. In our example, the transition "*Approved for Shipping*" represents the rule that we cannot begin shipping an order until payment is approved.

3.7.3 Business Rules

Business rules constrain several components of the business model: objects, processes, organizations, and the interactions between them. They may be constraints explicitly expressed by our models, for example, the definition that *customers are people who place orders with us*. We may need to explicitly define some business constraints, for example, *if we cannot ship an entire order within two days, we must send a backorder notice for the portions that could not be shipped.*

We need to define business rules regardless of the modeling technique we choose to use. In the object-oriented world, we may later implement business rules as part of methods. In the relational world, we may implement them as stored procedures or as part of the user interface. However, at the strategy level, the eventual implementation is not important. Our focus, instead, is on defining them.

Remember that at the strategy level, we are modeling the business from the executives' perspective. So, the rules may be assertions about the way business *should be*. Later, during project-specific analysis, we may discover the rules about the way business *is*. The difference between what *should be* and what *is* provides the justification for a BPR project. If the executives are good at their work, they probably suspect the difference, but may not have a measure of its impact. Our task, during the strategy study, is to uncover such suspicions and use them to justify further study. By the way, some management consultants use this technique to conduct a strategy study in a very short period to discover and justify the initiation of large projects.

There are published conventions to precisely model business rules and associate them with formal models like entity relationship diagrams. I find these conventions invaluable during the detailed analysis work. At the strategy level, I prefer to express them in simple business terms, as unambiguously as possible given the idiosyncrasies of our language. I place more emphasis on capturing the rule in a way that executives can understand and verify than whether it can precisely express the logic that needs to be implemented. In the next chapter, we will examine some of the formal notations for business rules.

There are four categories of business rules, as defined by the *Business Rules Project* of the Guide organization:

- Definition of business terms, that is, definition of how people think about things. These terms may be definitions of objects, entities, or attributes in our models.

- Facts relating terms to each other, that is, relationships, attributes, associations, or structures of things. These facts may be the detailed definitions of our objects and their relationships to each other.

- Action assertions, that is, constraints on the behavior of the enterprise. These assertions constrain the interaction between the objects and business processes.

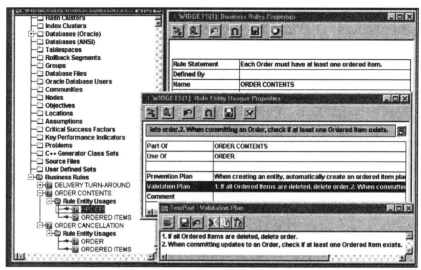

Figure 3-6: Business Rule Definition

- Derivations, that is, how knowledge in one form is transformed into other forms. Some examples of these derivations may be algorithms for calculation or aggregation, or the meaning of the status of an object. For example, once an order is completely shipped, it is eligible to be billed.

The document published by the Guide group addresses only row-three perspective from the Zachman Framework—that is, rules about facts that are recorded and changed as part of information systems. The next chapter addresses this row in the framework. In this chapter, we are addressing the row-two perspective from the Zachman Framework. We will establish the foundation for developing detailed definitions in the next chapter.

We discover rules during interviews or group sessions. We may express some rules in our object models. For example, models using subtypes express business rules. Attributes that apply to specific subtypes are facts about that subtype—a category of business rules. We may need to explicitly state other rules which an object model does not express. For example, the conditions that must be met for a particular subtype to be created is a business rule that a typical model does not express.

Start by making a simple list of statements that are candidate business rules. Examine them in view of your models. If your model expresses a specific rule, discard that statement. Remember that the statement may not be an atomic rule—that is you may be able to decompose it into component business rules. In many cases, one or more of the components may be expressed in your model and the remainder may need to be expressed elsewhere.

Oracle Designer does not provide explicit facilities to record business rules. Some practitioners have evolved ways of documenting rules in the repository. One method

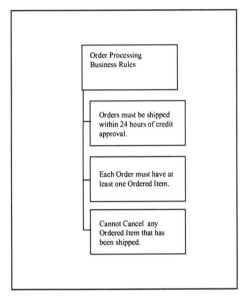

Figure 3-7: Rules as a Function Type

uses the User Extensibility features of Oracle Designer to define a new element called "Business Rule" with appropriate properties. The rule element is then associated with the data model elements, entities, and relationships. Figure 3-6 illustrates an example definition in Oracle Designer using its User Extensibility features.

Another approach uses a separate set of functions to express business rules. In this approach, one rule is a single function. You can use the function hierarchy feature to group rules into logical sets for convenience. Each function can be associated with data elements such as entities and attributes, using the matrix diagrammer utility. Thus, you can express the impact of a rule on data. The rule itself is expressed as a statement in the scripting language of your choice. Figure 3-7 illustrates an example definition in Oracle Designer. In this approach, you can use the Transformer Wizards to generate module definitions that correspond to these rules for implementation later. We discuss Transformer Wizards in Chapter 6 Database Design For Performance.

I should emphasize that business rules are *not* functions or processes. They are constraints imposed on processes or associations between data objects or their methods. Some examples of the constraints that business rules dictate are

- The conditions that must be met for a particular activity to occur.

- Policies on when particular objects may exist.

- When an object may respond to particular messages.

Business rules are not static—they may and *do* change as business conditions change. They are dependent on many modeling choices. For example, the rule that a department must be a part of a division in our company is only necessary if we model an abstraction of the organization structure such as illustrated in Figure 3-8.

Notice that such rules may be internal to an object type based on the object's internal implementation. At the strategy level, we need not be overly concerned with such rules. We should pay particular attention to business policies and rules that constrain interaction between object types. For example, we may find rules that govern when particular events may occur, or rules that dictate when a particular process can

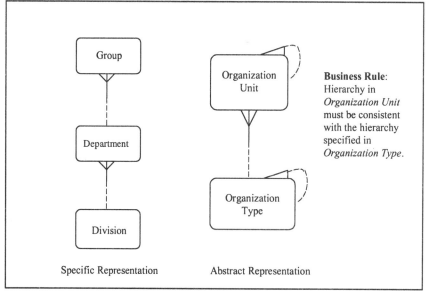

Figure 3-8: Organization Model

complete. My usual suggestion is to focus on rules that describe the external behavior of objects at the strategy level.

3.8 Mapping Models into Oracle Designer

Oracle Designer provides a business process flow diagrammer; however, it does not support object models for strategy-level modeling at the time of writing. Its repository does have a sufficiently rich meta model to allow us to map our strategy-level model. Here are some suggestions on ways to use older versions of Oracle Designer or other tools that do not yet support object models. Once it supports object models, you may not need to use such mappings.

Oracle Designer and the repository object navigator require you to define applications, which are typically a single functional area of an organization. This concept helps to modularize your model.

3.8.1 Object Types to Entities

Older releases of Oracle Designer do not provide object modeling tools. They provide a rich entity relationship model which can represent many of the components from an object model albeit less conveniently. For example, there is no direct analog to a method in the repository elements. Here are some suggestions on mapping object models. In the next chapter, we will explore in more detail a method to derive entity relationship models from object models.

You can map object types to entities in Oracle Designer. Attributes of object types will then be attributes of the corresponding entity. Since object types are more complex structures than entities, you may need to bend the rules for entity relationship diagrams. For example, an object type can have as an attribute a list of items. In conventional entity relationship modeling, this attribute would become a separate entity. At the strategy level, I suggest that you ignore the normalization requirements of entity relationship modeling, for the purposes of saving time. Instead, leave such *list* attributes as attributes to be refined in later analysis projects.

Associations can be relationships between entities—although you may have to refine relationship names depending on your object modeling conventions. Some associations, namely *is-a* relationships are represented simply as entity subtypes—these are not represented as a separate relationship in Oracle Designer conventions. However, you may choose not to use the entity subtype mapping, and use an explicit one-to-one relationship instead. Container relationships, namely *part of - made up of*, can be one-to-many relationships with the appropriate names. Aggregation relationships are anathema in normalized entity relationship models. However, the tools do not prevent you from drawing them.

Representing methods in the current repository metamodel is the challenging part. There are a couple of approaches. In one approach, you could treat methods as a new category of functions which are associated with just one object type (or entity). The association could be a new type of association defined using the User Extensibility features. You will also need to define a new property for functions, function category, that allows you to distinguish a method from an ordinary business function.

In another approach, you could define a completely new element using Designer's User Extensibility feature, called *Method*. You could then add properties to this element including the name of the object type for which it is a method.

One caveat for the User Extensibility features is that you will need to evaluate their impact each time you upgrade the Oracle Designer repository. Unless you have expert assistance in maintaining the repository, I would suggest you avoid using these features.

3.8.2 Processes or Object Interactions

One approach to modeling object interactions is process modeling as described earlier. Oracle Designer supports this approach.

Other models for object interactions, such as UseCases, can be mapped into the business process model. If you map methods into functions—with a specific category property—you can represent these models using the business process modeler.

There is no direct analogy for a sequence diagram that illustrates the sequence in which methods are invoked. The sequence would have to be implied in the order of the business processes in the diagram.

3.8.3 State Diagrams

Oracle Designer currently has no facilities to draw state diagrams for an object. You could, however, document the different states of an object by using a domain definition. Create one domain to represent the states of each object type. Set its allowable values list to reflect the states which are possible for that object type. This mapping does not allow you to document the transitions between states and which method causes the transition.

3.9 Formulating Your Strategy

Having defined the components of the strategy study, we are ready to formulate a strategy. You need to exercise your judgment extensively in this task. There are no recipes.

Compare your business process, object, and business rule models to your existing systems. Outline the parts that these systems cover. Undoubtedly there will be gaps and overlaps. Here are some of the areas you need to pinpoint:

- Are there suspected differences between business rules that *should be* and that *are* in practice? Estimate the impact of these differences on the business. If the estimate shows significant impact, plan to initiate a BPR project to redesign these business areas.

- Are there innovations that your company's competitors have that you might benefit from? Our goal is not simply me-too technology, but that which genuinely benefits the company or improves its perceived positioning in the market.

- Is there duplicate data between two or more systems? What is the cost of this duplication? For example, duplicate customer data between sales and accounting systems means double data entry.

- How is this duplicate data kept synchronized? If it is not synchronized, what kinds of extra work results? There are probably customers in the accounting system which do not appear in the sales system, or even worse, vice versa!

- Examine the gripes you heard during interviews. Why don't the current systems address these issues? Would it take too long to change?

- How often are requests for change or enhancements received for existing systems? A good clue to an inadequate system is a large volume of requests for change.

- How long does servicing a request for change take, on average? Would using Oracle's, third-party client-server tools, or intranet technology speed up this process in the future?

Combine the answers to these questions with the company priorities outlined in the previous chapter. With this combination, try to divide the models into possible system boundaries. Keep in mind current skills and strengths of your group. Use the cross-reference matrices to determine who benefits from each of the identified systems and who provides data in each. The group providing data must benefit in return; otherwise, they will be reluctant to participate.

Consider the potential effects of the draft system boundaries. Will you need to change hardware architectures as well as software? How will the user organizations react? Are organizational changes needed for effective implementation? Consult the high-level executives for their input and opinions. You should know whether they will be receptive to your strategy before you finalize it.

Don't forget to publish your information technology strategy once you have formulated it. This document will provide company executives an overview of your IT goals and the architecture of systems to support their business plans. The document is usually very short—typically two or three pages. It should focus on providing the overview graphically where possible. For example, a diagram of the high-level systems architecture is more effective than pages of descriptive text. This publication is also essential to prevent your staff from getting distracted by buzzwords or their pet project. Here are some of the items you should include in the IT strategy document:

- Statement of IT mission – long-term and short-term.

- A graphical representation of the architecture of all systems.

- A graphical representation of technology in use or planned.

- A brief discussion of proposed benefits from the short-term mission.

- A list of projects necessary to implement the short-term mission.

Your strategy will, of course, change as business plans change. Republish it whenever you change it. Keep it short and it will give the impression that you are in control rather than just spouting buzzwords. In companies that are geographically dispersed, a brief presentation can be an effective communication tool.

Case Study: WI Strategy Study

In this section, I present the key components of the Widgets, Inc. model, as an object model and business process flow diagram. In a strategy study, I typically use up to three levels of decomposition. This keeps it simple enough so that most high-level executives can comprehend it quickly. The intent, in this phase, is to focus their attention on parts that are of strategic importance to the business. Those are the candidates for the detailed analysis phase, especially if the company executives can prioritize them.

Similarly, the object models also represent only the important object types. So, you will see numerous many-to-many relationships. Details, such as developing the complete set of attributes, I defer until the detailed analysis phase. Remember that you are under pressure to show results quickly at this phase, so don't spend much time worrying about capturing the details. This way, you can keep the strategy study phase short and useful. It can be customized to suit the needs of the company.

During the strategy phase, we interviewed only the high-level executives of Widgets, Inc.: the president, who decided on sales strategies; the vice president of marketing, who chose product line strategies; and the chief financial officer. Keeping the number of interviews small is very important. I have seen many strategy studies which suffered from analysis paralysis. They took too long to complete, leading to heavy pressure to deliver quickly in later phases. In one to two cases, the developers decided to skip the design phase completely to make up the time. You can guess the quality of the end result! Typically, a strategy study should take less than one quarter of the time estimated for the entire project.

Documenting the Models

We used Solutron, Inc's Publisher/2000 product to compose several of our reports. This product provides convenient predefined phase end reports that can become part of your standard methodology. The advantage of using this product is that you can get consistent reports in word processor or web format that represent your project standards. You may modify the supplied rulesets to add or remove elements that your standard specifies. The repository reports supplied with Designer require significant rework to make them pretty.

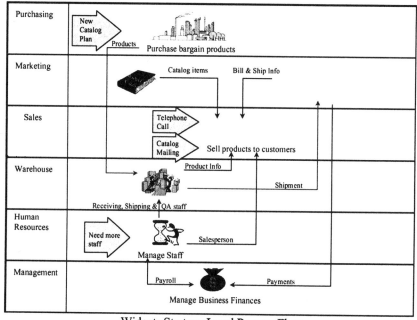

Widgets Strategy Level Process Flow

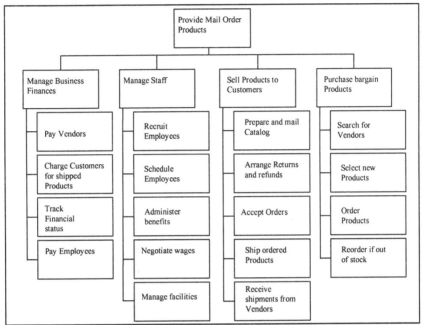

Widgets Strategy level Function Hierarchy

Notes on Process Models

- We use the terms "function" and "process" interchangeably here. Oracle Designer does so also.

- Start the strategic analysis with a top-level functions. The president provided us with the company's mission statement in the first meeting.

- We sketched out the departments to give us a tentative second level of the function decomposition. This gave us six functions, one for each organization shown on the left in the process flow diagram. Each organization usually represents a *swim lane* in a process flow.

- Aim to keep the function decomposition to only three levels. The fourth level typically means too much detail. Check to see if your grouping of functions is incorrect and if regrouping brings you back on track.

- Notice however, that we have only four major functions: marketing, sales and warehouse organizations collaborate to service just one (*very!*) essential function "*Selling products to Customers.*"

- During interviews, we followed each second-level function into more depth. We asked our three interviewees to contribute their understanding in each of the departments. If we had a lot more interviewees, we would have restricted discussions with each to departments they were responsible for. We did get a lot of repeated information, but an occasional pearl made it worth the tedious wait. These interviews also helped increase our credibility with these executives, since our questions quickly homed in on the business issues that were important to them.

- This sounds like interviews took days of discussions. They did not! Each interview was less than two hours—but two hours of intense discussion. Organizing notes after each interview took nearly a whole day.

- When we sketched in the detailed third level of the function decomposition, we realized that the sales and warehousing departments are very closely knit operations. So, we merged the warehousing function into sales in the hierarchy. Expect to rearrange your function groups frequently throughout the strategy phase. This is the reason why you should build trial models after each interview—it helps assimilate the information and clarifies interdependencies. The business process flows were invaluable in detecting these closely integrated functions.

Here is an excerpt of the report produced using Publisher/2000. The business process flow diagram was in fact inserted by the product—I edited it out to preserve the layout format of this book:

---

2 Process Model
2.1 Process Hierarchy
    SALES- Sell products to customers
    CATALOG- Prepare catalog
    REFUND- Send refund to customer for returned goods
    OE- Accept orders
    MAIL-LIST- Prepare mailing lists
    MAILING- Send catalog to customers
    CREDITCHK- Check credit and get approval
    RETURNS- Examine Returned goods
    PAYMENTS- Accept Payment
    REFUND- Send refund to customer for returned goods
    ORDERS- Place Order
    <Other subfunctions intentionally removed – Ulka>

Publisher/2000:Process Model Report Excerpt

2.2 Diagram: ELECTRONIC SALES
<Diagram excerpt intentionally removed – Ulka >
Figure1 Business Process Model: ELECTRONIC SALES
2.2.1 Input Events

2.2.2 Business Units

2.2.2.1 Business Unit: ACCOUNTING

Description: Responsible for revenue receipts, payments to vendors, payroll, and other bookkeeping functions.

Functions: PAYMENTS
REFUND
BILLING
CC-BILL

2.2.2.2 Business Unit: PURCHASING

Description: Responsible for all ordering of products from vendors

Functions: SEARCH
SELECT
BUY
REORDER
REORDER

2.2.2.3 Business Unit: TELESALES

Description: Responsible for traditional telephone sales, call center, and related functions.

Functions: REFUND
OE
CREDITCHK
ALTERNATE
REMINDER

<Other definitions intentionally removed – Ulka >

Publisher/2000: Process Model Report Excerpt

2.2.3 Processes

2.2.3.1 Business Function: ALTERNATE

Description: alternate order item selection

The product may be unavailable either due to long backorder cycle or because it is no longer made or contract has expired. In such cases, it may be possible to substitute an alternate product. Sales makes the decision on whether to contact the customer or just ship an alternate and then takes action as appropriate. In some cases the "terribly sorry" letter needs to be sent saying that we cannot fill the order

Frequency: 5/hour

Input Dataflow(s): unavailable re-orders

Output Dataflow(s): new-order

revised additional order

Associated Business Units TELESALES

Entity Usages

Entity	Create	Retrieve	Update	Delete
CUSTOMER	✓	✓	✓	✓
IN-STOCK PRODUCT		✓		
ORDER	✓	✓	✓	✓

Attribute Usages

Attribute	Create	Retrieve	Update	Delete
DATE ORDERED of Entity ORDER	✓	✓	✓	✓
ID of Entity IN-STOCK PRODUCT		✓		
NAME of Entity CUSTOMER	✓		✓	✓
NAME of Entity CUSTOMER		✓		

2.2.3.2 Business Function: BILLING

Description: Send Invoices

< Other function defintions intentionally removed – Ulka >

Publisher/2000: Process Model Report Excerpt

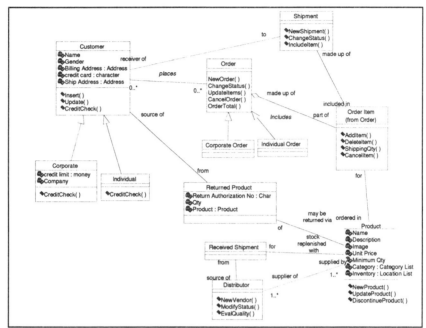

Widgets Strategy: Sales Object Type Model

Notes on Object Type Models

We developed these diagrams in parallel with the process flows. This is not the strict object-oriented approach advocated by the gurus. However, the business process flows served an extremely valuable comunication tool to encourage discussions with the executives. They had difficulty in understanding the object type models even when we tried interaction diagrams. UseCase diagrams came closer to depicting the issues under discussion but threatened to get bogged down in detail. Even in a small company like Widgets, the executives were a little removed from the minute details of daily operation. So, we decided to reserve the UseCase diagrams for use during detailed analysis.

Parallel modeling of object types and business processes ensured that we have identified functions which refer to these objects. We developed one diagram for each major business area, a total of four object type diagrams. We used the Rational Rose® to model object types using UML notation. We also developed similar entity relationship models using Oracle Designer. Both kinds of diagrams are shown here.

Notice that these are strategy-level models. We have rather sketchy details on each object. Attempting to gather more detail is too time consuming for this level and yields little overall benefit. In fact, the trap of collecting detail is a major cause of strategy studies that take too long. The Widgets strategy study, including feedback and documentation, required 4 people approximately 6 weeks to complete.

Each of the major business area in this example corresponds to a potential application. Depending on the complexity of the business rules, you may choose to further divide them into smaller applications. You need to use one Oracle Designer repository application to group each of the second-level processes and object types. This way, you can get reports for all corresponding elements in one application with the Requirements Specification report. I show a fragment of this report here.

Notice how the report constructs sentences from our relationships. This is a good way to check if we named the relationships correctly.

2.1 Entities and Attributes

This section provides a Description and Attribute list for each Entity.

2.1.1 Entity: CATALOG

Plural CATALOGS

Alias

Description A set of products offered for sale by Widgets Inc at a particular price. Widgets produces several catalogs per year. More than one catalog may offer the same product. Widgets plans to produce seasonal and targeted catalogs in the future.

Attributes

	Name	Datatype Description	Domain	Default
o	ID	NUMBER (10)	IDENTIFIER	
		Assigned identifier		
o	TITLE	CHAR (250)	SHORT TEXT	
		Title for the catalog e.g. Fall sale, Buyers Club Fall Special...		

Relationships

Each CATALOG must be for one or more IN-STOCK PRODUCTS
Each CATALOG may be used for one and only one ORDER
Each CATALOG may be copied to one or more CUSTOMERS

2.1.2 Entity: CLOTHING

Plural CLOTHING

<Additional text intentionally removed – Ulka>

Publisher/2000 Data Model Report Excerpt

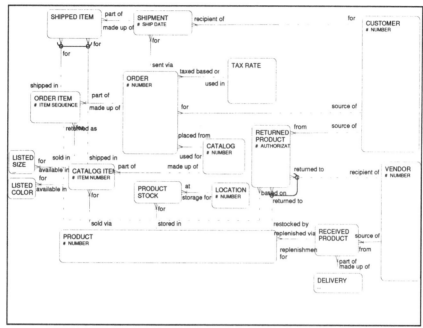

Widgets Strategy: Sales ER Diagram

Notes on the Purchasing Object Type Diagram

This business area is in its infancy at Widgets. Their current function, buying products from distributors, is only a small part of their future plans. So our models reflect the future plans, including the category analysis they intend to use as a basis for finding new products in the future.

Object types like Product Category, Customer Category, and Market exist only in the executives' minds. So at this level, we have little detail on them. Later, our business area analysis will explore them. From our current understanding, this group will require historical data for analyzing trends and demographical preferences of the customers. Our strategy therefore includes a data warehouse to support such analyses.

There is no data on these object types in current operations. This means that when tackling the purchasing application, we have to find ways of defining these categories and automated tools for categorizing existing object instances. These categories are likely to be very volatile. We should be able to create and categorize objects at will, not just during their creation.

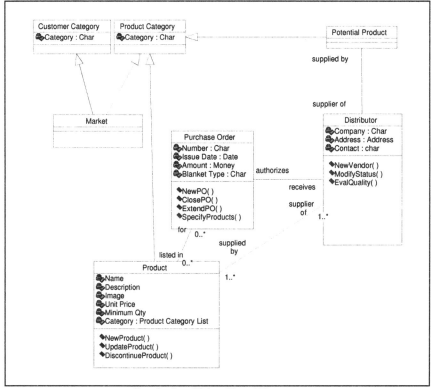

Purchasing Object Type Diagram

In the corresponding entity relationship diagram, notice there are several many-to-many relationships. Purists will argue that we ought to resolve them now, before proceeding further. However, such activities would add little to our architectural insights at this level. So we defer them until we are ready to tackle a detailed business area analysis.

Keep the strategy project short! I really cannot stress this enough. Remember your focus is to gain an understanding of the entire company. Broad strokes are sufficient to set the scope for later detailed analysis. Correctness of relationships and detail are tpics for detailed analysis, not strategy.

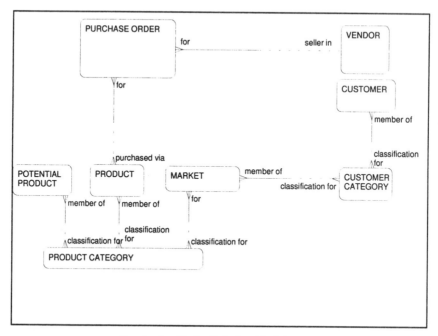

Purchasing Entity Relationship Diagram

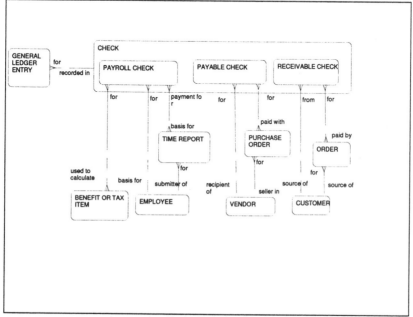

Accounting Entity Relationship Diagram

Notes on the Accounting Object Type Diagram

Notice the object type *Check* and its subtypes. This is a correct abstract representation which simplifies the understanding of the functions of the accounting department. Our representation in the entity relationship model is clumsy by comparison. Detailed analysis may choose to discard it later, if there is little similarity between the attributes of subtypes.

Object types like Sales Order and Purchase Order are shared between multiple organizations. We made the corresponding entities shared between the Oracle Designer repository applications. These shared entities may become shared tables when we design the database later. By realizing the relationships of shared entities to entities in each aspect of the business, we hope to design integrated applications that avoid duplicate data entry.

Notes on the Personnel Object Type Diagram

The *Job Standards* object type actually specifies a job grade and a list of benefits that

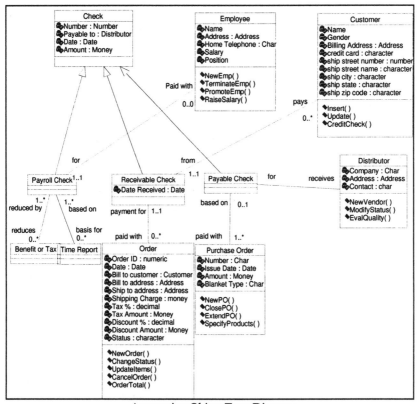

Accounting Object Type Diagram

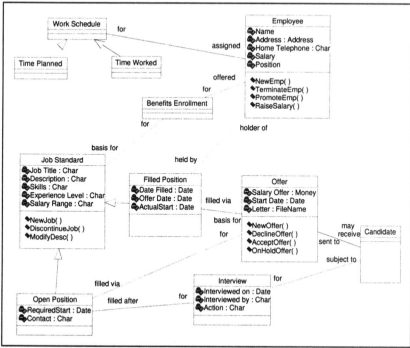

Personnel Object Type Diagram

are associated with the grade. This is another example of the detail orientation of the entity relationship technique. We may later normalize the *Job Standard* entity to two entities during analysis. We simply note this idea in the entity comment field in the repository for later review. The natural use of a plural name also gives us this hint, since by convention, entity and attribute names must be singular nouns.

Notice the mandatory relationship (solid line) between Employee and Schedule entities. This implies that we have no employees that are not scheduled for work time. Apparently, vacation time is also scheduled at Widgets, Inc. Sick time, again, is a category on the schedule.

We were given a similar argument for the relationship between Employee Position and Employee. Widgets, Inc. does not hire unless there is a defined position open.

Business Policies

During our conversations with the executive management and line managers, we heard a number of policies expressed. We captured as many of these as we could in this section. The played an important role in determining the complexity of business area processes, and hence influenced our application boundaries. In the Analysis phase, we will decompose these policies into business rules that our applications will

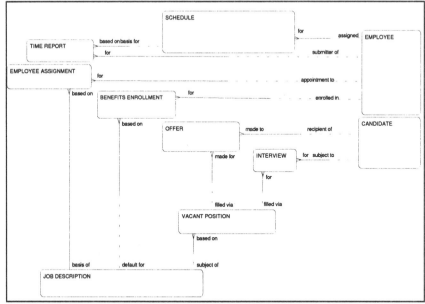

Personnel Entity Relationship Diagram

need to enforce. Some of these policies may be atomic, that is, rules that cannot be further decomposed.

We chose to use the Oracle Designer business functions to record business rules rather than using the repository User Extensibility features. This choice allowed us, in later phases, to use the existing Oracle Designer tools, such as the application transformer to carry our analysis elements into design and later into development. Here again, we used Solutron's Publisher/2000 product to produce the Business Rules report.

3.9.1.1 Policy: BP_SALE1

Individual customers must pay the entire balance due before their order is shipped.

3.9.1.2 Policy: BP_SALE2

Corporate customers must have sufficient balance available in their credit limit to cover their order before their order is shipped.

3.9.1.3 Policy: BP_SALE3

The customer is always charged the lowest price in effect at the time of order.

3.9.1.4 Policy: BP_SALE4

30-day money back warranty: Products may be returned within 30 days for a full refund.

Widgets IT Strategy

This document is an example of a published information systems strategy report. You may add other sections to this as appropriate. It should also include the strategy study findings documented in Chapter 2 as well as models as appendices.

Executive Summary

Widgets Inc is experiencing significant growth and their business plans should result in increasing their growth rate. Their current information systems are inadequate in supporting their current business. They also cannot support the plans for growth in the future.

Widgets undertook an information systems strategy study to analyze the current and known future requirements and to recommend a systems and infrastructure strategy. This document is the culmination of this strategy study.

This strategy report outlines the architecture recommended to support Widgets' current and known future plans. There are two aspects of the architecture: The systems and the infrastructure such as hardware and networks. A summary of the benefits of the recommendation is also included. The report summarizes several projects that should be undertaken to implement the recommendation.

Information Technology Mission

The information technology at Widgets need to support the business vision in the short and long term. This support is an on-going process, however, the infrastructure design must allow periodic review and change of direction. The new application architecture must support the needs of individual business areas as well as provide appropriate summaries for use at the corporate level. To this end, some of the essential characteristics are

- Adaptability of the components of the infrastructure to allow changes in base platforms or technology at a business area level. The infrastructure must be modular to permit such transition.

- The systems and technology architecture design must include transition plans for data, functions, and business users.

Systems Architecture

Widgets requires several application systems that need to be closely integrated. There are two applications that constitute the foundation of these integrated systems: accounting and inventory management. All other applications depend on these

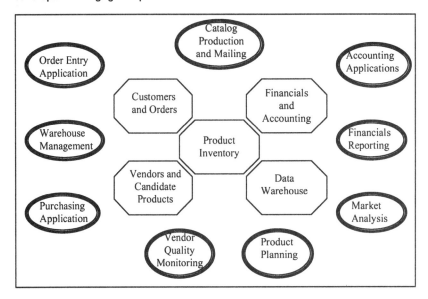

systems for successful operation. The diagram below illustrates the applications needed to support the business objectives stated by Widgets executives.

After a review of the existing systems at Widgets, the team concluded that these existing applications are inadequate to support the current and future operations of Widgets. These systems were implemented piecemeal and provide little opportunity for integrated operation. Business requirements such as informing the customer of stock availability as part of taking orders cannot be supported without complete integration between Order Entry and Warehouse applications. Furthermore, the estimated cost of enhancing these older systems to provide such integration is comparable to the cost of new development.

Some of the key requirements for applications are the ability to handle international transactions including currency variations, customs and excise regulations and accounting standards. Widgets applications will run the US and Europe. A portion of the order entry application will be available via the Internet to the global market. The applications also must be sufficiently integrated to permit smooth consolidation of data into the data warehouse. The proposed architecture will ensure this integration.

Technology Architecture

Widgets needs a local area network based architecture within each geographical location, the U.S. and Europe. Each location has a distinct set of customers and products. These locations should therefore be autonomous. The country regulations require that the European location be registered as a separate legal entity, perhaps as a wholly owned subsidiary. Also, the customs regulations make a transshipment between these locations similar to an inter-company sale.

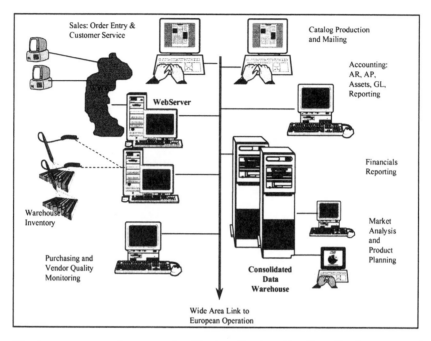

The team recommends separate localized applications for all applications except the Internet based public order entry and customer service applications. In addition, the data warehouse will include data from both locations.

The warehouse and inventory areas will use barcodes extensively to reduce manual entry during receiving and shipment. The aim is to provide an easy to use interface that requires minimal computer knowledge from these users.

Planned Benefits and Goals

Implementing these applications will provide several major benefits:

- Warehouse automation is expected to reduce shipping time. The goal is to achieve the business objective of 24 hour turnaround of an order.

- Using the Internet to provide customer service information is expected to result in cost savings on the support calls.

- The Internet based ordering system is expected to increase revenue with minimal additional labor cost. Long term, it is expected to reduce sales costs.

- Integration of the order entry and inventory systems is expected to reduce the number of items on backorder. This reduction is expected to improve customer satisfaction.

- Integrated order entry and automated warehouse systems is expected to reduce inventory by allowing future use of drop shipments from vendors or just-in-time delivery of items.

- Integration of credit card checking with order entry is expected to reduce lost revenues due to write-offs.

- The data warehouse will provide trend analyses of customer purchasing patterns and will assist in composing targeted catalogs. Targeted catalogs are expected to have a higher percentage of sales.

- The analyses possible from the data warehouse will allow informed selection of products based on seasonality cycles, trends and so on. This is expected to increase the ratio of catalog mailing to sales.

These are some of the key benefits expected from implementing the Widgets IT architecture. This list is not exhaustive but provides the support for making the decision to proceed with this architecture. The architecture team will design specific measurements to monitor the benefits from each application implemented.

Proposed Projects

The team recommends that the implementation begins with the foundation projects that will provide the most benefit. These include three applications to be developed and implemented as an integrated environment: accounting, inventory management, and order entry.

The accounting application shall be the first to be implemented. However, there are no immediately measurable benefits from this application. The inventory management system shall be the next target. The only benefits apparent from this implementation may be a reduction in the time to reorder products. These applications are both prerequisites for the success of the Order Entry application.

Benefits will not be measurable until the implementation of Order Entry application. The plan to first build the application for in-house telesales group. In addition to this, Widgets shall implement an Internet based order status inquiry system. This initial function should reduce the burden on customer service staff. Later, this interface shall be enhanced to provide an online Widgets catalog and direct order entry.

During transition, the initial input to the accounting application shall be manual, where appropriate. Entries pertaining to customer orders shall be bulk loaded once per day.

Analysis Techniques

The detailed analysis phase addresses a much smaller portion of the company than the strategic business analysis phase. It uses the outputs of the strategy study to make sure other, future projects mesh properly. The shared objects are of particular value in ensuring easy connections between applications.

This chapter discusses the techniques used for modeling during detailed analysis. Remember that we are now concerned with how business objectives are actually achieved, if at all, rather than what those objectives are. Similar to the previous chapter, we will restrict our discussion to the overall principles of techniques. For further detail refer to the texts in the bibliography or other books. The topics discussed in this chapter are

- Structuring your project for your chosen RAD or Waterfall methodology. We will examine some work breakdown structures for each approach.

- Techniques for refining the object models developed during the strategy study to gain better insight into the issues.

- Traditional techniques used in detailed analysis including function hierarchy, entity relationship diagrams, data flow diagrams, normalization, and cross-checks for completeness.

- How to develop models for stable systems. With experience, these techniques yield a flexible model. Such models require little change, even though business needs change over time.

- How to determine if your analysis has captured all of the requirements. Even in a RAD cycle, these completeness checks ensure that you don't miss some vital need.

4.1 Project Methodology

Having set the scope of projects in your strategy study, you are ready to start specific projects. The scope should define the business process cycle addressed by the project as well as dependent administrative tasks that need to be part of the project. The project definition document should also specify which object types the project owns and which ones will be external. In short, here are the key elements of a project scope definition:

- Core business processes addressed by project.

- New or existing administrative tasks that support the included processes.

- Core object types to be developed by project

- External object types—that is, owned by other applications or projects and external to the project in question.

- Requirements for interfaces.

- Business goals to be supported by project.

Within a project, you can choose the development process used. Though you may have a current corporate standard such as RAD or Waterfall, you cannot blindly apply one standard to all projects. Here are some key tests to determine if a project is appropriate for a particular approach:

- Does the project have easily defined groups of functions that comprise a logically complete business activity? For example, order entry functions form a logically complete activity, but shipment of products between warehouses is not complete.

- Do the groups of functions illustrate heavy dependence on object types owned by other groups? For example, shipment of products between warehouses depends on object types that are central to all inventory management functions.

- Can you implement the group of functions into production to be usable by the business, or will the business users need several other groups of functions before they can meaningfully use them?

- Is the group of functions small enough to be developed and implemented in a short time-frame, for example, in eight to ten weeks?

Be careful to choose an approach that is appropriate to the characteristics of your project. I have seen some expensive misapplication of approaches resulting in ineffective projects.

I emphasize the fact that RAD and Waterfall are styles of project structure. They do not inherently imply the use of a particular modeling technique or development tool. Individual methodologies *do* specify the techniques you may use. For example,

Information Engineering specifies the use of the entity relationship modeling technique.

4.1.1 RAD Approach

RAD is based on the incremental development principle. It involves iterating through the analysis, design, and build cycles, quickly albeit with incomplete information. The assumption is that with significant user interaction at the end of each iteration cycle, you build a system that is closer to the real requirements of the users.

To effectively use the RAD approach, you need a project that easily subdivides into relatively independent sub-projects. The characteristics of sub-projects are

- Independent ownership of objects.

- Clearly definable interface to objects not owned by the sub-project.

- Addresses a group of business functions that is usable on completion of development.

- Short estimated development time for each sub-project.

- Supporting administrative tasks can be included within the group of functions.

- Interfaces to external objects are flexible—that is, they can be redefined based on scheduled completion of other sub-projects.

An example of a characteristic that indicates that you should not use a RAD approach is a central shared set of object types manipulated by all sub-projects. Another example is where you require rigorous documentation for traceability from requirements to implementation such as for military systems or systems audited by regulatory agencies. Quick iterations through the analysis and design, in practice, means sketchy documentation of requirements and design decisions no matter what the methodology defines.

By now, my message that RAD is appropriate for small, relatively stand-alone projects should be clear. RAD basically uses the same techniques as a Waterfall model, but in an iterative fashion. For example, in a RAD project, we may perform some analysis, design as best we can, and develop an initial cut prototype. This process may uncover issues which we resolve in the second iteration analysis and repeat the cycle. I don't mean to imply that RAD is simply an unstructured approach. The techniques described in this chapter are just as useful in RAD, but we do not complete each phase before proceeding to the next.

Some RAD methods have a formal definition of what components shall be defined in which iteration and the number of iterations required to complete the project. For example, one method defines a brief analysis, followed by a design of the user interface in the first iteration, business rules in the second iteration, and testing in the third iteration to complete the project. The total duration of the project and that of each iteration is pre-defined as part of using the *timebox* style of project management.

Whether you use a formal structure like the example above or an informal iterative approach, you need to set a limit on when the development will be considered complete. Since you have no rigorous definition of requirements before starting development in the RAD approach, the limit should be based on either time or number of iterations.

Some projects are inherently unsuited for the RAD approach. Any project where you cannot decompose functions into independent sub-projects is a poor fit for RAD. Another poor choice is where the data structures are common between all sub-projects.

RAD assumes that your data structures can be built incrementally, just as functions can be built incrementally. In RAD, you develop the data model as you proceed through the iterations. So, you cannot completely model the database and design it before building the applications. Even in an object-oriented analysis method, you cannot build an object type until you have a fairly complete definition. Your definition may not be complete unless you consider the requirements of all subsystems. For example, a clinical trials application development project is a poor choice for RAD. In this type of project, the functions are deceptively decomposable into protocol setup, data entry, data cleanup, statistical analysis, and so on. The catch is that all of these subsets share the same data structures. You really need to model the data completely before you can build any of the subsystems.

Use the few rules of thumb I proposed earlier to judge whether your project is appropriate. Applied to appropriate projects, RAD allows you to deliver successful systems that meet users' needs.

4.1.2 Waterfall Approach

This approach is the traditional methodology that consists of several sequential phases including analysis, design, development, transition, and so on. This approach was popularized by industry gurus like James Martin in Information Engineering, Ed Yourdon in the Yourdon Method, and so on. Figure 4-1 illustrates the typical phases in such methodologies.

The approach derives its name from the assumption that you complete one phase before starting the next. Completing a phase implied that no further changes are required for the phase once complete. You do not revisit a phase once complete. For example, a change in requirements discovered in the build phase could not be accommodated easily. Clearly, in this approach, an error in analysis or design phases discovered during a later phase would be expensive to correct. So, the approach includes many techniques to ensure that you consider all requirements in the current phase before moving on to the next phase. Today, we use some of these techniques regardless of our development approach.

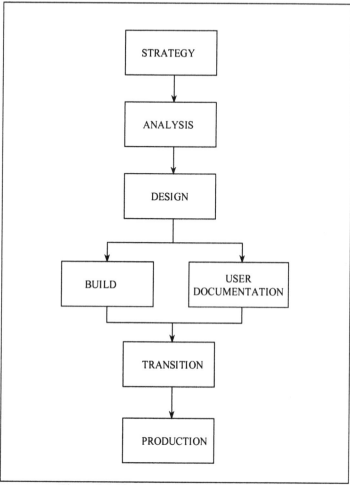

Figure 4-1: Phases of a Waterfall Methodology

On a superficial level, all life-cycle development methodologies follow a similar structured approach with similar techniques. An application is viewed by all as going through several phases in its lifetime, hence, the name life-cycle development. There are separate phases for analysis, design, programming, testing, conversion, and implementation (or production). Each phase uses a certain set of techniques and tools. The techniques vary in flavor and depth based on the methodology and the founder of the technique.

The principle employed in the engineered systems approach is divide and conquer. You probably have first-hand experience in getting overwhelmed with enterprise-wide systems. Relax. Only the strategy phase need consider the entire company. Each subsequent phase divides the scope into manageable chunks such as just one functional area. The strategy deliverables help keep all of the latter separate portions linked. Without the big picture, you would have too many peripheral functions to cover each time you tackle an application area.

Methodologies are rarely a recipe for system development. You rarely follow one straight out of the box, except at first. After gaining some experience, you can adapt it to your environment by adding or ignoring specific portions. The idea is to always maintain a structured approach—primarily to perform tasks methodically and to facilitate clear communication between all parties. Realize that it is very difficult to learn a methodology from a book. Instructors at training classes add real-world knowledge which is difficult to gain from books. Books are useful as reference material. You might find useful additions to your practice of techniques from books.

Much literature exists that describes each of the popular Waterfall methods in detail. In the remainder of this chapter, I will review some of the common techniques of these methods. My intention is to give you sufficient flavor of these techniques to appreciate their benefits in systems development.

4.1.3 Component-Based Development

This approach is a development of the object-oriented analysis and design methods. When we apply object-oriented techniques in real-life projects, we immediately see that it is not practical to work on one object type at a time. Since each object type provides services that other related object types use, we need to understand the requirements of other object types before defining these services. Such groups of closely related objects are the basis of a component. In other words, we have a formal means of defining the scope of a sub-project in terms of closely related objects.

A component can be any size—from a single object to an entire subsystem. In my experience, analyzing one subsystem at a time is much more productive than attempting to analyze single objects. However, we may design and build one object at a time. So a component at analysis may be further divided into smaller components during the design and build iterations.

When developing components, you may choose any style of project structure: RAD or Waterfall. The acclaimed advantage of object-oriented modeling is that the models map directly to implementation elements in the OO language. You do not need to transform the models from analysis to design as you would in entity relationship models that transform to relational tables. I suggest, however, that you may need some transformation even in the OO implementation due to performance or distribution considerations. The tools are rarely as capable as theory would like them to be.

4.1.4 Detailed Analysis Phase

The detailed analysis phase usually addresses one application at a time. The order in which you undertake applications depends on your information systems strategy and available resources. If you need a sales system for company growth and only have two analysts available, you cannot address sales and warehousing systems at the same time.

In the absence of an information systems strategy, you may find this phase to be the starting point for many projects. As a result, the project scope may be poorly defined or nonexistent. For example, a requirements document that consists of plain text descriptions of the functions covered by the project is a poor definition because of language ambiguity. However, such a document based on formal data and process models would better define the scope.

If your project starts at this phase without the benefit of strategy-level models, consider prefacing the project with a short strategy phase. This strategy phase would be application-specific and would not encompass the entire organization. Its purpose would be to construct models and test the boundaries specified in the textual description. The models will help clarify the specific interfaces needed to other, possibly existing, systems.

4.1.5 Gathering Information

The approach taken in the detailed analysis phase is bottom-up. We aim to analyze an area of operation together with the key doers in that area. Typically, we interview line managers, supervisors, or their right-hand people in our investigations. These people have direct responsibility for the day-to-day work, although they may not perform it themselves.

We take a bottom-up approach to ensure that we do not miss any detail as is possible in a top-down approach. However, the bottom-up approach alone cannot take into account company objectives, plans, and goals. The top-down approach provides this information without going too much into the actual workings of the company. During detailed analysis, we discover business rules that *are* rather than the rules executive management think *should be*.

The work plan in this phase is similar in structure to the strategy phase. We interview selected company staff in the chosen area. We model based on notes from these interviews using techniques appropriate to our methodology. We then feed back our models to verify their correctness. The specific technique may be refined UseCases, object models, process flows, entity relationship diagrams, or data flow diagrams based on the chosen methodology.

Detailed analysis phase interviews are with people who perform the work. In these interviews, we discover how the company actually works, as opposed to strategy-phase interviews when we model the way the company is supposed to work. These interviews take more time since we need all the details of each function. We collect, for example, all forms and reports currently used and make sure we understand their contents in the interviews. We obtain algorithms for any processing needed as well as frequency and volumes for all data and processing. Realize that users at this level have in-depth knowledge, but little breadth. So, you will discover additional interviewees through earlier interviews. Schedule sufficient time in your project plan to cover such extra interviews.

There are a lot more interviews to conduct in the detailed analysis phase than in the strategy phase, even though we tackle a smaller functional area. Each interview also takes much longer. In this phase, we are not only gathering information about how work is done, we also look for performance expectations, cost justification, and acceptance criteria. For example, suppose the users expect to increase their productivity because the system is supposed to provide data much faster. Ask them for the worth of hourly availability of data currently available overnight, or within minutes for data which they get once an hour today. Answers to such questions not only provides ideas for cost justification, but also describes their expectations.

Use an interview as an opportunity to set realistic expectations. When you provide examples of the potential new system, understate the possibilities. Set user expectations lower than you know is feasible without disappointing them. You should not underplay the possibilities so much that users lose enthusiasm, but be realistic. Then, if the system exceeds expectations, your users will be happy.

4.1.6 Models during Analysis

The models developed during the analysis phase are refinements of those developed in the strategy phase. However, you will develop in-depth models. You may have glossed over some areas during strategy. Now is the time to investigate them in-depth.

In the object-oriented methods, we refine the object models we started to construct in the strategy phase. For example, we may have identified the set of UseCases that form our project scope. Now we need to flesh them out with detailed events, actions, and exceptions. In object type models, we focused on the external interfaces of objects during strategy. Now we focus on the internal structure as well as the external view.

In some traditional methodologies, we use function hierarchy diagrams for modeling processes and entity relationship diagrams to model data. You might still use these techniques during strategy studies. In analysis, you would refine the entity relationship diagrams with detailed attributes and business rules. You might supplement the function hierarchy models with data flow diagrams. We also normalize the data details from the data flow diagrams. The normalized data model should be close to the entity relationship model, albeit more detailed.

Many methodologies use data flow diagrams as a primary analysis technique. Data flow diagrams were popularized by Chris Gane and Trish Sarson in the late 1970's and early 1980's. The Yourdon methodology specifies data flow diagrams as a primary analysis technique, although this methodology requires more rigor than the one proposed by Gane and Sarson. Until the mid-1980's, this method was used together with normalization techniques, without the support of entity relationship diagrams (ERDs). ERDs have added method to data analysis in the same way that data flow diagrams helped process analysis.

Today, the process flow diagram serves as a substitute for the data flow diagram. The methods for developing the diagrams apply equally to both process flows and data flow diagrams. The process flows have additional useful features—for example, they can represent physical material flows that are not shown in data flow diagrams, making communication with businesspeople easier. In Oracle Designer, process flow diagrams have multimedia features that are useful when presenting to (and persuading) a business audience.

You can check the models for completeness by comparing what we found in the strategy phase and detailed analysis phase. So, continuing with the models started in the strategy phase is a good idea. If you choose to change the techniques, for example, from object models to entity relationship models, the checks for completeness will be a little harder to apply.

4.1.7 Object-oriented Analysis

In the strategy study, our object models concentrated on defining the external view and behavior of the object types. In detailed analysis, we refine these interfaces and flesh out the internal structures of each object type. We will design their implementation in subsequent chapters.

To refine the internal structure of object types, we bring together several concepts described separately: normalization, business rules, and integrity constraints. Normalization and integrity rules apply to the definition of attributes of an object. Business rules apply to its methods. Let us examine how these concepts work together in the object-oriented models.

Although many attempts have been made to define what an *Object* is, there still is no clear, crisp definition even in the books authored by gurus like Booch, Rumbaugh and Jacobsen. Here is my attempt, with apologies to the purists:

> *An object is a thing of significance to the business that combines data and operations to manipulate that data and transform the object from one state to another. An object has integrity in the sense that its data is internally consistent. Data manipulation operations maintain the internal consistency and will not permit integrity violation.*

Note that this definition is a little more precise than the definition of business objects used in Chapter 3. As we progress through the stages of definition and implementation, we progressively refine our object model in the same way that I refine the definition of an object.

An object is described by a set of properties—that is, its attributes. An attribute may be a single fact about the object, a reference to another object, an embedded object, or

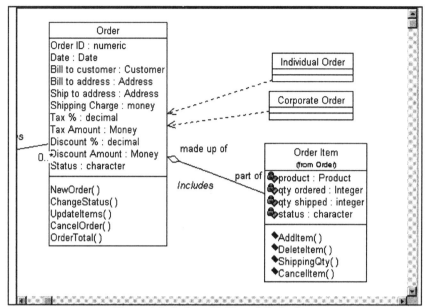

Figure 4-2: Order with Nested Order Item

a list of any of these. Figure 4-2 illustrates the *Order* object type with examples of each kind of attribute. Notice that according to this definition, objects are not normalized in the way entities in entity relationship diagrams are normalized.

It is beneficial to apply normalization rules, described in Section 4.5 Normalization, to attribute definitions to understand whether an attribute is just a list of single facts or an embedded object. For example, in the *Order* object, the attribute *telephone* is a list of telephone numbers—that is, a list of single facts.

The attribute *items*, on the other hand, is a list of an embedded object which has its own attributes: product reference, quantity ordered, product discount, and so on. Normalization forces us to examine any attributes that are lists of facts to determine whether it is a list of single facts or an embedded object. For embedded objects, we need further analysis to determine its attributes and methods.

In an entity relationship diagram, we would show *Order* and *Order items* as separate entities with their respective attributes. Intersect entities from an entity relationship diagram are likely to be embedded objects in an object model.

I mentioned earlier that an object may change its state when an operation is performed. An example is the status of *Order*. The object may maintain its status internally or make it visible via the external interface. For example, the status of Order needs to be visible externally so that the business may communicate it to the customer.

The status of the *Order* object is dependent on the collective statuses of its embedded *items* objects. For example, an *Order* is not complete until each embedded *item* has the status of either *complete* or *canceled*. So, the status may be derived from some operation on the object's attributes.

By the way, this dependence of the order status is a *business rule*. The rule is enforced by the method that retrieves the order status. Thus, in object-oriented models, we need to associate business rules with methods. In this case, the business rule is about deriving a fact about an object and hence may apply to only one object type. Of course, the rule may be inherited by its descendants just like any other part of the object.

Methods of an object specify the possible manipulations that you may perform on the object. For example, an *Order* may be created, canceled, shipped, paid for, and so on. We may specify one method for each of these manipulations. In each method, there are preconditions that must be satisfied before the method can execute. Such pre-conditions are business rules.

Similarly, a method may fail during execution because some post-condition cannot be satisfied. For example an order cannot be canceled if one or more of its embedded items are already shipped. Such post-conditions are also business rules.

In Chapter 3, we described four kinds of business rules specified by the *GUIDE* Business Rules Project. We also described two kinds of business rules applied to object models, namely, definition of facts and structural assertions. We have just described the other two of these four kinds of rules as applied to object-oriented models. Business rules that specify pre- and post-conditions are action assertions that constrain the actions. These kinds of business rules may use information from one or more object types. Rules that derive facts from other facts may also use information from more than one object type.

Realize that the business rules defined at the strategy-level may be too general or abstract to apply at the detailed analysis level. We may need to decompose them into their component parts before deciding whether they apply to a method, an association, or an attribute. Later in this chapter, we will examine some techniques for decomposing business rules.

4.2 Entity relationship Models

In this section, I will describe briefly the concepts underlying an entity relationship diagram. It is intended for those of you who are inexperienced in these concepts and would like some basic understanding. Those of you who are proficient modelers in this technique, please glance through these concepts. There may be some differences in our views. Being aware of these differences will help you understand my perspective throughout the remainder of the book.

An entity relationship diagram models data and how the business views its structure. An *entity* is something about which we want to hold information. For example, at

Widgets, Inc., we want to hold information about customers, products, and so on. These are examples of entities. Relationships between entities, represented on the diagram, describe the dependencies between them. Customers each buy at least one, and sometimes more, products. Customers also pay for each product that they buy (well, most of the time!). An entity relationship diagram (ERD) is a shorthand representation of such relationships. These can be drawn using the Oracle Designer entity diagrammer facility. Figure 4-3 illustrates a simple entity relationship diagram.

The specific information we want to hold about entities are called *attributes*. For example, we want to hold customer name, address, credit limit, and so on. These are attributes of the entity *Customer*. Even a few attributes help in ensuring that we correctly identify an entity. In particular, you should identify all attributes that are unique identifiers for each entity. Unique identifier attributes have values which uniquely identify an instance of an entity. The entity/attribute property sheet in the diagrammer allows us to define entity details as well as attributes of an entity. Entity details include synonyms, volume information, and a description. Attribute details include the format, optionality, domain, unique identifier, and a short note. In addition, we can define unique identifiers that are made up of multiple attributes.

Each relationship, in Oracle Designer conventions, is drawn as a line between two entities. Each line actually represents two relationships, one from the first entity to the second, and another in the reverse direction. A solid line near an entity denotes that each occurrence of that entity has a mandatory relationship with the second entity. We read this as *Each <entity 1> must be..* A dotted line indicates an optional relationship, that is, *Each <entity 1> may be..* The type of relationship is written as the relationship name at the end nearest the entity. In our sentence construction, the relationship name follows

> *Each <entity 1> must be <relationship name 1>.. ...*

The other end of a relationship line may be a single line, indicating an association with exactly one occurrence of the second entity. Crow's feet at the end of the relationship line indicate an association with one or more occurrences. Again these conditions appear in our sentence as

> *Each <entity 1> must be <relationship name 1> one and only one <entity 2>.*
> *Or*
> *Each <entity 1> must be <relationship name 1> one or more <entity 2>.*

The second relationship is read in a similar manner in the reverse direction, that is, from entity 2 to entity 1. In this case, we use the relationship name closest to the second entity. So, the relationship between *Customer* and *Product* entities in Figure 4-3 read as

> *Each customer may be the buyer of one or more Products.*

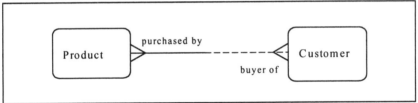

Figure 4-3: A Sample Entity relationship Diagram

and

Each product must be purchased by one or more Customers.

Why do we care about relationships between entities? A relationship defines a business reason for association between two pieces of data. With these drawing conventions, we can form structured English statements from the relationship definitions. Thus, we can ask users to verify our understanding by asking them to correct our English statements. For example, we can ask users if it is possible to have *Products* which are not purchased by any *Customers*. If the answer is "Yes," then we can correct the second relationship by changing must be to may be, that is, change from a solid line to a dotted line nearest the product entity. In such questioning, we improve our understanding of the business.

Relationship names obviously play a very important part in obtaining meaningful responses from your users. Finding the most suitable relationship names requires a lot of effort. Similar to our discussion of function descriptions, avoid using noise words such as process. Sentences like *"Each product may be processed by one or more salesperson"* will get user agreement, even though we have not identified the kind of processing a salesperson performs. We may be missing important information by glossing over the kind of processing involved.

Relationships come in several flavors:

- **One-to-one**: This type is rare. It usually indicates misunderstanding of one or both of the entities. Try defining some attributes for each entity. You might find that one of the entities is actually an attribute of the other.

- **One-to-many**: This type is the most common. Typically the crow's feet end is mandatory, and the other optional.

- **Many-to-many**: This type is fairly common. However, you really ought to normalize this further by adding an *intersect* entity between the two entities. The intersect entity is often something the business recognizes by name. For example, a many to many relationship between *Customer* and *Product* breaks out as shown in Figure 4-4(a). In this case, the intersect entity is an *Order*. In this entity, we have a place to hold, as an attribute, a shipping address if it is different from the

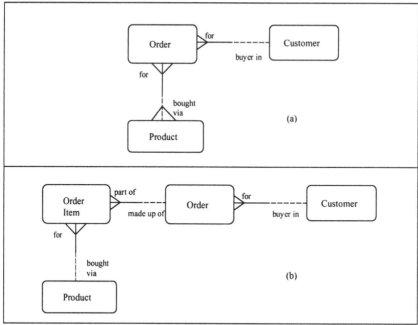

Figure 4-4: Intersect Entities

Customer's address. The shipping address might even be different for each order, such as when a Customer buys Christmas presents!

Unfortunately, there is still a many-to-many relationship between the *Order* and *Product* entities. Further breakdown leads to *Order item* as another intersect entity, as shown in Figure 4-4(b). Thus, we discover two more entities which we might have missed. Finding the names for intersect entities is not always as easy as this example implies. You often need to conduct several discussions with users and to investigate their current paperwork.

In addition to drawing relationships in the Oracle Designer Entity Diagrammer, we use the repository object navigator to define cardinality specifics, volume information, and to make notes on each relationship. A repository report, *Relationships,* in the data model section, shows the English statements constructed from relationship information. Note that relationships, like entities, belong to an application. However, defining entity sharing between applications makes associated relationships shared. No explicit sharing need be defined.

There can be more than one relationship between two entities, although many times there is only one. Arcs between two relationships from one entity indicate an exclusive-or condition. The ends of the relationship participating in an arc must be both mandatory or both optional, otherwise the condition does not make sense. As an exercise, try reading such a nonsensical combination using sentences composed by Oracle Designer. Oracle Designer will report such poor relationship names in its

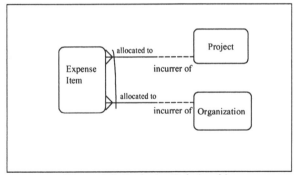

Figure 4-5: Exclusive Relationship

quality check reports. The other end of each of the relationships that are in an arc may be different entities or the same entity. Figure 4-5 illustrates an exclusive arc relationship.

Some entities may be made up of sub-categories. For example, suppose Widgets' products have sub-categories: tools, kitchen appliances, and clothing. These sub-categories are *subtypes* of the entity *Products*. The *Products* entity is called a *supertype*. Subtypes are mutually exclusive and must cover all occurrences of the entity between them. Subtypes are usually shown on the diagram as entities inside the supertype entity as shown in Figure 4-6.

Subtypes inherit all attributes and relationships from the supertype. For example, if *Product* has an attribute called *catalog number*, the subtypes tool, kitchen appliance, and clothing each inherits this attribute. Inheritance rules also apply to relationships. Some subtypes may have attributes that are different from other subtypes of one entity. For example, clothing may have an attribute *sex* indicating whether an item is male, female, or unisex clothing. Such an attribute obviously does not apply to the tool and kitchen appliance subtypes. A similar argument holds for relationships which apply to one subtype but not to others. This provides a convenient way to group similar objects. In fact, this technique is the key to convergent modeling as we will see in the next chapter.

If there are a large number of sub-classes, say, more than five or six, the diagram gets very cluttered. Create a new entity in such cases. In our example, we could have the entity *Product Type* as shown in Figure 4-7.

Entity subtypes are similar to sub-classes in the object-oriented models. One important difference is that entity subtypes in Oracle Designer are mutually exclusive. A subtype can

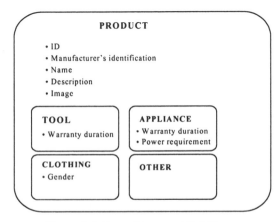

Figure 4-6: Super Types and Sub Types

only inherit from one parent. In object-oriented models, multiple inheritance permits a sub-class to inherit properties from multiple parents.

A common convention for the layout of an entity relationship diagram is to arrange entities such that all crow's feet point up or to the left. Diagrams in our case study follow this convention. This convention makes your layout follow a pattern. All base entities, that is, those that have mostly single lines starting from them, filter to either the right or to the bottom of the page. All transaction entities, that is, those that intersect between two or more entities, collect in the middle and left. If you then put all person or organization-related entities to the right and product-related entities along the bottom, your diagrams become regular. You can, of course, choose your own convention for layout, say, crow's feet pointing to the bottom or to the right. Consistent conventions are important for improved communication between members of your team. Oracle Designer does not enforce any restrictions on layout—you may place entities and relationships exactly as you choose.

When modeling several parts of a business, drawing everything in a single diagram is almost impossible. Even if you manage to do so, the diagram is probably useless, as it will be too complex to comprehend. So I suggest a breakdown based on business views. A business view is a group of entities which are of interest to a particular group of people in the company. For example, salespeople are interested only in sales-related information, entities like *Customer*, *Order*, *Order Line Items*, and so on. They have little interest in purchasing information like *Supplier*, *Purchase Order*, *Receipt*, and so on. There will be overlaps, of course. Both groups share the entity, *Product*, since they want to know the quantity in stock. Oracle Designer allows you to draw multiple diagrams which contain the same entities. You do not need to re-create entities—simply *include* existing entities into a new diagram.

To check completeness of your diagrams, use the Oracle Designer Matrix Diagrammer. With this tool, you can define which business function uses which entities as a cross-reference matrix. For each business function, you can specify whether the function creates, retrieves, updates, or deletes an entity. You can also comment on the usage, for example, a comment might be "*Retrieve sorted by Customer name*". There is more on the subject of cross-reference matrices in Section 4.9 Completeness Checks.

Diagrams are communication aids. So, pay attention to their layout and readability. The Oracle Designer facilities can help make your diagram easy to understand and memorable. You will need to define some layout

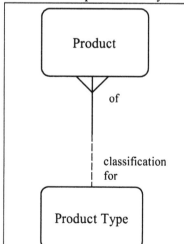
Figure 4-7: Alternative to Subtypes

conventions, especially for placement of key entities on your diagram; for example, always placing the *Products* or *Service* entities along the bottom of the page. Here are some hints to make your diagram easily readable:

- Do not bend relationship lines—following relationship lines around entities is difficult. Instead, try rearranging entities in the diagram or alter the size of the entity box.

- Use larger size boxes to draw attention to important entities. Less important entities, such as product type, can have small boxes.

- In a feedback session, build up entities and relationships over many overhead foils or pages. Showing the entire diagram at once overwhelms users and distracts their attention from the point you are trying to make.

There are many useful reports and quality checks in the repository reports. Explore these reports when you need to find some specific information. One of the most useful reports is the System Glossary. This report includes all of the entity descriptions as well as definitions of terms. Thus, you can document your understanding of any specialized terms of the business.

4.3 Function Hierarchy Diagram

A function hierarchy is a representation of business functions, that is, what a business does or needs to do. For example, Widgets, Inc. might have the following functions:

- Accept customer order.

- Send invoice for customer order.

- Ship ordered products to customer.

Simply listing all functions would make the business very difficult to understand. So, we organize functions into logical groups as a hierarchy within the business. In such a hierarchy, higher-level functions describe a broader area than lower-level functions. The highest-level function in a business is the mission statement for the business. Oracle Designer contains a diagrammer to develop function hierarchies. A hierarchical organization of functions is also called a *function decomposition* by some methodologies. Don't confuse this with a program structure chart decomposition, however. Here, we work with business functions, not program subroutines or functions.

You can, of course, move functions from one application to another, or share functions between multiple applications. Use your own judgment in deciding the boundaries between applications. Be aware, however, that access to information across applications becomes difficult based on your choices. This breakdown also prevents you from getting a view of all functions regardless of which application they belong to.

Figure 4-8 illustrates a function hierarchy drawn using Oracle Designer Function Diagrammer for the highest level of Widgets, Inc. The case study contains a complete function hierarchy for Widgets, Inc. The hierarchical organization of functions originated in James Martin's Information Engineering methodology. For more information, refer to the texts in the bibliography.

How far do you decompose business functions? This is a difficult decision. Ideally, the lowest level in the function hierarchy should contain only business functions which cannot be decomposed further, that is, *elementary business functions*. Stop decomposing when you reach a function which, once started, must continue to completion, or be aborted. There are no intermediate points. For example, once you start the function to "*Send invoice for a customer order*", the invoice is sent or not sent. The invoice cannot be half-sent!

You might argue that sending an invoice involves many functions such as print invoice, stuff envelope, address envelope, stamp envelope, and so on. However, such functions are very specific to a *mechanism*, in this case, envelopes in the mail.. Avoid describing functions in terms of mechanisms because mechanisms depend on technology which changes frequently. For example, if the company starts sending invoices by electronic mail—there are no paper invoices to print or envelopes to stuff! A simple change in technology makes your business model out-of-date.

Start function descriptions with an active verb followed by nouns which are the subject and object of the verb. This structure leads to simple wording and clear, concise descriptions. Avoid

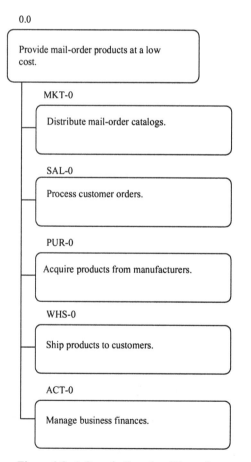

Figure 4-8: A Sample Function Hierarchy

ambiguous verbs or those that do not specify an action. For example, the verb "process" can mean different actions in each context. The simple rule is: Say what you mean, without any dressing up. There is another benefit to this method—the nouns in a function description are entities, an example of an entity, a state of an entity, or an attribute of an entity.

Occasionally, you might need to add conditional statements to clarify when a function occurs. Use a dotted line for a function requiring a condition to indicate that it is optional. The function description must state the conditions under which the function is performed.

Oracle Designer's Function Diagrammer lets you rearrange function hierarchies. Use this facility to draw and redraw your hierarchies until the organization makes sense to you. You can also define functions as being common on more than one function hierarchy diagram. Function labels aid you in tracking the sequence within a branch of the hierarchy. Of course, the function property sheet allows you to add a more detailed description of each function, or you may use the repository object navigator to so. The frequency of occurrence, response requirements, and business algorithms are some of the details you can define for a function. This may be a good place to record the current mechanisms used for carrying out a function.

4.4 Process and Data Flow Models

Process flow models are an essential part of BPR. However, the principles used by BPR analysts have been around for a long time under the guise of data flow diagrams. The diagrams may differ in conventions, but the following principles are common to both:

- Constructing an as-is model to represent the current business process

- Deriving an essential process model free of assumptions and technology-based constraints.

- Designing the new process model based on the new technology to be implemented.

Data flow diagrams are a bottom-up approach to process modeling. This technique has been in use since the 1970's. We can also apply the principles used in data flow models to business process flows. So, even if you consider this technique outdated, understand the methods used here so that you can apply them elsewhere.

We usually start by developing data flow diagrams representing the current operations and based on current mechanisms. Then, we derive an essential or logical model from the physical model. The essential model is free of technology and mechanisms. It should be very close to the elementary business functions we develop in the function hierarchy technique. Unlike the intuitive methods we used in the function hierarchy technique, data flow diagrams provide a more rigorous approach. Such rigor is

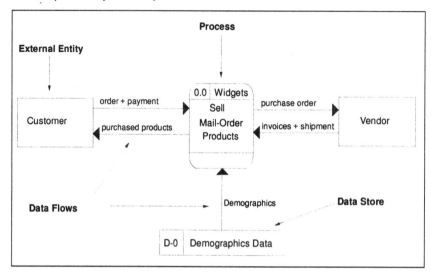

Figure 4-9: A Context Data Flow Diagram

necessary for analyzing the details. Since we tackle a much smaller portion of the company in the detailed analysis phase, such attention to detail is possible.

4.4.1 The As-is Flow Model

A flow diagram is a model which shows how data flows through business processes and how each process manipulates the data. These processes may be manual, automated, or some combination of the two. They are also a tool for communicating our understanding to users who actually do the work. Data flow diagrams focus primarily on the manipulation and transformation of data, while BPR process flows focus on the processes themselves. BPR models collect in-depth information about each process including its frequency of execution, metrics about its execution, costs, yields, and so on. We discussed the use of these metrics in Chapter 3.

A data flow diagram, illustrated in Figure 4-9, is made up of

- Processes, which are analogous to functions in a hierarchy. We describe how to manipulate incoming data into the outgoing data in a process.

- External entities, which supply all of the input and receive output of the system. Typical examples of external entities include customer, supplier, and so on. Do not confuse them with the entity relationship diagram—these are terminators of all information rather than a definition of what information we wish to hold. Sometimes they are also called sources and sinks.

- Data flows, which indicate movement of data between processes and data stores. They are drawn as lines between two processes, with arrows indicating the direction of flow. Data in the data flows may be elementary, that is, not processed or derived, that is, processed in some way.

- Data stores which are repositories of information over time or for later use. Information stored in a data store is the basis of our entity relationship diagram.

Describing an entire system in a single diagram makes the diagram very complex and almost impossible to understand. So, we develop it in several levels. Higher levels establish the context of the system, and each subsequent lower level shows more detail. Thus, the highest level, the context-level, consists of a single process with all external incoming and outgoing data flows. The next lower level explodes this process into a few major component processes, and another level lower, each of these processes explodes into more detailed processes, and so on. Figure 4-10 illustrates an exploded process. Process explosion in data flow diagrams is similar to function decomposition in our function hierarchy diagrams.

Each explosion of a process should result in no more than seven or eight processes. Restricting each level of explosion to this number makes each explosion easy to understand as well as manageable. Of course, every data flow to or from the exploded process must be shown on the lower-level diagram. Figure 4-10 shows an explosion of the example process from Figure 4-9. Checking that a lower-level explosion accounts for every data flow from the higher level is called level balancing.

This description implies that we develop data flow diagrams in a top-down fashion. This is not always true—developing lower-levels first and then leveling upward is quite common for initial diagrams. One way to start may be to break down the context-level process by the physical organization of the area being analyzed. Remember that we start with a model of the way work is done today, so partitioning based on current structure is okay. This may not be the best partitioning for the new system, but we'll worry about that later when we derive the essential model.

Oracle Designer provides a facility to draw data flow diagrams in a top-down fashion, that is, by exploding higher-level processes. In this facility, each explosion is a new diagram. Level balancing is easy in this tool since each explosion shows the higher-level process and all of its data flow connection to other entities, data stores, or processes. It also prevents mistakes such as drawing a data flow directly from an external entity to a data store. There must always be a process to receive and manipulate data from an external entity before storing it in a data store.

We define process details, a data flow, and a data store via their respective property sheets. As you draw items on a data flow diagram, they automatically get stored in the Oracle Designer repository. You can then add detail using forms accessible from either a diagrammer or the repository object navigator. Data flow and data store details in Oracle Designer are given in terms of entities and attributes. Thus, you can create them in the data flow diagrammer with just names. But before defining their contents, you must complete the entity relationship diagram details.

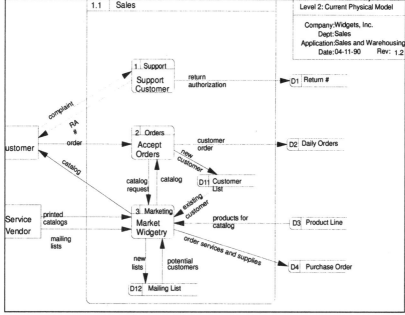

Figure 4-10: Process Explosion

Process details explain the data manipulations performed. There are no restrictions on the format of this explanation in Oracle Designer repository. Other third-party products include structured English, action diagrams, or state transition diagrams as techniques for detailed process descriptions. Oracle Designer may include similar techniques in the future.

How many levels do you need? A rule of thumb is until you can completely describe a process in about half a page. In many cases, this means at least three levels, and typically no more than five. In our case, slightly longer process descriptions are acceptable since we plan to use the Oracle Designer generators for development.

Remember the power of the SQL query language. Some of my consulting clients could dispense with the lowest-level data flow diagrams because of the complex processing a single SQL statement performs. They needed even less decomposition with Oracle Developer. If you understand how these tools work, you can judge when you have sufficient detail. Concentrate on getting accurate details on your data entities and attributes. Most of Oracle Developer tools are data-driven. Attention to detail on data pays off in the long run, especially if you plan to use the generators for application generation.

The Oracle Designer data flow diagramming facility serves for drawing both physical and logical data flow diagrams. Developing a physical data flow diagram from interviews is straightforward. The case study at the end of this chapter shows the physical data flow diagrams for Widgets' sales system. After completing the diagrams, conduct a feedback session to verify its correctness. These diagrams illustrate how the company works at present.

4.4.2 The Essential Model

In the function hierarchy technique we derived essential functions mostly by intuition. In this approach, we use much more rigorous methods. The end result is an essential model which is verified with users for its correctness. Don't try to derive the essential model before completing and verifying the physical model, however. Without a verified physical model, you cannot be sure of its completeness.

An essential model is the way our system would work if it used perfect internal technology. With perfect internal technology, there are no resource limitations. There is no need for communication—once some piece of data is known to one part of the system, it is available to all of it. Perfect technology does not require translation from one medium to another, or storage merely for processing as a batch. An essential model consists only of essential activities, or functions, and data flows between them. After we derive an essential model, we design the new system by adding the proposed technological and procedural changes to it.

Once we have a set of leveled diagrams for the current physical model, we start by joining together all of the lowest-level diagrams. Discard the higher-level diagrams. Connect the data flows of the lowest-level diagrams and consolidate common data stores and external entities. By the way, our method described here is the reason why the actual partitioning of the higher-level diagrams in the physical model is of small importance. After determining the essential processes, we level upward to derive new higher-level diagrams.

To derive essential processes, we discard any physical aspects or technology from our connected data flow diagram. For example, suppose one of our processes sorts orders received in the mail from all other mail. Discard this process as it implies the physical arrival of mail as a batch of letters. After discarding this process, connect the data flows incoming to that process to its outgoing flows as if the process never existed. Here is a summary of other types of processes to discard

- **Transporter processes**: These processes merely move data from one location to another without transforming it in any way. For example, processes to send mail, receive faxes, and so on. In most cases, they imply a technology or a mechanism and are easy to detect.

- **Translator processes**: Some processes translate data from one medium to another. For example, the process Enter customer order translates data from paper to a computer system. Discard these processes as they do not transform data.

- **Batching processes**: We often find processes which collect a number of transactions as a batch before processing them. Such processes are particularly common in manual systems. Discard these processes, again, because they do not transform data.

- **Edit processes**: Processes for editing that are internal to the system verify the correctness of information and possibly correct errors. In perfect technology, no errors occur and format conversions are unnecessary. Since we plan to change such methods in the new system, we discard such processes. Instead, the editing criteria are part of the definition of the data.

- **Audit or approval processes**: These processes represent the current methods for reviewing or approving data. Discard them. In perfect internal technology, there are no errors. In the new system, we design new procedures for them.

We also discard other items from the data flow diagram. We discard data flows that carry no information, data stores that merely exist to collect batches of data, historical storage, or duplicate copies of data used for backup. Here is a summary of some of these:

- **Data flows for physical movement**: These flows represent some physical item moving from one location to another, but carry no information. For example, a data flow representing an assembly moving from one test station to another is a physical movement data flow. In perfect internal technology, we do not need to move physical items.

- **Batch or buffer data stores**: These stores are merely repositories for collecting data into batches. In perfect internal technology, we process data instantaneously—as soon as we receive it—there are no time limitations or restrictions on the number of processors available. Discard these data stores. Connect any incoming data flows directly to outgoing data flows.

- **Magic hat data stores**: Data stores which only have outgoing data flows are suspect. Where does the data come from? They may be disguised batch data stores where you forgot a data flow coming from an external entity.

- **Black hole data stores**: Data stores which only have incoming data flows simply collect information that no one needs. Be careful, you may be missing a process which uses it. If no such processes exist, eliminate these data stores and the associated data flows. They are redundant.

As you eliminate each item from the data flow, make sure you do not lose any data. When you eliminate a process or a data store, connect incoming data flows to outgoing data flows. Draw and redraw your diagram and compare it with the original physical model until you are sure you have captured everything without any implied technology. Typically, the majority of processes should either retrieve data from a data store and pass processed data to an external entity, or vice versa.

Group the remaining processes, data stores, and data flows by events. Events in detailed analysis are probably more numerous than in the strategy phase. Start by drawing a separate diagram for each event. All responses to that event must be on the diagram. Then, level upward using sequences of events to obtain a logical group. In a functionally organized company, the logical grouping is likely to be quite close to the organization structure.

The essential processes derived in this process ought to match very closely with the elementary business functions. In fact, Oracle Designer treats the two as synonymous. This is a good check to make sure your model is complete. Another check is to define the cross-reference matrices between functions, entities, and business units. Now that we have a lot more detail, we should be able to define all usage completely. Each entity must be created, updated, and retrieved by some function. You may need to add processes to purge entities. The logic described in the process descriptions should match the usage described in the cross-reference matrix.

This process of developing a current physical model and then reducing it to an essential model seems a little long-winded. However, the methodical approach produces better results than the intuitive approach, even if you have very talented, experienced analysts. Even good people make mistakes sometimes. We all know the cost of discovering a mistake or misunderstanding later in the life-cycle.

4.4.3 The *To-Be* Flow Model

Once we have an essential model that is free of assumptions that are attributable to the current mechanisms, we are ready to redesign our processes. We need to add the restrictions of the new technology into the model. For example, in the Widgets company, we need to add the restrictions of the new Web technology to design the *to–be* data flow.

Of course, the new technology also implies *mechanisms* different from our current ones. The assumptions and constraints of these mechanisms are likely to be different from the ones we had before. We needed the essential model to understand our processes without the clutter of restrictions. Now we can clearly identify the processes that are the target of the new restrictions.

Realize that new technology may drastically change some processes. For example, if Widgets allows customers to enter their own order via the Web interface, it will not need order entry as a process performed by an internal organization. The order entry process itself still exists as an essential process, but it may now be performed by people outside our realm of control.

When such a change occurs, several of our service metrics—for example, average time spent on the telephone by a sales associate while taking an order, become obsolete. If our management processes depended on such statistics, we need to change them. Thus, not only have we initiated a change in the daily operations, we also have changed some of the goals of our data warehouse.

Although a strategy study is usually the only prerequisite to a data warehouse project, we can impact its goals through the process changes implemented in the to–be model.

This model, then, is the keystone to the detailed information system architecture. Yet, we often have to make project decisions long before this model is available. The key to making this model available sooner is a BPR project.

Here are some examples of items we may need to add to the essential model to account for the new model:

- **Security**: The new technology may impose new security requirements that were not needed in our current systems. For example, when an internal department entered credit card numbers as part of the order entry process, we did not need to secure their entry. When customers enter their credit card numbers for an order placed via the Internet, these numbers need to be secured against fraudulent access.

- **Audit**: An order placed via the Internet may need additional audit or approval prior to fulfillment. For example, we may need to compare the new order with previous purchases patterns for potential fraud. For drastically dissimilar patterns, we may call the customer back to verify authenticity. Such audits are common security measures in the credit card industry; we may now need them for big-ticket catalog orders.

4.5 Normalization

In the bottom-up approach, we end up with a lot of data elements. They appear in data stores and data flows. Of course this list is much more complete than the attributes we identified in the strategy phase. Now, we normalize the list, plug attributes into appropriate entities, and perhaps create a few more entities. Realize that entity relationship diagrams naturally lead to a normalized model, although that is largely dependent on the analyst's skills. The normalization process is usually more rigorous.

There are many introductory texts on how to normalize data using the two methods, decomposition and synthesis. So, we skip the details of the process. Instead, here are some informal tests for the normal forms.

There are five normal forms formally defined at present, although only the first three are most commonly applicable in database design. These normal forms, called first normal form, second normal form, and so on, form a layered onion. The first normal form is the outermost layer of the onion, and the fifth normal form is the innermost. The inner layers of the onion automatically pass the test of any layer outside them. Thus a relation in the second normal form is automatically in the first normal form. The converse does not, however, apply; that is, a first normal form is only in the second normal form if it passes the test for the second normal form. The normalization process aims to decompose data up to the most sensible inner layer.

4.5.1 First Normal Form (1NF)

The test for first normal form is whether each attribute in the relation takes only atomic values. By atomic values, we mean individual values such as those taken by attributes like *customer number* and *customer name*. A first normal form relation cannot have any attribute which takes multiple values packed into a single attribute. Note that a date could be treated as an atomic value whether as a combination of day, month, and year or as three separate attributes of day, month, and year. Whether to separate or not depends on your business needs.

4.5.2 Second Normal Form (2NF)

The test for whether a first normal form relation is also in the second normal form depends on identifying the key attribute of the relation. Each value of the key must uniquely identify a row in the table. For example, in a *customer order* relation, the key is obviously *ord_no*. The test for second normal form is whether every non-key attribute depends on the key.

4.5.3 Third Normal Form (3NF)

The test for whether a second normal form relation is also in the third normal form checks for any dependencies between non-key attributes. The end result is attributes that depend on the key (unique identifier) and nothing else.

The Boyce/Codd normal form actually has a stricter definition of a third normal form, but it applies rather rarely in a business application. For details on the difference between this form and the third normal form, refer to the book *An Introduction to Database Systems*, by C. J. Date.

4.5.4 Fourth Normal Form (4NF)

In most everyday databases, third normal form is a sufficient level of decomposition. Occasionally you might even notice update problems in third normal form, when there is a multi-valued dependency. In this case, some non-key attribute has multiple values for each key value, independent of other attributes. For example, each *seminar* uses more than one *textbook*, but has one title only. We decompose, in such cases, into two separate relations, *seminars* and *seminar texts*.

4.6 Analysis of Business Rules

At the strategy level, we gathered many assertions about the constraints on the business. These constraints were declarative statements about what the business must or must not do. At that level, these assertions implied some impact on the persistent data. However, it was unclear how they constrained or what data was constrained.

During detailed analysis, we need to relate business rules to the data and processes. For the object model, we discussed the role of business rules as pre- and post-conditions of methods for an object type. For traditional models, we need to incorporate them in a more complex way—by constraining the persistent data and cross-referencing the rule to the processes that must enforce the constraint. However, before we can do so, we must express the business rule in a technology-neutral way. The processes that enforce the rule may implement the rule based on a specific technology-dependent manner. So, in detailed analysis, we need to

- Break down the business rule into its component atomic parts

- Express it in terms of our data model—entity relationship or object models.

- Cross-reference it to the processes (or methods) that must enforce it.

- Express the consequences of violating the rule, that is exception handling requirements.

Our rules at the strategy level could be atomic or compound facts. At the analysis level, we need to break down all rules into their atomic components. For example, consider the rule "*We give credit to customers who have a good credit record.*" This rule could be sub-divided into several atomic rules, all relating to the business' definition of the phrase "*good credit record:*"

Strategy level rule:

We give credit to customers who have a good credit record.

Corresponding analysis-level atomic rules:

If the customer has prior purchase history, we give credit if this customer

⇒ *has always paid for purchases in less than 15 days, or*

⇒ *provides a credit card number that approves us blocking the amount of credit.*

If the customer has no prior purchase history, we give credit if this customer

⇒ *gives us a credit reference letter from a bank, or*

⇒ *has applied for an been approved for a line of credit with the company credit department, or*

⇒ *has a net worth of over $250,000.*

These atomic rules can be expressed in terms of our data models. There are many conventions and notations, for example, that popularized by Ronald Ross for expressing such rules. Figure 4-11 illustrates an example using Ross notation on an entity relationship diagram. This notation could probably be extended for use in object models, although there are no known attempts at such extensions.

In UseCase analysis, we would identify business rules explicitly so that we could analyze the consequences of violating the rule. For instance, our example rule might be part of an *order entry interaction* UseCase. We would explore the actions taken by the *sales associate* actor if the customer had poor credit record. Traditional models use a combination of techniques, such as state diagrams or entity life history models, to express these consequences. However, since few analysts developed these models sufficiently, usually due to lack of time on projects, we rarely specify exception handling in detail.

In Oracle Designer, we have a couple of alternatives for recording these rules. One approach is to create a separate function hierarchy, or a function list, to express a rule statement. We can differentiate these functions from business processes by adding a property called *function type*. This property may have one of two allowable values, process or rule. We can use the Oracle Designer User Extensibility facility to add this

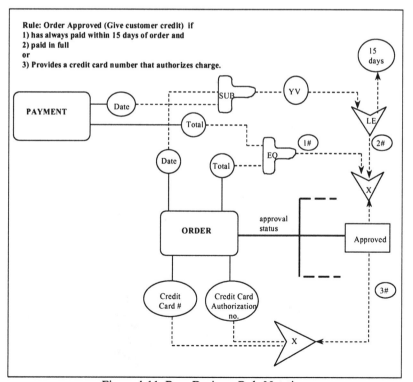

Figure 4-11: Ross Business Rule Notation

new property to the repository element type called function.

In this approach, we can use standard utilities such as the Matrix Diagrammer to create function-entity and function-attribute matrices. As we associate functions with entities and attributes, we state the condition expressed visually by Ross notation. The Ross method calls the associated entity an *anchor*, and the participating attributes *correspondents*. This approach of using Oracle Designer elements offers significant benefits during design and implementation using Oracle Designer wizards and generators. We will discuss some of these utilities in later chapters.

An alternative is to use the Oracle Designer User Extensibility feature to create a completely new element type called *business rule*. We would also create a new association, called *rule dependence*, between the new element type and the existing element type, entity. The *rule dependence* association represents the conditions of the rule expressed in the Ross notation between entities. One restriction of this approach is that we cannot make an explicit association between the *business rule* element type and attributes of entities. This restriction is due to the internal design constraints of the current Oracle Designer repository. The text of the association between the rule and entities must state any attributes involved.

This approach offers the ability to record business rules at the analysis level in the Oracle Designer repository. We cannot propagate this documentation further into the

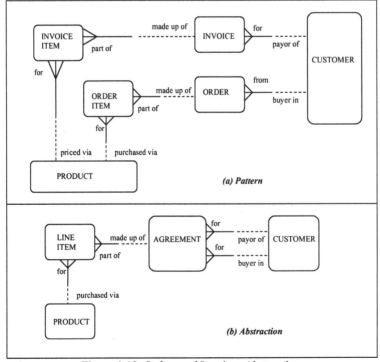

Figure 4-12: Orders and Invoices Abstraction

design and generator utilities.

4.7 Models for Flexibility

So far, we have only looked at models for specific things encountered in our analysis. We could base our design on such models; however, a relatively small change in business practices could alter our model. In traditional methodologies, we relegate such changes to the maintenance phase. What if we could make our models more flexible so that we could accommodate changes in the business? This exercise is called convergent modeling.

Convergent modeling applies equally to object models and entity relationship models. In object modeling terminology, it is sometimes called abstraction or generalization. In fact, this technique is the cause of discovering class hierarchies in an object model.

4.8 Convergent Modeling

The main principle in this approach is to look for patterns in our models. We then try to merge similar patterns. Our convention of diagram layout really helps in making patterns noticeable. The end result is usually a simpler overall model which actually accommodates unforeseen changes without restructuring our model or our design.

Consider the example in Figure 4-12(a), which illustrates the entity relationship diagram of *Orders* and *Invoices*. Don't the patterns look similar? The question to ask is: Can we represent both patterns with one set of entities? Before doing so, we need to make sure that we can account for all of the attributes in each entity by a common set. In this case, we can. So, the merged entities are shown in Figure 4-12(b).

Let's take this one step further. Compare the examples in Figures 4-4(b) and 4-12. Similar patterns again, except that *Customer* is a separate entity. What happens now if one of our vendors becomes a customer? We really would need to keep that information once as the *Vendor* entity and again as the *Customer* entity. Suppose, we invent a supertype called party with *Customer* and *Vendor* as subtypes. Our generalized transaction entity can now cover our dealings with customers as well as vendors. Actually, the relationships define in which transaction someone is a vendor as opposed to a customer, so we don't really need the subtypes *Customer* and *Vendor*. Instead, we might differentiate between individuals and organizations, so that we can deal with both types of vendors and customers. This pattern is shown in Figure 4-13.

As we generalize our models, we abstract data in our entity relationship model. This abstraction makes our models more difficult to understand. They are further removed from our users' perceptions. However, these models are much more flexible and powerful. In our transaction example, we can represent any transaction involving parties pertaining to a product. In fact, we could easily extend the *Product* entity in the future to include services not supplied today without changing the model.

The techniques here are equally applicable to object modeling. In fact, object models offer better features, such as inheritance of attributes and associations, as well as

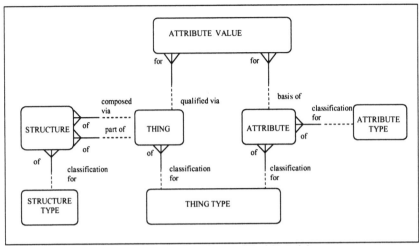

Figure 4-14: The Abstract World Model

methods. There have been several attempts at discovering patterns in object models. The bibliography cites several books on this subject.

There is of course a price to pay if we implement these abstract patterns in our physical database—more difficult access and lower performance. These issues are topics for a later chapter. Don't dismiss the power of these abstractions out-of-hand. Oracle tools provide some extensions which might relieve some of our worries. We need a methodical assessment of what our performance needs are before we design our databases.

4.8.1 Abstraction to the nth Degree

The process of abstraction can get extreme if you are not careful. We can actually model anything in the world with the general model illustrated in Figure 4-14. In some cases this may make sense, as it does for the model underlying the Oracle Designer repository. Some real-world examples for which it makes sense are clinical trials and document structure and indexing applications. In these real-world cases, such a model reduces development significantly. However, exercise extreme caution before adopting it!

There is an additional consideration when you develop abstract models like these. We lose the business rules that were embodied in the specific model. For example, the associations between entities is now through data; they are not expressed as explicit relationships. Rules must now be procedurally enforced. In object models, we need to develop separate methods for each subtype. Inheritance of methods is of little use since the business rules for subtypes are different from those of the supertype.

4.8.2 Abstraction and Generalization

Abstraction is the process of determining similarities between objects and constructing a class hierarchy of similar objects. This process is a key foundation of the object model. The very definition of a class, that it is a set of objects with similar content and behavior, embodies this concept.

However, there are no formal techniques for discovering members of a class. Most of the methods describe this as an intuitive process. In other words, as with any craft, it is dependent on the skill of the analyst.

My experience shows that if we correlate the object model to the traditional entity relationship model, we can use the patterns described in Section 4.8 Convergent Modeling. Thus, if we normalize the internal structure of objects using entity relationship diagrams, we can use layout conventions to observe similarities. In the object model, we have the added advantage of examining the methods of each similar object to determine whether they belong in one class hierarchy.

Abstraction is as useful in object models as it is in entity relationship models. Abstraction makes it possible for us to build adaptable systems. This does not mean that we can build systems that require no further programming or enhancements. Good abstraction principles may significantly reduce the enhancement process. Abstraction also makes it possible to build systems incrementally rather than undertaking large unwieldy projects.

4.9 Completeness Checks

Despite our attempts at turning the analysis process into a science, it is still a craft. Experience of the analyst is the key to successful and useful analysis. Methodologies can describe techniques, but cannot ensure success. Completeness checks help you determine if you have covered all of the requirements during your analysis. Our aim with these checks is to discover any holes in our models.

There are two kinds of completeness checks:

1. Checks for quality of a model, which may uncover incomplete or vague analysis.

2. Checks that cross-reference two or more kinds of models.

Oracle Designer has many standard reports for checking the quality of traditional models. For example, we can check entity relationship models by obtaining a report of entities that have no attributes. Such entities are rare and may indicate an area of incomplete analysis. Another example is entities that have no primary unique identifier. If you cannot define a unique identifier for an entity, you probably have not fully understood the entity.

Checks that cross-reference models involve verifying that all information of one kind represented in one model exists in the other model: for example, to check that all data elements identified as part of data flows or data stores exists in our entity relationship model as either entities or attributes. In Oracle Designer, we would perform this cross-check by defining each data flow and data store in terms of entities and attributes. Note that in a data flow diagram, we can name and draw data flows and data stores without specifying their components. Unless we define the component elements in each case, we cannot be sure that we have captured all data.

There are many examples of cross-model checks. Instead of describing them all, here is a list of the ones I find useful. You may develop your own additional checks.

- Define a function-entity CRUD (Create, Retrieve, Update, Delete) matrix to determine if you have at least one function that performs each operation on every entity. For example, if you find an entity which has no function that creates it, you may have found a hole in your functional model.

- Define an organization-entity CRUD matrix to determine if every entity has at least one organization that performs each operation on every entity.

- Similar checks can be applied in a object model. Every method defined for an object must be used by at least one other object. If you determine methods for an object based on UseCase analysis, it is unlikely that you should have dangling methods.

- Another check in object models is to determine whether every state of each object is achieved through one or more methods. If methods discovered in this check are not invoked by any object, we may have a gap in our analysis.

Case Study: Widgets' Sales System

As we presented the findings of the strategy study to the Widgets, Inc. executives, we started getting a lot of questions. "It seems that you understand how we work," they said, "but how will this help us meet our business goals?" We then outlined the next phase of the project—to analyze the sales and warehousing application. We explained why warehousing could not be left out of the picture, and how we could judge this from the strategy study.

The highest-priority business objectives were to offer specialist catalogs and more targeted marketing. To address these, we needed structures for tracking customer buying patterns. That is, we needed to build a data warehouse. This warehouse would allow marketing to investigate buying patterns. But, before such a data warehouse could be useful, we needed the ability to consolidate customer data and make it consistent. To lay a foundation for such a warehouse, we had to tackle the way Widgets handles their customer information.

In addition, this project lets us seek ways to reduce order-to-shipping time to 24 hours. There are notes with the models which explain how we came to the conclusion that sales and warehousing must be treated as a single project.

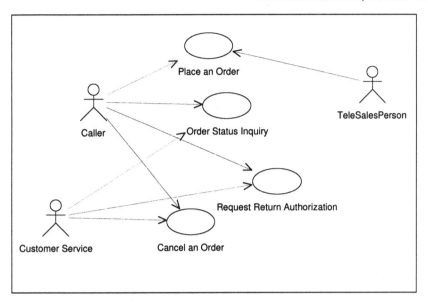

Sample UseCases

UseCase Models

We determined that the sales application consisted of many usecases. Included here are a few sample usecases. An exhaustive coverage, with explanations, would constitute a book in its own right. We used the Rational Rose product to develop these diagrams.

Widgets Sales UseCases

Some of the other usecases, not shown in the Widgets Case study, include

- Respond to a customer call and direct it to the proper group.

- Order dispute call

- Ship an order

- Receive returned product

- Receive shipment of products

For each usecase, we document the flow of events and associated activities. In Rational Rose, these are contained in an external document.

A usecase describes the flow of interaction within a transaction, including exception detection and resolution. Superficially, they may appear to be analogous to a data flow diagram. There are, however, several differences. A data flow diagram ignores order of processing—a usecase elaborates the order explicitly. Data flow diagrams typically ignore event triggers and control flows—usecases describe their occurrence and impact. One way to understand usecases is by considering them to be detailed design of the interaction between a user and the system. Action diagrams in Information Engineering are probably the closest, but not exact, analogy to event flow descriptions in usecases. Following is the flow of events for Order Status Inquiry usecase.

Order Status Inquiry Flow of Events

This usecase begins when the customer service representative enters the order number. The system verifies that the the entered number are valid, and displays the customer information for verification with the customer. The system then prompts the customer service representative to select one of the following activities:

- Change an ordered product

- Cancel the entire order

Alternate Flow

If the customer knows the customer number but not the order number, the customer service representative may enter the customer number.

If the customer does not know the customer number or the order number, the customer service representative may enter the telephone number of the customer.

In both of these cases, the customer must be asked their address for security

State Transitions for an Order

verification (Business Policy).

Note that we discover business policies and rules as part of this process. We need to document these rules. Later, during design, we will associate rules with anchoring object types and determine which methods should enforce them.

Change an Ordered Product

The customer may request the following changes:

- Change the quantity ordered.

- Cancel the ordered product.

- Change attributes of product e.g. color, size, finish etc.

If quantity is changed, the system must recalculate the order total. If a product is canceled, the system must recalculate the new order total. Any change to the order total means that the payment must be approved again (Business Rule).

Alternate Flow

If customer increases product quantity, and the product is out-of-stock, the additional quantity shall be backordered (Business Rule).

Alternate Flow

If the canceled product is already fully or partially shipped, it must be returned before cancellation becomes effective, that is, before refund can be given (Business Rule).

Alternate Flow

If the product with the new attribute (color, size, finish) is out of stock, the item shall be backordered (Business Rule).

Cancel the Entire Order

The customer requests that the Order be canceled. This request will be successful if no product in that order has been shipped yet (Business Rule). If the order is partially shipped, these items must be returned before order can be canceled (Business Rule). Refund will be given as products are returned (Business Rule). The valid paths to canceling an Order are illustrated in the state transition diagram below.

Object Type Model

We refined the object type model from the strategy level. The main effort was to add many more attributes and operations. Notice that the overall types did not change significantly. We did not need to add new object types, because we could accommodate all the known requirements with the types identified during strategy. A major reason for this was the flexibility of attribute types—they could be simple scalar types or complex like lists, object types, nested object types, or lists of object type.

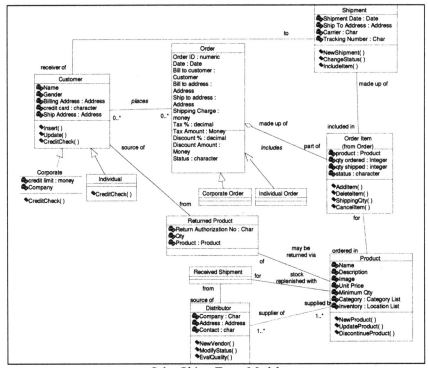

Sales Object Types Model

During strategy, we had identified *Corporate Order* and *Individual Order* as subtypes of *Order*. However, during analysis, we could find no distinguishing characteristic for either of them. We kept them on the diagram for clarity, but the real difference between them is due to kind of customer who places the order.

Traditional Models

The traditional models include function hierarchy diagrams, matrix diagrams, data flow diagram, and entity relationship models. You need not develop all of these diagrams just to use Oracle Designer for code generation. For example, a function hierarchy, an entity relationship model, together with function-to-entity matrix provides sufficient detail for the application design transformer utility. Alternatively, you may use data flow diagrams cross referenced with entity relationship models to provide similar detail.

Data flow diagrams are a little dated. Business process flow diagrams are currently in vogue. As we said before, the approach for developing business process flows is much the same as for data flow diagrams. You may also use them for presentations to users. We include data flow diagrams here for completeness of our case study illustrations.

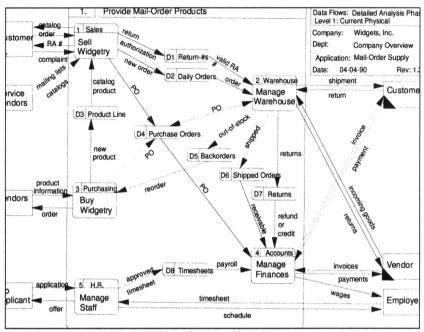

"As is" Level 1 Data Flow Diagram

The initial three diagrams show the detailed workings of Widgets' sales and warehousing operations at present. We gathered this information after another set of interviews—this time with lower echelons of the company. The second and third diagrams are explosions of the first, shown on the facing page.

- Don't be surprised at the clutter on these diagrams. Paper-based systems, or even poorly partitioned applications, are always messy. If yours is neat, you have probably missed something, such as exceptions, or you have made assumptions which simplified it. Beware of making unwarranted assumptions—they will return to haunt you in some later phase.

- Processes in these diagrams are synonymous with functions in the function hierarchy. Data flows are associated with them in the data flow diagrammer or directly in the repository object navigator.

- Draw data flows with just names, initially. Then, after you complete the detailed entity relationship diagram, fill in the detail. Data flow detail consists of the entities and their attributes that make up the data flow. You cannot define a data flow with any other components.

We used the Publisher/2000 business function reports together with these diagrams. Remember that diagrams alone are insufficient, you need the narrative associated with it to get user verification. The narrative should be concise and to the point in stating *what* happens without specifying *how* it is implemented.

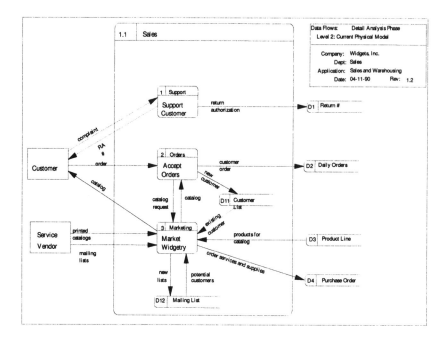

"As Is" Level 2 Sales Process Diagram

Notes on the Sales Process Explosion

- By this time, we are down to interviewing people on the shop floor, usually at the supervisory level. This is so we can find out what really happens, as opposed to what company management would like to believe.

- We identified two new internal data stores: customer list and mailing list. They are not used by other departments. There are many similarities between them.

- This was our first chance to get real users involved in the analysis. Marketing staff came up with a bunch of ideas on improving their work. These ideas will affect the way we build the proposed functions and database.

- Remember to give credit to users who supplied ideas. This gets them enthusiastic about what the new system will be able to do.

- Throughout this process, sell the concept of the new system—not for money, but for successful implementation later! Enthusiastic users are essential to success.

- Sales had no idea of the current inventory position.

- Currently, there is no way to differentiate between real customers, that is, those who purchased something, and mailing list customers. The mailing list is internal to the marketing department.

- Note that within one group, the diagram is much less chaotic. This shows a well-run group—only its interfaces to other groups are numerous and complex.

Notes on the Warehousing Process Explosion

- When we completed the sales data flow, there were a lot of data stores shared with warehousing. We suspected this during the strategy phase by looking at the mandatory relationships in the sales and warehousing entity relationship diagram. We already had management approval to consider warehousing as part of this project, so we set out to investigate this department in depth.

- Unfortunately, the warehouse manager was not very cooperative. He was miffed at being the target of a productivity improvement project, as our project objective was described within the company. "I run a very tight shop," he said, "There is no room for improvement here." This was the dragon on this project. There is always at least one on every project.

- After much flattery, we got a tour of the warehouse and were introduced to the supervisor. This person was our workaround. We had to get the actual detailed

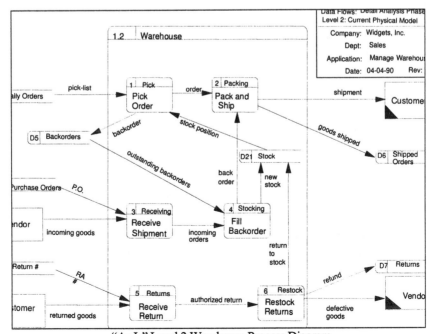

"As Is" Level 2 Warehouse Process Diagram

workings somehow. The high pile of paperwork on his desk was a good sign that our project could help him.

- Follow the tips mentioned earlier on drawing these data flows initially. Fill in the detail later. The reports you get are the same regardless of the level of the data flow diagram.

- The warehousing group has no means of anticipating sales until they get the actual order forms. Then, it is too difficult to analyze them. They are under too much pressure to get the shipments out to worry about how many of each product there are orders for. They are too busy to optimize their picking and packing operations.

Notes on the Combined Essential Model

This is where the fun starts. We pasted together the level 2 data flow diagrams on a large piece of paper; we then started eliminating processes and data stores.

- We eliminated batch data stores to start with: *Daily Orders* (these are just unshipped orders) and *Shipped Orders* (these are just marked as shipped by warehousing). *Shipped Order* is simply an attribute of the *Order Items* entity. Accounting will be able to query them online when payments are being reconciled. So, we eliminated a lot of paper shuffling and multi-part order forms.

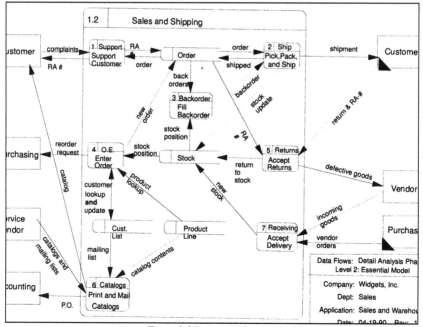

Essential Process Diagram

- Picking and packing processes are one logical function. The data flow between them is a physical transport of products. So, we eliminated this data flow.

We added a few facilities to improve the working conditions of the sales and warehousing staff based on suggestions made by them during interviews.

- The current physical system has no means for the customer support staff to verify an order and date shipped before issuing a return authorization number. We could not estimate the losses to Widgets due to this oversight. However, in the essential model, we added the facility for verification. Note that the *RA #* is just an attribute of the *Order Items* entity.

- Order entry now has direct access to the current stock position to verify that an ordered item is in stock. The *Product* entity provides online descriptions of products, so they no longer need a paper copy of a catalog.

- Customer support did not have a catalog—at least officially. Many times, they could not even be sure that a return was for a product that Widgets sold. In practice, they sneaked a copy of the catalog from someone's desk every so often. In the new system, they can look up an item online.

- We combined the mailing list and customer data stores so they are shared by order entry and catalog mailing personnel.

- Order entry can request a catalog for a customer by simply updating the customer list. Since this list is shared, the customer automatically gets the next catalog.

- Warehousing can query and get a summary of products and shipping quantities for a set of orders (pick, pack, and ship process). This process will help optimize their picking function. It will allow them to carry a larger number of each product from the shelves to the packing area. They will also get a better handle on the day's shipping volume and improve warehouse staff schedules better.

Notes on the Detailed Entity relationship Diagram

- We drew this diagram as we conducted interviews. Once we completed it, we could see a lot of similar patterns. This diagram is shown only to help you appreciate how we derived the convergent model. Notice the disparity in the number of entities in this diagram and the convergent model shown next.

- Notice the complicated handling of returned items. Returned Items might be shipped back to the vendor or, if there is nothing wrong with them, returned to stock. Watch for arcs, indicating an exclusive or relationship. These lead to complex database design.

- We differentiated between orders from customers to Widgets and orders from Widgets to vendors. This is the easy way, initially. However, the diagram

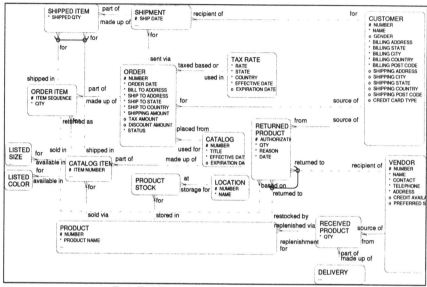

Detailed Entity Relationship Diagram

becomes quite complex as a result of being so specific. But, it helps us to notice the patterns.

Notes on the Convergent Entity relationship Diagram

- From the previous diagram, we noted similar patterns in the interaction with customers and vendors. In both cases, we have *Orders*, *Order Items*, *Shipments*, and *Shipment Items*. So, we merged these entities.

- We also merged the *Customer* and *Vendor* entities using a supertype, *Party*. With this new entity, we can use relationships to define the from and to parties.

- These two steps simplified the diagram a lot. We have fewer entities overall.

- One side effect of this abstraction was that we discovered that some of the items received at the dock were actually for office use at Widgets. For example, the file cabinet ordered for a manager's office was received by warehousing. Our convergent model could deal with these exceptions with two minor changes: the relationship between *Order Item* and *Stock Item* became optional, that is, a dotted line rather than the solid line shown here; also, *Stock Item* becomes a subtype of a new supertype entity called *Asset Item*. A new subtype called *Office Item* is part of this supertype. *Office Item* has information about items ordered for internal use. This entity will eventually form a part of the asset control system for office equipment. Of course, no such system exists at present—but our analysis uncovered the need for it. The asset control application was deferred as a topic for another project.

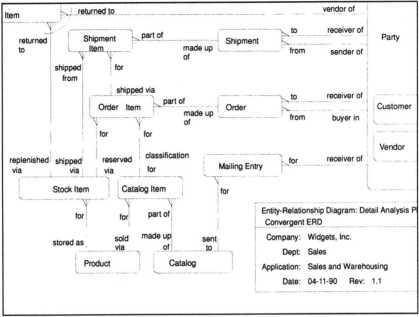

Convergent Entity-Relationship Diagram

Application Architecture

As part of developing an Information Systems strategy, you have to formulate an overall architecture appropriate to your company. This architecture is a framework for all your applications. It defines company-wide constraints such as the desktop systems, the network infrastructure, and so on. Within this framework, each application has many choices, depending on the specific application needs. In this chapter, we will discuss these choices. We intend to increase your awareness of the kinds of architectural decisions that need to be made for each application rather than a discussion of particular products. This chapter covers

- The typical architecture of the systems of the 1990's and earlier. We will examine the application development tasks that were made easier due to these architectures.

- The requirements of the systems of the future and the architectures needed to support them. We will compare these to the traditional architectures to examine the types of tasks that are more challenging in these environments.

- What are two-tier and three-tier architectures? We will review some of the middleware in use today and the directions of the future. Are these issues application-specific or are they a company-wide standard?

- Should you choose a tool appropriate for each application or make a company-wide choice? There are management, technical, and personnel issues involved in making this decision.

- When you roll out an application into production, what kind of support structure will you need? We will describe support infrastructure requirements that may need additional development.

5.1 The System Environment

Traditionally, our information systems were centrally located. Our data files and databases lived on some mainframe or server machine. Our programs were stored on these machines as well as being executed on them. In this systems environment model, we had a common location for installing all software for an application. We installed modifications to the software, whether bug fixes or enhancements, in one location. Most of our applications were designed for terminal-based interactions.

We accommodated distant users of an application by implementing fast links via leased lines between geographic sites. We used terminal servers to efficiently use these expensive links. But our applications still used terminals as the basis of interaction.

The personal computer revolution changed some of our methods. We went through a radical infrastructure change. We began using PCs for activities like word processing. We gradually placed PCs on every desk instead of terminals. We implemented local area networks (LANs) to connect PCs to a common shared file server. Our distant links now supported wide area networks (WANs) for better accessibility. Most of our applications remained terminal-based. We simply used PCs to emulate terminals. A large number of applications at the time of writing, surprisingly, still use PCs to emulate terminals as the interface to applications.

The client-server principals caused a radical change in our application infrastructure. We debated the benefits of client-centric and server-centric applications—that is, whether the processing should take place in the client desktop machine or the (database) server machine. The runtime environment of the client tools became more and more sophisticated—and so did the server database management systems. As we experimented with these tools, we realized that there were several constraints:

- Network bandwidth could severely constrain the client-server applications. Poorly designed client-server applications could use up all of the available bandwidth.

- Network traffic volume affected perceived response of the client application. High traffic resulted in slower response as the client exchanged information with the server. Since user actions determined traffic volume, the peaks and valleys in response could not be controlled by the IS support staff.

- Early client tools simply performed all processing in the client. They generated massive network traffic because they transported data across the network for processing. Enhanced server-side processing, through stored procedures and triggers, was needed to improve efficiency and performance. The aim here was to process data where it resided rather than on a client across the network.

- Client tools worked well over local area networks. They were somewhat acceptable over wide-area networks based on leased lines. However, they were abysmal over intermittent slow connections like the public telephone system because of the low bandwidth of these connections.

- The graphical user interfaces (GUIs) of these tools demanded an increasing amount of horsepower and memory on the desktop. The traditional business model that upgraded the desktop infrastructure every 5 to 10 years was simply unusable. Upgrades could be delayed for at most two years. This increased frequency of infrastructure upgrades strained company budgets.

The client-server model also challenged our application administration environment. Installing our application programs in a single central location may lead to slow startup response as each program is transported across the network. We may no longer have a single location for all of our application programs. In geographically distant sites, we install copies of our applications to localize access. Even within one location, we may install multiple copies of our programs to localize network traffic within sub-nets. All of these strategies mean that we have to plan and coordinate updates to programs more formally. The ad-hoc scheme used by many of our clients in the single mainframe environment is no longer appropriate. Updates have to be propagated to all of the installed sites at the same time.

The development of World Wide Web technology challenges our client server architecture models yet again. We can use this technology from outside the company via the Internet or from within—that is, using an intranet. The runtime environment with these applications is the Internet browser familiar to most people. The programs are again in a central location, the web server site, and may be stand-alone or may connect to our corporate databases. In fact, our programs may be divided into pieces, some of which execute as *applets* in the browser, and others which execute on the central web server.

This development makes it significantly easier to implement applications that are not only at our company sites but also on the portable notebook computers used by our traveling staff. However, no one technology is suitable for all of our applications. For example, the web-based interfaces are too slow for applications that require heads-down data entry—that is, applications that involve high-volume data entry daily. Such data entry applications require immediate validation of data and quick response to errors.

Another technology that simplifies many of our design tasks is the data warehouse concept. Before we started building data warehouses, our design for an application had to accommodate both operational and historical data. Now, we move the history over to a data warehouse, simplifying the design of our operational system. Figure 5-1 illustrates a generic architecture for a typical application. We need to add the extra steps necessary to transfer the data on an on-going basis. We may have additional work if the data warehouse contains integrated data from many applications. For example, we may need to transform our application's data to match the expectations

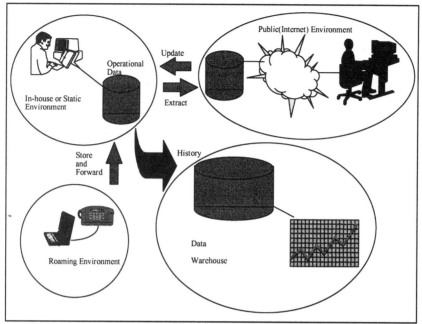

Figure 5-1: Generic Application Architecture

of the data warehouse. In addition, we need to make the storage division transparent to the users.

All of these developments mean that we need to understand the environment in which our applications will run. We no longer assume the simple environment of terminal-based systems. We need to determine whether our applications involve high-volume data entry and which portions of the application need it. We need to determine which portion of our application may be used by casual users—making it a candidate for a web-based interface. We need to determine which portion of our application requires power query or data manipulation capabilities—making it a candidate for GUI client-server tools.

Thus, we may need to divide our development based on the type of interface required, as well as the functional requirements. The effort to roll out each portion of the application may be different. For example, the GUI client-server tools will require significant user training prior to rollout. The high-volume data entry portion may require significant testing and performance tuning as part of the rollout. The web interface may need less training for the interface but we may still need to provide assistance in understanding the data and rules implemented in that portion. The rollout plans for our applications need to take all of these aspects into account.

5.2 Desktop and Roaming Requirements

Traditional analysis covers the business aspects of defining requirements. These definitions tell us what the system should do. However, we also need to know the environment in which the system will do these tasks before we can design the system. The environmental requirements specify whether a given process will be used by users who have a permanent connection to the network or whether they may be travelers that can only connect intermittently. We also need to determine if there are any tasks accessible to the general public. For example, order entry for Widgets' Internet catalog is a process accessible to the general public.

There are three types of potential environments: static, roaming, and public. The *Static* environment is the typical office-based desk workstation that many of us use. The characteristics of this environment are

- One user generally uses the same desktop machine every day.

- They perform a specific set of application tasks which don't vary very often.

- Their application tasks may be repetitive like data entry or may be casual like querying for data.

- They have a permanent connection to the area network, usually a LAN.

- They have certain predetermined hours of operation with rare exceptions.

A *Roaming* environment is typical of a traveling salesperson. In these environments, the user may call into the system from an unpredictable location, perform a few tasks, and then disconnecting. They may use their own equipment or someone else's, depending on company policy. The characteristics of this environment are

- The user may connect at unpredictable times from unpredictable locations.

- They perform a set of application tasks which need to be completed in a short duration.

- They may get disconnected partway through performing their tasks and need the ability to reconnect and continue.

- They may use the public telephone system to connect with the consequent network speed and cost constraints.

- We can identify users in advance, for example, through an enrollment or subscription process.

- The data accessed may be proprietary, confidential, or otherwise sensitive.

The *Public* environment is typical of web applications like an online catalog, which do not require users to pre-qualify for access. In this environment, we cannot usually determine who the users are in advance. We have little or no control over the equipment or software used for access. The characteristics of this environment are

- Users perform a limited part of the application.

- Data accessed may not be sensitive, but the data provided by users may be sensitive depending on the application.

- They may access at unpredictable times and from unpredictable locations.

- We cannot identify users in advance.

- We cannot obtain specific interface requirements other than through public opinion gathering mechanisms like focus groups and surveys.

We have much experience in designing systems for the static environment. We can choose our favorite GUI tools, generate code, get users involved in testing, and so on. We can contemplate complex server-based validation or implementation of business rules in this environment because users are continuously connected to the server. There are two kinds of tasks in this environment that have different requirements: high-volume data entry and casual interaction.

The high-volume data entry tasks require facilities that speed entry. For example, instead of forcing the use of value lists for entry into certain fields, we need to provide abbreviations that get translated into the actual values. Any facilities that reduce keystrokes are desirable as they will speed entry. We may have to suspend the use of many GUI interaction features like radio buttons and check boxes in favor of a keyboard-based interaction. After all, moving your hand to the mouse for mouse clicks slows down data entry. We will have a need for this type of task in many applications until we can find a way to enter data at the source—that is, before it arrives in our application.

Casual interaction is the most common interface in any type of application. This may involve data entry tasks also, but not at the volume in the previous discussion. Speed is important, but it is not measured in keystrokes per minute. A more important requirement is to provide an intuitive interface—that is, one that is easy to learn and remember. Most GUI interface features are aimed at this type of task.

Roaming environments are becoming prevalent since notebook PCs have become affordable and more portable. We have less experience in building for this environment, but the tools are improving. The principle criteria to determine in this environment is whether you need to be connected to the central database server system while performing these tasks. Many tools used to build applications today insist that you be connected throughout the session.

Ideally, for many tasks in this environment, we should provide a store and forward mechanism with facilities to work offline. With these mechanisms, the user could connect to the server to download some data, disconnect to work offline on the retrieved data, and then connect again to upload the completed work. This concept is becoming more common with e-mail systems. If we provide this style of interaction, the user would be less dependent on the quality of the connection, and we would reduce the cost of lengthy telephone calls. However, the challenge is to provide an intuitive interface that requires little support. Users in this environment probably work strange hours around the world. We do have opportunities to train these users in our application, but such training may be too expensive.

Public environments are a very recent development. The challenge in these environments is to get an untrained user to perform many tasks which today are done by internal organizations. For example, ordering goods from the online catalog requires a call to a sales associate today. If we obtain the data in an electronic form, we can eliminate entry errors and reduce our costs. However, we need to provide this access without compromising confidential or proprietary data from our systems. Applications built to operate via the Internet provide many opportunities to meet these needs but we must understand their requirements before diving into implementation.

In the static and roaming environments, we provide access to sensitive company data. We need to specify the types of security necessary to protect the information. In the public environment, we need security controls to isolate the data visible to the outside world. This requirement will impact our database design significantly.

Broach this subject with care. Users typically want extensive security in computer systems, usually far beyond that provided in a non-computerized environment. For example, they don't consider leaving a sensitive sales report on their desk at night a security issue, but will be upset if you suggest that sales data be made readable by anyone with authorization to access the sales system. As a general rule, try to arrange security restrictions such that read access is based on access to an application, and modification access is controlled based on some criteria.

Try to maintain restrictions to as high a level as possible. Finer granularity of security control often results in unwieldy systems. I have seen many applications where the unwieldy security controls (built as specified by users!) were completely bypassed in practice. For example, one application controlled access at the data element (column) level. Administering security in this application was so complex that users simply gave each other their passwords rather than reconfigure the security. In a short time, everyone knew each others' passwords. So much for security!

In my experience, object type-based access is often sufficient to what the users need. Access to the high-level object type should imply access to its component objects— that is, any embedded objects. In terms of entity-relationship models, the entities to control are reference entities like *Customer*, *Product*, *Inventory Stock*, and so on. We should not need separate controls for modifications to *Customer Addresses*, *Contact Lists*, and *Credit References*.

When we complete analysis, we need to consider these additional requirements. Partition the application based on the environment appropriate for each task. Then, define the criteria appropriate for each environment. Don't be surprised to find that you need to support a particular task in more than one environment. For example, just because Widgets provides an online catalog does not mean that they eliminate their telephone order entry requirement. In fact, they are always likely to operate both. Does this mean that you may have double development work ahead? Not necessarily. Choose your development tools once you realize the dilemma and you may be able to use a web-based interface for external and internal users. This is the foundation for intranet applications!

5.3 Two- or Three-tier Architecture

You may hear discussions regarding two- and three-tier architectures. These terms have been used in two contexts: hardware and software. A two-tier hardware architecture involves just clients PCs connected to a server machine. Two-tier software architecture is our prevalent client-server model—a client application such as Oracle Forms connected to the Oracle server. Figure 5-2 illustrates a typical two-tier architecture with its components.

Three-tier architectures are a little less clear. Hardware tiers are the desktop PC, local file or database server, and a central mainframe. Software tiers are the client executing in the PC, a middle interaction tier, and the database server. Figure 5-3 illustrates a typical three-tier architecture with some common components. We focus on the software tiers only in our discussion.

We have been using two-tier architectures for some time. Why should we consider a three-tier architecture? There are a few potential reasons. Some of the new types of

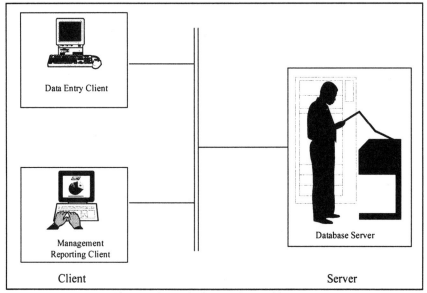

Figure 5-2: Typical Two-tier Architecture

environments make it impossible to operate with the two-tier architecture model. The simplest case for a middle interaction-tier is apparent in the roaming environment that implements a store and forward mechanism. The software that manages the store and forward control is an additional tier. In the Oracle product suite, the mobile agent software serves this role. The webserver software, one of Oracle's offerings in the Internet environment, is also middleware—providing a three-tier architecture.

Another reason for a three-tier architecture may be for separating integrity constraints from individual applications. Good candidates are business rules that need to be enforced in multiple applications. Rather than implementing the rules in each application, we may consider a rule server that intercepts all modification requests to the database and applies the appropriate rules to validate the interaction. This rule server may be a third-party product or you may build it as part of your project. It may even use the facilities of the database server, for example, by implementing rule logic as stored procedures.

Another example of a middleware application is for login authentication in a network environment. In such an environment, we often have a user id for the network, another one for the workstation, one for each database instance account, one for each application to which we have access ...—the list goes on. As it gets harder to keep track of all the user ids we have, we start practices that help us remember passwords,

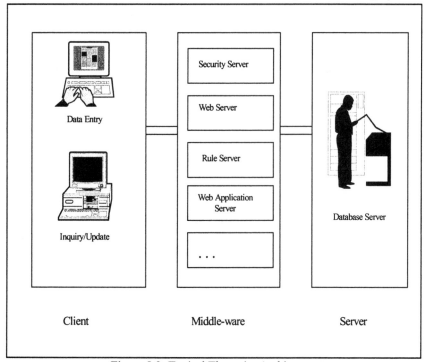

Figure 5-3: Typical Three-tier Architecture

but lead to poor security control. For example, we might write our passwords in some easily accessible place. The bureaucracy needed to administer such security controls is unwieldy! There are middle-ware products that provide a better solution. They provide a single logon authentication service, and then propagate the user id and passwords to all the required access points. This permits us to use the same user id and password in all applications that require security controls.

Unfortunately, there are many products that act as middleware. Each product provides a different service that may be unrelated to other middle tier products. Conceptually, whenever you use any of them, you are implementing a middle tier. But, you really cannot decide at the strategy level whether you should use a two-tier or three-tier architecture. The choice is determined by the needs of your application.

Even within one application, you may have parts requiring a two-tier architecture and other parts that require a three-tier architecture. If your application has a static environment, you may not need a middle tier—a two-tier, client-server architecture may suffice. In roaming and public environments, you may have no choice but to use a three-tier architecture. The environment and tools you need to use drive your choice.

5.4 Protocol Choices

At the strategy level, you may decide to use a particular network protocol, for example TCP/IP. This is merely the foundation upon which networking applications build. At the application level, your chosen tools may use Oracle's networking layer, Net8, or the industry de-facto standard ODBC for access to the database. These are your two main choices. Until recently, there were many other options which have since taken a back seat and are therefore no longer significant.

Should you choose a client or server tool based on which protocol it supports? In the next section, we will discuss some of the pros and cons of using Oracle's products and some third-party products. There are technical pros and cons to using ODBC or Net8. We will not examine these in depth here. I suggest you follow up through the books in the bibliography.

Oracle's Net8 has the obvious benefit that it provides a one-stop solution. It is closely integrated with the database server. Therefore, it allows you to take advantage of its finely-tuned facilities. All of Oracle's client products use this protocol as standard. Some of these products also support ODBC.

Third-party tools that are closely allied to Oracle also support Net8. However, you may have to purchase additional components to make use of them. Many products, like PowerBuilder, come standard with ODBC drivers, but you must purchase additional database drivers to use Net8. Since ODBC is a Microsoft standard, most desktop PCs running Microsoft Windows software can support it.

There are administrative issues involved in choosing products that use different protocols. For example, if one application chooses ODBC and another chooses Net8, you must employ staff with appropriate skills in both to support the applications. You must provide appropriate training to these staff. You must also plan for upgrading each component software as and when it becomes available.

Remember that in each case there is a software component that you must install in each client. By standardizing the protocol drivers across applications, you can reduce some unnecessary overhead.

5.5 Choosing the Tools

Many corporations choose client server tools as a corporate standard. For example, they may choose Oracle as the database server for all of their applications. This makes sense for the database server. It enables you to promote consistency and connectivity among all applications.

Choosing client tools is not always possible, although many corporations do. The benefit of choosing a single product as the corporate standard allows you to build staff with experience in the product. You would be able to provide development as well as maintenance expertise through such staff. The complex array of features offered by any client GUI product makes this approach very lucrative.

However, one product rarely meets all of the needs of all of the environments that your applications must support. For example, Oracle's Forms product is not suitable for applications that support a *public* environment, as discussed earlier in Section 5.2 Desktop and Roaming Requirements. The WebForms component requires you to install a plug-in—acceptable for an intranet client, that is, a user in a static environment. But, we cannot predict the browser used by the general public, and so we cannot be certain that the plug-in would be compatible.

A better corporate strategy provides a limited choice of products as standards which meet certain corporate-level criteria. For example, you might choose the entire suite of Oracle products—for one stop purchasing power, as well as one other third-party product in each of the static, roaming, and public environments—for features not supported by Oracle's set.

5.5.1 Desktop Client

Client GUI tools allow you to develop impressive multimedia interfaces. These tools are much more sophisticated than our terminal interfaces. We can now include graphics, images, sound, and other types of information as part of our application. We can also link to other applications—for example, a viewer and editor for a scanned image as a separate window concurrent to our data entry window. The possibilities today are endless.

However, there is a price to pay for these features. The configuration requirements of these products increase with every release. For example, Oracle Forms currently claims a minimum of 16MB of memory for a small application. This requirement increases significantly for real-life applications involving several windows. And, you will need even more memory if your users wish to run other applications like Word or Excel in other windows at the same time! The speed of the processor is equally important for the usability of the application. The requirements for third-party products are similar.

This type of client tool is called a *fat* client. Such tools perform a great deal of processing in the client. They manipulate and cache data in the local memory. They execute complex validation logic using their proprietary scripting language or, in the case of Oracle products, PL/SQL. Before displaying bitmap graphics, they must read and store them in memory. So, it is not surprising that they require as much memory horsepower as you can supply on the desktop and beg for more.

Fat clients have generated a tremendous demand to upgrade desktop PCs. If your application is targeted at a small number of users, the upgrades may not impose a significant burden on your budget. However, many of our applications today are aimed at hundreds of users—sometimes even thousands. The upgrade now makes a significant hole in the budget.

Another issue is training users of these applications. GUI features are no guarantee of an intuitive interface. It is up to the design standards imposed by your application, if not at the corporate level, that your interface will be intuitive. Even then, users of these tools will require training. We will discuss the issues of administration and installation of these tools in Section 5.6.3 Administration and Support Environment.

The alternative is to use a *thin* client, for example, a web browser together with server-side processing software like Oracle's Application Server. A thin client performs little more than the display and user interaction part of a fat client. It defers most of the processing to the server-side software. Thus, it requires much less resources than a fat client.

The benefit of using a tool such as a web browser is that users are already familiar with it. They use their browser to surf the Internet. So, we should not need to provide training in the mechanics of using the tool. We can focus on providing application-specific training.

However, Web browser tools appear to be also adding more and more functionality, for example, local processing in the client through Java applets or JavaScript. If you want to keep the thin client thin, avoid excessive use of these features. Alternatively, use an integrated product like Oracle's WebServer, that can execute Java at the server side.

5.5.2 Roaming Tools

Roaming tools run the gamut from software that runs on ordinary MS Windows notebooks to specialized palmtops with custom-built software. Which hardware you choose depends entirely on your application's requirements for portability, access, support capabilities and so on. It is simply not possible to set a corporate-level strategy for such tools. In addition to diverse products, the technology in this environment is developing at an incredible pace. Any tools discussed in this book will be obsolete even prior to printing.

The issues you should consider in this environment are usability and integration. If your company salespeople already carry notebooks, it makes sense to put more software on the same machine. In my opinion, the only justification for custom palmtops is reduction in user training. For example, if you plan to provide these devices to delivery staff who have no prior experience with Windows PCs, a custom palmtop makes sense—especially if it hides the operating system interface completely. Of course, you need to deploy them in large quantities to make the cost of custom development worthwhile.

Many custom palmtops have proprietary development tools. Thus, you would lose the advantage provided by standard notebook PCs—they can run your standard client tools. Remember, however, that the standard client tool may assume that the user has a continuous connection to the server database. You need client tools that can support the *store and forward* concept.

The design for an application that implements a store and forward concept is also different. We will discuss these design issues in a later chapter. Realize, however, that your choice of store and forward middleware will affect the application design. The middleware should be a standard component rather than chosen by individual applications.

This software should provide a bi-directional forwarding mechanism not just from the client. It should allow the client to invoke a task, such as initiating a report, and the disconnect, leaving the task running on the server side. This capability is analogous to running programs in batch—the initiating user need not remain logged into the application. When the task is complete, it stores the result and runtime logs that are forwarded to the client at the next connect session. Of course, it should offer the client a choice of downloading when the next session is started. If it downloads without offering a choice, users are likely to get frustrated by the lengthy startup time!

5.5.3 Web Application Tools

This technology has caught the information systems industry off-guard in a similar way that the PC revolution did in the early 1980's. Because of its intensely visual and marketing-oriented traits, the first-generation web applications involved the information systems staff peripherally only. The principle developers were graphic artists and publishing experts. In fact, the key phrase throughout this era of web applications was *web publishing*.

While these first generation web applications were visually appealing, they suffered from the same technical drawbacks as the software developed prior to modeling and methodologies. They consisted of hand written code, in HTML or Java. They stored results in flat data files and rarely performed data integrity checks. For example, most

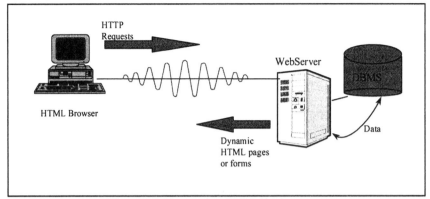

HTTP
Requests

WebServer

DBMS

HTML Browser

Dynamic
HTML pages
or forms

Data

Figure 5-4: Transactional Web Environment

such applications hard-coded choice list values. Then, if a value in a list changed, all code had to be modified. Impact analysis tools were not even considered in advance.

Second-generation tools are transaction-oriented—albeit with some differences from the traditional transaction model. These tools include web servers that execute some programming language, like PL/SQL, and dynamically generate the HTML or Java processed by the browser. Figure 5-4 illustrates the architecture of these transactional tools. There are third-party engines that also operate in a similar manner.

Tools in this environment are evolving so rapidly that any discussion of specific features would be obsolete before publication. The key feature to examine is whether your CASE tool can support a particular tool. If it does, then it might be worth foregoing bleeding-edge features in favor of maintainability of the level of your normal development. Do not compromise your organization's software development maturity level for a little glitter.

For the foreseeable future, I suggest that you perform a short evaluation of the available products when building each application. The choice for your previous application may no longer be appropriate for the next one. Be prepared to change your choice frequently, although not at the risk to your application development deliverables. You may have to support multiple products while the technology settles down. For some period of time, the furious pace of innovation in this environment makes any corporate strategy obsolete before you can write it down.

5.5.4 Reporting Tools

There are two kinds of reporting tools: power development tools intended for programmers and ad-hoc reporting tools intended for end users. There are many products in each category, even several from Oracle. You need to evaluate several products before setting a corporate-level limited choice strategy.

Ad-hoc development tools often require significant effort in developing an end user model of the data rather than the database structures. The end user model may simplify the database structures by pre-joining certain tables, providing longer, less cryptic names for tables and columns, and so on. The effort involved in this definition is often significantly reduced if you have a repository like Oracle Designer. If you have an object model, end user views of data may be easier to identify. Some tools provide an API that allows you to automate the loading of the end user model rather than manually entering it.

There is much literature about reporting tools. Trade publications frequently evaluate tools with the latest feature function lists. There are even services like Patty Seybold's *Seybold Report,* published periodically, that may provide you with excellent reference material.

5.5.5 OLAP Tools

Online transaction processing (OLAP) tools provide three types of services:

- Complex query and reporting facilities.

- Data scrubbing, transformation and loading facilities.

- Data storage and processing.

Query tools combine the features of reporting tools with the ability to perform complex queries. Multi-dimensional databases are tools that provide data storage services similar to those of a DBMS. These dimensional databases also include the capability to massage data, for example, through summarization, roll-ups, and aggregation algorithms. We will discuss analysis and design needs for these databases later in a separate chapter.

5.6 Infrastructure Design

If your organization is already at Level 3 maturity (or higher) on Watts Humphrey's capability maturity model, your project team has a head start. Such organizations already have a methodology in use, trained staff, and project management structure. Your project team still needs to construct project plans and prepare an environment. But, with the structure already defined, startup should require little time.

If you are still working on improving your organization's maturity level, here are some of activities you will need as part of startup:

- **Project methodology**: You may need to establish the methodology and techniques to be used in your project. The first step is to train all the team members in its use. Another important step is to hire an expert to be the team's mentor in methodology. This person will help jump-start the strategy or analysis process and speed the progress by providing experiences from other similar projects. After the initial period, this person can provide part-time quality assurance on models and can detect and resolve modeling conflicts.

Stage	Description
Innocent	New to Oracle, CASE, and Oracle Designer.
Aware	Heard of Oracle, Oracle Developer; knows Oracle Designer exists.
Apprentice	Has taken a class, attended a Oracle Designer Workshop, and has experience in other tools.
Practitioner	Tried it at least once; has started Oracle Designer-based development, not completed it.
Journeyman	Succeeded at least once; at least one Oracle Designer-based project in production.
Master	Uses routinely, knows shortcuts; uses data abstraction techniques.
Expert	Expands use to other disciplines.

Table 5-1: Meilir Page-Jones' Stages of Expertise

- **Waterfall or RAD approach**: Decide whether your project will use a Waterfall or RAD process. Should you use a timebox approach for controlling scope creep? Do all team members understand these concepts? Can they apply them? Prepare your team appropriately and you will have cohesion that is much more effective than throwing a bunch of people together.

- **Team skills**: In any project team, you need a combination of skills. Table 5-1 illustrates the stages of expertise defined by Meilir Page-Jones. The ideal project has a group of experts who can work together. Such staff can easily swap roles and fill gaps for each other. In practice, the ideal team is just a goal to strive towards. You will need to construct a team made up of novices, journeymen, and perhaps one master. Figure 5-5 illustrates a potential skill matrix you could construct to assess the gaps in the project skill set.

In addition to structuring the team and the project architecture, you need to organize the physical working environment. Again, in an organization of Level 3 maturity or higher, you will already have these environments operational. Otherwise, you need to construct them for the first project and then propagate them to projects that follow.

5.6.1 Development Environment

You need to separate the personal and team working areas—that is, designate directories where each individual's *experiments* will be held and where the team's *finished* products will be held. Here are some of the things for which you need separate areas:

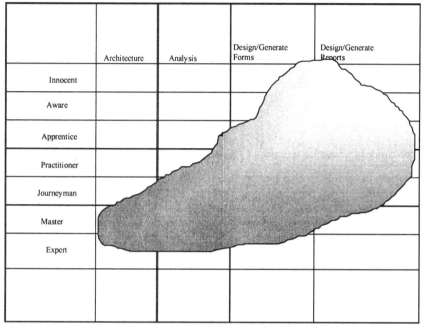

Figure 5-5: Sample Skill Requirements for Project

- Directories for notes, schedules, memoranda, project plans, documentation, and so on.

- Oracle Designer applications for individual experiments and tests.

- Oracle Designer applications for project work.

- Directory structure for programs—binary and source, separated by subsystem or development language. This structure should mirror the production environment.

- Directories for sample test data together with their database load scripts.

- Database schema and accounts for personal testing and experiments and a shared schema for common testing.

The team's common area should be controlled in some way to reduce garbage. Alternatively, you can designate a project librarian to monitor and collect products of the team. You need to devise test data loading utilities for the shared common database schema. These utilities, together with a saved test data set, should allow you to reconstruct a clean test database even if it gets corrupted during development.

Another environmental requirement is a source code control mechanism such as provided by third-party products. You will need these even during initial development to be able to reconstruct some deliverable after a few modifications. Source code control utilities should be able to keep deltas of the modifications. They should also provide the ability to reconstruct a specific version.

Investigate the use of Oracle Designer utilities for version control of repository models. However, they may not be very useful if you have many shared objects between applications. More on this subject in a later chapter.

One of the most neglected areas in projects, in my experience, is the mechanism for managing test data. Neglect here costs many wasted hours. Basic Oracle utilities such as *export/import* are insufficient in a fast-changing development environment. These utilities cannot be used if the database structure changes between the time of export and the time of import—a frequent occurrence in the RAD approach. Without utilities to manage the process of reloading test data often, the team wastes a great deal of time tracking down apparent bugs that are merely data errors caused by another person's testing.

5.6.2 Rollout Environment

Many projects ignore this area until development is complete. Unfortunately, many inconsistencies about the users' needs and stated requirements show up at this point in the project. I recommend that you consider these issues as a concurrent part of the project plan:

- **Data conversion**: Plan the legacy data that should be converted to the new system. Cut your teeth on conversion—and get some real test data as you go along. By the way, put some of your really smart people on these tasks, with a skill stage of Practitioner at least. A lower skill level person, working on their own, will likely miss some key conflicts. They may not raise red flags so that you are forced to reexamine your models and rules.

- **Implementing reengineered processes**: BPR implementation is much harder than analysis. It involves much more than user training. BPR implementation starts concurrent to application design. While the technical staff are building the system, BPR implementers cajole and persuade businesspeople to understand why the processes need changing. Their important task is to get the business staff to buy into the change. Then we can train them in the new system and resultant processes.

- **User transition training**: Start planning the transition as soon as you have a handle on data conversion. You need early deliverables to get the ball rolling. My suggestion is to have at least one deliverable every three months. Each deliverable should include some usable functionality, even if does not serve everyone's needs or even all of one organization's needs. Your application design should allow incremental delivery of the functionality. This way, users can use the partial system long before the entire application is complete. This approach can ease the transition with on-going training and involvement.

5.6.3 Administration and Support Environment

Development methodology is not enough for long-term maintenance activities. We need to adapt it for this fast-paced environment. To keep your organization from slipping back into Level 1 maturity from a higher level, a methodology is essential. structured approach to problem-solving helps reduce the fire-fighting. After all, errors during production runs are just problems that we can solve.

We need to make an important separation between development and support. Support involves short-term, intense work interspersed with periods of quiet. Some managers try to make use of these periods of quiet by giving support staff development tasks. Unfortunately, this approach takes away the time to regroup and rethink issues. An important lesson is to keep support staff focused on support. They must be free to drop the task at hand to solve some problem. The quiet periods are essential for them to get a sense of achievement. Any development tasks that they must drop in favor of support issues lead to frustration.

You can always cycle staff between periods of support and periods of development. However, during any particular period, they should be focused on the particular type of task. Frequent interruptions in development are a primary cause of poorly developed applications.

Source code control is even more important in this environment. There could be many people involved in modifying code to fix problems. Occasionally, they may introduce other problems. You must have the capability to back out of any change within a short time-frame.

Better yet, package several reported problems and their fixes into a release of your application. Plan periodic releases, for example, two or three times per year. Then, you can test several fixes together.

You can even pool regression testing for bugs in a release together to save some testing time. However, to support regression testing, you must build up a database of bug reports, example test data to demonstrate the bug, and the correct data. Building this kind of database is an on-going activity. You must have tools that allow you to add to your test data through the life of your application.

Another issue you will need to plan for is software upgrade. The type of environment determines how easily you can upgrade client software. The static environment is the hardest because you will need to coordinate upgrade for all users together. If these users use other applications, you will need to test the different components to make sure that there will be no conflicts on the desktop. The roaming environment may also need coordinated upgrade of the client software. Logistically this is difficult. The public environment may be the easiest to handle—it has centrally-located software. There are third-party management tools that help administer remote distribution of software. This software can test the client machine to determine versions and offer an option to update if appropriate.

Case Study: WI Sales Application Architecture

The team reviewed the requirements discovered during the strategy and analysis phases. We also reviewed the models and reports from the Oracle Designer repository. Based on these inputs, the team recommended an architecture for Widgets. Clearly, there are alternative architectures that would also meet Widgets' needs. The team chose the Microsoft-based solution to satisfy Widgets' corporate policy.

Infrastructure Design

Widgets sales currently has one office in Timbuctoo with a staff of 50 telesales representatives and 5 customer support representatives. A second office is planned for its European operations with an initial staff of 10 telesales representatives. The Timbuctoo warehouse has 10 shipping clerks and the accounting group has 5 staff. The table below defines the service level requirements of these groups at Timbuctoo.

Application	Service Level	Users	Transactions
Sales	7x24	50 x Telesales	6,000 /day OLTP
		5 x Customer Service	
Warehouse	6x16	10 x Shipping Clerks	Interactive
Accounting	6x12	5 x Accounting Staff	Interactive

The recommendation for these offices is a combination of two-tier and three-tier client-server architecture consisting of:

- **Desktop Client:** A PC compatible running Microsoft Windows. The sales Order Entry application will be implemented with Oracle Forms, and the remainder of the application will be based on the web server tools. This choice means each telesales representative needs to be trained in the software. However, the performance of this function is critical and the current web tools are at the bleeding edge.

  Customer service representatives needs are less performance critical. Many of these functions will also be available via the Internet. For example, the order status inquiry function will be the first function provided on the WidgetsNet. For compatibility, these applications will be implemented based on the web server.

  The client application software will be installed on a network file server and the Forms runtime software will be installed on every client PC. The startup delay caused by installing the Forms runtime software on the network file server is considered unacceptable for this environment. In addition, standard software installed on these client PCs will include e-mail, and Internet browser software.

- **Network File Server:** A PC-compatible machine running Microsoft Windows NT. There will be two file servers dedicated for each Sales location.

- **Network:** The local area network within each Widgets location will consist of a single shared backbone with branches for each department. Departmental file servers will be placed on the appropriate branch of the network. Routers at each branch will isolate local traffic from clogging the backbone. Widgets will standardize on the TCP/IP protocol.

  A wide-area network will connect the U.S. location to the European location. Due to the relative isolation of the product lines and customers, the traffic on this network should be minimal except when distributed database synchronization is scheduled.

- **Database Server**: The Oracle database will run on a PC compatible multi-processor machine running Microsoft Windows NT. For performance purposes, the database will be on a separate machine from the file servers. The initial rollout of the sales and warehouse systems should share a single server machine. The server can be enhanced with additional memory, processors and disk based on growth plans. Each location, U.S. and Europe, will have its own database server. As more applications are rolled out into production, the growth path is to add more database server machines or switch to a larger machine. Depending on the data integration requirements, shared data may be distributed using snapshots or replication.

  There will be a separate database server machine for supporting the Widgets data warehouse. The intensive queries anticipated for this warehouse need to be thus isolated from the performance critical order entry application.

  The development team will have an additional database server for their development and test environment.

- **Web server**: The web server will provide a middle tier to the intranet web-based applications on a separate Microsoft Windows NT machine. This approach will reduce the load on the database server since all web server users connect under a single Oracle account.

- **WidgetsNet Service**: The public Internet-based customer service functions will require a separate machine for security. Initially, this machine will run the public instance of the Oracle database as well as the web server software. The separate Oracle instance is needed for isolating access to confidential data contained in the corporate databases.

Environment

The in-house sales orders database and warehouse database will be initially supported by a single production instance of Oracle. The WidgetsNet customer service application will run from a separate Oracle instance. It will contain an subset of the production orders and warehouse data that excludes any confidential information such as product cost to Widgets.

Production Instance Configuration

Each user will have a unique user identification on the production instance. Access security will be controlled via roles that provide read or write access to the sales and warehouse data. The default logon to an user's account will only provide read access to the tables. This default will be sufficient to service any ad-hoc query or reporting needs.

The Order Entry and Warehouse applications will contain password protected roles that allow insert, update, and delete access to their respective tables. These security roles will be granted, but disabled, to each user account. Each application will activate its respective security role at run time allowing users to perform insert, update or delete actions from the application's controlled interface. The controlled interface is responsible for maintaining data integrity by enforcing business rules and constraints.

Each application schema will be owned by a separate Oracle account. Shared tables such as product will be set up in their own schema. Public synonyms will hide any specific reference to the schema owner account. This design implies that all table names must be unique within the Widgets integrated databases.

Development instance configuration

Each developer will have a unique account for their use. Application database objects may be created in these accounts at any time by using the Oracle Designer server generator. These objects will be private to the owning developer who will be responsible for updating them as necessary. Developers must create private synonyms to reference these objects whenever they wish to override the public synonyms that point to the shared schema.

A shared development account for each application will be available to all developers. This account will own the latest development release schema of the application. Public synonyms on the development instance will reference objects in this schema.

The development DBA will be responsible for updates to the shared schema and loading the available test data. Developers will be responsible for constructing the test data and updating it based on changes to the schema. Changes to the test data should be tested in the developer's private schema. The test data will be purged once a week. Development release of the application schema will be created from Oracle Designer server generator at this time. Clean test data will be reloaded after the purge.

In addition, there will be a test account containing the latest testing release schema available to all developers. Developers must use private synonyms to reference objects in this schema. The development DBA will be responsible for maintaining the script to drop and create these synonyms.

Part

2

Designing Oracle Applications

This is where the rubber hits the road. All of those castles in the air that you built while analyzing user requirements need to come down to earth. To accomplish this transformation with the skill of a magician, we need experience in the tool set used for implementation. Theoretical knowledge, while laudable, is no substitute for battle scars.

Ironically, this phase is where many people start when building an application. So we could design an isolated, stand-alone system starting from here. Unfortunately, our applications are rarely stand-alone. They need to exchange data, or share a client workstation, or are used by the same person. So we need the earlier phases — to help us avoid kludgy interfaces and associated headaches.

Automated tools help us quite a bit in this phase. Primarily, we use Oracle Designer to manage applications boundaries and objects shared across them. There is significant support for mapping the analysis objects to the implementation objects though the transformation utilities in the product. We will focus on the reasons and kinds of transformation rather than the mechanics of driving the tool. Here is what design is all about!

Database Design for Performance

Bitter experience shows that you have to design an application for performance, because retrofitting performance is not only painful but time-consuming. And, after all that work, success cannot be guaranteed! DBMSs like Oracle make shuffling tables and columns very easy. Unfortunately, your programs are not immune to the cascading effects of restructuring the database. The time required for modifying forms and reports, even when you use Oracle Designer to generate code, is significant.

In this chapter, we examine the variables which control the performance of an application. You must tackle performance issues in the design phase so you can establish appropriate measures for database structure, program specification, and coding. These measures are your primary standards and conventions for development. We examine five major themes in this chapter:

- User requirements analysis, to determine their real needs as opposed to what they say they want. We will examine how the performance needs for the static, roaming, and public environments differ.

- Designing a relational database from an object model. The design considerations involve more than just the ability to map the object model into Oracle Designer elements.

- Database design using the Oracle Designer utilities, including analysis of the volume information collected in the detailed analysis phase. We continue the controversy of denormalization as an aid to improved performance.

- Application design, including the types of constructions that lead to slower performance in Oracle.

- Designing access security, including uses of Oracle security facilities.

6.1 Real-time, Real Quick, or Human Time

In my inexperienced past, I once asked a supervisor what the performance expectations were. Obviously (although it wasn't obvious then!) the reply was, "We need a real-time system." This supervisor was thoroughly fed up with waiting several seconds each time the staff ran some program. Knowing the capabilities of the system we were designing, I started back-peddling furiously. Fortunately, my more experienced teammate suggested further analysis. We found that actually 4 or 5 seconds was quite satisfactory for the work done by these users. In one or two functions, anything up to 15 seconds was okay.

Why is there such disparity? The media in our industry frequently misrepresent the technical meaning of the term "real-time." I differentiate between these concepts by calling them real-time, real quick, and human time. Real-time is time at the nanosecond or millisecond level, where only machines dare to tread. This is the stuff of missile guidance, robotics, process-controlled manufacturing, and so on. Real quick, on the other hand, is a range between a fraction of a second to a few seconds. It is the time-frame which people think of as very quick. Typically, the maximum in this category is 1 or 2 seconds. We need this type of response in telephone order entry, hotel checkout desks, or airline reservations. Human time is any length of time longer than real quick. We use this measurement for any activity that can complete within a reasonable time, but longer times have no direct impact on the user's work. For example, a collections department chasing receivables has plenty of time to prepare their questions before calling delinquent customers.

So, instead of asking users directly, here is what we can do. For each function or process performed by a user, we should observe how long it takes at present. Ideally, we have a model of the business processes where we can record these observed averages. Then we can question the impact of the current length of time on their work. For example, a data entry clerk whose performance is measured by the number of keystrokes per minute, receives a poor performance record, and hence less pay, due to a slow system. On the other hand, a telephone salesclerk who conducts 10 or 15 calls per hour does not suffer.

Be very careful when justifying a system based on productivity gains. Productivity gains obtained from removing redundant functions do not imply faster system performance. In other cases, you may promise faster performance from the new system but the users cannot benefit from it. Make sure users want *and* can benefit from speed improvement. In certain types of work, improving speed has no impact on productivity.

An important issue is whether users can change their way of working to take advantage of new facilities. If they do not develop work habits which take advantage of faster systems, productivity gains will not occur. Careful transition plans for new procedures are essential in this case, as well as increasing users' enthusiasm for the new methods.

We can characterize performance needs in each of our three environments, static, roaming, and public, if we assume the types of interaction ideal in each environment. The static environment has the most varied performance needs because we implement most of our applications in this environment. So, we need to separate performance needs by the kind of work: online transaction processing (OLTP), casual queries, reporting, and online analytical processing (OLAP).

OLTP work generally requires real quick response. However, each action in this kind of work involves small amounts of workfor example, querying the order status of an order, updating the balance of a bank account, and so on. Small amounts of data are modified and committed in each transaction. Today, inquiry actions in this environment are often automated rather than being mediated by a person. For example, Widgets could provide an order inquiry service to consumers that allows the customer to type the order number on the phone keypad and receive the current status of the order. Such automated telephone response systems include a voice synthesis system that reads the status of the order over the telephone.

The data entry portions of OLTP might use a public environment—that is, an Internet-based interface to provide consumers with more direct control over ordering. However, there will always be a need for a data entry application in the static environment to support the telephone sales staff. Such data entry applications will need real quick response also.

Casual data entry and inquiry typically have less critical response time requirements. The emphasis in this kind of work should be ease of use. Use the GUI features of the client tools to make such an application intuitive to use. Aim for a typical interaction response time of 3-5 seconds for a perceived real quick performance. Remember that an interaction can be an information message or a dialog requiring user action, not necessarily the complete transaction.

Reporting tasks have two different kinds of performance expectations. Real quick when entering the parameters, but human time while generating the report. In the case of reports that execute in batch, the completion time may be measured in many minutes or hours. The trend in this kind of work is for individual users to request short reports—that is, reports that request small amounts of data. Periodic long reports are scheduled to run automatically at slow times, such as at night, with the results posted on the intranet. Users can then retrieve them online for viewing or printing.

The roaming environment really is a combination of two environments: static when working on the application offline and public when connecting to the central server for upload and download activities. The portion of the application that interacts with users offline, that is, without a connection to the central server, should have the same performance design criteria as those in the static environment. However, the store and forward mechanism manages the result.

When the user connects to the central server, the store and forward mechanism downloads these results to the database server. The store and forward agent at the database server then applies them to the database. The response expectation of the download or upload is in the human time-frame. Completion time of several minutes is acceptable. Longer time is acceptable if the user can disconnect on completion of the download without waiting for the store and forward agent at the database server to complete its processing.

An example is where the user defines report selection criteria offline, connects to the central server to initiate the report generation, and disconnects. The report executes after the user disconnects and stores the results. When the user next connects to the central server, the store and forward agent uploads the report results. The expected response from the disconnected report execution is, in this environment, similar to batch run reports—from several minutes to hours.

The public environment operates a little differently. When servicing a user over the public Internet, designers have no control over the time for transmitting the display data. The control is over how fast the web server responds to the request. This response needs to be in the real quick category. The web server can often be a bottleneck if you get more traffic than anticipated. The traffic is almost impossible to predict, however. So, your best bet is to design the architecture best as you can and then plan for upgrades by monitoring the traffic.

When servicing users over a private intranet, you can predict traffic. Use the process frequency and transaction volume estimates collected during analysis. You may still need to upgrade, but in a more predictable fashion. The response levels need to be similar to those in the static environment for comparable activities.

6.2 Deriving a Design from Object Models

The touted advantage of using object modeling techniques is that you can implement the model. In the Oracle environment, you cannot do this until you upgrade to Oracle8. You may have to make some compromises for those objects that already exist in the legacy relational systems. You have four choices for implementation:

- Implement using a third-party object DBMS and interface to Oracle.

- Implement using Oracle8 object management facilities together with their ability to present relational tables as objects through the Object Views features.

- Implement using object-oriented tools, but store the database in an RDBMS.

- Map object-oriented models to relational and implement entirely in Oracle environment.

6.2.1 Third-party Object DBMS

Object DBMS products are maturing quickly. You need to build up your maturity in using them quickly also. In fact, it would be a good idea to pilot some small projects during the transition to Oracle8 prior to developing mission-critical applications.

There are several third-party object DBMS products on the market, Informix-Illustra, Object/Store, Gemstone, UniSQL—just to name a few. You will need to evaluate them prior to selection as part of your architecture design. We will focus on the database design issues in this chapter.

Of course, each DBMS has its own approach to storing data. You will need to determine whether the products are flexible enough to meet the needs of your application. Most of these products have incorporated the research of the past several years. They typically provide multi-user concurrency control, two-phase commits for distributed access, CORBA compliance, and so on. The products have been on the market long enough to be mature through practical use. There are numerous publications that address the capabilities of these products.

There is more to design than defining objects. You need to convey volume and frequency analysis to the database management system. Although we cannot discuss the details of using each product, here are some additional design considerations:

- **Storage Design**: Design distribution of data across multiple disks to distribute I/O. How will you make optimal use of the storage space and retrieval mechanisms to maximize performance? How will you partition application objects to keep them physically separate from each other within the database?

- **Database Sizing**: Use an algorithm to estimate physical storage requirements from the logical models. For example, how much extra space should you allow for overhead?

- **User account management**: Should you create one account per user or a single account for the application? What administration burden does this generate?

- **Security**: How will you design database security to tie into user accounts? Does access to an object imply access to its embedded objects? If you need a finer granularity of access protection, for example, attribute-level protection, how will you implement it?

- **Interface to Legacy Systems**: How will you exchange data with your application if the data resides in a relational database? There are third-party products that will *wrap* relational data together with methods to make them look like objects. Would you use such a product for your application? An alternative is to exchange data on a periodic basis between the object and relational databases. Your design should specify how the exchange will occur, how often, and any exceptions that need special handling. How will you maintain integrity between legacy data and your object database?

- **Interface to the Data Warehouse**: How will you exchange data from the application database to the data warehouse database? You may need to design transformation algorithms for potentially converting to a multi-dimensional database or to a relational database.

These considerations are similar to those for designing relational databases, although there is less of a requirement for transforming from the logical model to the physical database. It does not even matter whether you use the RAD or Waterfall approach. Most of these considerations address the production environment, not the development environment. However, their design may radically impact the development choices. For example, if you choose to implement very fine granularity security controls—such as attribute-level protection—you may need to define many additional pre- and post-conditions to methods on the protected objects. You may also need additional special methods to access all attributes of the object, rather than simple reference to the attributes.

6.2.2 Oracle8 Implementation

Oracle8 is an Object Relational database management system (ORDBMS). It enhances many of the relational facilities of its predecessor, Oracle7, particularly for supporting distributed and parallel processing. In addition, it provides the ability to implement object-oriented applications mixed with legacy relational applications.

Oracle8 provides almost a direct mapping from the object models we have discussed so far to the database *object types*. An *object type* or *abstract data type* in Oracle8 is a class definition. It specifies the structure of a set of objects including the attributes with data types and methods.

We will, however, have a few design decisions to make. We need to determine the appropriate data type to use when implementing the models. We will discuss the architecture of Oracle8 later in this chapter and the options for implementation in Section 6.6 Oracle8 Architecture.

Later releases of Oracle Designer provide some support for objects in its repository. It includes object modeling facilities using the UML notation. It can then generate Oracle8 physical database definitions and the scripts to generate the objects. You can also use the Object Data Designer to model and generate Oracle8 objects. The added benefit of using Oracle Designer is that you can manage the object definitions as well as the legacy relational applications and mapping between the two approaches.

6.2.3 Object-oriented Tools with Relational Oracle

In this option, you would use object-oriented development tools for developing interactive client-side programs and relational Oracle for data management. There are many client tools on the market, including some from Oracle. For example, Oracle provides PowerObjects for OO development support. The Oracle Developer tools provide some OO capabilities, such as property classes and inheritance, which will be enhanced over time.

This option is possible with pre-Oracle8 technology. In fact, Oracle Designer provides some support for implementing this option, although not as extensive as for the Oracle Developer tools. In Release 1.3, Oracle Designer provides a generator for C++ classes and Java. Future releases may provide support for PowerObjects in addition to Java. If you choose third-party development tools, the development effort is entirely manual and without the benefit of using a CASE tool.

Your first step in this option is to map the object models into relational structures. We discussed this mapping in Chapter 3. Once you map the object model into analysis elements in the Oracle Designer repository, you can proceed to design the relational database as described in this chapter. The C++ generator uses the analysis elements to generate C++ class structures. Of course, you will need to manually code the methods for the generated class structures. So, you will need additional development effort.

6.2.4 Map to Relational Oracle

This option means that you revert to the traditional Oracle development using Oracle Designer. It leads to the highest level of repository-based support for development using earlier release of Oracle Designer. You can use any of the Oracle Designer facilities once you map your object model to the analysis models supported—namely, entity relationship diagrams, business process flows, matrix diagrams and so on.

In chapter 3, we discussed some of the ways you could map object model elements to the Oracle Designer repository. You could also use the Object modeler features of Oracle Designer to model the object types and then generating a relational database based on it. Portions of this chapter describe how you would proceed once the mapping is complete.

6.3 From Models to Database Design

6.3.1 Object Models to Oracle8 Design

Object definitions in Oracle8 are type definitions. They do not physically create a storage mechanism for objects. So, you have a two-step creation process: create the type definition and then create a table of that type. A table in this context is a set of object instances that will be managed together. A row in this table is an instance of the object type.

Object type definitions correspond closely to our object models. Each attribute of the object may have simple or complex data types, as illustrated in Figure 6-1:

- **Atomic data types**: These are standard database types such as character or numeric. They correspond to the relational column data types supported by Oracle.

- **Nested object data types**: These are attributes that are complex objects with their own attributes. For example, the address of a customer is an object type itself consisting of street, city, state, and zip code information. In Figure

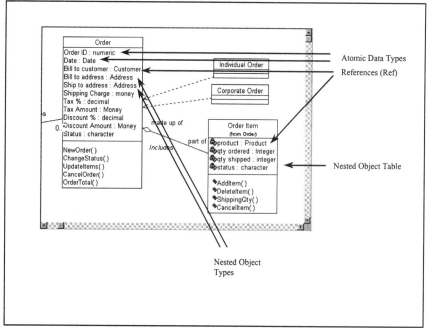

Figure 6-1: Kinds of Data Types

6-1, we denote these simply by declaring the attribute data type to be the object type.

- **Reference data types**: These are attributes that are simply pointers to object instances. Their relational equivalent is a foreign key column.

- **Array data types**: These arrays have a fixed maximum number of elements specified as part of their definition. An array may be of atomic data types or object types.

- **Nested arrays of object types**: If you declare an attribute to be a varray and its data type is an object type, you get an array of object types nested into the primary (outer) object type. This option is a combination of array and nested object data types.

- **Nested tables**: If an attribute has as its data type the name of a table, you get a nested table. The table may be created based on an object type definition. This is different from nested arrays of objects which have a declared maximum number of elements. A nested table does not limit the number of elements that can be associated with the instance of its outer object.

Now you have the foundation on which to base your design decisions. The issues you need to decide concern when you should use each of the attribute data types. The logical object model assists a little, if you put some effort into the attribute definitions.

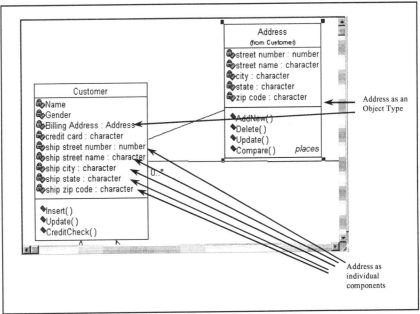

Figure 6-2: Two Approaches to Definition

Be prepared to refine your model to better represent the attribute data type choices available to you and their physical implementation impact.

As an example, during logical modeling you have the choice of defining *Address* as its component attributes or as an object type as shown in Figure 6-2. You may decide to change your approach based on the implementation impact. Here are some factors to consider when deciding whether to nest an object inside another or to simply create associations between them through reference attributes.

A nested object does not have its own identity. You may reference it only as part of its parent. For example, the city attribute (defined in the *address* object type definition) of the address of a customer must be referenced as *address.city*. A table of object types contains a unique object identifier (OID) for each instance of the object type. You may obtain the reference to an object (using the *Ref* function), store the reference in another table, and use it to access attributes of the referenced object. For example, if you created a separate table of address types, you would reference the city attribute of a customer's address as *customer.address.city*. Consider using independent tables when you may need to access them independently of the primary object.

When should you use an array data type rather than a nested table? An array data type (*varray*) places a maximum limit on the number of elements in the list. A nested table places no such limits. If you know the maximum limit, an array data type is appropriate. For example, if a student may only enroll in six credit courses in a semester due to time constraints or a business rule constraint, you might consider creating course enrollment as an array data type. Another example is payments within a payment plan offered by Widgets allows a maximum of six payments over six months. Such payments would be appropriate to implement as an array data type. The Order Items table is a good example of an object type that you might implement as a nested table because you would not limit the number of items a customer may order at a time.

You need to define the detailed implementation of each method on the object types. The standard methods on each object type include: constructor (insert) , destructor (delete), selector (select), and modifier (update). In addition to these, you need to define to Oracle *map* and *comparison* methods for each object type. Because object types represent a set of components, Oracle does not know how to compare one object instance to another.

A *map* function maps an object instance to a value represented by a scalar type, e.g., number, that Oracle knows. For example, you may provide a function that maps *publication* object types to the title of the publication, that is, a text string containing the value of its title attribute. Oracle would then use this mapped value for all comparisons. Thus, two publications with the same title would be equal.

A *comparison* function performs a comparison and provides the result, that is, whether one object instance is equal to, greater than, or less than the other. In our address object type example, the comparison function might say two instances are equal when each corresponding component matches exactly, that is, the street address, city, state, and zip codes match exactly between two instances of address. One instance may be *less than* the other when the street number in one address instance is less than that of the other, but the remainder of the address components match.

In both kinds of methods, you have to define a lot of rules about comparing two object instances. Your logical model provides little assistance in defining them. They are an essential part of your application and database design. In object type implementation, the line between application and database design is quite gray.

The earlier versions of Oracle8 do not provide explicit support for subtypes. So, you have another design decision about whether to implement each subtype as a separate object table, or to just use rules enforced by methods to distinguish between subtypes.

Subtypes have two key requirements: attributes that are specific to the subtype, and methods that are specific to the subtype.

Any objects in your model which represent existing relational tables in an Oracle database need some extra work. You interface design choices include:

- **Duplicate Data:** You might simply choose to copy data from the source application into the new application. You need to establish methods for synchronizing the updated data between the two applications. This option is appropriate when currency of data is not an issue, or slightly outdated data is acceptable. There are many implementation options for supporting this approach including Oracle's replication and snapshot facilities.

- **Object Views:** You can define views on relational tables that make them appear to be object types. These views define methods as well as attributes of the object type. The methods interpret the required operation on the view and implement the corresponding specific operation on the underlying relational tables.

Your decision depends on your future direction as well as the logistics of data access by users. Supporting this kind of decision is where your analysis efforts pay off.

6.3.2 Entity Relationship Models to Relational Design

If you used Oracle Designer for the strategy and analysis phases, you should have entity relationship models. If you completed their definition, an initial database design is fairly easy. Here is a checklist of the elements you need before database design can be done:

- Entities.

- Attributes with format and/or domains.

- Relationships with most many-to-many relationships eliminated.

- Primary unique identifiers consisting of attributes and/or relationships.

- Secondary unique identifiers, if necessary.

Essentially, each entity in the entity relationship diagram becomes a table in the application database. Of course, if you are concerned about performance in your application, you need to do a little more work. Let us discuss the simple case first, that is, converting from entities to tables as a one-to-one correspondence. Use the database design transformer wizard to perform the default mapping from entities to tables and generate column definitions from attribute and relationship definitions.

This process gives you a simple database design in which there is a table that corresponds to each entity. The columns of the table are either a transformation of the attributes of the corresponding entity or a derivation based on a relationship with another entity.

Oracle Designer uses relationship information to derive foreign key columns automatically. The generated column names are long-winded, especially for foreign key columns. So, edit them to your liking. You will need to define tablespaces discussed in Section 6.7.2 Storage Parameter Definition. But, your simple database design is essentially complete. The simple database design yields a normalized database, provided your entity relationship model was normalized. You may then construct a data schema diagram that illustrates the physical database.

Note that for simple applications involving small databases, this approach is sufficient. The default database and index design is adequate for these cases. If your application contains large volumes of data, you really ought to look further. Oracle Designer allows you to map more than one entity to a table or one entity to multiple tables. You need this facility for designing high-performance databases where you choose to denormalize tables. Ignore the protests of theorists who insist on pure relational normalized models and at least investigate some of the other avenues before making your decision.

6.4 When to Denormalize?

Designing a database for performance involves assessing the trade-offs between faster access and duplicated data. Duplicated data requires more complex data integrity enforcement algorithms and hence, more complex programs. To speed access, we examine the types of access needed by the performance-critical functions and the impact of using normalized structures.

Concentrate your efforts primarily on the performance-critical functions, that is, functions requiring real quick response times. In most applications, these functions comprise a small portion of the entire application. For each of these functions, identify the entities accessed or modified by the function. In addition, you need information on the frequency of function execution and entity volumes involved, that is, number of rows affected. You should obtain reports from the repository for these frequencies and volumes, if you recorded them in earlier phases.

The types of operations that potentially slow the execution of a transaction are:

- The number of tables (or entities) to be joined. For a self-join, count the table once for each occurrence in the join. For example, if a table is joined to itself once, count two occurrences.

- Calculation of derived data values, where the base column values do not change. For example, once we complete entering an order, the order items do not change. Thus, our calculation for order total has base columns, e.g., the amount column in order item, which do not change. Such calculations performed on a large number of rows at runtime slows response time. These calculations may not be significant in an OLTP application, but are critical in data warehouse design.

- Joining with many reference data entities such as organization type, customer type, and so on where we obtain some textual description from reference data entities. Such entities increase the number of tables in a single join. In a data warehouse, we may wish to denormalize such descriptions into the related fact table so that we retain historical context as well as reducing joins.

- Any retrieval from a large table which does not use an index. Without an index, Oracle has to read every row in the entire table to select the data requested. We discuss indexes in the Section 6.5.2 Access Methods, as well as how SQL statements affect their use in a later chapter.

- Access contention when more than one user tries to update the same set of rows in a table. Oracle controls concurrency by locking rows being updated by one user. All other users must wait until the first user releases these locks. This contention has a significant impact on response time in Oracle7. We discuss locking mechanisms in Section 6.5.2.3 Concurrency Control Options:.

Normalization reduces the complexity of maintaining data integrity by removing duplicate data. However, it typically increases the number of tables accessed by a function. Take, for example, the computer industry's habit of using codes with everything. We use codes for color, category, class, grade, in fact, we use codes for every item that offers a choice from a pre-defined list. In a normalized database structure, codes require a reference data table which includes a description for each code. Our purpose with such normalization is that if a description changes, we need to make the change in only one place.

But, do items in such lists actually change? Suppose a car manufacturer chooses cyan as a new color. Is blue, the old color, no longer valid? In a data warehouse, we would want the reference to the old color, blue, for the old cars, and refer to cyan for the new cars. In practice, we add to such lists rather than replace one description with another. We could store the description in our main table as well as in the reference data table. The reference data table is still useful for validation purposes. By the way, the old argument of preventing typographic errors becomes meaningless when we use pick-lists for entering descriptions. The reference data table is needed for presenting pick-lists.

Assess the trade-offs carefully before you choose to denormalize. Putting all of your data into two or three large tables is as bad as using dozens of tables. Denormalization techniques aim to improve performance by one of the following:

- Reducing the number of tables in a join operation.

- Reducing the number of rows in a table.

- Reducing the number of calculations performed at runtime.

Do not get carried away by denormalizing everything, however. Take into account the size of the row in the denormalized table. If this size is large, very few rows may fit into one block on disk. Thus, retrievals will be slow simply because you have to retrieve a large number of disk blocks to get your required rows.

6.5 Oracle7 Architecture

In this chapter, we will discuss Oracle's architecture from the perspective of a developer. Database administrators need more in-depth information that we will discuss in Chapter 8.

Why should designers and developers care about the Oracle7 architecture? Without a basic understanding of Oracle7, you can only produce a textbook design. Textbook designs are great for classrooms, but in real life they are inadequate. In addition to defining tables, columns, and indexes, you need to define their storage characteristics. You have to convey to Oracle7 the information deduced from the data volume and access frequency patterns you obtained during analysis. From your analysis information and an understanding of Oracle7 architecture, you can design storage parameters for your application tables and indexes. This is an integral part of physical database design.

Oracle uses one or more operating system files for data storage. The size of each of these files is specified when you assign it to Oracle. Once assigned, Oracle treats the storage space in all of these files as a single contiguous space for data storage. Space is then assigned to a table as needed. Prior to Oracle7 release 7.3, Oracle did not extend a file when the database ran out of free space. Instead, the DBA had to detect this condition before it happened and supply additional space by adding another operating system file to the database. Since Oracle 7 release 7.3, you can use extendable files that will grow if more space is needed.

This explanation is, of course, a simplified view of how Oracle manages storage. In practice, Oracle allows you a great deal of control over how it chooses to apportion space to database objects and where each object resides. The mechanics of this control depend on the version of Oracle and are detailed in these sections.

Oracle made several architectural changes to the DBMS kernel in Oracle7. For example, the background processes that constitute an instance of Oracle are different. Data storage is similar to Version 6, although there are a few terminology changes. There are also several additional administrative facilities to help DBAs manage storage and partial backup and recovery of the database—especially where large databases are concerned. The primary changes are mostly transparent to programmers and users. DBAs need to understand some of these changes since database tuning considerations are quite different.

The major enhancements in this release improve Oracle's data warehousing capabilities and support for parallel queries. These changes improve performance significantly in some applications. Before discussing the design issues for this architecture, we need to be familiar with its concepts.

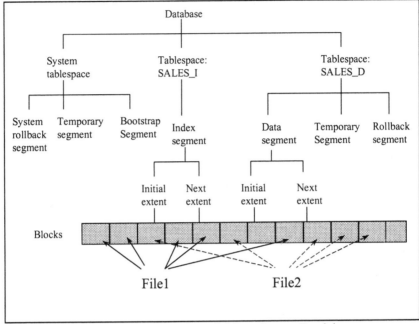

Figure 6-3: Oracle7 and Oracle8 Data Storage Breakdown

6.5.1 Storage Structure

Oracle7 has some architectural changes which improve the database administration process. The storage structure implements the concept of a database using multiple operating system files. Figure 6-3 illustrates this storage architecture. Oracle7 implements SQL statements, such as create database and alter database, to manipulate parameters associated with a database such as its name. In addition, the Enterprise Manager Utility provides a GUI interface for database administrators.

An instance is a set of processes and shared memory which make a database accessible to users. An instance can open exactly one database. On some operating systems, notably VMS on clustered VAX machines, more than one instance can open the same database. We discuss the instance processes in Section 6.5.3 Process Architecture.

The physical storage of a database consists of one or more operating system files. Each operating system file is part of one tablespace. You can place tables, indexes, and other objects in a specified tablespace. Oracle database dictionary tables and associated indexes always go into a default tablespace called system. The system tablespace also holds any objects created without specifying a tablespace. You can create new tablespaces and change their parameters via the following SQL statements: *create tablespace*, *alter tablespace*, and *drop tablespace*.

Tablespaces provide rudimentary security control. You can associate tablespaces with users by granting them access privileges on tablespaces. You can assign a default tablespace for a user to hold any tables or indexes created by the user without specifying the name of a tablespace. You can define a quota for a user to control potential space hogs. You can also define a tablespace as the default temporary tablespace to hold any temporary tables created by Oracle when executing that user's queries.

A tablespace can be taken offline for backup without affecting users who are accessing data from other tablespaces. Thus, you could perform maintenance functions without ever shutting down the entire database.

A single table cannot span tablespaces. However, a table can span multiple disks due to the operating system files that make up a tablespace. You can place an index on columns in a table in a different tablespace from the one holding the table. Thus, you can balance I/O between separate disks by the placement of tables within tablespaces and the placement of indexes on columns of these tables. Distributing I/O across physical disks in this manner helps improve performance. We will discuss these and other database administrator issues in Chapter 8.

A tablespace is divided into segments. A data segment holds data for one table. Creating a table implies creation of its data segment. Similarly, an index segment holds data for one index. Oracle automatically creates temporary segments when you execute a query that needs storage of intermediate results.

You can choose where a new table should reside, but once defined, you can relocate it only by copying it. So, the tablespace architecture for your application is really an integral part of designing your database. Typically, you should work with your database administrator in designing this architecture. Other areas for consulting with your DBA include designing the architecture for data distribution, data warehouse, and secure Internet applications.

6.5.2 Access Methods

6.5.2.1 B-Tree Access:

The standard Oracle indexes are B-tree indexes. This type of index is very versatile. Oracle also supports compressed B-tree indexes.

Oracle stores indexes together with the table data in a tablespace. Remember these parameters when you create an index. You can locate the index in the same tablespace as the table data or in a separate one. If you have multiple disks available, it is a good idea to locate table data and indexes on separate disks.

For optimal access, an index should fit mostly into the *initial* extent. Making the size of the *initial* extent sufficiently large for an index ensures that the index occupies contiguous blocks. This strategy assists the operating system's read-ahead facilities and also reduces the chances of fragmentation in the tablespace.

An index can consist of several fields concatenated to form a composite key. The maximum limit for an index key is 16 columns. The fields comprising a composite index need not be in any particular order within the record. Each field can be ordered in either ascending or descending order; by default, they will be in ascending order.

There is no limit on the number of indexes you can create on a single table. But, assess the performance trade-offs between improved speed of data retrieval vs. degradation in speed of insertion and updates. Each time you insert a row or update an indexed column, Oracle has to update all of the corresponding indexes.

6.5.2.2 Clustered Storage:

Oracle provides multi-table clustering, that is, storing data from more than one table close together. Typically, tables that share a column are ideal for clustering. Storing this data close together may minimize the amount of disk I/O Oracle needs to perform when accessing the data from both tables together.

Oracle implements clustering by means of a cluster key. This key can consist of up to 16 fields corresponding to the appropriate fields in the tables to be clustered. In our customer orders example, we might choose order number as a cluster key to join the *Order* and *Order items* table. Oracle can cluster a maximum of 32 tables in a single cluster. The steps in creating and using a cluster are

1. Create a cluster using the SQL create cluster statement. Note that you can associate a cluster with a space definition.

2. Create each table to be clustered with the create table statement, including the cluster clause. Note that you have to specify the table's cluster key in the cluster clause.

3. Load data into the clustered tables.

Given enough spare space in the database, you can cluster an existing table. The basic principle is to create the desired cluster definition, followed by creating each table under a different name. In this case, Steps 2 and 3 can be combined into a single SQL statement to load the data from the existing table into the new table during creation. Then, you can drop the old table and rename the new table to the desired table name. You need extra spare space because until you drop the old table, the database actually contains two copies of the data.

It is possible to cluster just one table with this clustering scheme, that is, intrafile clustering. This type of clustering is useful only when the key columns can contain many duplicate values. A single-table cluster forces Oracle to keep the data *sorted* by the cluster key and so improves range-scans on that key dramatically. However, you may be wasting some disk space in return.

Clustering data really involves rearranging the way data is stored. Thus, changing existing tables to a cluster involves a significant shuffling of data. Clearly, you perform this type of database restructuring while others are using the database at your own peril.

6.5.2.3 Concurrency Control Options:

Oracle implements its own concurrency control mechanisms using the system global area, SGA, under UNIX. It provides explicit and implicit locking mechanisms for a transaction, at table and row levels. These mechanisms work automatically, without requiring explicit coding by the programmer. Occasionally, you may wish to use explicit locks, for example, to run a lengthy report involving many separate queries.

The default locking level on Oracle Forms update is by row. Internal Oracle functions, such as the data dictionary cache, also use locking. We will discuss the various types of internal locks in Chapter 8 Database Administration.

Oracle provides several types of locks: row share, row exclusive, share, share row exclusive, and exclusive. By default, Oracle provides a *committed read* level of isolation (called read consistency in manuals). It uses rollback segments to contain a copy of data at the time of executing a query if that data is modified after starting the query. Hence, a user always obtains a consistent view of data even though others might have updated the same rows in the database. A *dirty read* level of isolation is not possible in the Oracle implementation.

The *cursor stability* level of isolation is rather more complex. You must use a *share update* (synonymous with a *row share*) lock that operates at row level. An example of using this level of isolation is a long-running report or batch update that requires point-in-time data consistency. For long-running reports, Oracle provides the *Set Transaction Read-only* statement that indicates to Oracle to provide consistent data as of the start time. In the case of updates, you need manual locking. You would obtain this type of a lock using any one of these statements:

Lock table <table-name> in share update mode [nowait]

or

Lock table <table-name> in row share mode [nowait]

or

Select .... for update of <column-name>

This type of lock prevents someone else from updating the data you are working on and from explicitly locking the entire table in exclusive mode. It prohibits others from reading the selected data. Other users can obtain share update locks on the same tables.

There are two ways of achieving the *repeatable read* level of isolation. One way is by using the *share* lock which operates at the table level only. In this case, you are preventing other users from performing any updates on the entire table, although they may read from it, until you release the lock. The other way is by using a *share update* lock, which operates as an intention lock at row level. With this lock, other users can still obtain a *share update* lock on different rows, but their updates will not be applied to the database until you release the shared lock on the table.

You would only use an explicit *exclusive* lock on a table if you wanted to make extensive changes affecting a lot of rows. Obviously, while a table is locked, no one can update any data in it, so you would not do this at peak database usage times. Note that even with an *exclusive* lock, other users can still read data from the locked table. Implicit exclusive locks occur automatically whenever you change anything in a table, that is, when you use an insert, update, or delete statement. Implicit locks occur whenever you use a SQL statement, whether embedded in a programming language interface, in SQL*Plus, or in Oracle Developer tools.

If you cannot obtain the lock you want, Oracle normally just waits until the lock becomes available. You can control this default, however, by specifying the nowait option. There is no way of specifying a time-out period, that is, to wait for the specified time and then, if the lock does not become available during this period, return. You can simulate this yourself with a *busy-wait* loop in your program.

Oracle also provides mechanisms for transaction-level controls based on the use of locks and the SQL commit and rollback statements. Note that Oracle does not supply a specific start of transaction statement. The start of a transaction is implied by the first executable SQL statement. The end of the transaction can be a commit statement, a rollback— that is, abort transaction—any data definition statement such as create or rename, or when you log off from Oracle. Oracle can also unravel transactions in progress when errors such as deadlocks or abnormal termination occur.

The *archivelog* facility supplied by Oracle can be used to keep a continuous record of changes to the database. With this facility, you can recover from disastrous situations such as disk head crashes which destroy all database data. You may use such a facility in conjunction with regular backups of the database. After a disastrous loss of your database, you will consider the effort expended in backups and journaling well worth it! Even users who complain of the overhead of using journaling will appreciate not having to manually repeat all transactions since the latest backup. We will discuss these issues in depth in Chapter 8.

There are actually two additional types of locks: latches, which control access to the shared memory structures, and internal locks, which control access to internal objects from the system tablespace such as the data dictionary.

6.5.3 Process Architecture

Figure 6-4 illustrates the process architecture of Oracle7. Here is a description of how these processes interact.

When you start up the database, the system global area (SGA) is initialized and the background processes start running. Oracle uses the init.ora parameters and control file to initialize the database. At this time, there will be minimal information in the system global area, for example, which operating system files comprise the database.

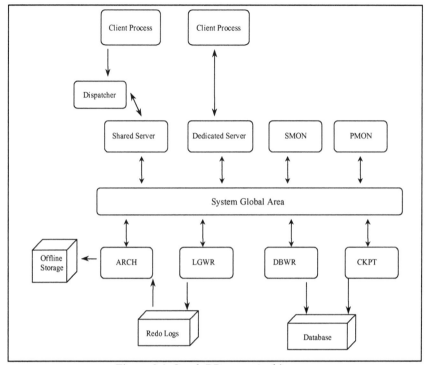

Figure 6-4: Oracle7 Process Architecture

Oracle uses the control file throughout the time when the database is up and running. The background processes are also up and running throughout.

When a user connects to the database via some interface utility such as Oracle Forms, the user client process starts and attempts a connection via SQL*Net. Its connection request is heard by a process called a *network listener* that runs on the database server. The listener connects the requestor to a back-end Oracle process called a dispatcher process. In a client-server architecture, the dispatcher is on the database server and the user process is on the client PC. When the client and dispatcher are on the same machine, this two-process architecture is sometimes called a two-task installation. There can be many dispatchers on a machine.

As the user retrieves some data by performing a query, the dispatcher process schedules the request in the server queue. A shared server process retrieves the results into the data buffers of the system global area. It also retrieves the related dictionary definitions into the dictionary cache. The dispatcher passes the result data to the client process from the data buffers. If another user also requests the same data, the server process retrieves it from the system global area, rather than going to the disk files.

The dispatcher serves all clients—that is, it is shared between them. You may dedicate a server to a specific client process, in which case, there is no dispatcher. The

DBA can configure multiple server processes depending on the resources available. Each shared server works on a single request from the queue at a time, but is not associated with a particular client.

Note that under the UNIX operating system, the dispatcher process must have special privileges to allow it to access protected database memory structures. This process typically runs with the same privileges as the background database processes such as the database writer (DBWR).

Oracle writes any updates applied by a user client process into the system global area. At the same time, it copies the relevant information to the rollback segment, so that Oracle can reconstruct the old data if necessary.

When the user commits the updates, the server process marks the updates as committed in the SGA and writes the committed data into the redo buffers. Then it triggers the redo log file writer (LGWR) to write all changes pending in its buffers to the redo log file. It may write pending uncommitted transactions from other users as part of this write. Commit processing is complete as soon as redo logs are written, and the user can proceed with other operations. If the LGWR needs to switch to another redo log file, it initiates a checkpoint, that is, wakes up the database writer to synchronize SGA buffers with database files.

Throughout this time, the database writer (DBWR) process periodically checks for changed data buffers. The user's shadow process may also awaken the DBWR if the shadow process is unable to find free data buffers. The DBWR writes the least recently used SGA buffers to the database files, and marks these buffers as free. Notice that there may be a time lag between the commit processing and the database writer process writing the change to the physical files. The physical database files may not always be up-to-date with respect to committed transactions. However, the database recovery processes can always use the redo logs for up-to-the minute transaction recovery.

In distributed and parallel database configurations, there may be two additional processes: the Recoverer (RECO) and lock server (LCK). We will discuss these in later chapters. They are more an issue for a database administrator than a developer.

6.6 Oracle8 Architecture

As stated previously, Oracle8 is an object relational database management system. As such, its underlying architecture has not changed substantially between Oracle7 and Oracle8. Oracle8 provides several enhancements to the Oracle7 relational architecture to better support large databases. These include improvements to the query optimizer, parallel queries, and facilities like partitioned tables. We will discuss many of these improvements in Chapter 14 Distributed Databases.

In this section, we will focus on the extensions that support the object-oriented features of Oracle8.

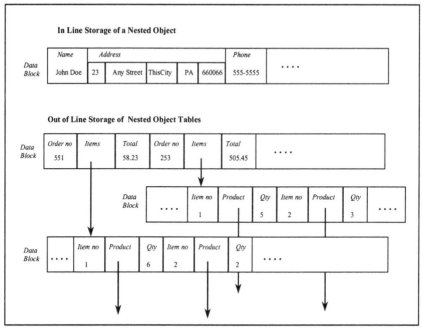

Figure 6-5: In-line and Out of Line Storage of Object Types

6.6.1 Object Types Storage Structure

Object type definitions, like view definitions, are logical constructs. They do not allocate any storage space, other than for the definition itself. When you create a table based on an object type, you allocate storage space in the database. The *create* statement also allows you to define storage parameters as supported in Oracle7.

Storage of embedded object types is a little more involved. Nested object types within an object type definition do not have a separate identity. The nested object instances are stored *in-line*—that is, as if they were a column within a table. These object instances occupy the same tablespace and extents as their outer object instance. Such object instances are sometimes called column objects.

The only exceptions to this storage restriction are object instances that are stored in a nested table. Nested tables are stored *out-of-line*. Object instances stored in a nested table have a separate identity. You can define storage parameters for a nested table as part of the statement for creating the *store* table. Think of this as a way of linking independently stored tables without defining explicit foreign keys. Such object instances are sometimes called row objects. Figure 6-5 illustrates the concept of in-line and out of line storage.

Each object instance is assigned a unique identifier, called an *OID*. This identifier is assigned by Oracle8 and is guaranteed to be unique regardless of the object type. Oracle8 promises to handle up to $2**128$ unique object instances. When you specify an attribute data type of *ref*—that is a reference to another object instance, you are specifying an attribute that will store the *OID* of the referenced object instance.

OIDs can be used as pointers to object instances. So, you can define tables which contain pointers to object instances, or just attributes that contain OIDs. You can de-reference these pointers within SQL statements to access the values.

6.6.2 Object Views

Object views are a wrapper around relational tables to make them appear to be object types. Object view definitions include the facilities to define methods which translate the required operation on the object type to the corresponding operation on its underlying tables.

Object instances implemented via an object view can have an OID. You must create the view with the appropriate specification, *with OID*, to obtain this feature. You might use this feature if you need to reference or nest tables of these object instances within another object type definition. For example, if your new object-oriented application references the product definition implemented in a legacy relational system, you might create an object view on products *with OID*.

Keep in mind that you cannot change the storage architecture of existing relational tables. So, it would make sense to implement references to object views based on existing tables as *out-of-line*, or row, objects. Your two choices for this approach are to use nested object tables, or reference attributes that point to instances obtained from an object view.

Another key feature which allows object views, and in fact any view, to be updateable is the *instead of* trigger. This trigger allows us to redefine the functionality of standard operations on a view, such as insert, update, or delete. Thus, we can hide the constraint requirements of the underlying tables of a view in the code of the *instead of* trigger.

6.6.3 SQL Extensions

Oracle8 includes a few key extensions to SQL to support object-oriented constructs. There are extensions to the DDL statements to allow creation of type definitions and permit the use of types as data types for an attribute. There are extensions to DML statements to allow references to object type attributes, whether atomic, complex or nested. There are also extensions to the access security model to allow granting of privileges associated with creating, populating, and accessing object tables. Rather than reiterate the syntax conventions from the Oracle manuals, we will discuss only their concepts here.

You can refer to an attribute of an object table in the normal SQL DML statements just like the columns of any other table. So, for atomic attributes, you see little difference. Complex data types, such as nested object types, may require reference to parts of the column object, for example, the city component of an address column.

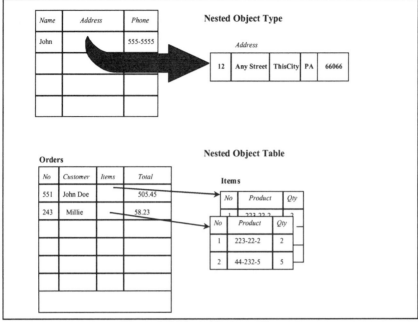

Figure 6-6: Nested Instance Concept

Oracle8 provides the dot notation (**.**) to reference parts of object types such as nested object types. You refer to the city component of address as simply *address.city* in any DML statement.

Array types require an additional index reference to specify the particular element of the array in the column. Alternatively, you may reference the entire array provided that the destination of the data can accept it. For example, when retrieving data into PL/SQL variables, you must make sure that the receiving variable also has the appropriate object type.

Access to instances in nested tables is a little more complex. Figure 6-6 illustrates the concept of nested instances. Think of it as a set of nested rows for each instance of the parent object. You need to specify a subquery to pinpoint the set of nested rows. Oracle8 implements such a reference through a mechanism called a flattened subquery, through the keyword *THE*. *THE* syntax is similar to a function, enclosing the subquery within parentheses. You can use this anywhere you may normally reference a column, hence its name *flattened subquery*. Figure 6-6 illustrates the insert statement using THE.

6.7 Physical Design Considerations

There are two areas of design you should pay particular attention to: database design and physical implementation design. Database design considerations include table definitions, indexes on tables, and how well indexes serve the application's access needs. Physical implementation considerations include how to place database files on disks, backup and recovery plans, and integrating with the operating system facilities.

Database design considerations differ in the development environment and the production environment. So your development instance may be organized differently from the planned production instance. Because of such differences, your project may use a different database administrator to support the development team from the DBA who supports the production environment.

Table definitions and indexes have an enormous impact on the performance of the application. The optimum design requires a careful assessment of the trade-off which database designers and application designers need to scrutinize very closely. Unfortunately, most large corporations divide the design functions between two rather independent groups: database administration and application development. Both groups need hands-on experience in both sides of the project. The best design team will have members from both groups dedicated to the particular application at hand, regardless of their separate reporting hierarchies.

One large corporation that I came across insisted on separating the design tasks. Their application designer was a recent university graduate and had little practical experience in building applications, even less in building relational database applications. The DBA group consisted of two people who had a lot of data modeling experience. Unfortunately, they had little knowledge of their operating environment or of physical implementation issues and the internals of Oracle. After numerous meetings and status reports, they eventually completed development.

Their first database design was fully normalized (just like the book says!) and had no index definitions at all (physical considerations are not important in relational technology!). Needless to say, they ran into snags when the first critical batch reporting program took 28 hours to run. Just creating the appropriate indexes reduced the runtime of this report to under two hours. Rearrangement of their data distribution on disks reduced another hour. We received many commendations from the operations group who had headaches watching the available resources dwindle on their system monitor.

Determining the best indexing scheme for each table is not quite as simple as the Oracle Designer transformer leads you to believe. You can use the result of this wizard as a starting point. However, review the application access needs extensively before finalizing the index design. Here are some tips:

6.7.1 Indexes on Table Columns

As a minimum, you need an index on each unique identifier (primary key) of the table, and on each foreign key. The primary and unique constraints allow you to specify that you want to use an index when you create the constraint. Thus, you should not need an explicit index for these constraints. Foreign key constraints do not create an index, however. So, you should explicitly create an index on each foreign key. While this suggestion may seem excessive, keep in mind that without these indexes, Oracle will lock the entire master table (in share mode) whenever you update a row in the corresponding detail table.

Primary, unique, and foreign keys may be made up of more than one column, in which case, the indexes are called concatenated indexes. The trick to using indexes is in the order of columns in a concatenated index.

Rather than the intuitive sequence of columns in a concatenated index, use the column producing the most reduction first in the sequence. For example, consider an index consisting of the columns company code, account number, and transaction type in a journal entry table of an accounting database. If there are only two companies, the account number column reduces resulting rows much more than the company code column. Similarly, transaction type further reduces the resulting rows more than the company code. So, the sequence of columns in your index should be account code, transaction type, and company code. Creating optimum indexes can make an order of magnitude difference in the execution time of a query.

6.7.2 Storage Parameter Definition

With each table definition, we can specify certain storage parameters. For each table and index, we can define storage parameters including the size of the initial and next extents. The *initial* extent size is space that Oracle reserves when you first create a table. After this extent is full, Oracle will obtain a *next* extent to extend the table. The same principle applies to the allocation of space for indexes, except that the sizes used are based on the index storage parameters. The space obtained may not be exactly the size specified by the next extent parameter. Oracle applies internal rules to efficiently use fragments of space and avoid creating unusable fragments. For example, rather than leave a one block-fragment free when obtaining a next extent, Oracle will include it. Thus, the next extent may be larger than expected. Oracle also uses the *pctincrease* parameter, if specified, to increase the size of the next extent from the size of the previous extent obtained.

When you omit storage parameters for a table or index, it inherits the storage parameters from the tablespace where it will be located. The default storage definition from the system tablespace is used whenever you omit specification of storage parameters for a tablespace.

When you define storage parameters, you are really providing hints to Oracle on how to allocate the space in a tablespace. The sizes for the extents in storage parameters are in terms of number of blocks, which relate directly to Oracle's basic unit of disk I/O. This is why you need to choose carefully the storage parameters for a table. You can, of course, change these parameters at any time, but they do not affect tables already created with the older parameter values. The new parameters only affect tables created after the change.

Strive to store the entire table in contiguous blocks, so that you minimize disk head movement delays. You can use default values for each of these parameters, but to improve speed, define storage parameters appropriate to the volume of table data. There are similar parameters for index definitions also.

Oracle uses the minimum space for missing or null data values. Oracle7 uses one byte of storage per null value whenever one occurs in the middle of a row. When these null values are replaced by data, Oracle must expand the row to include it.

Third-party products, like *ts_reorg* consolidate table data by copying it. The only way to defragment your database is to take a complete export, initialize the tablespace, and then import the data back. This process may be reasonable on small databases, but for large databases spanning many disks, it is a nightmare. So, it is worth spending some time thinking about this issue.

6.7.3 Physical Implementation Considerations

Since the previous publishing of this book, several technological changes have occurred. These changes significantly affect the considerations for performance. So, our physical layout strategies need to change. Here are some of the changes that affect our physical layout design:

- Disk architectures have changed —RAID technology, onboard caching, faster rotation speeds—all have resulted in much faster throughput than possible just a few years ago. So, the issue affecting performance attributable to disks is seek delay, not data reads.

- Disk striping facilities both by the hardware subsystem and operating system are excellent. These facilities are reducing the need to manually distribute I/O between disks.

- Operating systems improved their file storage subsystems. For example, all major implementations of the UNIX filesystem now support the write-through feature. This feature allows Oracle to maintain disk consistency when processing database commits and checkpoints. Maximum file size has also increased tremendously—reducing the need to use raw files.

- Hardware architectures that permit larger amounts of memory—even gigabytes of it—are now common. Of course, the drop in memory prices have helped. The result is that you can design a larger SGA for Oracle and still have room for operating system read-ahead buffers.

In this section, we consider how to integrate the Oracle database issues with the operating system. We will discuss where to place Oracle database files in the operating system, how to plan backup and recovery procedures, and how to set up batch and interactive access in Chapter 8 Database Administration. Database administrators can tune many factors to improve performance that are omitted from this chapter. Here is a brief overview of the issues:

- **Database Files:** In each database, you need data files which are associated with each tablespace in the database. To distribute I/O between disks, you can use the striping facilities provided by the operating system—for example, the stripe set under Windows/NT. Alternatively, locate these data files on a separate disk to distribute disk I/O manually. Remember that a table must fit within one tablespace. So be sure to use your volume estimates to size your tablespaces.

- **Distribution of Tables Among Tablespaces:** A common convention is to create two separate tablesaces—one for data and one for indexes. You will need to define the tablespace as the default for each user of the application and grant them appropriate access privileges.

- **Use of Operating System Files:** This consideration is closely related to the distribution of tables among tablespaces. You can use operating system striping mechanisms to distribute I/O. This feature, in conjunction with the read-ahead facilities, can dramatically improve throughput.

- **Distribution of Data Among Oracle Extents**: To maximize the benefits of Oracle's multi-block reads and the read-ahead buffering mechanisms of the operating system, you need good use of storage parameters on tables. Use the storage clause of the *create table* statement to enforce these parameters.

The performance issues tackled by a good storage parameter design are fragmentation and chaining. By striving to store as much of the table in an initial extent as is reasonable, we avoid fragmentation. Appropriate definition of *pctused* and *pctfree* parameters help you avoid row chaining.

6.8 The Database Transformer

Oracle Designer provides a utility that generates candidate database element definitions from the entity relationship models stored in its repository. Note that it merely creates repository definitions of the candidate database. You may modify these definitions prior to generating the DDL and creating the actual database. For example, after generating the candidate database elements, you might modify column names to conform to your project's naming conventions. Table 6-1 illustrates some example transformations performed by this wizard.

You can use this utility in both the Waterfall and RAD approaches to development. In the waterfall approach, you would select the entire model as the transformation set. In the RAD approach, you would select a few entities at a time as the transformation set. When you modify the analysis, as part of a RAD iteration, make the changes in the analysis model—that is, the entity, attribute, and relationship definitions. Then, run the transformer utility again to propagate those changes to the database definition in the repository.

Analysis Element	Design Element	Comment
Entity	Table	Table name is derived from the plural of the entity name.
Attribute	Column	Simple case
UID Attribute	Foreign Key Component Column	Derived at the many end of a one-to-many relationship.
Entity Short Name, Relationship name	Foreign Key Constraint Name	Derived from the short name of the related entity or relationship name.
Entity Short Name	Intersect Table Name	Derived from the short names of the related entities.
Entity Class Name	C++ Class name	You must supply this if you use the C++ generator.
Candidate Key	ID	Generated when unique identifier is not available for the entity being mapped to a table. An Oracle sequence is associated with it.
	Oracle Sequence	Generated for candidate keys, otherwise you need to define them.
Secondary Unique Identifier	Unique Constraint and its Component Columns	Derived.
One to Many Relationship	Index and its Component Columns	Generated based on runtime options.

Table 6-1: Some Sample Transformations

Note that you need to set the appropriate transformation options each time you run the transformation utility. For example, to propagate changes to attributes into the database design, you need to set the *modify columns* option. To propagate new attributes, you need to set the *add columns* option. If you deleted attributes, however, you would need to manually remove the corresponding columns in the database element definition.

An alternative to propagating specific changes from analysis to design definitions is to delete the design elements and create new ones. Deleting tables can be time-consuming, especially if you have them referenced in module data usages. Oracle Designer will not delete tables that are referenced by a module. A *force delete* utility is available for use when you want to delete elements including any references.

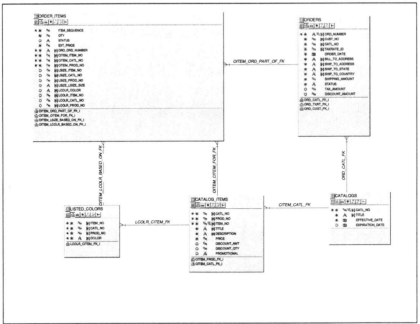

Figure 6-7: Multiple FK Column Propagation

A database transformation may not produce the entire database design that meets your requirements. It takes care of most of the drudgery. You can then focus on special cases where you need additional work. For example, if you use concatenated columns as primary keys often, you may end up with the same column reference under different generated column names in an intersect entity. Figure 6-7 illustrates one example of this with its corresponding schema diagram. The database transformer may generate such multiple columns where each is part of a different foreign key. You may need to remove additional references, leaving just one such column reference— and use in all of the foreign key constraints.

When the database elements meet your requirements, you may generate the data definition language script using the DDL generation utility. Oracle Designer will offer you an option to execute the DDL when the scripts are complete. You can preserve the DDL for repeated use—for example, to create private test schemas for individual developers or to create development and test databases. In a production environment, your DBAs may insist that you hand over the DDL script for them to create the schema. Typically they guard production instances zealously and may not grant developers sufficient privileges for such activities.

Oracle Designer allows you to design and specify tablespace and storage specifications as part of the Design Editor Admin definitions. Each tablespace and storage specification is defined separately in a schema. Then, you may associate them with an implementation of a table or an index in that schema. In practice, you will need to design two sets of storage parameter specifications: one for the development environment and one for the production environment. You should define these two environments as two different schemas. Realize that the development and production instances may have different tablespace names for use by your application. Also, a development database is usually small, containing only a subset of the data in the production instance. So, your storage specifications ought to reflect these differences in the appropriate schema.

One common way to accommodate these different instances is to use the tablespace default storage parameters for the development environment so that you do not associate a storage parameter definition with any tables or indexes in the Oracle Designer repository. Prior to the production rollout, you will associate the appropriate storage parameter definition with each table and regenerate the DDL scripts. There is a drawback to this approach, however. You cannot test the final DDL until the production rollout. I highly recommend that you test the script prior to the actual production rollout. Your production DBAs will thank you for the extra effort which will save them much frustration and debugging of your DDL script!

6.9 Designing Security

There are several facets to designing security: user identification, database access control, function access control, and physical access control. Of these facets, physical access control, that is, controlling access to the physical computer, is beyond the scope of this book. We will focus our design efforts on options for identifying users and controlling database and application function access.

6.9.1 User Identification

An important design consideration is whether you provide individual user accounts or a single account for all users of your application. With individual user accounts, you can track who did what for audit trail purposes. However, you have a greater administrative burden on database or application administrators. This option is necessary if your application updates sensitive or business-critical data. Using a single account for all users means that you cannot track individual users' actions. This option is useful for applications that require unsecured access, for example, an inquiry application or a public environment order entry application.

Within one application, you may have different security control requirements. For example, the Widgets order entry application comes in two flavors of security: public order entry and internal order entry. In public order entry, we only provide functions to create new orders. So, we need no access security—anyone can create an order. We could use a single user account, for example, *guest*, that everyone can use.

In the internal order entry application, we want to automatically enter the order entry clerk's identification on the order. In addition, we may have additional functions such as modifying orders available to our internal staff. In each case, we would track who modified the order and when. This audit trail could be maintained automatically if we assign separate user accounts to each clerk.

Notice that if you use a single Oracle account, but use a custom login mechanism to identify individuals, you are effectively assigning individual user accounts. Your application would track these individuals through a custom user administration function.

As part of your security design, you need to design an administrative function to enroll users into your application, remove them, or change their privilege. Oracle provides many facilities to build such a function. This function may allow your users to take charge of administering user accounts and privileges instead of burdening your DBAs and system administrators with these tasks. Many applications, in my experience, have successfully trained departmental secretaries to perform such administrative tasks.

6.9.2 Database Access

It is common for your application to maintain data integrity by implementing rules. These may be part of the application logic, implemented in the server, or in the middleware layer. Direct access to the data may lead to data updates which violate the integrity rules. If you permit data modification outside the application, you usually cannot control data integrity, even if you make extensive use of database triggers and stored procedures. So, you might prevent access to the application data outside the control of your application.

However, in these days of user empowerment, we would like users to use ad-hoc query tools so that we don't have to write one-time use reports for them. We thus encourage them to use one or more of the query tools we support. Unfortunately, these query tools imply access outside the control of the application. Several of these tools provide facilities to modify the data as well as query facilities.

Your design needs to accommodate these two conflicting security requirements. With Oracle there are several alternate approaches. Before discussing them, here is an overview of Oracle's database security architecture.

Oracle provides a user account and password as a primary identification mechanism. Security privileges such as access to tables and procedures is associated with the user account. Oracle provides controls for select, update and delete access privileges to a table, and an execute privilege to stored procedures. Oracle also provides many other privileges that we are less interested in for designing application security. You may grant a privilege directly to a user account or indirectly via a role. A role is a name give to a set of granted privileges. You can name roles to represent the functional roles of your business users or a similar logical group of access privileges within your application. Designing these roles would be part of your security design.

A role-based security design would consist of a minimum of two roles: a default role, giving select access only, and a update role, giving access for modification. The default role would be active for each enrolled user. So, if they access the database via an ad-hoc query tool, they may select the data. This default role would not permit any update or delete access.

The application should control the activation of the update role. You could password-protect the role so that users could not activate it through a tool like SQL*Plus. Of course, the application needs to know the password. The role should be activated on initial entry to the application before any programs within the application are executed. In the Windows client environment, you may need to build a custom launch window which activates the role and then allows the user to invoke each program. You could only provide separate icons for each program if you could activate the role prior to executing each program.

Another approach is to use a secondary login effected by the application. In this approach, each individual has an Oracle account which has select access only to the application database. Users would employ their individual accounts when using an ad-hoc query tool. At startup, the application would log into another Oracle account which has update privileges. The secondary logon is transparent to the users. This method is useful where some technical reason prevents granting of privileges via roles. This method was popular in older versions of Oracle that did not support role-based security.

Security based on application data requires more sophisticated design, for example, one of my clients needed business object-based security. In this scenario, the owner or creator of an object could modify any information in that object and its dependent information. For example, the *owner* of a particular customer—such as the sales representative—could update any information about that customer including multiple addresses, contact persons, organization units, and so on. However, they could not update information for a customer owned by another sales representative unless given explicit access by the owner.

This type of security requires us to design additional database tables to track the potential multiple owners of each core object such as customer. Note that we do not need to identify owners of dependent tables such as address and contact persons. Dependent tables contain a foreign key reference to the customer. The owner of the core table implies ownership of all of its dependent tables. We must also program procedures that would verify ownership prior to allowing update or delete operations. The Widgets case study illustrates this example.

6.9.3 Function Access

Users need access to tasks that are part of their responsibilities but not others. In fact, they should be prevented from accessing functions for which they are not trained. During analysis, you should have obtained these access requirements and recorded them in the organization function matrix. Now we need to design an environment to enforce the requirements.

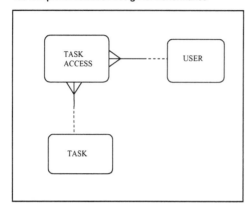

Figure 6-8: Task Access Security Model

In a terminal-based environment, we could control this functionaccess via a menu system. Menu items represented user tasks. If a task was not allowed for a particular user, the corresponding menu item either disappeared or was disabled. In a windowing environment, we don't have an application menu. However, we can construct a custom application window that presents a set of icons for the programs accessible to the user. You could develop a common launch window for all of your programs. Then, based on task access, the program would gray out icons for functions not available to the current user.

To implement task access control, you need to add a user profile table with a child table listing the tasks permitted for a user. Figure 6-8 illustrates the entity relationship model for this approach.

Some projects insist on more sophisticated security controls. For example, a client may insist on a data entry program to allow some users to only perform queries, others to only update, and still others to update and delete data. Implementation of such controls can seriously impact performance. Instead, you could develop three separate programs with the appropriate operations allowed. This duplicate forms development is tedious if you are developing manually, but with the assistance of the Oracle Designer repository and generators, it is not a great effort. Your initial module may permit all operations. You then copy this initial module to create a similar module, but disable the delete operation in the copy. The generator then produces a similar program without the delete operation allowed.

To reiterate the caution mentioned in earlier chapters: Keep security simple. Complex security, even though listed as a top requirement by users, does not get used. For example, one of my clients developed an application with elaborate security that defined column-level access privileges—at the express request of the key users. They even built an administration interface to make it easy to administer. After the application had been in production for about one year, we found that users were ignoring the security system. Instead of granting access to specific columns as needed, they were simply giving each other passwords to perform the task they wanted.

CASE Study: Widgets Sales Database

The team needs to design the architecture and the database instance in parallel with the database objects. Some architectural decisions can impact the design of database objects as well as the application programs. For example, the decision to use distributed databases with partitioned tables implies that a simple *create table* statement is insufficient. The initial architecture for Widgets requires little such complex design.

Placement of objects in a particular tablespace is a significant decision that depends on the instance design. Typically, a database administrator needs to be involved in making these decisions. So the discussion of tablespaces and placement of objects in these tablespaces is deferred until Chapter 8. The design here focuses on the needs of the production environment, not the development environment. For example, the development environment may keep all tables in the same tablespace but in the production environment, they may be separated by application to ease backup and recovery procedures.

Illustrated in this case study are the proposed object schema in Oracle8 and the relational schema possible in earlier versions as well as Oracle8. Later chapters will assume the relational schema, because of the limitations of the Oracle Designer and Oracle Developer toolsets at the time publishing. These tools will undoubtedly be upgraded to support the object environment in the future.

The Oracle8 Object Schema

Mapping the object model to Oracle was straight forward. Illustrated here is a portion of the schema to illustrate the transformation from the logical model to the physical database implementation. We did not specify all of the constraints needed on this schema for brevity's sake. Keep in mind that we have to specify all constraints when creating the table, including *null/not null* as a check constraint on every mandatory attribute. Type definitions do not permit constraints as part of the definition statement. The major design considerations were:

- Whether to use nested types or just reference them. The rule of thumb we followed was that intersect object types, that is types that relate to more than one base type should be nested within the type that it is most closely related to. For example, inventory type is more closely related to product than the location.

- Whether to use variable array types or nested tables. The rule of thumb we followed was to use nested tables if we could not determine the precise number of instances of the nested type. This option allows the most flexibility in access to the nested object instances. Variable array types restrict the maximum number of object instances. We did not need to preserve the order of creation of object instances in this schema, a feature that would have dictated the use of variable arrays. The order of creation of order items is not significant in our case study.

```
create or replace type address_type as object (
Name                    varchar2(80),
```

```
address_1                    varchar2(80),
address_2                    varchar2(80),
city                         varchar2(80),
state                        varchar2(80),
post_code                    varchar2(15),
country                      varchar2(80)
)
/
```

/* Notice the use of nested address_type attribute data type.   */
/* The map member function cust_map just uses cust_id for sequencing */

```
create or replace type customer_type as object (
cust_id                      number,
name                         varchar2(256),
gender                       varchar2(1),
billing_address              address_type,
credit_card                  number(25),
ship_address                 address_type,
map member function cust_map return number
)
/
create or replace type body customer_type is
  map member function cust_map return number is
  Begin
      return cust_id;
  End;
End;
/
create or replace type cat_type as object (
cat_id                       number,
category                     varchar2(10),
description                  varchar2(2000),
map member function cat_map return number
)
/
create or replace type body cat_type is
  map member function cat_map return number is
  Begin
      return cat_id;
  End;
End;
/
```

/* We have to create a type definition for the table before using it as */
/* an attribute data type, in product_type **/*

```
create or replace type cat_table_type as table of cat_type
/
create or replace type location_type as object (
loc_id                    number,
warehouse                 varchar2(25),
section                   varchar2(25),
aisle                     varchar2(25),
shelf                     varchar2(25),
map member function location_map return number
)
/
create or replace type body location_type is
  map member function location_map return number is
  Begin
      return loc_id;
  End;
End;
/
```

/* Notice the nested tables category and inventory. */
/* Notice the reference to location_type. *Without the* ref *we would */*
/* have just an attribute of type location_type. *After creating tables */*
/* of these objects, we can restrict the scope of the location attribute */
/* to that table. */

```
create or replace type invent_type as object (
product_num               number,
location                  ref location_type,
qty_stock                 number,
qty_reserved              number,
qty_missing               number
)
/
create or replace type invent_table_type as table of invent_type
/
```

/* Notice the nested tables category and inventory. */

```
create or replace type product_type as object(
product_num               number,
name                      varchar2(60),
image_file                varchar2(256),
unit_price                number(8,2),
```

```
        min_ord_qty              number,
        category                 cat_table_type,
        inventory                invent_table_type
        )
        /


        create or replace type oitem_type as object (
        order_id                 number,
        product                  ref product_type,
        qty_ordered              number,
        qty_shipped              number,
        status                   varchar2(20)
        )
        /
        create or replace type oitems_table_type as table of oitem_type
        /


        create or replace type order_type as object (
        order_id                 number,
        order_date               date,
        bill_to_customer         ref customer_type,
        ship_to_customer         ref customer_type,
        bill_to_address          address_type,
        ship_to_address          address_type,
        shipping_charge          number(8,2),
        tax_rate                 number(4,2),
        tax_amount               number(8,2),
        discount_rate            number(4,2),
        discount_amount          number(8,2),
        status                   varchar2(20),
        items                    oitems_table_type
        )
        /
```

/* Here are the tables based on the object type definitions.   */
/* Notice how we add constraints, type definitions do not have them.   */

```
        create table product_categories of cat_type
        primary key cat_id
        /
        create table locations of location_type
        primary key loc_id
        /
        create table Customers of Customer_type
        primary key cust_id
        /
```

```
create sequence cust_seq start with 1 increment by 1
/
```

/* *Specify the storage table name for nested tables for clustered storage.* */

```
create table products of product_type
nested table category store as nest_categories
nested table inventory store as nest_inventory
/
create sequence prod_seq start with 1 increment by 1
/
create table orders of order_type
nested table items store as nest_items
/
```

The Relational Schema Diagram

We used the database design transformer wizard from Oracle Designer to develop the relational schema. We made minor modifications to the resulting schema. We also drew its data schema diagram illustrated here, rather than list the DDL statements for every table.

A data schema diagram (DSD) is a representation of the physical database. Some developers use the entity relationship diagram for this purpose. The key differences

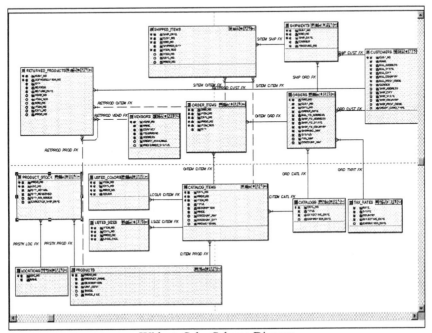

Widgets Sales Schema Diagram

between these two diagrams is the meaning of the associations: in an ERD associations are relationships between entities; in an DSD, associations represent foreign key constraints between tables.

Sample Table Definitions

The table definitions shown in the data schema diagram were associated with a particular schema, Widgets. In this schema, tablespaces and storage parameters were specified for each table. You can *implement* the same table definitions in more than one schema. The tablespace associations and storage parameter definitions can be different in each schema. So, you can create one schema representing the development environment with small storage extents, and another representing the production environment with larger extents as appropriate. You can even represent snapshots and replicas in this manner.

Illustrated below are DDL statements for a few tables. We did not include all schema tables here for brevity. Oracle Designer generates separate files for each type of DDL statement: table creation, constraints, indexes, triggers, and so on. These illustrations contain excerpts from many such files.

```
/* Notice the NOT NULL and DEFAULT constraints specified in line.    */
/* Comments are based on the Column Comment property which in turn    */
/* is derived from the analysis level Attribute Comment property.     */
```

```
CREATE TABLE ORDERS
(ORD_NO                VARCHAR2(25)     NOT NULL
,CUST_NO               NUMBER(15)       NOT NULL
,CATL_NO               NUMBER(15)       NOT NULL
,ORDER_DATE            DATE             NOT NULL
,BILL_TO_ADDRESS       VARCHAR2(2000)   NOT NULL
,SHIP_TO_ADDRESS       VARCHAR2(2000)   NOT NULL
,SHIP_TO_STATE         VARCHAR2(30)     NOT NULL
,SHIP_TO_COUNTRY       VARCHAR2(30)     NOT NULL
,SHIPPING_AMT          NUMBER(6,2)      DEFAULT 0
                                        NOT NULL
,STATUS                VARCHAR2(30)     NOT NULL
,TAX_AMT               NUMBER(6,2)      DEFAULT 0
                                        NULL
,DISCOUNT_AMT          NUMBER(6,2)      DEFAULT 0
                                        NULL
)
TABLESPACE SALES_D
STORAGE(
INITIAL 1 M
NEXT 1 M
MINEXTENTS 1
```

```
 MAXEXTENTS 199);
COMMENT ON COLUMN ORDERS.ORD_NO IS 'Order number';
COMMENT ON COLUMN ORDERS.CUST_NO IS 'Customer number';
COMMENT ON COLUMN ORDERS.CATL_NO IS 'Catalog Number';
COMMENT ON COLUMN ORDERS.ORDER_DATE IS 'Date Ordered';

CREATE TABLE ORDER_ITEMS
(ORD_NO                    VARCHAR2(25)     NOT NULL
,ITEM_NO                   NUMBER(15)       NOT NULL
,CATL_NO                   NUMBER(15)       NOT NULL
,PROD_NO                   NUMBER(15)       NOT NULL
,ITEM_SEQ                  NUMBER(2,0)      DEFAULT 0
                                           NOT NULL
,QTY                       NUMBER(8,2)      DEFAULT 0
                                           NOT NULL

)
TABLESPACE SALES_D
STORAGE(
INITIAL 1 M
NEXT 1 M
MINEXTENTS 1
MAXEXTENTS 199);
COMMENT ON COLUMN ORDER_ITEMS.ORD_NO IS 'Order number';
COMMENT ON COLUMN ORDER_ITEMS.ITEM_NO IS 'Number in the
catalog';
COMMENT ON COLUMN ORDER_ITEMS.CATL_NO IS 'Catalog Number';
COMMENT ON COLUMN ORDER_ITEMS.ITEM_SEQ IS 'Order sequence of
item within the order';
COMMENT ON COLUMN ORDER_ITEMS.QTY IS 'Qty ordered';

ALTER TABLE ORDERS
ADD CONSTRAINT ORD_PK PRIMARY KEY  (ORD_NO)
USING INDEX  TABLESPACE SALES_I
STORAGE(
INITIAL 1  M
NEXT 1 M
MINEXTENTS 1
MAXEXTENTS 199) ;
```

/* Oracle Designer generates primary and unique key constraints on all */
/* tables before generating the foreign key constraints that are based   */
/* on them to avoid referencing non-existent keys. Notice the use of   */
/* indexes in the DDL for before constraints. It also specifies the   */
/* tablespace to use for these indexes.   */

```
ALTER TABLE ORDER_ITEMS
```

```
ADD CONSTRAINT OITEM_PK PRIMARY KEY
(ITEM_SEQ
,ORD_NO
,ITEM_NO
,CATL_NO
,PROD_NO)
USING INDEX  TABLESPACE SALES_I
STORAGE(
INITIAL 1 M
NEXT 1 M
MINEXTENTS 1
MAXEXTENTS 199) ;


ALTER TABLE ORDERS
ADD CONSTRAINT ORD_CUST_FK
FOREIGN KEY                (CUST_NO)
REFERENCES CUSTOMERS       (CUST_NO)
ADD CONSTRAINT ORD_CATL_FK
FOREIGN KEY                (CATL_NO)
REFERENCES CATALOGS        (CATL_NO);


ALTER TABLE ORDER_ITEMS
ADD CONSTRAINT OITEM_ORD_FK
FOREIGN KEY                (ORD_NO)
REFERENCES ORDERS          (ORD_NO)
ADD CONSTRAINT OITEM_CITEM_FK
FOREIGN KEY
(ITEM_NO
,CATL_NO
,PROD_NO)
REFERENCES CATALOG_ITEMS
(ITEM_NO
,CATL_NO
,PROD_NO);
```

/* Notice the naming conventions of foreign key indexes—It makes it easy   */
/* to match it to its corresponding FK constraint. Also note that indexes are */
/* in a separate tablespace SALES_I per the design specified in Chapter 8   */

```
CREATE  INDEX ORD_CUST_FK_I ON ORDERS
(CUST_NO)
STORAGE(
INITIAL 1 M
NEXT 1 M
MINEXTENTS 1
MAXEXTENTS 199)
```

```
TABLESPACE SALES_I;


CREATE  INDEX ORD_CATL_FK_I ON ORDERS
(CATL_NO)
STORAGE(
INITIAL 1 M
NEXT 1 M
MINEXTENTS 1
MAXEXTENTS 199)
TABLESPACE SALES_I;


CREATE  INDEX OITEM_ORD_FK_I ON ORDER_ITEMS
(ORD_NO)
STORAGE(
INITIAL 1 M
NEXT 1 M
MINEXTENTS 1
MAXEXTENTS 199)
TABLESPACE SALES_I;

CREATE  INDEX OITEM_CITEM_FK_I ON ORDER_ITEMS
(ITEM_NO
,CATL_NO
,PROD_NO)
STORAGE(
INITIAL 1 M
NEXT 1 M
MINEXTENTS 1
MAXEXTENTS 199)
TABLESPACE SALES_I;
```

/* *Notice the following excerpt from the .avt file generated together with*   */
/* *the table DDL. This file contains allowable values defined in domains*   */
/* *that are associated with the generated tables. All allowable values from*   */
/* *domains and columns are stored in the CG_Ref_codes table.*   */

```
DELETE FROM CG_REF_CODES

WHERE RV_DOMAIN = 'GENDER'

/
```

```
INSERT INTO CG_REF_CODES (RV_DOMAIN, RV_LOW_VALUE,
RV_HIGH_VALUE, RV_ABBREVIATION, RV_MEANING)

VALUES ('GENDER', 'MALE', NULL, NULL, 'Male')

/

INSERT INTO CG_REF_CODES (RV_DOMAIN, RV_LOW_VALUE,
RV_HIGH_VALUE, RV_ABBREVIATION, RV_MEANING)

VALUES ('GENDER', 'FEMALE', NULL, NULL, 'Female')

/
```

Application Design for Performance

We all know that poor design of a program results in poor performance. So, what makes for a good design? With the GUI tools available with Oracle, the answer is no longer just structured design. You need to discard the techniques which were (and still are!) suitable for programming in a procedural language.

This chapter describes some useful Oracle tool techniques. Some of the specifications depend on the interface environment. For example, the parts of the application that must run in the mobile environment need to specify how the disconnected interface should operate. In the public environment, we need to specify how to handle conflicts due to its optimistic locking style. Realize that we cannot easily change the user interface style defined by Oracle Forms. In this tool, we can only react to user actions, not control their sequence. Our specifications, therefore, focus on reactions. The high productivity claims for these tools depend on fitting your requirements to their capabilities. We cover the following topics:

- Forms specification techniques, which focus on defining what data to present to users, and what manipulations to perform based on user actions. We will review the specifications used by the Oracle Designer Generator for Forms.

- Report specification techniques, with an overview of the Oracle Designer Generator for Oracle Reports.

- Specification techniques for batch or procedural modules, which might be written in a third-generation language or PL/SQL. We will discuss how business rules might fit into this category.

7.1 Performance Considerations

A good design is simple and elegant. However, we occasionally need to make compromises for faster performance. Such compromises must match the development tool used for a particular implementation. Also, we must make a reasoned decision about where to compromise during the design phase. Patchy solutions devised during development—or worse, during testing—can only yield inadequate solutions.

A primary requirement for good design is to know the style and mold of each of the tools you plan to use in development. We introduce the concepts implemented by some of the tools in this section. Later chapters discuss forms management and report writing tools in detail. Successful designers need to be experienced in using these tools to be aware of their features and limitations.

Another requirement is to understand the types of program actions possible and their impact on performance. Client-server tools are very powerful—you can make them do a lot of work with very few statements. Unfortunately, fewer statements do not mean less work when they execute! When performance is critical in your application, understand the amount of work involved in executing each statement. Then, you can judge the appropriate timing and offer good perceived response to your users.

Oracle Forms implements data-driven interaction. It performs best when your interaction model closely fits its style of working. For example, a block of data in a window roughly corresponds to one table in the database. Insertions, updates, and deletions from this block operate on its corresponding table. Programming in Oracle Forms involves defining reactions to events initiated by user actions. For example, when the cursor is in the *Order Date* field and the user clicks the mouse cursor in the *Item no* field, you may want to prevent entry of order items if the customer has not yet been specified in the *Customer Name* field. Oracle Forms calls such reactions *triggers*.

You can, of course, implement multiple tables in one window. You can make such blocks and their underlying tables transparent to users through program triggers. However, the amount of work in such an application might defeat your time estimates and performance objectives. For example, a trigger consisting of several statements is inherently slower than if it consists of a single statement. Triggers causing database access are slower than are those which move the cursor around. My experience shows that increasing complexity of programming in triggers generally leads to slower execution. Thus, implementing a data entry screen which uses complex validation and which will be used by power typists is not a very good idea. Complex validation triggers will probably slow the response sufficiently to frustrate classic data entry clerks, especially if their performance is measured by keystrokes per minute! Remember, only a very slight degradation in response causes such users frustration.

Access to an Oracle database is via SQL. All of the application development tools with Oracle use SQL for database access. Even Visual Basic, a C program, or third-party utilities such as SQL/Windows from Gupta, or PowerBuilder from Powersoft, must use it. So you must understand the power of SQL as well as its limitations for a good design. Using traditional techniques such as programmatically matching two files one record at a time will not run as fast as a join in SQL.

Some other pitfalls occur in unoptimized coding or inadequate database design. A database retrieval which does not take advantage of indexes will be slower. So, pay close attention to your retrieval requirements, index design, and volume of rows retrieved. It is rarely a good idea to design your application independent of the database design. The two are very closely related.

Other pitfalls are network traffic generated by your client code. For example, suppose your order entry form running on a client PC displays a list of products. If you have several thousand products, the client may transport the data for all products across the network before displaying the first 20 products. The resulting delay will lead to perceived slow performance! You could prevent this from happening by a simple design requirement to impose selection restriction prior to displaying the list.

When client-server GUI tools are inappropriate for the task, you can use a programming language, such as PL/SQL, C++, C, Fortran, or COBOL. SQL is embedded into your program statements in such instances. In addition, Oracle provides an array processing feature to improve performance in these languages. Using arrays, you can retrieve multiple rows at a time into your program's memory area. Thus, you will reduce the interaction with the database and improve speed of execution. You can also design the use of stored procedures and triggers rather than performing all business logic and rules enforcement in the client. If appropriately designed, this approach gives you reusable components as well as reducing movement of data over the network.

Oracle allows sharing of the database between multiple users. However, careful design of concurrency control is essential for good performance. Tools such as Forms have their own built-in model for when rows are locked and committed. Make sure you are aware of these models and their impact, although you really have little control over them. You can control when activities that may create concurrency conflicts occur. These are common sense measures—for example, schedule any bulk updates when your OLTP users are inactive.

There are other design decisions that affect performance in a client-server architecture. Watch out for database access across the network. Network access is typically much slower than accessing a database on the local machine's disk. In addition, be careful of multi-step processing of data. Try to use PL/SQL for processing all steps on the database server and only transmitting the final result over the network. Otherwise, the intermediate results of each step cause the network traffic to be the performance bottleneck.

Architect your applications such that your OLAP users are isolated from the OLTP users. We already examined a typical architecture that achieves this in Chapter 5. OLTP activities are typically performance-critical. Data warehouse users, on the other hand, are analytical. They perform queries that explore historical data; for example, to look for patterns, or to perform trend analysis. OLAP activities not only churn large volumes of data, they also involve complex manipulations. All in all, OLAP activities can use up all the computing power you can make available. Mixing this activity with your day-to-day operational transactions will likely lead to serious performance impact.

Designing data warehouse applications is very different from OLTP applications. So, we will reserve its discussion until a later chapter. In this chapter, we will focus on designing operational systems only.

7.2 Designing Programs

Some of the programs that comprise your application are represented by business functions. Others are business rules that we defined during analysis. Still others are created during the design of the application. Your methodology for transforming analysis elements into design elements must encompass all three kinds of programs. Let us examine these mapping processes and the considerations peculiar to each.

7.2.1 Deriving Programs from Business Functions

The first task in application design is to determine the boundaries of each program from your logical model. (Note: I use the term "*program*" to mean an independently executable unit. Do not confuse it with other common uses of this term such as a source file containing code.) This translation is one of the hardest in a project, and yet methodologies provide little guidance in the task. We use only the lowest-level explosions for processes from our process flows, function hierarchies, and atomic business rules. Higher levels were necessary for understanding the big picture and for presenting it to our users.

We need to consider two aspects of a business function when deciding program boundaries: processes which are always performed together by one person and the tool used to implement the program. A good rule of thumb is: One program uses one tool, or in process-based architectures such as UNIX, one program is one process. The crux of the problem is: Which business functions should become a program? Let's review the information we have that will help us determine program boundaries.

From the process logical model, we have a set of business functions which are essential to running the business. A single business function or a group of business functions becomes a single executable program. So, start by separating business functions that represent manual activities in the new system. Typically, manual activities involve some physical movement, such as packing a shipment, or some person-to-person contact. They are closely tied to the new mechanisms you plan to implement in the new system. By this stage of the project, your users should be working very closely with you to design such new mechanisms. After all, they will carry out the designed manual procedures. Your role is to make your users aware of which business functions to include in the new automated system. These functions may be partly automated in the existing legacy systems, but not in a way conducive to

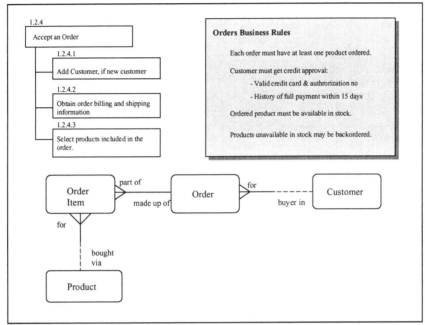

Figure 7-1: Candidate Group for a Program

the redesigned procedures. By the way, this type of design is where joint application development (JAD) techniques work very well. Practitioners of business process reengineering have several techniques for conducting focused sessions that address the detailed design needs.

What do you do with the business functions you decided to automate in the new system? We need to group them logically. One way of determining a logical group is by using our function-entity cross-reference matrices together with the business rules. For each business function, gather the list of entities used. Then, study the relationships between these entities in our entity relationship diagram. Business functions affecting entities with mandatory relationships (solid line relationship) should be grouped together. Watch out that you don't end up with a single program implementing all of the business functions! Take into account the type of access each business function makes to these entities.

Group together business functions which insert new data. A group might insert into several entities with a mandatory relationship between them. For example, consider the entity relationship diagram and associated business functions in Figure 7-1. Business Function 1.2.4 adds new occurrences to the order entity. There is a mandatory relationship between order and order item entities. So, we group Business Function 1.2.4.2 with 1.2.4.3. The relationship between order and customer entities is also mandatory. Thus, we add Business Function 1.2.4.1 to the group. This grouping is, of course, intuitively obvious to a user: We should be able to add a new customer when taking an order. Our grouping allows us to enforce the constraint rules defined in the entity relationship diagram and implements a natural progression of work.

Now, what about the business functions that update these same entities, such as updating order item shipping status? Obviously we group them together as well. But should this *update* group be different from the *add* group? The answer depends on what your development tool provides. Some tools, such as Oracle Forms, allow add, update, retrieve, and delete functions on any screen form you develop. In fact, you have to disable any of these deliberately if you want to offer them as separate menu options to users. So, if you plan to use Oracle Forms, add and update groups should be one program.

Consider, as an alternative, Prolifics' forms utility JAM or Gupta's SQLWindows. With these tools, you have to write separate code to add and update database tables. So, you can choose to use the same screen definition with two separate sets of code: once to add new occurrences and once to allow updates. Each of these sets might appear as a separate option on the user's menu.

Now consider the business processes that these activities represent. Does an order entry clerk typically delete an order? At Widgets, in the old process model, the order entry salesperson performed all of these activities. In the new model, a separate customer service representative deletes an order if the customer cancels a previously placed order. Actually, Widgets management would like to keep a historical record of such cancellations for further analysis. If a customer simply backs out of placing the order while conversing with the order entry salesperson, we simply back out of the order. The new process model allows handling of orders placed via the new Internet-based interface as well as via the telephone. The point here is that we need two separate programs: one for the order entry salesperson and one for the customer service representative. You need to consider such division of labor when designing the program boundaries.

There is, of course, a separate business function to maintain customer data. This business function has overlapping functions with the foregoing order entry group. Ideally, we should be able to develop the customer entry and update form in a reusable fashion. With Oracle Forms, develop this as an independent form which is called up by the order entry program. If the response time for calling up a separate form is too long, then consider duplicating the code with separate pages within a single Forms executable. To make such design decisions, you need intimate familiarity with your development tools and the architecture of your static environment. In fact, a rule of thumb I find effective during design is: If in doubt, try it out! Don't wait until the coding phase to discover that you misunderstood a capability of your development tool. This is the real purpose of prototypes in engineering! Then, write down your experiment—and give it to the programmer as hints at coding time.

Report business functions, if they appear in your analysis models at all, are rather more straightforward. Typically these business functions retrieve entities which are related to each other in some manner, mandatory or optional. If a business function

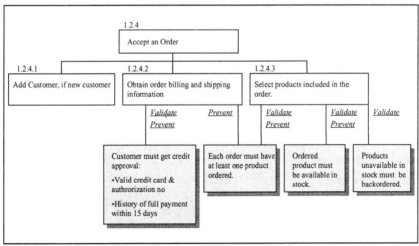

Figure 7-2: Business Rules Enforcement

appears to retrieve entities which are only distantly related—that is, with many intervening entities not included—ask your users to clarify the anomaly. You may be missing some relationship, or may be an implicit algorithm for the intervening entities which you do not know about.

7.2.2 Designing Programs from Business Rules

If you followed the approach described in earlier chapters, you have a multi-level model of business rules, with business policies at the highest level and atomic business rules at the lowest level. In addition, we should have these rules cross-referenced with business functions to indicate which functions should enforce each atomic rule. Figure 7-2 illustrates a sample fragment of the business rules model.

The design of the programs that represent business rules depends on the kind of rule. Facts and some constraints are simply database elements like tables, columns and integrity constraints. Other constraints may need a procedural validation. Still others may require a prevention action to ensure that the rule is not violated as well as validated. Let us consider some examples:

If the customer has prior purchase history, we give credit if this customer

$\Rightarrow$ *has always paid for purchases in less than 15 days.*

This constraint requires us to check past payments from this customer to see if they were within the 15-day requirement. We need a procedural constraint to implement this rule. We have a choice of implementing it as a database trigger that rejects an order if it violates this rule and other related rules. For good user interface design, this rule should be checked also by the order entry program. So, a better design would be to implement a stored procedure for validation which would be invoked by both the database trigger and the order entry form.

Rules may not be always implemented as a procedure or a trigger. Suppose that the response resulting from the credit check procedure we described earlier is too slow for the fast pace of order entry. There is a good case for our example rule to be implemented by creating another column in the customer table. This column would represent whether the customer is creditworthy. It could be populated with a value of *positive credit* until the first late notice is sent. The first overdue payment would change the credit status to *negative credit*. Then, perhaps, after two years of timely payments would reset it back to *positive credit*. This is another method for implementing this business rule while satisfying the performance requirements.

> *A vendor must exist before a payment can be made to it.*

This constraint requires us to check that the vendor marked as the recipient of a payment exists before we commit the payment to the database. In addition, we could create the vendor every time a payment to a new vendor is created so that we prevent the violation of the business rule.

7.2.3 Designing Systems Programs

During design, we may create programs that are not directly derived from business functions. Such programs may be utilities needed to support other programs or reusable components other than business rules. We might also design scripts or programs that run in batches or during off-hours, processing such as data extraction and loading into a data warehouse. Such programs are needed to support the architecture of our application but have no direct association with the business model.

Grouping programs for periodic or batch runs follows a similar logic to the grouping of business functions. Remember to account for the time factor in your decision process: programs to be run daily are a separate natural group from weekly or monthly groups. The tools you might consider for implementing these programs include PL/SQL, a third-generation language interface with PRO* precompilers, or a third-party tool such as SQR.

Typically, we give very little consideration to how to administer the application once it goes into production. But, such utilities are an important part of designing an application. We should include the following in our design definitions:

- Administration of user ids and passwords.

- Integration of these Oracle user names and passwords with the application user ids and passwords. After all, making users sign on more than once is a very poor user interface. Why should your users have to appreciate the difference between an application and an Oracle database?

- Assignment of access security privileges to new users and reassignment when user roles change.

- Scripts for backing up your application data, programs, and user setups.

- Procedures for recovering data in case of a disaster.

Design of these functions is really specific to your application's needs, although you may set company standards that permit many applications to implement the same scheme. Designing these functions and developing them is a relatively small effort that pays off handsomely in later stages, particularly in impressing user management with your efficiency.

As an application developer in a large data processing shop, you might consider design of these functions beyond your job description. But, they are an important part of your project. Recruit staff from the appropriate organization, the database administration group or systems programming group, to design and build these functions. I have seen too many applications seriously delayed because we overlooked such functions at design time and did not include them as tasks in our project plan.

In a small organization, designing these functions in this phase is even more important. You cannot afford the chaos of putting the application into production without any of them in place. Ignore them at the risk of burning a lot of midnight oil— and losing credibility in the view of your users.

You may find that including tasks in the project plan for designing and building these functions raises many eyebrows. Management resistance is highest when development time is rather short. However, the smooth transition from development to test and then into production convinces even the worst skeptic. In one of my projects, we smoothly installed turnkey systems at dozens of installations across the US without any on-site UNIX expertise—or any technical knowledge. The manager was convinced only after we expended several weeks installing the first system and recovering from disasters stemming from trivial user typos!

7.2.4 The Application Transformer

Once you have determined the mapping of functions to implementation modules, you are ready to use the Oracle Designer application design wizard. This utility transforms

Table Property	Setting a Standard
Display Title	Block title in Forms or web page, frame title in reports. Consistent naming.
User/Help Text	Used by the MS Help generator. Consistent help descriptions across tools.

Table 7-1: Sample Properties Propagated by the Application Transformer

Column Property	Setting a Standard
Prompt	Field label in Forms or web page, Column heading in reports. Consistent naming.
Uppercase	Converts input to all uppercase characters. Consistent treatment for case insensitive retrieval.
Display	Whether column is typically displayed. Set generated key columns to not displayed for better user interface.
Display type	Data type to use for display e.g. radio button, check box, and so on. Consistent user interface.

Table 7-1: Sample Properties Propagated by the Application Transformer *(continued)*

selected business functions into implementation modules. Prior to running this utility, you must have definitions of the database including tables, columns, and constraints in the repository. You may use the database transformer to obtain such a database design.

There are a number of database objects properties that you may specify prior to running the application transformer. The transformer will propagate these design specifications further to each use of these objects in modules. Table 7-1 illustrates some of the common properties we may define to facilitate the setting of standards in module data usages. These properties are just illustrations and not an exhaustive list.

You must indicate the specific portion of the function hierarchy that it may transform. This portion may be a single function or an entire branch of the hierarchy. For each function, this utility creates a corresponding module. It also creates module table and column usages corresponding to the entity and attribute usages of the function.

In the waterfall approach, you may use this utility at the end of the analysis phase to transition into the design phase. In the RAD approach, you may use this utility repeatedly in each iteration from analysis to design. Thus, you may propagate the information gathered during analysis into the design and implementation of the application.

7.3 Forms Specification

Once you are aware of the capabilities of the tools, you will find writing specifications relatively simple. Functions which you might implement using Oracle Forms characteristically have verbs such as maintain, add, update, delete, and enter in their descriptions. If you were less rigorous in the analysis phase, look for function names that contain verbs like *process* used in descriptions, These might be hiding some interactive forms based processing.

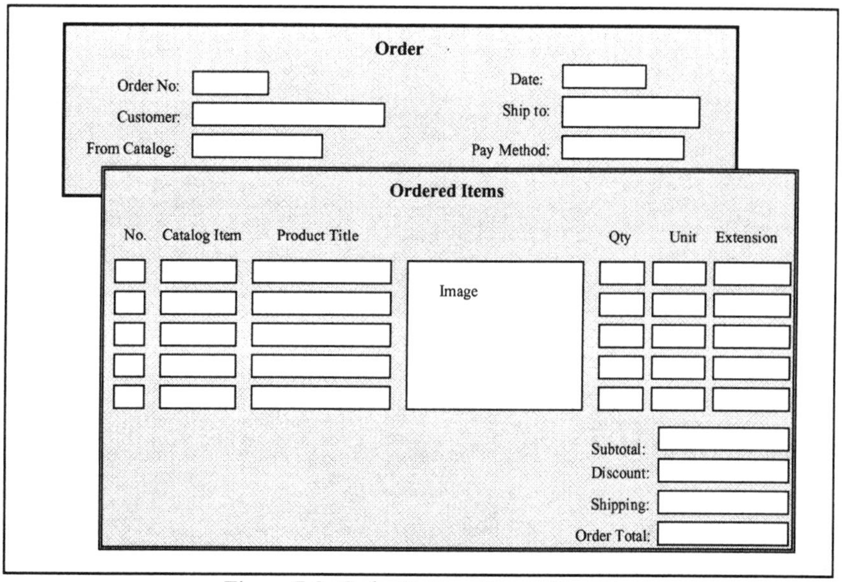

Figure 7-3: Order Entry—Forms Layout

A forms specification needs to cover the following basics:

- Layout of data on the screen, specifying multiple canvases or windows.

- Relationship of the different blocks, such as master/detail, and the behavior of detail rows for each operation on the master. Such behavior is frequently called block coordination.

- Data correctness and integrity requirements, including validation of individual data elements, cross-element validation, foreign key constraints, and so on.

- Enforcement of business rules through validation to ensure conformance or positive action to avoid violation of the business rule.

- Navigation details, such as which fields have lists, and navigation between blocks, pages, windows, and forms.

- Operations available from each form and details specific to the operation. These operations may be presented as menu options or a set of iconic buttons.

One module usually denotes one form in Oracle Designer. The module may manipulate data in one or more tables. We may choose to navigate from one form to another—that is, a parent child calling relationship between otherwise independent modules. Some of the children modules in the structure may be business rules that the parent module needs to enforce. These rule modules may be implemented as procedures. We discuss specification of procedural modules in Section 7.5 Procedural Program Specification.

There are four parts to a module specification in Oracle Designer: the structure of the modules in the group, the detailed specification of each data element that will be displayed, the interface layout including the windows, and the interaction rules that govern the form. Figure 7-3 illustrates a potential layout of the order entry module. In earlier releases, you would use individual tools to perform each of the design tasks. In Release 2.1 and later, you can perform all of these design tasks using Oracle Designer's Design Editor tool. We shall examine each of these components in detail in Chapter 9. Here is an overview of the components.

7.3.1 Relationships Between Modules

A module network illustrates the relationship between the group of functions we determined earlier. The root (or parent) module will be the form that we generate and the children modules may be forms or reports that we may wish to call or navigate to from the root form. Figure 7-4 illustrates a sample module network for a menu module calling a couple of forms modules. Part of the design process is to design the navigation between forms as well as between elements of a form based on user's interface needs. Oracle Designer provides a *display view* for the module data diagram for this purpose. Although this view is not a WYSIWYG display of the module, it provides boxes indicating the window, tab pages, and canvas boundaries. It also uses arrows to indicate navigation between these elements.

7.3.2 Relationships Between Tables in a Module

The module data diagrammer (MDD) provides facilities for specifying layout as well as relationships between the tables used within the module. It uses positional conventions to indicate master detail and lookup relationships between tables used by

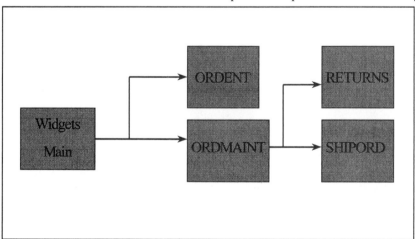

Figure 7-4: A Sample Module Network

the module. Master detail components are arranged top to bottom with each master component above its detail component. There is one base table in each component and are the primary targets of any data manipulation supported by the form. This layout is illustrated in Figure 7-5. We will discuss module diagrams in detail in Chapter 9.

In earlier releases of Oracle Designer, modules contained data usages directly. In Release 2.0, a module is made up of one or more module components. Each base table forms the basis of one module component. Module components can contain data elements from this table, any tables for which it contains foreign key columns, or new data elements not related to the database that you define, called unbound items. Module components can be specific to a module or reusable in more than one module.

7.3.3 Using Constraints in Design

The design must specify the type of coordination required for insert, updates, and deletes between module components. There are three ways to influence the generated code: properties specified on a constraint definition, properties of data usages of a module component, and generator preferences. The relevant properties are dependent on the kind of rule you wish to implement. I suggest an iterative approach to using the generators: setting properties a few at a time, generating code, testing the resulting behavior, and back to setting or resetting properties. The discussion in this section concerns the overall design decisions. The properties and preference settings are discussed in Chapter 9.

For insert or update operations, specify whether a master row without any detail rows is acceptable. As an example, we accept rows in the *Customer* table without any rows in the *Orders* table. On the other hand, an order without any order items has no meaning (usually!). The business rules expressed by the entity relationship diagram should be very helpful in

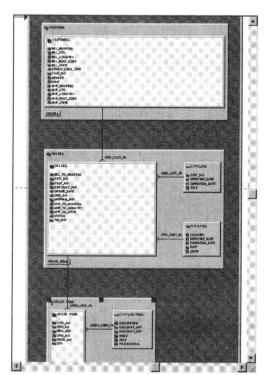

Figure 7-5: A Module Diagram

determining such design issues.

Delete operations in coordinated blocks should also specify how to enforce the business rules. Can we allow detail rows which are not attached to any master row, that is, orphan rows? To specify this, we use the *Nullify* option on the constraint property. Of course, if the foreign key column is part of the primary key in the detail table, we cannot implement this option because columns in a primary key cannot contain a null. Should a deletion of the master row imply deletion of all associated detail rows, that is, cascade the deletions? To specify this, we use the *Cascade* option. Alternatively, should we deny deletion of the master if associated detail rows exist? We specify this using the *Restrict* option.

Updating a key column is forbidden in the database. So, if the foreign key column from the master table is part of the primary key in the detail table, you cannot specify an update on such a column. In fact, Oracle Designer tools will warn you if you attempt to violate this rule. Besides, if the foreign key constraint is based on the primary key constraint of the master table, we cannot update columns that are in the primary key of the master table anyway! So, here are the prerequisites for specifying any update cascade options:

- The foreign key constraint of the detail table must be based on a *Unique* key constraint rather than the primary key constraint of the master table.

- The foreign key column should allow null values if you intend to specify the *Nullify* option.

When the foreign key column is not in the primary key of the detail table, we have several options for cascading the modified value from the master. The *Cascade* option will update the foreign key columns in all dependent rows if the value in the master is updated. The *Nullify* option will set the foreign key column to null whenever the master table column is updated to any value. The *Restrict* option will prevent you from updating the column in the master table.

Foreign key data integrity checks are always lookups into another table. With the Forms Generator, you know which table is the origin for the foreign key since you know the relationships between the source entities. So, all you need to specify is whether to enforce referential integrity. You also need to account for the master/detail processing specified. For example, if we allow orphan detail rows, should the foreign key value in such rows be null or some default value?

7.3.4 Properties of Tables in a Module

In the module data diagrammer, we can edit the properties of the base and lookup tables. For base tables, we would specify the permitted kinds of usage, such as insert, update, and delete, as well as display characteristics. We would specify the usage of columns from their tables, such as insert, modify, or nullify, and the display characteristics of each column. We would also specify any derived columns and the derivation expression.

You need to specify which tables and columns each form uses. The initial specification may be propagated from the function definition in the corresponding business function. The module transformer wizard propagates such usage information when creating module definitions.

For each column, you need to define validation criteria. If you were thorough in the detailed analysis phase, you already have these criteria. For the Oracle Designer Forms Generator, you will need to define range checks, a list of valid values, and so on. If you plan to use the Forms Generator, you may specify validation criteria as properties of a column in a table. If you do this specification prior to using the application design transformer, the criteria will be propogated to each module. You may override some of them in the column usage for the module. For validation against a list of values, specify a database table as a lookup table. Another alternative is to use domains—appropriate when the valid list is short and static. Remember, however, that a database table lookup at runtime will slow down the form's response. So, avoid using a table based lookup lists when designing forms for performance critical data entry, unless the requirements demand it.

You need specifications for each insert, update, delete, and retrieve operation where you want the program behavior to be different from the tool's common behavior. For example, the default retrieval in Oracle Forms retrieves rows in random order. If you require the rows to be sorted in a particular order, you should specify it in the column properties.

If you need an audit trail for all changes to a particular table in your form, specify the requirement to journal the table. Note that once you specify journaling on a particular table, the DDL Generator produces the corresponding *create table* statements and the Forms Generator produces the code to write journal rows whenever the specified modification occurs.

7.3.5 GUI Layout

Note that we can visually arrange our tables into windows, separate pages, or pop-ups on the same page. Ideally, you should define company standards for such GUI elements as colors, windows, scroll bar size and placement, radio groups, check boxes, lists of values and buttons, layout of list forms, and so on. The appendix contains a set of example standards which you may modify for use in your company. This is the only way you will get any real consistency.

7.3.6 Interaction Specification

An important point to keep in mind when defining interactions is that actions should appear in the sequence that is natural to the users' work. It is often useful, if you are unfamiliar with the tasks involved, to observe one or more users at their normal work. Of course, the sequence can be changed under some circumstances—based on a BPR project—but normally you should stick to the one already in use.

One example where you may alter the sequence is when some technological requirement drives the change. For example, a telemarketing salesperson may ask for credit card information prior to obtaining or verifying the customer's shipping address. This allows the credit verification process to proceed concurrently while the address information is being checked. This may not be a natural sequence at present, but a little training could change the process. Such considerations may also influence the placement of items in windows so that the user is guided through the process.

OO analysis describes a technique called an interaction diagram which explores interactions between objects. James Martin defines a technique called a dialog design diagram which illustrates navigation between screens. Both of these techniques let you define the order of events within a form. In addition to these diagrams, in each interaction, the design should specify whether a user action triggers the interaction or a program. Examples of user actions that trigger interaction might be pressing a button, moving the cursor into a screen item using a mouse, and so on. Then, our design should define the GUI components used for the user actions, for example, buttons, scroll bars, menu item, check box, and so on.

Each user interface technique has different performance characteristics. For example, starting up new windows within a form is real quick. A new window based on a new form, however, will require longer because it has to load and initialize the new form in memory. If the new form resides on a file server, add some time for transporting it over the network to the client.

Designing a list of values based on a hard-coded query is real quick. You can also display a list based on a query of one or more tables. This list will require more time because of the interaction between the client and the server database. You can specify a *where* condition in the query based on a screen item value—so the database server will filter the result rows before transferring them to the client. This approach will be real quick. If you do not specify the *where* clause, any runtime filtering will occur in the client. Filtering rows in the client will be slower because all rows in the query table must be transported over the network to the client before any filtering occurs.

In an early implementation of a generated form on one project, we suffered through this issue when displaying a list based on *products*. The list displayed instantaneously in the development system—which only had a few hundred products. When we installed the developed software into the demonstration environment, the form virtually died when retrieving the list. This environment had many hundreds of thousands of products! When we specified a filtering *where* clause on the query in the record group definition, the list was displayed real quick.

7.4 Report Specification

A report is any function that retrieves information from the database and formats it for presentation. The output medium of the function is irrelevant—it may be to a screen, a printer, web page, a plotter, microfiche, 35mm slide, and so on. A report only retrieves data, as opposed to a form which retrieves information to allow the user to

Prog: Sales by Product Category— **Date:** April 1, 1990 <u>Rev:</u> 1.0	
Dept: Sales	
Application: Sales & Marketing	
Utility: Oracle Reports (or SQR)	
Table Access:	
orders, order_items, customer, product, product_category, state	
Report Type: Matrix	
Matrix Definition:	
Product Categories as columns across page, States as rows down the page, Cell is volume of sales for the state in a product category.	
Column Handling:	

Name	Description
State Total	Total sales over all categories for a state.
Category Total	Total sales over all states for a product category.
Grand Total	Total sales for company over all states and all categories.

Figure 7-6: Report Specification Items for a 4GL

change it. A report may transform the retrieved data before writing its output but does not change the data in the database. You may run a report interactively—that is, initiate its run from the client, respond to its prompts, and wait until it completes. You may also run reports in background—for example, submit them to a queue for an overnight run. By this definition, the *invoice customers* function is a report, and so is the *list customers* function. Reporting functions characteristically lie between a data store and an external entity in a data flow diagram.

A report specification needs to cover the following basics, as detailed in Figure 7-6:

- Layout of data in the report. You might base this specification on some of the standard formats described in this section. Company or project standards for such layouts are essential.

- Runtime selection criteria to obtain from the user. The method to obtain these criteria could be another company standard. Ideally, the interface is via a form.

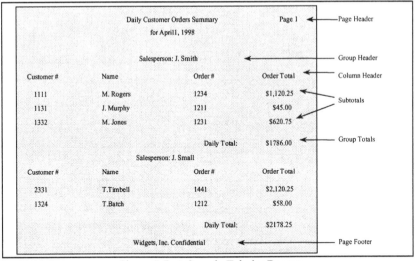

Figure 7-7: A Sample Tabular Report

- Tables retrieved, with selection criteria as well as relationships between them. In addition, you need to specify the sort order of the retrieved data.

- Control breaks for the data, if any, with associated layout and processing information.

- Derived data to present together with their derivation algorithms.

Few utilities paint a report layout, unlike screen painters. If you have existing tools which you use, such as COBOL report layout charts, use them for these report specifications too. You could try using Oracle Reports as a prototyping tool for laying out your reports. However, layout in this tool effectively involves writing almost the entire report. Besides, you need to have your database design complete and the tables implemented before using it. Similar arguments apply to the idea of using SQL*Plus. You may use both effectively for reports required after the application is in production.

You might obtain runtime selection criteria from users either by prompting for them one at a time (ugh! Don't do it!) or by presenting an entry screen which initiates the report. All Oracle tools for report generation, for instance, Oracle Reports and Plus8, have facilities for obtaining selection criteria. There is no limit on the number of selection criteria obtained at runtime. However, they do not support validation of these criteria and cannot present lists of values associated with them. You could design a form module for each report in Oracle Designer for the selection criteria. We will discuss techniques for such forms modules in a later chapter.

Obviously, you need to specify which tables and columns the report uses. You also need to describe how the selection criteria affect retrieval of data from these tables. In addition, you need to specify any calculations or transformations necessary on the retrieved data. The types of calculations and transformations determine which report generation tool you could use. Selection of the most suitable tool also depends on the type of layout requirements.

- **Tabular reports:** This category covers the majority of analysis reports in a typical business. It is made up of columns of data items across the page with totals for data grouped over some column value. Figure 7-7 illustrates a tabular report.

  SQL*Plus is a good tool for these types of reports provided that you can retrieve all required columns in a single SQL statement even if the data comes from several different tables. Computed values should be based on control breaks—that is, whenever the value of a particular column changes; for example, order totals by order and customer columns. Any SQL constructs which prevent sorting of data on control break columns prevent the use of SQL*Plus. Computations should be on individual columns without requiring inter-column comparisons or comparisons between row values and group totals. For example, you would not use SQL*Plus for a report that requires a column where the order item price is expressed as a percentage of order total. The performance of such processing in SQL*Plus is typically slow. Instead, consider using Oracle Reports or a third-party tool for better performance.

- **Form reports:** This category covers most of a business's interaction with the outside world. It includes any report based on a form, preprinted or otherwise, such as invoices, checks, labels, and so on. With preprinted forms, alignment will be necessary and the report generator must provide data for alignment. You may need to print serial numbers, as needed on checks, and may have strict formatting requirements. Using Oracle Reports is the best choice for such reports. SQL*Plus usually is less flexible in its formatting options and has no alignment facilities. If you use modern laser printers, you may have special templates for use with this report which you must include in the specification.

- **Matrix reports:** This type of report looks similar to a spreadsheet. Typically, the column categories and row come from tables in the database. When the report consists of a very few column categories which rarely change, you might consider using SQL*Plus reporting facilities. In this case, categories will be hard-coded in the report definition, so you compromise flexibility for faster development. Figure 7-8 illustrates a matrix report.

  Your specification for a matrix report should include a definition of which data items make up the column headings and row titles. In addition, specify the data for the cells. In each case, define which tables the data comes from and any calculations necessary before presenting the output.

	Sales by Product Category for April 1, 1998			
State	**Appliance**	**Clothing**	**Tools**	**State Total**
New Jersey	500	1000	580	2080
Pennsylvania	100	300	5000	5400
New York	300	200	1000	1500
Category Total	900	1500	6580	9980
Widgets, Inc. Confidential				

Figure 7-8: A Sample Matrix Report

Oracle Reports has specially-designed facilities for developing matrix reports. However, these facilities insist that each cell value come from a single SQL statement. Any third-party tool should implement control breaks and automatic totaling facilities to be suitable for this kind of a report.

- **Embedded data reports**: Typical of this category is a form letter where we embed data from the database within some text. This type of report is common in bulk mailings of personalized junk mail such as letters announcing, "You may have already won $50,000." Page formatting and fancy fonts are of paramount importance in such reports. You will need to specify the type of margin justifications, default fonts, font changes, paragraph characteristics, and so on. These specifications will be similar to those for a desktop publishing package.

Early mailings used preprinted letters with your name inserted with a regular printer in an obviously computerese font. Today, I relegate such tacky presentation to the garbage file instantly. Fast laser printers make it possible to present a uniform font style and page formatting. The best presentation among my most recent junk mail was one that included my name in the caption of a cartoon! Obviously my name in their database indicated me to be a computer aficionado. Oracle Reports is probably essential for at least text-oriented reports, since it provides better font manipulation capabilities than do any of the other choices. In future releases, it promises to support even more facilities for desktop publishing-style capabilities as well as web output.

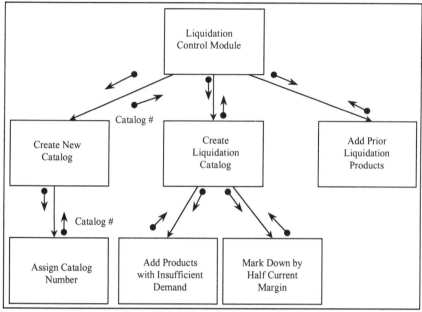

Figure 7-9: A Sample Structure Chart

7.5 Procedural Program Specification

If some parts of your application need procedural processing, you can resort to using a procedural fourth-generation language or a third-generation language interface to Oracle. Typically, you might use PL/SQL or a third-party language like Pro*Reports for batch updates to the database or a batch integrity checker, and so on. Writing in these languages will be much faster than writing the same code in a third-generation language. You can even write a series of SQL statements in a SQL*Plus script to do some kinds of processing.

Consider using a third-generation language when processing huge volumes of data in a limited-time window. Oracle's PRO* interfaces offer array processing features which improve performance when you access a lot of rows returned from one SQL statement. Use these interfaces for temporary downloading or uploading of data between the new application and other databases. There is little difference between writing specifications for these procedural programs and our traditional programs. Do remember, however, that any interaction with the Oracle database will use SQL. So, the amount of code in these programs will be somewhat less than in traditional file-based systems.

One of the popular techniques used for specifying procedural code is using a structure chart. Figure 7-9 illustrates a sample structure chart. There are formal techniques for decomposing a problem into such a hierarchical solution. The primary concept underlying this structure is to have clear division of data manipulation between modules. Each module receives as input, shown as data couples, the data it should manipulate. In turn, it returns a status, shown as a control couple, as well as processed data. Typically, all input and output is segregated into separate modules. Ideally, all communication with a module is via passed parameters. Unfortunately, many programming languages, notably COBOL, make it very difficult to implement such segregation.

Oracle Designer allows you to define one module to be a sub-module of another in its Module Data Diagram. Thus, you may define hierarchies of modules. You can also define recursive calls to a module, that is, a module calling itself. Any number of modules may call the same sub-module, allowing you to define reusable library components. Thus, the Oracle Designer repository acts as a documentation tool. This documentation is particularly valuable in maintenance mode for determining the potential impact of a change. However, keeping the documentation up-to-date with this tool can be very tedious.

A structure chart is a good way to document an overview of the program structure. However, we also need to specify the detailed logic for each module in the chart. There are many formal methods for this specification, although Oracle Designer does not support any. The most popular ones include pseudocode, structured English, decision trees, decision tables, action diagrams, state transition diagrams, and several others. Several of these techniques are useful in specific contexts only. For example, decision trees and decision tables are useful when program actions depend on a set of conditions.

Action diagrams and state transition diagrams are two of the most commonly automated techniques. You can think of an action diagram as one step up from pseudocode or structured English. They can be used for both high-level definition of modules and low-level logic of each module.

In action diagrams, we draw blocks to identify a module or block of processing. A block is used in a similar fashion to its meaning in structured programming: a function, subroutine, each clause for a condition, and so on. Figure 7-10 illustrates a simple action diagram. This representation is uncomfortably close to writing actual code—but necessary if your function really requires a procedural solution. An example of a suitable function is one introduced due to a design decision to store derived data: an integrity check and recalculation function for running overnight.

We can map higher-level action diagrams to structure charts on a one-to-one basis. Detailed action diagrams are, however, just like pseudocode with blocks delineated. This similarity is probably one reason for their popularity in code generation CASE tools.

State transition diagrams, drawn using Yourdon conventions, may look similar to data flow diagrams. There is a very important distinction: They are really not procedural! Typically, these diagrams are common in designing software where asynchronous processing occurs, that is, events can occur at any moment and our process must react

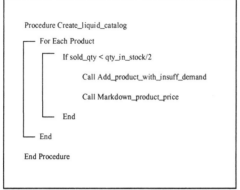

Figure 7-10: A Sample Action Diagram

to them promptly. State transition diagrams have wider application, especially in object-oriented implementations.

Realize that Oracle Designer allows only free-form module logic definition. There are no diagramming tools to support action diagrams or state transition diagrams. The rapid improvement of these tools by Oracle means that these facilities or similar ones may be added. Notice, however, that Oracle's tools have a distinct preference for declarative specification rather than procedural—so the likelihood of new tools for procedural specification in Oracle Designer may occur only after a cultural change in their product design strategies.

7.6 Reusable Tools Design

The most common elements that are good candidates for reuse are the code for business rules, and interface to the core objects such as customers, products and so on. An important decision is how and where each reusable component may reside for the most effective use in the project. Our choices include

- Procedures & packages that may reside on the database server or as libraries on the client-side,

- Client-side object definitions that may reside in object libraries or generator templates,

- Project-wide libraries and templates or module-specific libraries and templates.

- Business rules implemented as procedures in libraries or as module-specific application logic defined in the repository.

These are hard choices that will affect the maintainability of the resulting application. There is one simple rule of thumb to follow: Centralize! Whenever possible, move manually written procedural code away from individual client-side programs into shareable sources like libraries or database server. Of course, choose the source such that the code may be executed in the client as well as the server as appropriate to the user interface. For example, a stored procedure in the database server may be executed from the client program as well as by a database trigger. Reusability means that the code needs to be made a little more generic than absolutely necessary. However, it may save you from re-inventing the wheel in many programs.

An important criteria for deciding whether code should reside client side or server side is the level of database access it needs. When possible, any code that requires database access should reside server side. This strategy will help reduce network traffic for transporting database data and should result in significantly improved overall performance. Restrict client side code to code that references client side elements, such as screen form items, and server side procedures or functions. A side effect of this strategy is a better likelihood of reusable code in the server side procedures and functions. Since you are forced to design parameterized passing of data to these pieces of code, the result is less use of global variables with values assigned in many different program units in the client!

A critical requirement for successful reusability is management of the reusable components so that they are easily found. I have seen many really good beginnings flounder because the developers found it easier to write their own code rather than research the libraries for an existing reusable object. I find peer reviews have a wonderful side effect of publicizing reusable objects available in the library.

7.7 Project Controls

There are a few components of a design that we have not dealt with explicitly. We need definitions of the application environment, security, and administrative functions. The architecture design provided most of the guidelines for our hardware and software architecture. However, we must add detail to the environment in the design phase. Similarly, we analyzed the requirements for security and administrative functions during the detailed analysis phase. In this phase, we need to detail how our design would fulfill these requirements.

7.7.1 Access Security

Throughout analysis, you probably emphasized the security requirements of the users. Almost every project I have worked on emphasized the importance of access controls—and in every case, no one wanted to pin down the details. So, take the time to define your details. Remember that security restrictions at the database level are frequently insufficient. You will require controls at the application level as well.

We discussed database-level controls in the previous chapter. Oracle enforces these controls only when a user attempts an operation against the database. For example, users with no access to a particular table will discover this restriction only when they attempt to retrieve data from it. Instead of showing them a screen only to deny them access to the data, I recommend that your application prevent access to the screen itself. You may use Oracle Forms menus to implement such a control, assuming you can synchronize user names and access control roles between the menu and database. Alternatively, you might define your own security database and application controls which must be hidden from all users.

7.7.2 Standards and Conventions

Oracle Designer provides powerful tools for analysis, design, and development. However, you need project standards to use them most effectively. The Repository

Object Navigator allows you to define and manage applications. All dictionary elements, including entities, functions, relationships, and so on, are owned by applications. Other applications can share dictionary elements, although they have severely restricted privileges for modifying these elements.

It is easy to dream up applications and define them in the Repository Object Navigator. However, the subsequent administration can become a nightmare, if you do not lay down project standards and conventions. For example, distinguishing between the name of an entity and its corresponding table with some simple convention saves your development team countless hours. I have outlined some sample standards in the appendix which you could use as a starter kit for your company.

Remember to document the exact setup for your project team's working areas. Defining directories or the appropriate equivalent for source, binary, and test files; providing tools for accessing them with minimum effort; and other small utilities will keep your team organized. I usually appoint a chief architect on each project who becomes my right hand in building such utilities and enforcing their use. Ideally, such tools would be built and maintained by a project support group, possibly a subset of the systems programming group in large corporations. The support group could then define and maintain corporation-wide standard—establishing a corporate programming culture: the technical equivalent of (the very effective) blue pinstripe suits.

Case Study: Orders Module Design

During this design process, we discovered a couple of oversights in our analysis. Since this is a real life case study, we decided to discuss it as in its appropriate place, rather than correcting earlier models. Be prepared to find such oversights during your projects. The key is to know how to correct the errors, once discovered, and to do it quickly by using the features of the Oracle Designer tools.

Our oversight was missing two relationships that indicated the *selected size* and *color* of the ordered items. The selections are made from *listed size* and *color* properties of a catalog item. As a result, we were missing two important foreign key columns in the order items table. When specifying the detailed interaction of the order, we discovered that we could not record the choice made by the customer. The value of detailed dialog design should be now abundantly clear. Bear in mind, that a RAD approach often skips this step as unnecessary. Oversights in a RAD project are often discovered when demonstrating to the users. Unfortunately, if your users simply nod their heads at your prototype, the discovery may not occur until later. On one RAD projects, we did not discover a few missing data elements until we tried to roll out the application to its second location!

We were able to fix the analysis model to include these attributes. Then we used the database design transformer in custom mode to propagate these modifications.

Fortunately, this utility allows us to specify that we only wanted new columns created with associated foreign keys and indexes.

Orders Module Specification

There are two parts to the module specification: the data driven specification and the interaction specification. Oracle Designer records the data driven specification which will illustrate in Chapter 9. In this section, we illustrate the interaction specification which could be recorded as *Module Description* or *Module Notes* in the Oracle Designer repository. In object methodology, a UseCase would provide similar information.

Dialog Approach:

> From the order form, query and display customer information.

> Mark changes to customer information as part of the order. Do not navigate to a separate window for customer update. Note navigation to a separate window increases the time a telesales representative must keep the customer on the phone. Longer telephone time affects productivity and also affects customer satisfaction.

> Request credit information as soon as customer is identified and begin internal credit approval process. Credit card authorization cannot be performed until order total is known.

Transaction Controls:

> Commit customer information when navigating out of window. Do not commit order and items information until "Complete" action is pressed.

Static Display:

> Current User Name, Date/Time of starting the session.

Customer:

> **New**: Copy Shipping address from billing address (default).
> Set credit status to "Negative Credit".
> Action button: Initiate a credit check process.

> **Modify:** Cannot update credit status interactively.

> **Delete:** Only mark as delete, for archiving to the warehouse.

> **Navigation:** New Order

Order:

> **New**: Determine whether individual or corporate customer
> Use customer number code from catalog to verify prior history. If customer number is not available, use telephone number to attempt to identify the customer. Otherwise, use the combination of name and zip code or postcode.
> Get credit card information for individual customer

Activate credit check process in background

Select Catalog for pricing

Copy shipping address from billing address as default.

Modify:

Cannot change Catalog, or customer name if order status is "Approved"

Delete: Only mark as delete (set status = cancelled) after commit.

Navigation: Order Items, Customer

Order Items:

New: Display description from catalog item, not product.

Verify product quantity is in stock,

If unable to verify product quantity, set item status = unconfirmed.

Note: This requirement will allow us to take warehouse data offline even though sales orders continue to be taken.

If insufficient product quantity in stock, set item status = backordered

If sufficient product quantity, set item status = confirmed.

Action items: *select color* and *select size*:

Active if applicable to the catalog item, inactive otherwise.

Modify: Allow changes to color, size and quantity

Delete: Set item status= cancelled after commit.

Normal delete until "complete" button pressed.

Navigation: Customer, Order

Database Administration

The tasks of the DBA are pretty much ignored in application development. Developers consider DBAs to be somewhere between operators and wand-waving magicians that miraculously keep the database running. However, these experts have a vital role to play on any development team. Of course, a DBA performs different duties based on whether the team is developing new applications or maintaining a system already in production.

Another common confusion is about data administrators and database administrators. These two are very different animals. Data administrators manage the data itself, while database administrators manage the storage of and access to that data using products such as Oracle. In this chapter, we will describe the responsibilities of data administrators and database administrators and some of the differences between their activities. This chapter is not a comprehensive discussion of administration issues, merely an overview of the following topics:

- The responsibilities of the guardians of data use, the data administrators. We will discuss data models, standards for data management, and the kinds of procedures needed for implementation.

- Database administration in an development environment vs. in a production environment. We will discuss the tools needed to support the continuous changes that occur during development.

- Designing an Oracle environment to support multiple applications with some shared data. The emphasis will be on maximizing performance and providing reliable operation.

- How to plan for recovering from disaster. It is not sufficient to back up your database. Plan for hardware and network outage as well as data loss.

8.1 Data and Database Administration

Data administrators are guardians of data in a corporation. They are primarily business modelers who map the data assets of the corporation. Database administrators, on the other hand, are guardians in charge of storing data. They are technical experts who make the data accessible to those who need it.

The responsibilities of both groups span applications and departments. There is often much cross-fertilization between them. In some large corporations, they may both report to the same director. This organization structure may be the source of confusion between the tasks of the two groups.

Data administrators (DAs) are modelers. DAs create and maintain strategic and tactical data models. They work with modeling and repository products like Oracle Designer. Database administrators (DBAs) work with database management products like the Oracle DBMS. DBAs create and shuffle tables, constraints, and other physical objects.

DAs track use of data by different organizations and applications. The repository products they work with provide facilities to map the usage of data between business views and implementation views. DBAs use the maps developed by the DAs in designing the physical layout of the databases. They monitor actual access to data in a database. They work with access and traffic monitoring tools like AdHawk and DBVision.

DAs aim to keep data definitions consistent between the different uses of the data elements. They aim to maintain the semantic integrity of data. DBAs actually keep formats and referential integrity of stored data. DAs establish standards and conventions to help maintain semantic consistency. They use a repository as a tool for recording and communicating these consistent definitions across all information systems professionals and business users. DBAs establish standards for naming and domain specifications to maintain storage format consistency. They use product facilities like primary and foreign key constraints, which may be industry-standard facilities.

DAs are involved in strategy-level modeling as well as application-level models. They elaborate the models with business policies and rules. A DBA is usually involved only in application-level implementation of the model. DBAs implement business rules as stored procedures, triggers, or object methods in the database. Of course, application developers may also implement business rules within the application. DBAs may utilize strategy-level models when designing the company-wide database architecture.

DAs often use entity-relationship diagrams when modeling the data of an enterprise. DBAs may use this same technique to model database schemas. This dual use of entity-relationship diagrams leads to much debate and perhaps confusion. Oracle Designer distinguishes between an analysis-level model and implementation-level schema model. Analysis-level models are drawn using entity-relationship diagrams. Implementation schema models are drawn using data schema diagrams.

8.2 Development versus Production DBA

Just like there is a significant difference between new development and maintenance of an existing application, a DBA who supports new development has different duties than one who supports an application already in production. What they have in common is knowledge of the specific database management product, namely Oracle. This common knowledge includes an understanding of the internal structure of the Oracle server: its processes, storage methods, space management methods, and other rules of the product.

8.2.1 Supporting Development

One of the initial tasks when starting application development is to set up the environment for the team. This environment must allow individual developers to test their work with their own test data. In addition, the team needs a central shared database containing common test data that is used for formal testing as well as integration testing between modules.

When the team uses Oracle Designer routinely, it is easy to maintain individual sets of tables as well as the common set. Of course, you must institute rigorous procedures among your development staff, to change the database design only within the Oracle Designer environment. There is no support for an environment where only the designated DBAs change the structure. Besides, the DBA should not control each developer's individual environment. The DBA can, and should, control the shared test environment.

Typically, individuals should use their own Oracle accounts to set up the test database with their own data. In a large team, individual test environments are critical to avoid conflicts between testing. There are too many hours wasted tracking down some apparent bug, only to discover it was due to unexpected modification to the test data by another developer. In a small team, developers might be able to coordinate their testing to avoid conflict in a shared database environment.

Some formal communication is necessary when you provide individual environments. For example, changes to the database structure must be broadcast to everyone. You may want to establish a formal schedule for releasing database structure changes within the team. Depending on the size of the database and team, the schedule may range from daily releases to weekly releases. In a RAD approach, such a schedule imposes a discipline on the team and sets the ground rules for collaboration. Each developer is responsible for updating their individual environment at their convenience.

The administrator should also provide some tools for migrating test data from one release of the database structure to the next. Actually, these tools also help the DBA to migrate test data in the shared database. The standard Oracle tools, import and export or SQL*Loader, are insufficient on their own. These tools need additional capabilities such as mapping data from the older structure to the new, inserting default values where appropriate, transforming the data types, loading from one table in the old structure to a different one in the new structure, and so on. There are many third-party tools available on the market to support these activities. You will need to explore their capabilities prior to selecting one.

An alternative is for the DBA to construct a custom set of scripts for each release. Many teams take this approach if they expect few or infrequent changes to the structure. Custom scripts are not very practical in a RAD environment where the change release interval is short. One of the major hurdles the DBA must overcome in these scripts is maintaining the referential integrity of the data from one release of the database schema to the next. If your database schema includes constraints, you may not be able to simply disable them to make the structural changes. You may need to drop constraints and recreate them after you move the test data.

A shared database environment has a few additional requirements. You need to maintain multiple versions of the shared database, typically three or four versions or more if you make frequent releases. This requirement allows developers to choose when to move their development and testing to the new release. Just because you release the new schema does not mean all developers can start using it right away!

Another requirement is to publish the changes and their impact on the test data provided in the shared database. For example, if you added a new mandatory column, what will its value be in the test data in the new release? If you changed a previously optional column to be mandatory, what values will be in those rows that previously had null for this column? The test data issues get even more complex—consider a column that becomes a foreign key column in the new release because you decided to associate a lookup list with it. All programs that used that column will now need to be modified!

You usually construct test data to test valid as well as invalid conditions in a program. So, you need to be able to *initialize* the test database to predefined values so that you can test specific conditions. A DBA typically does not construct the data, the developers do that task. However, the DBA needs to provide utilities that will allow the developers to initialize their own test conditions prior to testing. In addition, developers need the capability to reconstruct their test conditions at will.

Whenever you establish a shared test database, you need to coordinate the use of its test data. Each developer needs specific data content to test their particular program. A good strategy to avoid conflict between developers is to coordinate their testing. Some strategies to coordinate testing when using only a shared test environment are

- Divide the developers' assignments such that they require little shared data other than reference or lookup data. This approach requires juggling task assignments based on dependencies in the data model. It really can only be done with a small team where the project leader is closely involved in all aspects of development.

- Divide the test data such that each developer is assigned a specific range of key values. The range is typically based on some key reference table, for example, a range of customer id values. The, all data that references the assigned range of customer id values is the sole domain of a developer. This approach is possible with a small or medium-sized team.

- Ad-hoc coordination between team members is also an effective method—but only among a closely knit team. Communications in such a team are easy and friendly, often conducted in the hallway or over the cubicle wall. Close quarters are a necessity for this approach to work.

It should be obvious from these discussions that supporting the development environment requires significant resources. One of the major tasks of the DBA is to plan for the needed resources: equipment, networks, software licenses, and others. Then, a concerted effort is needed to procure these resources—usually with some assistance from the project manager. The DBA may have to negotiate with vendors, obtain and evaluate products, and recommend purchases.

A development support DBA has many masters. In effect, all developers and designers demand services, occasionally in conflict with each other. It is vital that the DBA and project manager work in concert to facilitate the development. Diplomacy is a key attribute of a good development support DBA. These DBAs hold the reins to application development productivity in their hands—literally!

8.2.2 Production DBA

A production DBA usually gets involved in the project when you start planning its transition into production. Ideally, you start planning the transition as soon as database design begins in earnest. The transition plan should progress in parallel with the design and development activities. Make sure there is plenty of communication between the transition team and the development team to ensure that their respective designs are feasible. The production DBA is responsible for several activities as part of the transition team:

- Design the Oracle instances for the production sites. This task includes not only the physical location of the equipment, but also the location of data within an instance, the links and communications between instances, replication or snapshot design, and so on. The remainder of the chapter covers many of these design issues.

- Conversion of data from the source legacy systems to the new database. Although the development team will actually write the programs to perform the conversion, the DBA must provide facilities to perform the conversion. For example, the conversion team will need staging databases, test setups for testing the production instance design, and so on.

- Design the training environment database. This task involves designing the process of enrolling users when training begins, initializing the test database, cleaning up after each training session is complete, and providing administrative assistance during training.

- Plans for distributing the application and installing it on the target client sites. In cooperation with user training and business process implementers, the DBA needs to plan the enrollment of users and facilitate their access during both training and production rollout.

- Designing disaster recovery plans for the production environment. We will cover this in more detail later in this chapter.

- Designing the process to distribute and rollout the later releases of the application. This is one area ignored by many transition teams. Enhancements and maintenance releases of the application are more frequent in the early days of production than when the application is mature. Planning for this inevitable task avoids many crises later.

- Understanding the characteristics of the application database. In particular, the production DBA must plan the monitoring activities that will be necessary soon after rollout. This task requires close communication with the development DBA. Occasionally, production DBAs can point out design flaws early to avoid later performance problems, although the production DBA needs a thorough understanding of the application to make good suggestions.

A production DBA's responsibility once the application is in production is very different from a development DBA. Some of these tasks are

- Capacity planning for growth.

- Monitoring activity for performance characteristics.

- Administering users and access controls.

- Tuning the database.

- Determining the causes of performance problems.

- Managing database space.

- Upgrading instances to new versions of Oracle software.

- Rolling out maintenance releases and enhancements to the applications.

There are many good books that cover these areas in depth. With all my good intentions, it is not possible to provide the necessary in-depth discussions here. We will provide an overview of the issues in the remainder of this chapter. Our primary focus is the design of the database. So, our coverage of production issues merely scratches the surface.

8.3 Oracle Instance Architecture

An Oracle instance is made up of several components: processes, files, and memory structures. An instance can contain data for many applications. It can service many users concurrently while maintaining defined security controls. In a client-server environment, the users may access the instance across a network that is local or wide area. An instance can also provide links to data from another instance transparently so that users are not aware of the data location.

The instance processes run on the database server machine whenever the instance is running, whether or not any users are active. These processes manage movement of data between files and memory structures, and respond to access requests from clients.

The instance files contain data, transaction information, control information about the instance, and so on. There are three kinds of files in an instance. *Control* files correlate the operating system files within an instance and the logical names in the database dictionary. *Redo log* files contain information necessary in preserving the integrity of transactions on the database such that database writing can be asynchronous to the user's transaction processing. *Data* files contain the actual application data.

The shared memory structures, the *system global area (SGA)*, allows all processes to share data. These structures also contain other commonly used information, for example, the database data dictionary, parsed SQL statements for active transactions, and client request information. All client requests and data must pass through the SGA. Client processes cannot access the instance files directly.

8.3.1 Oracle Server Processes

In Chapter 6, we discussed how instance processes cooperate to execute a typical client request. A DBA can tune several parameters that affect the operation of these processes. There are additional processes that may occur due to the way an instance is set up. Figure 8-1 illustrates the potential processes in a multi-threaded server setup.

An administrator can control whether a client gets a dedicated server or a shared server. One of the tunable instance parameter controls the maximum number of shared sever processes on the instance. In simple terms, you increase shared servers to handle increases in client request traffic. Of course, you will need to balance the overhead of a shared server with requirements of other processes on your platform. Another trade-off is between number of shared servers and the speed of retrieving data from the database files. Your hardware configuration will limit the number of servers you can effectively run. Once you reach the limits of your platform, increasing the shared servers will show little improvement and may even cause degradation.

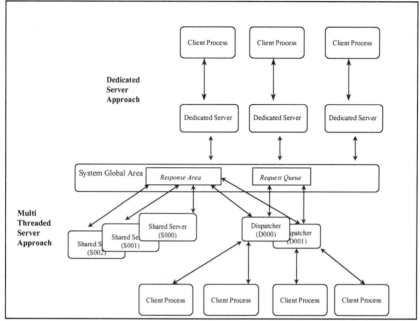

Figure 8-1: Processes for Server Approaches

Shared servers service one request at a time from a request queue. The request queue and response to a request all reside in the system global area. The shared server does not communicate directly with a client process. The dispatcher populates the request queue and communicates the response back to the client process. One shared server may service requests from many client processes over time. This configuration is the most common way to efficiently use memory resources on the server platform.

A dedicated server services only one client process, and there can be as many servers as there are clients. There is no dispatcher in this setup. The server communicates directly with the client process without any request or response queues. This configuration is reminiscent of the *shadow* process of earlier Oracle releases with similar issues. A primary issue is that it requires significant memory resources on the server platform. Supporting a large number of clients with this configuration requires large amounts of memory which cannot be shared between client processes.

The log writer (LGWR) process writes modifications to the log files, rotating through them in a circular fashion. If you configure *archivelog* mode on the instance, the archive (ARCH) process will copy any filled log file to the specified backup media. The copied log file then becomes available to the log writer. Remember that any modification in the database results in a transaction in the log file. A database *commit* guarantees that the log writer has written the changes to the log file, even if the database writer (DBWR) has not completed its work.

The database writer works asynchronously—writing changed blocks from the database buffer cache to the data files. It marks a block as available as soon as it completes writing it. On some platforms, you can configure multiple database writer processes if your instance appears to be lagging in clearing modified blocks. High transaction volume databases may require more than one database writer, especially if transactions involve significant amounts of modified data.

You can force the instance to checkpoint at regular intervals to ensure that data files are up-to-date. A timed checkpoint is basically a signal for the database writer process to wake up. The log writer can also cause a checkpoint if you configure a transaction volume based checkpoint, for example, after every one thousand transactions. Checkpoints reduce the amount of transactions we would need to roll forward from the redo log files, should we need to restart the database from a system crash. However, a checkpoint has a significant impact on performance and should be scheduled with caution. See the section on disaster recovery planning for more discussion.

In the parallel server configuration, there is an additional lock (LCK) process to manage inter-instance locking. We will discuss more on parallel servers and processes needed in a distributed environment in a later chapter.

8.3.2 Oracle Files

The three kinds of Oracle files, *control*, *redo log*, and *data* files, have different characteristics. They do have one requirement in common— to keep multiple copies spread across disks as a precaution against media failure.

Control files are usually quite small, but contain information critical to running the instance. These files are initially created when you create a database. They contain the names of all operating system files associated with an instance together with certain instance parameters that are set at the time of creating the instance.

Losing the control file is hazardous to your database's health. Keep at least two copies of the control file. Simply make additional copies while the database is shut down, and modify the instance parameters to indicate the location of each copy of the control file. You can also explicitly create additional files with the *create controlfile* statement. Oracle will keep all copies up-to-date. At least one copy should be on a separate physical disk.

You need to design the *redo log* files as part of the instance design. Their size and the number of log files you need depend on the number of concurrent users and the size of their transactions. Large numbers of concurrent users conducting small-sized retrievals each will require more log files. This is typical of an OLTP database. Similarly, a small number of users conducting large-sized updates will also need large log files. Don't forget those batch bulk updates that occur overnight—they generate redo logs too!

Keep the redo log files on a separate disk from the data files to insure against disk failure. Oracle can recover the database state from these redo logs if your data files were not up-to-date when an instance abruptly terminates. You can also maintain a mirrored redo log on a separate disk to guard against disk failure of the redo log files disk. Redo log files are also necessary to roll forward from a backup copy of your data.

If you choose to use the automatic archive log facility, be sure to place the archived log files on a different disk from your database. This way you won't lose your archived log file when a disk crash zaps your database disk. The *archivelog* process should back these up periodically for offline storage, or you may back them up manually. If you choose manual archiving, remember that if all log files are full, the database grinds to a halt.

The biggest space, by far, is in Oracle's data files. Their size depends on the size of your database. Each data file is part of a tablespace in the logical structure of the instance. You would extend the size of a tablespace by adding more data files. The size of the data file does not inherently place a restriction within the instance, except that a single extent must be within one data file.

Files may be part of the file system of your operating system, or may be raw partitions under the UNIX operating system. Just because you choose UNIX filesystem files does not mean that Oracle will extend the file size automatically. Prior to version 7.3, you could not extend files at all after creation. From version 7.3 onwards, you must specify to Oracle that it may extend the file. Once specified, Oracle will automatically extend the data file size as needed.

The argument against using the UNIX filesystem for Oracle files is that the space that Oracle considers contiguous may not in fact be so. A UNIX file is not guaranteed to be contiguous. As disk throughput increases due to advances in technology, this may not be a significant disadvantage. We must also weigh this disadvantage against the benefits of buffering and read-ahead intelligence provided by the filesystem. Provided we configure our Oracle server machine with plenty of memory, we can provide memory for filesystem read-ahead buffering as well as Oracle's memory structures.

Notice that Oracle likes to have a lot of disks. As a general rule, lots of small disks are better than one big one. Approaches to recovering from media failure are more complex if you use just one or two big disks. Unfortunately, the faster disks are also the big ones. So, you often end up with some wasted space.

8.3.3 Memory Structures

An Oracle instance uses shared memory to hold any information needed by more than one of its processes. The shared system global area contains buffers for data, redo log entries, data dictionary information, and so on. All communication of data between processes uses the SGA. When you create an Oracle instance, you get a small, default

SGA. Usually, you will tune it to make the best use of available resources. When designing the instance, you should pay particular attention to the configuration of the SGA. The important considerations are

- **Sufficient data buffers**: Oracle uses free data buffers based on a *least recently used* algorithm. *Dirty* buffers, that is, buffers containing modified data, are written to the disk by the database writer process and then placed in the free buffer list. If you do not have sufficient data buffers in the SGA, processes are less likely to find the requested data in these buffers. Hence, they will need to get it from the database files first—resulting in slower access. Realize, however, that increasing the data buffer cache beyond a certain size results in diminishing returns in terms of performance improvement. Use monitoring tools to track the number of cache misses, that is, access to database files, which occur before you further increase their size.

- **Sufficient dictionary cache**: Every time Oracle executes a SQL statement, it must access the database dictionary to obtain the schema information. Similar to the data buffers, Oracle must first load the dictionary definition into the dictionary cache buffers before the process can use it. A cache miss, that is, access to disk to obtain the dictionary information, results in slower performance. Since Oracle needs this information frequently, you should ensure you minimal cache misses.

- **Sufficient shared pool**: This area in the SGA holds parsed and compiled SQL statements, as well as the dictionary and library cache. Parsed statements are shared by multiple user processes that are executing the same SQL. Space in this area is deallocated based on a least recently used algorithm. If a process needs a statement that is already deallocated, it must reparse the statement again. Make sure you allow sufficient space in the shared pool for shared SQL and PL/SQL statements. This is particularly important in an OLTP environment where many users execute the same programs concurrently.

- **Sort area:** Oracle needs to sort data as part of processing database access requests. For example, when joining data from two tables, one of them will be sorted. A small sort area slows this kind of processing resulting in sluggish performance. The size of this area is important in both OLTP and OLAP environments.

There are many other tunable areas that are part of the SGA. The above four have the most impact initially on performance. Oracle can use as much memory as your money can buy. The more memory you allocate to the SGA, the more performance improvement you are likely to get.

8.4 Database Space Management

Space management tasks are somewhat different for an initial implementation of an Oracle system than for additional application implementation. You will need to set standards and style when you create the first instance of Oracle. Like it or not, these standards will stay in your organization for a long time!

When you initially create an instance for an application, you need to estimate the size, capacity, and growth of this database. These estimates should be part of the analysis information. If you recorded most of this information during analysis, the database design transformation wizards would derive it into the table definitions. You can use some of the standard reports from Oracle Designer to estimate the size and storage characteristics of each table. You may categorize tables by size into small, moderate, and large sizes.

One approach is to create one tablespace each to hold the small and moderate tables. Each of the large tables may merit a tablespace in its own right. You should pay special attention to the access characteristics of large tables. You may want to design storage to avoid chaining and fragmentation. You may design distributed I/O across disks. Small and moderate-sized tables should require little attention after initial design.

When you implement additional applications in the same instance, you may choose to use existing tablespaces or create new ones. A common approach is to create a set of tablespaces specifically for each application. This approach allows you to use the rudimentary access control options that a tablespace provides. Another advantage is that you may simplify backup and restore procedures for each application.

As you add each application, you may monitor the space usage and I/O patterns to determine whether you need take further action. Periodic monitoring is necessary to ensure sufficient free space is available. You should also try to anticipate and monitor the growth of each application. These monitoring tasks will allow early warnings for needed expansion of your database space.

8.4.1 Tablespace Allocation

An instance contains several tablespaces. The system tablespace is essential for an instance. The bootstrap segment resides in the system tablespace. Creating a database implicitly creates this segment. It holds the database dictionary information when an instance opens a database.

A tablespace may also hold segments called rollback segments. Rollback segments hold information about transactions in progress. When you roll back a transaction— that is, undo its effects on the database data—Oracle obtains information on that transaction's effect from the rollback segment in order to undo them.

The system tablespace contains the system rollback segment. You can create and change rollback segments with the SQL statements *create rollback segment, alter rollback segment*, and *drop rollback segment*. Multiple rollback segments may improve performance when you have more than one tablespace, or when many users concurrently use the database. Since these segments grow and shrink dynamically, it is a good idea to dedicate a tablespace to them.

Oracle also uses rollback segments for implementing read consistency. You can define multiple rollback segments for an instance. Each instance must have its own set of rollback segments. An instance claims rollback segments at start-up time. You can take rollback segments offline or place them online through the *alter rollback segment* statement. Rollback segments can be public or private. Most of your rollback segments should be public. You only need private rollback segments when you use multiple instances sharing a database, such as with clustered VAXs.

We suggested earlier that you should place most of a table in its initial extent to ensure contiguous allocation. However, if you have very large tables, storing entire tables in the initial extent is not practical or desirable.

For large tables that grow or shrink rapidly, you may design large-sized extents for subsequent allocations of space. You can use the *pctincrease* storage parameter to allow next extent sizes to increase as the size of a table grows. Reserve the use of *pctincrease* for tables that grow steadily to large sizes through high transaction volume. Using it for small tables or tables that grow very slowly may result in wasted space. For large tables, you may consider performance tuning options discussed in Section 8.4.2 Chaining and Fragmentation and Section 8.4.3 I/O Distribution among Disks.

You can, of course, simply use default settings for all tables. The defaults will always use the tablespace storage parameters. You can grow this tablespace by simply adding more files or using extendible files. A simple way to manage tables by their size would be to create three tablespaces: small with storage parameters to handle small tables like lookup lists, medium to handle tables that grow slowly, and large to handle very large tables. Then, place the tables based on their size in the appropriate tablespace, letting the tables inherit the storage parameters of the tablespace.

Once a table is created and associated with storage parameters, you cannot relocate it easily. For extra space, add more files to the tablespace. To relocate a table from one tablepace to another, save the data from the table, drop it, re-create it using a different storage definition, and then load the data back. An alternative, if you have sufficient disk space, is to create the new table under a dummy name with the appropriate storage definition, copy data from the old table, drop the old table, and rename the new table to the correct name.

Note that throughout these manipulations, you will need to remove any constraints on other tables that reference the table on which you are working. Disabling or removing these constraints can be more difficult than is first apparent. I often come across databases without any constraints—someone disabled or removed them while manipulating one or more tables, and forgot to enable or recreate them! Of course, you only discover resultant dirty data when you attempt to load it into your data warehouse.

If you plan to run multiple applications in a single database, I recommend that you define at least one separate tablespace for each application. A common convention is to create two separate tablesaces—one for data and one for indexes. You will need to

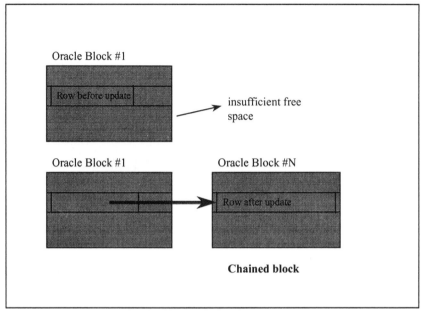

Oracle Block #1

Row before update

insufficient free
space

Oracle Block #1

Oracle Block #N

Row after update

Chained block

Figure 8-2: Block Chaining Concept

define the tablespace as the default for each user of the application and grant them appropriate access privileges. This scheme has the advantage that you can take individual tablespaces offline and back them up individually without affecting users of other applications. You also isolate the effects of contention for rollback segments by allocating them to individual tablespaces.

Be sure to allocate sufficient space in rollback segments to meet the needs of concurrent users' retrievals. Oracle7 rollback segments contain only changed data— that is, deltas of changes. The size needed depends on the environment. In an OLTP environment, the size of rollback segments need not be large. It is more important to create a sufficient number of rollback segments than worrying about the segment size. In an OLAP environment, you need large rollback segments because the typical query retrieves large amounts of data and runs for a long time.

8.4.2 Chaining and Fragmentation

The area of most concern in an OLTP database is the performance degradation due to chaining or fragmentation of the database. Figure 8-2 illustrates chained blocks. Chaining occurs when you update a previously created row resulting in an increased row size. If the block has insufficient free space to accommodate the increased row size, Oracle must grab another block to store the row and chain it to the original block. Oracle can only access the chained block by accessing the original data block and following the chain. Such increased I/O results in performance degradation.

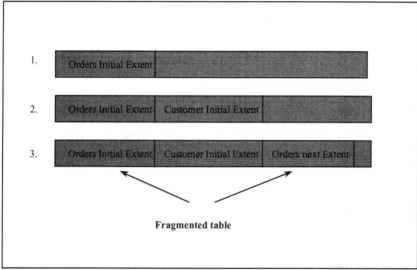

Figure 8-3: Fragmentation Concept

You can reduce the chances for chaining through good design of storage parameters, *pctfree* and *pctused*, on critical tables. Critical tables are those that have high transaction volumes and have rows that expand in size dramatically through updates.

Use the *pctfree* parameter when creating a table to reserve space within each block for expanding row sizes. You will need to understand the pattern of how the application creates rows and how it updates them to determine the potential growth in the size of a row. If row size grows beyond the available space in a block, Oracle chains another block to store the row.

Note that large rows that require multiple blocks to store also lead to chaining. Consider increasing the Oracle block size in these situations. Oracle implementations on many platforms support the use of block sizes of 16K, 32K, or occasionally 64K. Larger block sizes permit Oracle to read larger amounts of data in a single read which is then buffered in the system global area.

The *pctused* parameter determines when a block has space available for inserting new rows. Oracle will insert rows while actual free space is more than *pctfree* and until the *pctused* level is reached. Thus it attempts to reserve the *pctfree* amount of space for updates, and uses up to the *pctused* amount of space for inserts. Oracle maintains a list of blocks eligible for inserts and a list of blocks eligible for updates. Set *pctused* such that the block is reasonably full without using up reserved free space.

Fragmentation is when portions of data from a single table are stored in physically distant parts of the disk. Figure 8-3 illustrates the concept of fragmentation. Access to such data requires increased disk latency delay, resulting in slower I/O. Fragmentation of frequently accessed tables is the most critical. Again, good design of the storage parameters, *initial extent*, *next extent*, and *pctincrease*, helps to reduce fragmentation. Small and moderate-sized tables can avoid fragmentation. Use other tuning strategies for large tables since some fragmentation is inevitable in these tables. Realize that there is no defragmentation utility in Oracle.

8.4.3 I/O Distribution among Disks

There are three alternatives for balancing I/O among disks: manual distribution, Oracle striping, and platform striping. You must choose your alternative before you create the database instance. Once chosen, you cannot change easily—you will need to scrap the instance and start over.

Manual Distribution: To balance disk I/O between multiple disks, you need multiple tablespaces. Make administration easier for yourself by using a one-for-one correspondence between physical disks and tablespaces. For example, each tablespace should contain one or more operating system files from one physical disk. Then, place tables in tablespaces to evenly distribute I/O between disks. Function frequency and transaction size information is very useful in determining your distribution.

To manually optimize performance, you might wish to distribute database tables selectively over several physical disks. Here is one way to create a database with custom table distribution:

1. Estimate the size of each table and each of its indexes; include Oracle overheads.

2. Using the convention that a tablespace corresponds to one physical disk, create the appropriate number of tablespaces with suitable names in the Oracle database. For example, suppose the filesystems /db1 and /db2 represent two separate disks. You might create two tablespaces called tabspace_1 and tabspace_2.

3. Determine how you want to distribute the tables on physical disks.

4. Create the tablespaces with the appropriate file names. The *create tablespace* or *alter tablespace* statements will initialize the files.

In our example, we create the file data1 in the /db1 filesystem and data2 in the /db2 filesystem. Then we add data1 to tabspace_1 and data2 to tabspace_2. For optimal space usage, make these initial files somewhat larger than the total size of the tables you intend to store in them.

5. Ideally, most of the table should fit into the initial extent, unless you are concerned with I/O distribution on the table. In Oracle7, these parameters are part of the storage clause of the *create table* statement.

6. Create each table and all of its indexes specifying these storage parameters in the respective definitions.

Oracle striping: In this alternative, we use the fact that a tablespace is made up of one or more operating system files. We would create a tablespace with two data files, one from each disk. The tables placed in this tablespace, typically a large table, would be created such that it spans the data files. For example, we could create the table with an initial extent parameter large enough to force the next extent into the second data file. Remember that extents cannot span data files. Thus, the data in this table would be distributed across two disks.

Platform Striping: Another alternative is to let the operating system balance the I/O distribution for you. This alternative requires that your operating system provide a *disk striping* mechanism. If your operating system provides a disk striping mechanism, such as Microsoft Windows NT's *stripe set*, you may use this in lieu of deliberately calculated I/O distribution. Striping is also provided by some RAID configurations, normally known as RAID level-1. You will need to manage this configuration at the hardware or operating system level. If your DBAs do not have sufficient system-level privileges to configure these, make sure the system administrators work closely with the DBAs. Otherwise, your RAID striping may be turned off by an administrator ignorant of Oracle's requirements. These mechanisms are usually as effective at distributing I/O as anything you spend hours designing.

8.5 Database Monitoring

There are two reasons for monitoring the database: to establish a pattern of events that leads to performance problems, or to track the trend in capacity consumption. Monitoring to track down performance problems is very common. Oracle provides many database statistics, contained in the V$... tables, that you can use to determine the pattern of events that led to the performance degradation. However, many performance problems may be due to the SQL statements themselves. So, before you spend significant time monitoring to track down performance problems, examine the SQL statements in your programs. This type of monitoring can be useful in both the development and production environments. Few projects take the time to conduct performance benchmarks prior to releasing the application into production. So, in practice, you don't discover performance issues until after rollout. This is why the first few weeks after rollout are hectic—you have to fight the performance degradation fires.

The second reason for monitoring is to understand how the application is consuming database capacity. For example, you might want to monitor the free space available in the database over a period of time. After gathering data on the trend of space consumption, you can use the analysis to project when you might need to add more disk resources. You can similarly monitor consumption of other resources like processor utilization, memory utilization, and so on. This type of monitoring is necessary after the application is rolled out into production.

There are many tools available for monitoring. Some tools are appropriate for server monitoring. For example, they can detect and report on events occurring on the database server, such as database crash or resource consumption. Other tools are appropriate for ad-hoc monitoring such as trying to determine the cause of a particular performance issue. Discussion of these tools is beyond the scope of this book.

8.6 Disaster Recovery Planning

Few projects consider designing for disasters as part of their charter. They simply defer this to the production DBA. This planning often is delayed until just before application rollout. Keep in mind that one instance may often include several applications. Your disaster recovery plan must meet the service requirements of every application. The interdependencies between these applications make this task complex, for example, tables shared between them.

8.6.1 Service Level Requirements

One of the first steps in planning is to establish the service level required by each application. Here is a checklist:

- **Required up-time**: Is the application required 24 hours a day, 7 days a week? Do you have any window when the application can be unavailable? Some applications are required only during a normal working day in a particular time zone. Others span time zones and need to be available for 12 to 16 hours per day. Still others are global and cannot be down at all. The service level requirement determines the kind of backup approach you may choose.

- **Available backup window**: How long is the window of time when users are not actively using the application? Is this time reserved for bulk or batch processing? Is there any spare time? This window determines the kind of backup approach appropriate for your application.

- **Down time tolerance window**: How long can the application be unavailable before it impacts the business? If an application that supports telephone sales is down, the business impact is immediate. A warehouse going down may not impact the business for several hours or days. This window establishes the bounds for you recovery process.

8.6.2 Factors Affecting Backup Strategy

There are several other issues to consider when you design your backup strategy. These are dependent on the application characteristics rather than requirements that can be stated. For example:

- Database size: If your database is small, you might simply choose to back up the entire database. If your database is too large, a full backup might take longer than the available window. This issue is compounded when you have multiple applications within one instance. Your backup choices are restricted to application-level backup, incremental database backup, or rolling tablespace-level backup. Remember to match the redo log archives to the backups so that you have a matching set to recover from.

- **Hardware reliability (MTBF)**: Interpret this statistical measure of failure for your configuration. For example, suppose you have a 160-drive array and the MTBF for the drives is 50,000 hours. Then, expect a drive failure every 50,000 hours / (24 hours*160 drives), that is, something will crash about **twice a month!** Prepare your backup and recovery strategy appropriately.

- **Warehouse:** Usually, data warehouses have large databases and the potential to grow indefinitely. The growing database size makes it difficult to design a long-term backup strategy. Sometimes, it is faster to reconstruct a data warehouse—that is, reload all its data from the source, than to recover it from a backup. Test the recovery time for your favorite strategy before applying it to a warehouse.

8.6.3 Recovery Scenarios

The most common reason for a database crash is power failure. If you have no guard against power failure such as an uninterruptible power supply, don't bother reading any further until you get one. You will recover its cost in short order because you will save time otherwise wasted doing a lot of unnecessary recoveries. One of my Wall Street clients was paranoid about using a UPS. Then they moved their computer center, and of course, immediately guarded their computer with a UPS—but not the disk drives! Predictably, a power failure crashed several of their disks resulting in two days of downtime—nearly got their CIO fired. The moral is be aware of what you are guarding against and plan accordingly.

Another common occurrence is when someone unintentionally deletes a table. This happens more often than you realize! They request that the DBA recover this table from backup. Of course, it is not enough to just get the table back, you also need to apply to it all the modifications since the backup. Without these modifications, the data in the table will not be consistent with respect to its related tables. So, you need matched redo log archives before you can do roll forward recovery. Your backup and recovery strategy must allow recovery of single tables in such situations.

Can you recover data for each application individually? You might lose all data for an application if the schema owner is dropped! Your recovery strategy may be simply to restore the one user. If applications share tables, you need to determine whether your strategy will support recovery of one application without recovering other dependent applications.

How would you handle loss of a single data file, a control file, or a redo log archive? Are these scenarios possible based on the design of your instance? For example, if you use a Windows NT stripe set, all of your files are spread over the disks in the set. So, loss of a single data file is not likely. Determine which scenarios are possible in your configuration and then make sure you can recover from them. Don't worry about how unlikely the occurrence might be; if you don't plan for it—Murphy's Law will prevail!

Design your backup and recovery strategy to handle media failures. Make sure you have hardware fault tolerance, such as disk mirroring (RAID level-1) or RAID 5. As mentioned before, the larger your installation, the more likely that *something* will fail.

Finally, plan how you might test your backup and recovery strategies *before* a real occurrence. One of my DBA friends periodically visited their company's computer room and randomly pulled the power plug on various devices. Her objective was not only to see if a database could be recovered, but also how long it actually took and how organized the approach. She could then decide whether and which operations staff needed training. She could also address any recovery issues that did not meet the service level requirements. If you have time to only test one thing before the rollout of an application, test that your backup and recovery strategy actually works. Finding out the flaws in your backup when you are under the gun to recover from a real disaster is too late!

8.6.4 Backup Strategies

There are three basic strategies for backup: a cold backup, an online backup, or a combination of a full and incremental backup. A cold backup requires that your database is offline while the backup is in progress. Backup may use an operating system-provided utility, for example, under UNIX, you might use tar, cpio, or other similar utility. With Oracle 7.3 and later, you can use the Enterprise Manager utilities for backup. This physical backup together with redo log file backups will allow you to recover the database to the last committed transaction.

If you must provide 7x24 service, you can only use an online backup strategy. You need not take a tablespace offline prior to backing up the component operating system files. Online backup requires that you use the *archivelog* mode. You must also indicate the start and end of a backup using the *alter database begin backup/end backup* statements. This causes Oracle to mark the backup start and end points in the redo log files. These marks are used during recovery. Don't forget to archive the redo log files as part of the strategy. Recovery in this strategy is much more complicated.

There are more ways of recovering from corrupted databases with Oracle than you are likely to use. However, be aware that you can recover from most disasters with only a minor loss. Oracle automates certain types of recovery. For example, if your database crashes but there is no damage to any media or files, recovery is automatic when you start the database. Some of the more complex recovery methods, such as recovering to a specific time, are documented in the manuals.

8.7 Performance Tuning

A DBA invariably gets involved when an application has sluggish response. This may occur during development or anytime after the application goes into production. But, performance sluggishness may be due to either application code or the database setup.

Your first task is to first determine the symptoms experienced by the users and then investigate the causes.

Some examples of the characteristics you need to determine are: What is the form or report that experiences performance problems, what sequence of actions lead to sluggish performance, is the problem in the application or the database, is it easily reproducible or intermittent, what activities are going on in the database at the time of the problem, and so on. It is, of course, easier to pin down a reproducible problem than an intermittent one.

There are several tools available to investigate problem areas. Some tools focus on application code, while others allow you to examine the database. Code examination lets you determine the way in which a particular SQL statement will execute. For example, you can determine which indexes, if any, will be used in the statement being examined.

You can examine the proposed execution plan for a SQL statement with Oracle's *Explain Plan* utility or third-party tools like ExplainSQL. You will need to understand the impact of execution plan choices such as *merge-join* or *nested loops*. The third-party tools assist you in understanding the impact and determining if the execution plan chosen by the optimizer is the appropriate one. If your knowledge of the data suggests a better execution path, you may provide *hints* to the optimizer. For example, if you would like the optimizer to use a particular index, you may specify a hint in a comment embedded in the SQL statement. The optimizer uses such hints to modify the execution plan.

To understand the impact of executing a SQL statement, Oracle provides a couple of other utilities, *Trace* and *Tkprof*. *Trace* provides the actual execution path of a statement. *Tkprof* provides execution statistics in addition to the actual execution path. These statistics include database access information such as number of fetches. The Oracle Enterprise Manager also includes utilities to examine these statistics in a graphical manner. In addition, the Enterprise Manager provides facilities to monitor an instance to examine the activity in the instance.

Performance tuning an Oracle database is a complex topic. There are several books published to assist the database administrator. Instead of a detailed discussion of these issues, we will review the items that have the most impact on improving performance.

8.7.1 Top 5 Application Tuning Tips

When you experience a performance problem, investigate the application SQL statements first. Here are the areas that you should pay particular attention to:

- **Where clause construction:** Make sure that you use appropriate operators in the *where* clause. For example, try to use exact matches, if you can, rather than inequality operators or wildcards. State your conditions as positive restrictions rather than negative conditions such as *is not null* or *not equal to*.

- **Use indexes:** Using indexes speeds retrieval significantly. Where there are multiple indexes for the optimizer to choose from, try to provide hints for using a hash index. You can use a hash index for an exact match. If your index is based on concatenated columns, make sure the most restrictive column is positioned first in the concatenation sequence. However, there is a point of diminishing returns in the use of many indexes for a single statement.

- **Cost-based optimizer:** Use the cost-based optimizer whenever possible. But, remember to run *analyze* on the tables first. This optimizer needs the statistics gathered by the *analyze* utility to make reasonable decisions. Use *hints* to tell the optimizer what it does not know. After all, you probably understand the data distribution in your application better than an automated tool like the optimizer.

- **Joins:** Control the number of tables joined in a single statement. One rule of thumb is to have no more than 3-4 tables joined in a single statement. Of course, there may be occasions when you must do so. Depending on the size of the query result, you may combine the SQL statement with 3-4 tables joined with PL/SQL loops to produce the desired result.

- **Use a tool:** Use a tool like Explain Plan or a similar third-party tool. Don't spend time guessing. You may waste time unnecessarily.

8.7.2 Top 5 Database Tuning Tips

Tuning the database is another step in troubleshooting a performance problem. If the problem is intermittent or you cannot isolate the problem statement, you might use a database monitoring tool to investigate. Here are the primary areas to target your tuning efforts:

- **Analyze tables:** This utility collects statistics that are used by the optimizer. You need not analyze the entire table—especially large tables. Be sure to use a representative sample of data that illustrates the data distribution typical of each table.

- **Memory bottlenecks:** Tune the SGA to provide sufficient space for the concurrent activities in the database. In Section 8.3.3 Memory Structures, we discussed the important areas to tune.

- **Disk I/O bottlenecks:** Look for hot disks to pinpoint I/O bottlenecks. Most of the database monitoring tools provide facilities to do this. Look for ways to distribute I/O as we discussed in Section 8.4.3 I/O Distribution among Disks.

- **CPU bottlenecks:** Check out the CPU usage to make sure that less than 90% is utilized. The only solution to a CPU bottleneck, unfortunately, is to get a bigger machine or to add CPUs. You can set up periodic monitoring of the database to analyze the growth in CPU usage to plan for capacity growth.

- **Network bottlenecks:** Network traffic can cause delays if you transfer large volumes of data. You may develop such programs inadvertently, for example, an unrestricted list of values based on a query from a large table. The small databases used in the development environment may defer the discovery of such issues.

8.8 Planning for Rollout

Rolling out an application into production is a significant technical challenge. Good planning helps make it smooth. There are several things you must plan for:

- **Setting up the production database:** If you have good volume metrics from the analysis phase, this is relatively straightforward. Otherwise, you need to guesstimate the initial size and be prepared to grow it.

- **Data load:** Getting the initial data loaded into the database can be a challenge. You may need to transform or scrub data from legacy systems before loading into the new system. If the initial data does not meet the integrity constraints designed into the new database, plan what you will do with database constraint definitions. Oracle8 offers facilities to apply constraints only to new data, but will your application crash when retrieving unclean data?

- **Staging area:** You will need an area where you can practice data conversion and loading. This area may also be a test area for realistic testing and for training users just prior to production. You will need this area for testing the subsequent releases of your application containing bug fixes and enhancements. So, keep it around, unless it consumes an unacceptable portion of resources.

- **Infrastructure:** You will need to plan any changes to the infrastructure. For example, you may need to upgrade the PC on each user's desktop prior to installing the client-server application. Coordinate these changes with your system and network administrators. Don't forget to install the runtime software needed for your application.

- **Software distribution:** You need to install the application software for each user either on their file server or on each client's disk.

Your planning should begin just as you complete the initial database design. You may need to start a parallel project to define the conversion rules and begin building the data conversion utilities. You may discover important characteristics of the data during this process that you may want to communicate to the application design team.

Case Study: Widgets Database

Service Levels

There are two distinct kinds of service levels required by the Widgets applications. The sales application requires a 7 (days) x 24 (hours) operation while the warehouse and accounting applications only require 6 (days) x16 (hours). At first glance, this disparity in requirements suggests two separate database instances. However, further investigation revealed two key criteria:

- There are interdependencies between applications that were not apparent from the data models. The sales application retrieves inventory quantities and updates the quantity reserved value when the order is complete. For corporate orders, the sales application verifies that outstanding balance on the customer's account in the accounting application together with the current order total is within that customer's credit limit. These dependencies were captured in the business rules model. These dependencies mean that putting these three applications on a single instance would be convenient. Growth through adding database servers would require the use of distributed facilities of Oracle which we discuss in Chapter 14.

- The 7x24 service level is a requirement for availability of the application, not the availability of the database instance. As long as Widgets can continue the order entry process, the service level requirement is satisfied.

The team heaved a sigh of relief when they discovered these criteria. They could set up an extra machine to allow opportunities to upgrade application software and to provide a warm standby. Normally the standby would be synchronized with the production machine using the advanced replication features of Oracle. When scheduling the release of upgraded application software, the standby would be configured with the upgraded software. Its data would be synchronized with the old production machine on a periodic basis, because advanced replication might not be feasible with different releases of the application.

The plan for switch-over to the standby would be to log telesales representatives off the old machine a few at a time and have them log on to the standby database. They could continue entering new orders into the standby. The missing orders from the old machine would be loaded into the standby on completion of the switch-over.

There is a risk of inconsistent inventory position between beginning the switch and applying the missing orders from the old machine to the standby. After in-depth discussions with warehouse and sales management, the team decided that the inconsistencies could be resolved manually without significant detrimental effect on business. Widgets management accepted this small impact in exchange for implementing a cheap architecture that still provided a perceived 7x24 operation. Of course, the alternative was to freeze order entry software and use expensive fault tolerant, 7x24 capable hardware. Actually such inconsistent inventory position, with consequent back orders, is a common occurrence in current operations, so persuading management was not too difficult.

Application Activity Patterns

Before designing the instance, we need to analyze the patterns of the applications' activities. The sales application is a typical online transaction processing (OLTP) application. It adds product orders into the database and reserves the quantity ordered of the product against quantity available in inventory. These transactions are of relatively short duration, lasting at most a few minutes. System response in this application is critical. However, the requirement for providing a 7x24 operation means that backup must occur while the application is online.

The warehouse application is also an OLTP application, but requires only 7x16 operation. Backup of this application could be performed after the application is down. This application includes certain reports that are run in batch overnight. So the backup strategy must accommodate a batch window.

The accounting application is an OLTP application with a requirement for 7x12 operation. This application has a significant number of batch reports run daily.

Other applications to be integrated into these applications include: loading of the catalog with its price list on a periodic basis, daily extraction of orders data for the public web based system, weekly extraction of data for loading into the data warehouse, and electronic data interchange systems for product ordering from product distributors.

Instance Design

The instance design includes layout of tables and indexes among tablespaces, layout of tablespaces between disks, layout of tablespaces used by other system activities, and location of instance files on disks. This instance design is for the support of sales, warehouse and accounting applications. Other instances, such as for the data warehouse and web database, will be designed as needed.

It makes sense to isolate the performance critical sales application activities from those of the other applications while maintaining the data integration requirements. Each application will use its own tablespaces, one for data and one for indexes. This separation should reduce contention for locks and latches for access to database dictionary elements. In addition, users of the sales application will have a temporary tablespace separate from that allocated to the users of the other applications. In addition, a large rollback segment dedicated to the sales application will permit the necessary online backups. The other applications shall share a rollback segment.

The estimated size of the sales data is 10 gigabytes (6000 orders per day @ 10 K per order * 365 days * 5 *factor of safety*). The estimated size of warehouse and accounting data is 5 gigabytes. The disk requirements are double (*for luck!*) this size, that is, 30 gigabytes. Although typical disk sizes are increasing at a rapid rate, the team decided to use 4 disks to support the ability to stripe the disk. On an Windows NT system, these disks were allocated as a single stripe set. Files for all the tablespaces were created in the directory representing this stripe set. In addition, a separate disk directory was used to store the database and operating system software.

The team also decided to use *archivelog* mode on the instance to reduce the loss of transactions in the case of a system crash. The set of log files were also on the disk stripe set with a second (backup) set of log files on the software disk. Database control files were similarly duplicated between two physical disks. Logs were configured to switch every 10 minutes or a maximum of 1 megabytes of data. Automatic archiving of these log files was configured. The plan was to turn *archivelog* mode off during major data loading or update processes.

Backup and Recovery Plan

Backups would be scheduled during the low activity period of the sales application. Allowing for four time zones in the U.S.A. the best time to schedule backups is around 2 AM in Timbuctoo. Online backups freeze the data files but allow transactions to be recorded in the rollback segment. When backup is complete, the redo logs are applied to the data files. So a large rollback is essential for the sales application.

The other applications are inactive at the time of the scheduled backup and should generate minimal rollback traffic. However, their tablespaces cannot be taken offline because of the data shared with the sales application. So online backups of these applications must be integrated with the backup of sales data.

An alternative design would be that if the inventory data is unavailable, orders could be taken without reserving available stock. Similar accommodation could be engineered for credit checks against the accounting data. This design is probably necessary anyway to accommodate individual machine failure in the future growth path where sales and warehouse applications run on separate machines. Notice how such architectural considerations can impact application program design!

Part

3

Developing Oracle Applications

Now we get down to the nitty-gritty—how to build what we set out to do. The Oracle DBMS provides fourth-generation tools for building interactive forms, reports, and batch programs. We will focus on these tools in the following chapters.

You are not stuck with Oracle-supplied tools, however. Many third-party vendors make a living supplying forms utilities, report generators, and high-level procedural language interfaces to Oracle. So, to add a little spice, we examine some of these tools. I do not intend this to be an exhaustive survey of third-party products. There are too many good products which are changing too quickly to include in this book. Instead, I provide a flavor of what is available.

These chapters use the example programs we designed in the previous part of the book. So refer to them if you need details on layouts or processing design. I have chosen at least one example of each type of program.

There is little hand-holding, tutorial-style, step-by-step description in these chapters. Instead, I show heavily annotated code illustrating typical and nontypical techniques. Replacing Oracle's substantial set of manuals is not my intention. Expand on the techniques illustrated for your own applications. If you grasp the philosophy underlying them, you are well on your way to building successful applications.

Interactive Screen Programs

Interactive forms comprise a major portion of today's applications. They are not, by any means, merely interfaces for entering data, as in more traditional systems. Data entry is just one of the major functions served by these tools. They also allow users to query in a targeted manner—to find just the one piece of data they need. You might also use forms as a means to obtain data traditionally printed in reports.

The previous printing of this book showed design and development as distinct steps. In the Designer environment, the distinction between these phases is very faint. In fact, in a RAD approach, you will iterate through the design, build, and user test steps several times for each form. The code generators produce interfaces that are based on the behavior inherent in the underlying tool. So, you need to be familiar with the interface and restrictions of Oracle Forms.

One chapter cannot do justice to the facilities of these complex tools. We cover concepts in this chapter and leave detailed description of individual tools to the books listed in the bibliography. In particular, we cover the following topics:

- Defining a form and each of the typical components of a form. Components include canvases, blocks, items, and triggers to program-specific actions.

- Layout and navigation between multiple blocks, within one window or multiple windows. We will examine concepts such as spread tables for organizing items that allow us to show more data than a window can comfortably display.

- Generating forms using the Designer tools and customizing them for an intuitive interface. We will explore Designer facilities to add business logic.

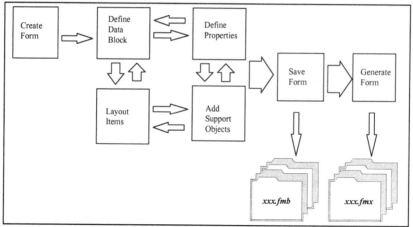

Figure 9-1: Definition Stages with Oracle Forms

9.1 Oracle Tools

Building interactive forms using a GUI development tool such as Oracle Forms is very different from using traditional procedural programming languages. Instead of coding each step of a user's navigation through the form, you let the utility do most of that work. Development, then, consists of defining the characteristics of each field and the program action when the cursor initially enters a field, or after it exits the field.

If you use Oracle Designer to generate application code, most of your programming team may ignore the mechanics of using the Oracle Forms toolset. You may need one or two experts to manage the standard libraries and reusable objects needed by your projects. These libraries can be incorporated into the code generator environment.

Our primary purpose with screen forms is to allow users access to the data in the database. For many tasks, Oracle tools provide multiple ways to do this. Forms provides a controlled interface for accessing data. It is suitable for well-defined, repetitive tasks, such as order entry or customer lookup. Other Oracle tools allow ad hoc access for the user who does not wish to wait until a program can be developed. They are particularly suited to one-off access. Unfortunately, they all depend on the user understanding the structure of the tables in the database, at least superficially. So, before you give these tools to the user, you must train them in the database structure, and perhaps use of SQL. Teaching non-technical users these structures is not a trivial task.

9.2 Oracle Forms Components

Oracle Forms is a developer's utility. It has a development interface, called Form Builder, and a runtime part, called Forms Runtime. In this section, we will briefly review the components of a form—enough to gain an appreciation of the concepts. Don't expect to become a Forms development expert through this review. However, it should give you an appreciation of the amount of work performed by the Forms generator in the Oracle Designer toolset.

Within Form Builder, there are wizards that assist you in developing specific components. After gaining some experience, you may, of course, bypass the wizards. When you develop a form, it goes through several distinct stages before you can run it. Figure 9-1 illustrates these stages and the associated location of your form definition.

When you start defining the form, its definition is in memory. You can save the definition in a file, the *.fmb* file, or in database tables. Then, you need to use the generate and compile options to transform it into the executable *.fmx* file. The compiled definition is always in an operating system file that is used for running the form. You may copy this file to any other machine that has the same application tables and run it using Forms Runtime. Developers can run the form without exiting Form Builder.

A form is made up of several elements that determine its layout, database access, behavior, interface, and so on. Each element has properties, appropriate to the kind of element, describing its layout, display characteristics, database correspondence and other qualities used by the Forms Runtime environment. Developing a form consists of defining these elements and their properties using the Form Builder utility. In our discussion here, we have grouped these elements by their common functions.

The first set of Forms components consist of layout elements. A form is made up of one or more pages, that is, canvases. A window shows a portion of the canvas and may provide scroll bars to pan around the canvas. You may also have canvases that are stacked over other canvases. Pages may be stacked using a staggered tab style of display—similar to file folder tabs we use in manual filing systems.

A second set of Forms components include data elements. Data elements in a form, called *items*, correspond to tables and columns. You may specify one or more blocks each relating to one base database table and one or more lookup tables. Blocks may also be based on views or PL/SQL procedures. A block must be contained within a canvas, but may be duplicated through the alternate layout feature in another canvas. Columns from lookup tables are called display items. You may have displayed or non-displayed items within a block.

A third set of Forms components are global variables that are storage areas available to any component of the form, including menus, toolbars, and control blocks which are not associated with any database table. These blocks might be used for displaying common data elements such as user identification, date, and so on.

A fourth set of Forms components are the support code objects. These include record groups to support lists of values, program units consisting of procedures and functions called from control points, perform validation such as checking for referential integrity, or dynamically modify the capabilities of the application conditionally based on the rules. These control points are called triggers. Triggers represent points at

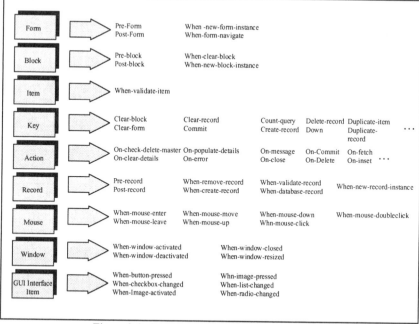

Figure 9-2: Sample Triggers and Control Points

which a form may react to an user's action, for example, a mouse click.. Figure 9-2 illustrates some sample categories of triggers and the control points provided by Forms.

9.2.1 Layout Objects

Figure 9-3 illustrates Forms layout components and their relationship to each other. The basic components for visual layout are contained within a window. It is a view on the canvas displayed from the form. At least one canvas must be displayed. The canvas may be larger than the window size. The size of the window defines the amount of a canvas that we can view at a time. We can provide horizontal and vertical scroll bars to allow us to *pan* around a larger canvas. Of course, at runtime, we can resize the window to fit our needs. Scroll bars are essential in these cases.

Canvases may be stacked on top of the other. Their properties allow us to specify their size and placement, as well as backdrops and colors. With these facilities, we can design each display component individually. Then we stack them appropriately on a background canvas to achieve the desired visual effect. With Developer Release 2.1 and later, we have tabbed pages—another way of stacking that leaves a staggered tab like a file folder tab for each page. Even at runtime, we can dynamically control, via trigger code, when and where we display pages, enable or disable tabs, and stack canvases.

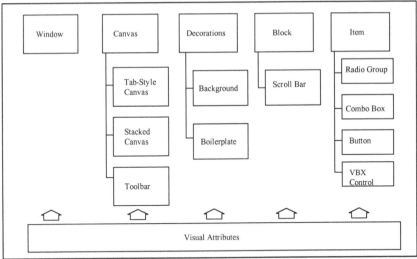

Figure 9-3: Forms Layout Elements

We can place blocks of data and corresponding prompts (or item labels) anywhere within a canvas. We commonly use some decorative effect such as a border or lowered rectangle to delineate elements in separate blocks. Such decorations are not mandatory. We can choose to place all blocks on a single canvas or place them one on each separate canvas. In a tab-style presentation, we must place data for each tab on a separate canvas.

Each item within a block has display characteristics. For example, we can display images, radio groups, poplists, OLE containers, and so on. Each button in the form is an item, whether it is based on a database column or is just a display item. We can associate icons with buttons via their iconic properties. Actions are associated with each button via trigger code.

We can standardize many display characteristics via support objects like visual attributes. One method is to develop libraries, or style templates, which provide starting points for our project or company standards. Oracle Forms provides object libraries and template forms for this purpose. Standardizing GUI elements such as colors, icons, and toolbars is critical if we are to achieve a consistent look and feel. Otherwise, we may end up with two programs where different programmers applied their own taste in colors—resulting in a multi-color application! There are several style guides available, or you may develop your own.

9.2.2 Data Objects

All database objects in a form are contained in blocks. A block is usually associated with a database table. *Control* blocks have no corresponding database table. A control block may contain items that establish context, such as user name and today's date, or

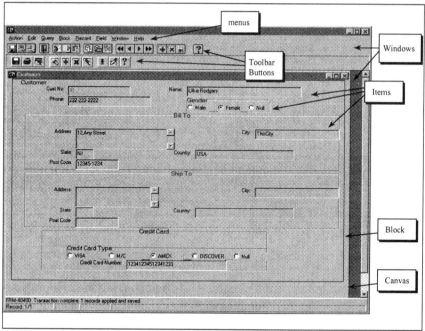

Figure 9-4: Data Elements in a Form

items without reference to any database tables. Figure 9-4 illustrates the data components of a form. A block may also be based on a database view, provided that insert, update, and delete actions can be executed on it as required by the form. A block may also be based on parameters of a procedure.

A block is made up of items, each of which may be based on a database column, may be a display-only item, or may be a hidden item. A display-only item is commonly used for displaying data when some change occurs in some other related item. For example, when a user enters a customer number, you might use a display-only item to display the corresponding customer name. A hidden item is not displayed on the screen at runtime, but might be necessary to hold data required for some operation transparent to the user, such as supplying query criteria for retrievals from the database or performing a calculation. For example, you might use a hidden item to hold the sales tax rate for calculating the sales tax on an order.

Block properties allow us to specify characteristics such as which table serves as a block's base table. For each block, specify whether you can insert, update, select, or delete rows from the underlying base table. We can also specify navigation restrictions or constrain the retrieval of rows from the base table by specifying a *where* clause. We can relate one block to another, for example, to specify a master detail relationship. Forms wizards assist in creating forms with such relationships easily.

Each item is specified by defining a set of properties. Item properties allow us to define display and access characteristics, that is, whether insert, update, and query actions are permitted on an item. You can specify these properties for each individual item, or define classes from which to copy properties to an individual item or to subclass it.

Item Property	Description
Type: Item Type	Kind of item, e.g., text, Image, VBX control, and so on.
Display: Canvas	Canvas on which this item is displayed. Other properties specify the item's position on the canvas.
Display: Visual Attribute	A standard attribute that sets the font, color, and other characteristics. The same visual attribute may be used for many items, for example, to set all mandatory items in a form to Bold Blue.
Data: Mirror Item	Name of an item to mirror the current item on. This allows us to display a value on multiple pages, for example, a customer name to establish context on multiple pages.
Data: Default Value	Value to set this item to in insert mode. You can override this value at runtime by simply typing over it.
Navigation: Navigable	Set to true if cursor is allowed to enter this item; set to false to prevent it. For example, set to false in a display-only item.
Database: Base Table Item	Does the item map to a column in the current database table? Items mapping to other database columns such as product description are not in the current table.
Database: Primary Key	Use this property to ensure uniqueness. This option can degrade performance of your form since it has to access the database table to enforce unique values.
Database: Case Insensitive Query	Disregard upper- or lower-case distinctions when querying using a user supplied value in this item. Forms may perform comparisons at the client end, resulting in a significant amount of network traffic, so beware of using this option.
Database: Update if NULL	Only allow entry if this field is empty. If a prior value exists, do not allow user to change it. Useful for one-time entry fields.

Table 9-1: Some Sample Item Properties

Functional: Case Restriction	Specify the case to which to convert input in this field as user enters characters. For example, setting it to upper-case causes conversion to upper case.
Functional: Autoskip	As soon as this field is full, move cursor to the next field without requiring user action.
Miscellaneous: LOV	A list of values to be associated with this item, that is, a list of allowable values from a table or hard coded.
Miscellaneous: Hint	A hint or brief description to be displayed at the bottom of the window for entry in this item.

Table 9-1: Some Sample Item Properties

Specifying an item for selection allows you, at runtime, to enter query criteria based on that item. The display length of an item can be different from its query length. This feature allows query conditions such as greater than or less than, which increase the space needed for an item value at runtime.

Item properties are grouped by functions, for example Type, Display, Database, Functional, Navigation, and so on. Table 9-1 illustrates some of the interesting properties for an item within each group. There are, of course, many more properties not listed here. This is not intended to be an exhaustive list. Some properties are dependent on the kind of Forms object and others are standard. New properties are added with each new release of the tools.

9.3 Global Objects

This set includes menus, toolbars, and other common elements displayed throughout your application. Oracle Developer Release 2 provides facilities for using template forms as starting points. These global objects are some of the elements that you might consider putting into a template form. Oracle Designer has always used the template form concept which we discuss in Section 9.4 Generating a Module.

Forms also provides global variables that make their values available throughout a session. Thus, a simple means of passing data between two forms that run in a single session is to put it into global variables. There are also system variables accessible during the session that contain information like the item under the current cursor position, status of the record or block, and so on.

9.3.1 Business Logic Objects

In addition to the declarative definitions, Forms provides procedural control facilities via triggers. Triggers contain PL/SQL code that executes when the associated control point is triggered due to some user action. Other procedural code facilities include program units such as functions and procedures which a trigger may invoke. We use triggers to alter the default behavior of Forms.

```
/* CGUI$GET_UNIQUE_ID */
/* Generate unique identifier value for item from unique source */
BEGIN
 IF (:CUSTOMERS.CUST_NO IS NULL) THEN
 BEGIN
  CGUI$GET_NEXT_CUST_NO_SEQ(
  —:CUSTOMERS.CUST_NO);  /* OUT: Next value from sequence ——*/
 EXCEPTION
   WHEN NO_DATA_FOUND THEN
  —MESSAGE('Internal Error: No row in table SYS.DUAL');
  —RAISE FORM_TRIGGER_FAILURE;
   WHEN TOO_MANY_ROWS THEN
  —MESSAGE('Internal Error: More than one row in table SYS.DUAL');
  —RAISE FORM_TRIGGER_FAILURE;
   WHEN OTHERS THEN
  —CGTE$OTHER_EXCEPTIONS;
 END;
 END IF;
END;
```

Figure 9-5: Sample Trigger Code

Remember that Forms assumes a particular style of behavior—for example, that we use a single form for query, insert, update and delete tasks. We use triggers extensively to build a different interface, composed of, say, three forms: one for specifying query criteria, a second for displaying a list of matching records, and a third for displaying and updating the detailed record.

A trigger is custom code that we can write to make Forms perform a particular task. The language is a slightly modified version of PL/SQL. Figure 9-5 illustrates trigger code for populating the *customer id* with a generated unique number. This is a *pre-insert* trigger on the customer block. Screen field names start with a : (colon). This trigger calls a *program unit*, which actually performs the task. Figure 9-6 illustrates the code in the program unit. The program unit could be executed from many triggers. Notice the comments that identify the generated code. These identifiers are consistent throughout the form, providing easier understanding of generated logic. Names of program units are also consistent. For example, the illustration shows a *get_*... program unit, which obtains the unique identifier. A unit which checks a constraint would be called *chk_*... You should aim to follow coding standards like these in any manual development to make maintenance easier.

Here are some more good habits: screen field names should match corresponding database fields. Block names should correspond to table names. These habits have saved me many hours of work when modifying a form. Forms is a good tool to use when you are developing a new form, but very difficult to navigate around when modifying a form developed by another developer. By the way, this is where generated code from Oracle Designer provides the biggest benefit. A generated form is so consistent that you can determine quickly where and what code to modify. Sometimes, I find it faster to generate a new form using Oracle Designer generators than to modify an existing hand-written form.

The trigger name defines when Forms will activate it. For example, a sequence number-generating trigger is called a *pre-insert* trigger—it is activated whenever a row is inserted. Note that there is no implication that the inserted data is *committed*—that requires a separate action.

You can associate triggers with any of the objects in a form, such as a window, tab page, item, block, or the form itself. In addition, you can associate a trigger with a key that a user may press, or a database access by Forms such as an insert, update, delete, or query. Figure 9-2 illustrates many of the form objects with which a trigger can be associated. Trigger names starting with *pre-* are activated just before Forms executes that action; similarly, names starting with *post-* are activated immediately after the action is complete. Thus, Forms activates a *pre-field* trigger just before the cursor enters the associated field. Forms activates a *post-delete* trigger immediately after executing the delete access, but before executing a database commit. Remember that you can perform a number of updates to the database which Oracle will not actually write to the database until you commit them. You may undo such updates with a rollback statement at any time prior to the commit.

Key-based navigation is important in some environments, for example, for forms used for heads-down data entry. When performance is measured by keystrokes or units of

```
/* CGUI$GET_NEXT_CUST_NO_SEQ */
PROCEDURE CGUI$GET_NEXT_CUST_NO_SEQ(
  P_NEXT_VALUE IN OUT NUMBER) IS  /* Next value from sequence */
/* Value in Item :%s.%s */
BEGIN
 DECLARE
  CURSOR C IS
—SELECT  CUST_NO_SEQ.NEXTVAL
—FROM   SYS.DUAL;
 BEGIN
  OPEN C;
  FETCH C
  INTO   P_NEXT_VALUE;
  IF C%NOTFOUND THEN
—CLOSE C;
—RAISE NO_DATA_FOUND;
  END IF;
  CLOSE C;
 END;
END;
```

Figure 9-6: Program Unit for Unique id

data entry, moving your hand to the mouse wastes precious time! Forms has dozens of different keys for shortcuts. Each key has a particular meaning, such as execute query, move cursor to the next block in the form, and so on. These keys correspond to many of the built-ins available in writing key-based triggers. By associating a trigger with a key, you can change the actions that Forms performs whenever a user types that key.

Simple triggers are sufficient for a simple Forms application. Consider, however, a form such as our order entry screen which has one block for *orders* and another for *order items*. Since there could be many items in each order, we defined the *order items* block as a multiple row block. We may want to allow the user to choose whether *order items* are automatically queried for each *order*, or queried only on request by user.

For automatic query, we could use the master-detail coordination facilities provided by Forms. However, to coordinate on request, we need trigger code to perform coordination. For example, if we perform a query in the *order* block, say, using the *order number*, Forms does not automatically display all of the associated rows in the *order items* block.

9.3.2 Master-Detail Blocks

Let's start by defining the way Forms behaves if we cordinate the *orders* and *order_items* blocks. We need to examine the required behavior for each type of operation: query, insert, update, and delete.

There are two ways a user can query in the *orders* block: by pressing the Query button twice on the toolbar to retrieve all rows; or by pressing the Query button once, entering a search condition in an item such as an order number, and then pressing the Query button again to retrieve specific rows. In either case, we would like the *order_items* block to show the items corresponding to the order displayed in the *orders* block. Of course, when we scroll through the retrieved orders using the Next Record and Previous Record buttons or the scrollbar, we would like the *order_items* block automatically to show the rows corresponding to the newly displayed order.

Similarly, inserting a new *order* should force the entry of *order_items* as well. In our example, we require that each order must have at least one order item. When the user deletes an order, we must first delete all of the associated *order items* and clear the *order_items* block, before deleting the order itself.

Order items rows contain the order number column, which is the foreign key to the *orders* block. You should hide this order number field in the *order_items* block from the user—so they do not get confused by seeing the order number appearing on every order item. One way is simply to define the field as not displayed in the attribute window.

You can apply similar logic for any form involving master-detail relationships. Notice that we have to anticipate each *event* that the user might possibly trigger at runtime and code an appropriate trigger code for it. Our code cannot force the sequence in which the user works. This peculiarity is common to most fourth-generation GUI forms development tools. It is important that you understand this method of coding for successful development using Forms.

You can use any PL/SQL statements or Forms built-in procedures in a trigger, provided you follow the restrictions placed by certain types of triggers, called restricted built-ins. These restrictions prevent you from using navigation statements that would invalidate the context maintained by Forms. For example, navigation to a different item from a *pre-item* trigger would invalidate the fact that the cursor is about to be placed in that item.

9.3.3 Trigger Scope

You are probably wondering by now how to decide whether a trigger should be item-level, block-level, or form-level. These levels are a nested set, with item-level triggers being the innermost set. Item-level triggers are active only when the cursor is actually in the item on which you defined the trigger. Block-level triggers, similarly are active only when the cursor is in an item within a block. Form-level triggers are active anywhere in the form.

If your define a trigger in an item and at the block level, the item-level trigger takes precedence when the focus is in that item. In all other items, the block-level trigger takes precedence. So, before you define a trigger, think about where the focus will be when the trigger is executed. If the focus will always be in a particular item, define your trigger on that item. This was the case in our trigger which retrieved the *product name* given a *product number*. If you cannot predict which item the focus will be in, define your trigger at block-level. For example, whenever the user clicks on a button, the focus is on the button item. We cannot guess which item the cursor was in when the user pressed the Execute Query button. So our query triggers for block coordination are block-level triggers. When deciding where to define a trigger, ask yourself the following questions:

- For a derived item value, when should a new value for this item be calculated? For example, we derive the *item total* item value from the *qty* field. Thus, every time this *qty* value changes, we should recalculate the *item total* value. So, we define a *When-validate-item* trigger on the *qty* field.

- To change the default action, we can precede the action with trigger code. These *When-* or *On-* triggers allow us to alter the default behavior of Forms. Make sure that your trigger code is not dependent on the focus—we cannot predict where the focus will be when the action is invoked.

- To change the action of a shortcut key under specific circumstances, where will the cursor be when this action is to be performed? What should occur when the user types this shortcut key? For example, after the user fills the *order* block, we would like the cursor to move to the first line in the *order_items* block. The cursor, at this point, will be in the last item in the *orders* block. So, when the user presses the *next item* key after entering this item, we would like the cursor to move to the *item_no* item in the *order_items* block. The trigger, then, must be called *Key-nxtfld* defined on the last item. In all other items, pressing the *next item* key should move the cursor to the next sequential item in the *orders* block.

Here are some more techniques for developing in Forms. Notice the *totals* block on the order entry screen. This block, called a control block, is not associated with any database table. It contains display only items. We define a trigger on the *item total* item to add the current value into the *subtotal* item. The *subtotal* item has a trigger which calculates the shipping and tax as a percentage of the current subtotal and then adds it to the subtotal to get the grand total. The trigger on the *item total* item calculates the new subtotal, which cascades to the trigger on the *subtotal* item, which in turn cascades to the *shipping* and *tax* items. Thus, triggers can cascade, causing multiple changes to the display.

This block contains data derived from previous items. In our database, we do not keep this derived data. However, it is nice to display this information as users enter orders, so that they can quote the final order total to the customer. Control blocks are a very useful technique for such data.

When you are using character mode software, another way to use control blocks is to create fake windows. Remember that versions earlier than version 3.0 of Forms did not allow you to pop-up lists of values windows or windows for called forms. So, this technique is only useful in the older version prevalent in some Oracle Applications suite. The order entry form calls another page to allow entry of customer data. The *orders* block seen partially in the back is just a control block. Form-level triggers copy the values into fields from the *orders* block.

We can extend the Widgets order entry example to many other industries. For example, suppose your order entry is more complex than just picking items from a catalog. What if you have to consider dependencies between products, as when configuring a computer system? The salespeople probably try out many different configurations before proposing one to the customer. You could implement such a scenario by using a scratch pad of tables. Then, your order entry would consist of writing trial configurations using the scratch pad and then copying the final order into the main tables.

In this example, assume that orders always use the trial scratch pad tables. You must therefore designate a Forms button or a shortcut key, such as the *commit* key, which the user must press to convert a trial order into a real order. Next, you should define a trigger on this action, *When-button-pressed* or *Key-commit*, at the form level, to copy the appropriate rows from the scratch pad tables to the main tables. You can keep the data in the scratch pad tables so that templates for other types of orders are available.

The scratch pad idea has many applications other than in order entry. For example, I have used it in a design for a security administration system. The scratch pad tables were actually for submitting the user id and security access information to a batch utility. The batch utility would run overnight to create the appropriate operating system ids, Oracle user names, security access views on tables, and so on from information stored in the scratch pad tables.

9.4 Generating a Module

The Oracle Designer forms generator adds a layer of consistency to the forms in your application. Realize that there is quite a lot of setup to generate usable modules. Some experienced developers may even claim the amount of Designer setup is comparable to the effort of developing a form directly in Forms Builder. The major benefits of using Oracle Designer are

- The consistency of the generated form.

- The ability to apply project or company standards to all forms in an application.

Consistent code produced by the generator makes forms maintenance much easier than manually developed forms with individual styles. For example, generated forms contain foreign key validation code in program units always called CGRI$<block name>. These program units are called from various triggers on the block. In a hand-built form, the programmer may have written the code in any one of these triggers, or may have missed one or two triggers. Even if the programmer wrote the validation code as program units, the names used in that form may not match the names for similar validation code in another form. Good project management and significant code reviews would be necessary to produce similarly consistent code in hand-built forms. On some of the projects I have been involved in, this consistency made it possible for us to assign enhancements and maintenance of forms to anyone on the team, without worrying about who originally developed the form. It also permitted us to structure development teams that utilized programming strengths during the training phase of the project.

Enforcing standards for look and feel of the application are essential for making the forms easy to use. Consistent look and feel helps reduce the user training required when rolling out the project. The GUI standards we discussed during design should be enforced during development to achieve this consistency. Oracle Designer provides several facilities to make this easy, as discussed in Section 9.5 Building a Common User Interface.

9.4.1 Module Definitions

The preliminary definitions of a module should exist after you use the application design transformer. Here, we will focus on modules to be implemented using the Forms Builder. Later chapters address modules to be implemented in the Report Builder and Web.

A module is made up of module components, as illustrated in Figure 9-7. A module component is a group of items that logically belong together and are typically displayed on a single canvas. It roughly corresponds to a block in the resulting form. It may contain:

- **Bound items:** These items correspond to a column in a database table. They may belong to the base table or one of the lookup tables. The generator produces code to populate and query from these items, as well as to interact with the database for insert, update, and delete access.

- **Unbound items:** These items are not associated with a table. They may contain anything that you wish to display without accessing the base table or its related tables. Some examples of unbound items are: current user's name, today's date, parameter values passed from a calling form, and so on. You can populate them by writing procedures and attaching them to events on which the value of the unbound item should be refreshed. For example, you may display the user's name on initial display of the form, and refresh it each time the form elements are cleared.

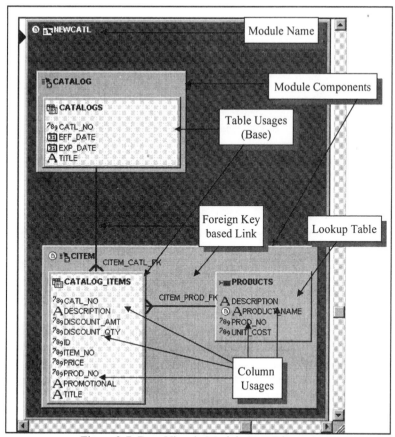

Figure 9-7: Data View in Module Data Diagram

- **Navigation items:** These items are not associated with a table. They are typically buttons that allow navigation to another module component, that is, another block or another module. In display view of the module diagram, you will see arrows indicating the navigation path.

- **Action items:** These items are similar to navigation items, except that they execute some application logic. You may program the logic as a named procedure. An example of an action item might be a button that converts a proposed computer configuration to an accepted order.

- **Application API:** These are a set of control points in the generated code where you may insert custom logic. For example, you may insert your own code before query, after query, and so on. These facilities allow you to execute procedures that implement business logic intermingled with generated code.

- **Application logic:** These are a set of control points in the forms event model where you may insert custom logic. Typical forms events are called triggers. For example, you may insert your own code at the beginning of the *When-button-pressed* trigger. You may create named procedures to be executed when this trigger fires at runtime.

You may also insert application logic at a table usage or item usage level. The rules of precedence, determined by the Forms scoping rules, are that lower-level item triggers override higher-level block or form trigger code.

You can relate module components to each other in two ways: by using a constraint link between the base tables of the respective modules, or by describing a shared data link between module components. A constraint link is based on an existing foreign key constraint between the data tables. The shared data link is based on non-database data elements and is used only to pass data displayed in one block to a graphics-based module.

Lookup tables are positioned to the right of the base tables. Foreign key constraints define the links between these tables. Figure 9-7 illustrates a sample module data diagram showing *data-based links* between module components. We can also view this diagram from a *display* perspective to understand the elements that will be displayed and any navigation links between the module components.

Figure 9-8 illustrates a display view of the module. You can switch between data and display views in the module diagrammer. The module display view is not really WYSIWYG—it indicates the elements that will be displayed, their grouping, if any, and their sequence. For example, we may define an *item group* called *Charges*, which contains tax, shipping, and discounts applied to the order. This view shows the window and page placement of each module component. This view may also show links for navigation; for example, the action item button *Items* navigates to the *items* module component. An action item may navigate to another module component or to another module. In our example, the action item *Products* navigates to the Products module.

Module components that contain only unbound items can be defined to display non-database information, that is, control block information. You may use such a control block to provide a separate query criteria display whenever the user presses the *Query* button on the toolbar. You may also embed unbound items within a module component based on a database table usage. For example, we might display the order total, calculated as the sum of its items, as part of the *Orders* module component.

The presentation of windows determines the ease of use of your application. Matching your presentation style to the environment that your users are familiar with can make the difference between days or hours of training. For example, a scrollbar to navigate multiple rows in a table format is intuitive to someone used to a Microsoft Windows environment. Providing a *Next Record* button instead of a scrollbar requires explanation. The generators impose their own style of presentation if you use them as delivered. However, you can customize the default styles using templates, object libraries, and preferences.

9.4.2 Customizing Elements

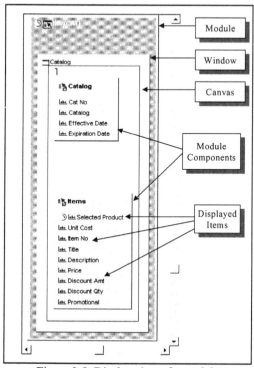

Figure 9-8: Display view of a module

One important aspect of your application is the look and feel. You need consistency in the presentation of graphical interface elements like windows, canvas, radio buttons and so on. The generator provides three facilities that affect the look and feel.

You can create standard definitions, or *styles*, for an element in an *object library*. The generator provides some default object libraries, but you can create your own. You can use the object library as a means of encoding project guidelines. Generated modules may override these guidelines on a case-by-case basis.

A second facility consists of a set of preferences which define layout controls. Preferences may be applied across all modules within an application, or on a module level. Within a module, preferences may be applied at more granular levels such as module component, table usage, item usage, and constraint usage. You can also define *preference sets*, which may be applied selectively to a module. Preference sets are useful for creating standard layout styles based on the kind of module: a set for master detail on a single canvas layout, a set for single row display module, a set for a multi-row display module, and so on.

A third facility involves the use of a *template* form. A template form is a form, developed manually in the Form Builder, that contains objects to be copied into each generated form. These objects may be code implementing business logic, control blocks, and other generic objects. They should not reference any specific database, form items, or blocks since they are copied without modification to the generated form. Oracle Designer supplies a few default template forms that contain several pre-defined objects. You may copy and modify these templates for your project's custom template. Some examples of objects in a template form are:

- Program units that implement generic business logic. You may reference these procedures and functions in application logic, or in application API code in specific modules.

- Control block definitions may contain generic items such as user identification, current date or time, module name, and so on. The default template forms supplied with Designer provide some of these generic items.

- Named visual attribute definitions in Release 1.3 and earlier allow you to define standard sets of colors for use in the properties and preferences of a module. For example, you may define a visual attribute to use for highlighting the current row in a multi-row display. Release 2.1 uses object library definitions to set properties.

- Toolbar definition may be used to define a canvas and buttons for use as a toolbar in every module. Each button will need to execute the appropriate action when pressed.

A typical project makes judicious use of all of these facilities. Object libraries provide a means of setting project and company standards. Where possible, you should subclass properties of objects from an object library. Note that object libraries are a feature of Oracle Forms and are useful whether or not you use the Designer code generators. You may override individual properties on specific objects if necessary.

Preferences are hierarchical from the application at the highest level to individual data usage items at the lowest. The rule of thumb is to apply preferences at the highest possible level. Within a project, you may create one or more named preference sets to define the style for a particular presentation. For example, if you prefer item labels above the item in a one-row-at-a-time form, you may create a named preference set that defines this presentation style. I have found it useful to define two or three presentation styles in many of my projects: single row at a time, multi-row

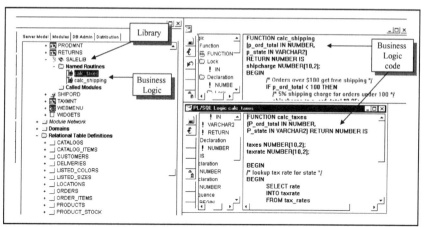

Figure 9-9: Library Module Definition

presentation, and a master-detail presentation. Of course, you also need to set certain data usage and module component properties to match the requirements of these styles.

In Release 1.3.2 and earlier, template forms were used as storage areas for custom code. Much of this custom code may be defined directly in the Designer repository as part of the module definition in Release 2.1 and later. However, template forms are still useful for common presentation elements that you would like to include in several forms. Note that a project may typically have more than one template form. The common elements may be window, canvas, and block definitions that may be copied into each form without modification. Note that control blocks need not be maintained in template forms—they may be defined and maintained as a reusable component. I find it useful to define reusable components for any custom blocks that may be required in a project's forms. I may make a private copy of the reusable component if customization for a particular module is necessary. The customization is then obvious and documented in the repository. Such definitions captured within template forms are less obvious. My recommendation is that using the repository facilities wherever possible is preferable to template forms, which must be maintained outside the repository.

9.4.3 Incorporating Business Rules Logic

In Chapter 7, Application Design for Performance, we discussed some design criteria for implementing business rules as the client- or server-side code. In this section, we discuss techniques for implementing client-side code only. Chapter 11 will discusse implementation of server-side code. In this section, we discuss how to incorporate calls to server-side procedures into generated forms.

There are several ways of implementing client-side business rules logic: a library module, object library, template form, or via application logic in a particular module.

Designer Release 2 supports generation of library modules, but object libraries and template forms need to be maintained manually outside the repository environment. The rule of thumb is to implement user interface-dependent code in these approaches: standard object-level logic in an object library and form-level common logic in a template form.

A recommended strategy is to place business rule logic in named procedures. These named procedures may be placed in an object library, library module, or in a server-side procedure or package as appropriate. Calls to these named procedures may be placed in the event model, Forms triggers, in this case, are placed in the object library, template, or module-specific application logic. Named procedures in a module should be used only for module-specific interface logic.

Note that any named procedure code in a library or template form needs to be called by a specific module for it to be executed. In this respect, a call to a library procedure or a call to a server-side procedure are similar. The execution of these procedures is different: Library code executes in the client and server-side code executes in the server.

A library module is a type of a module in the Designer repository. It may be attached to one or more modules that may call the code contained in it. The language property of the module determines whether the library is specific to Forms, Reports, or common to both. You will need to ensure that your use of built-ins is appropriate to the language specified in the code for the library module. Library modules may be repository-based, that is, the repository contains their code. You may use the module logic editor to define the code. Alternatively, you may create a library module to be

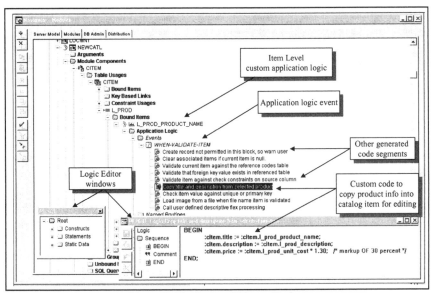

Figure 9-10: Custom Trigger Code

file-based, that is, it is simply a reference to a manually maintained library file that contains the code. Figure 9-9 illustrates the property dialog for defining a library module.

Since library code executes on the client, you should restrict it to contain user interface-related code. An example of user interface code is simple validation of items of date format type such as implementing the rule that expiration date must be later than effective date. Remember that any code that requires database access is best implemented as server-side code to eliminate unnecessary network traffic.

Module-specific code may be incorporated into the generator's environment by using language-specific event models supported by the module definition. Figure 9-10 illustrates an example of defining a module-specific trigger that calls a named procedure. Note that triggers defined at levels lower than the module, may specify an execution style; for example, they may override or executed before or after the higher-level trigger code. This style may be used to combine execution of code for the same trigger defined at a higher level, for example, at block-level, with code for that trigger defined at a lower level, for example, at item level. The default execution style is for lower-level trigger code to override higher-level trigger code.

If you use module-specific code to primarily incorporate calls to either client-side library code or server-side procedures, you may simply default trigger execution style to override higher level triggers. Note that other choices of execution style make it difficult to debug the form.

9.4.4 Reusable Components

A module component is the smallest independent unit in a Designer module definition. Its definition is rather data-centric—a base table and its associated lookup tables. A module component may also be based on a procedure or unbound items. So, you may compose module components such that they could be used as part of more than one module—that is, a reusable module component. For example, one of my projects was to develop a system to support stability testing of medicines. In this system, almost every form needed to display the stability lot and plan to establish the context. This display could be achieved using a reusable module component.

A module component may be included as part of a module definition like any other module component. You may edit it only with the reusable module component editor, instead of the usual module diagram or property dialogs. Note that if you edit the definition of a module component, the changes affect only those modules that are generated after the modification. So, to apply the modification to existing or previously generated modules, you may have to generate them again. It is good practice to use your best talent to develop reusable modules. These modules need to be thought through very carefully to make them sufficiently generic to be reusable and yet simple enough that they actually get used.

You create a reusable module component like any other module component—using the module data diagrammer or property dialogs. After creating a module component, you may reset its property to convert it to a reusable component. It is up to you, however, to make sure that a reusable component is self-contained. It should not contain references to any items outside its contents.

Occasionally, you may want to customize a reusable module component for use in a particular module. You can convert a reusable module component included in a particular module from *reusable* to *specific*. After resetting this property, any modifications apply only to that module. The custom module component is now an independent copy of the reusable module component. Other modules that include the previously reusable module are not affected by any modifications. I find this a useful approach for capturing many commonly used module components that differ slightly from one module to another. If we can understand the common elements and differences, we can create a reusable component with just the common elements. Each module that includes the reusable component may make its own custom copy as a specific component and define its custom code.

One example of a reusable component that differs slightly from module to module is a comment entry pop-up based on a table shared by several other tables. Each comment is assigned a unique identifier such as a generated sequence number. The referring table contains a foreign key reference to this unique identifier. Since several tables contain such a foreign key reference to the common comment table, the entry form must allow association and update of this foreign key column behind the scenes. So, each module that includes this comment entry pop-up needs some custom code to update the appropriate foreign key column. All other operations of the comment form are identical and are independent of the referring table.

Reusable module components are useful if used judiciously. They may provide a useful means of capturing code that otherwise might be manually maintained outside the repository. The original implementation of our example comment entry pop-up (in Forms 3.0 and Oracle CASE 5.0) was developed and maintained outside the repository. The features available in recent versions of Oracle Designer make it possible to manage more such utilities within the repository.

9.4.5 Linking Modules

So far our discussion has covered the ability to generate individual modules. Your application, however, is made up of several modules. We need some way of launching modules and often a means of navigating from within one module to other related modules. For example, we may need to navigate from the customer entry module to the maintenance module for market segments to create a new segment. We also need menus—for example, a menu for access by telesales staff that is different from the menu for access by accounting staff. Other kinds of links include navigation buttons from one module to invoke another module. A list of values button to invoke

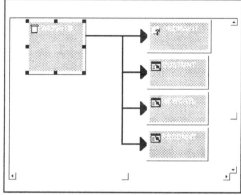

Figure 9-11: Menu Module Network

a module that provides the ability to select and return a value for an item is a special case of a navigation button. Each of these module links is defined in a different way.

A menu module defines a hierarchy of other modules. Figure 9-11 illustrates a menu hierarchy. These modules may represent additional menus or items that invoke a module. You may attach such a custom menu module to each Forms module. Menus appear as drop-down items at the top of a Forms window. Each form may attach a separate menu. In addition, you may include custom code to enable or disable menu items based on the form context or business rules.

An application system will typically need a few custom menu modules that provide navigation based on a user's functional roles. For example, you may define a menu that allows navigation to customer entry and market segment maintenance modules that are attached to order entry and query modules. Another menu may allow navigation to accounts payable and accounts receivable modules that may be attached to all billing modules. You may generate menu modules separately or as part of generating a Forms module with its attached menu.

You may enforce security in a module by associating modules with repository definitions for database roles or users. Figure 9-12 illustrates the module properties for defining security.

Occasionally, a module may provide convenient access to other modules by implementing navigation buttons to them. Figure 9-13 illustrates a navigation item definition that is represented as a module network link. You may also custom code navigation by creating an action item with application logic that invokes another

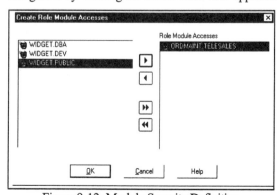

module. Such navigation would be difficult to track, however, as it is buried in custom code.

A launch pad is a module containing navigation buttons that invoke other modules. These navigation buttons may be part of a control block—that is, a block made up of just unbound navigation items.

Figure 9-12: Module Security Definition

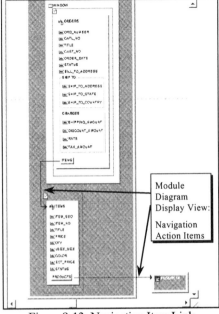

Figure 9-13: Navigation Item Link

Navigation items are shown in the module diagram as a link to the called module. Each navigation item may have an image associated with it that represents the icon for the module and/or a text label. You may enforce security in a launch pad module using the custom code facilities and your own security structures.

I recommend that you minimize the use of module-specific navigation item as they may lead to a spaghetti of module links. Remember that you may not remove a module definition until all links to it are removed. So, to replace one module with another, you would need to find and modify all links to the obsolete module—a tedious task. You would also need to regenerate each modified module with consequent testing and production release tasks.

When invoking a module, you may wish to pass certain item values to it to pre-query related data. For example, if you navigate to a market segment maintenance module from a customer entry module, you may wish to display the current customer's market segment on startup. You may define such parameters in the module definition from Oracle Designer Release 2.1 and later. Earlier releases allowed only report modules to have parameter definitions. Note that it is up to you to ensure that the appropriate data items are available in the module definition for passing, whether they are displayed or not. Figure 9-14 illustrates the parameter definition property sheet. List of values parameter passing is automatically generated for modules defined to be LOV format.

9.4.6 Third-party Utilities

There are a number of third-party products that improve the facilities available with Oracle Designer. Some provide pre-defined sets for presentation styles, others provide custom utilities that you may incorporate within your generated code. Some examples include:

- Display of a pop-up calendar for selecting a date on any data usage defined with the format of date.

Application Owner	WIDGETS
Module / PL/SQL Definition	ORDENT
Name	p_cust_id
Input Output	Input
Position	10
- Defined By	
Domain	
Datastructure	
Column	CUST_NO
Table Definition	
Oracle Type	
- Definition	
Datatype	
Length	
Decimal Places	
Default	
Optional ?	Yes
- Display	
Display ?	Yes
Prompt	
Dynamic List ?	No
Suggestion List ?	No
Input Mask	
- Menu Generation	
Substitution String	

Figure 9-14: Module Parameter Definition

- Utilities that compose a control block containing just queryable items on any form that permits query. This block is displayed when the user presses a button to enter query criteria.

- Utilities that provide list of values facilities during a query.

Examples of such packaged utilities are DesignAssist, Headstart, and Guidelines/2000. These packages can speed up your project development if you have expert assistance available. Effective use of these tools requires that you maintain at least one expert with in-depth understanding of the internal structure of the tool.

Other third-party software may provide documentation tools. One notable software, Solutron's Publisher, allows you to produce design and specification documents from the Designer repository. It uses rulesets that may encode your project standards for documentation. Documentation may be published in a word processor format or published on the web using their Publisher server tools. I find these reports a significant improvement over the standard repository reports available with Designer. To establish project standards and verify compliance to these documentation standards, I would definitely recommend the use of such tools.

9.5 Building a Common User Interface

When choosing your interface, or designing your runtime environment, you must consider the common elements that your application user is familiar with. Some considerations include:

- Current interface for performing the functions provided by the application. For example, is your application replacing an existing one? Is the current interface character-based or GUI?

- Other applications on the user's desktop. For example, if the accounting clerk uses a package that provides a Forms based interface, the user is familiar with this user interface. If, however, this package provides a browser-based interface, you would be adding yet another user interface style to the user's desktop by implementing your application in Forms.

- Hardware configuration changes necessary when implementing the application. For example, if the typical configuration would need a $1,000 upgrade and your application has 1000 users, you would spend $1,000,000 on hardware upgrades alone. This amount does not include the cost of support staff to perform the upgrades.

- Skills necessary to maintain the application once it is in production. If portions of the application are deployed using a browser-based interface, and the rest uses a client-server implementation, you have to manage and administer both environments. You may need to coordinate releases of application enhancements and bug corrections between both environments.

- Potential duplication of development effort between two environments. If some functionality needs to be implemented in the browser based and client-server implementation, you may duplicate development effort.

- If you choose a single tool for portions of the application that run in the web and the client-server environments, you may have to develop using the common denominator of facilities available in the two environments. In the web environment, network traffic is an even more serious consideration if the application is likely to run over the Internet.

Before you select your development tool, consider these issues. One option is to use tools that adapt to both a browser-based environment as well as client-server environments. For example, you may choose to run Oracle Forms in a browser-based as well as client-server environment. This may be a good choice if all of your users can be trained to use Forms. Chapter 15 addresses the pros and cons of these choices in more detail.

You may have to constrain some features if you intend to run Forms in both browser-based and client-server environments. For example, in the web environment, Forms triggers for mouse movement events are not supported. So, any custom code for these triggers will simply be ignored. Be aware also of item-level validation or other trigger actions. These generate a significant amount of traffic in the web environment.

A significant consideration should be the deployment environment. There is a high resource cost associated with running Forms programs in a web environment. Tools like Forms were engineered to work in a client-server environment. Their web version may consume almost as many resources as each client—but all on the Forms server machine instead. Developer Server creates one executable for each connected user. Even with reengineered runtime, supporting many hundreds of users may require big iron server machines. So, consider the tradeoff of centralized administration vs. the cost of centralized server machines. The consideration is only significant if you expect to serve large numbers of application users.

9.6 The Upgrade Issue

Development tools change significantly over time. Consider the radical changes between the terminal-based operation of Forms version 3 and the GUI interface of Oracle Forms today. The rate of such changes means a constant learning process is essential. The cost of training and re-training staff with each new release is expensive.

Many companies avoid the retraining costs for staff as tools change. Their systems continue to use older versions of tools. I know many clients who continue to use their character mode Forms 3 applications rather than convert them to the GUI version simply because of the retraining cost for staff who would continue to maintain them. Another reason for not converting applications is the cost of conversion and re-testing. Although each version of the tool provides conversion facilities from the previous version, this conversion rarely takes advantage of the new facilities. Staff must be retrained so that they can enhance the converted application to use any new features.

The downside of this procrastination includes potential high staff turnover as developers move to jobs where they can upgrade their skills. Another downside is termination of support by the tool vendor—which they must do to conserve their support resources. Most tools are dependent on other underlying products. Eventually, the underlying products also withdraw support, forcing you to rebuild the application.

One side effect of using a tool like Designer for developing applications is the ability to use its facilities to ease the upgrade process. One way is to use its generators to learn the best way to use the new features of each release. You may build small, new applications in order to facilitate the learning process. Then, you may apply the knowledge to existing applications for conversion as well as enhancement.

Another way may be to use the generators to build entire applications so that their definition is held in the repository. You may then use these definitions to rebuild your application in a new release of the tool or use them as a head start to rebuilding using a different tool. Of course, it takes a little more work than just pressing a few buttons to generate each program. However, the reduction in time for learning the new tools may make this effort worthwhile.

9.7 Development Management Issues

In a wave of feature-itis, many GUI development environments have ignored the issues of managing the development environment. Some of the development facilities you need include debugging environments, source code management facilities, and change management facilities. Forms provides you with some debugging facilities as well as integration with third-party tools for source code management.

Forms can be slow if you write long, complex triggers. Triggers are normally executed as soon as possible. Thus, complex triggers on fields will slow the movement of the cursor between fields. If possible, avoid such triggers. Alter your design and user expectations so that you can test complex conditions at the end of a block rather than after every field.

Forms definitions may live in the Forms tables in the database, as well as in the *.fmb* and *.fmx* files. If you practice source code control using the *.fmt* (documentation) files, be sure to load the form definition from these every time. Keeping the form definition in the database tables is tempting because you can then use reporting tools to print it. However, then you will find it difficult to track who made what changes to a form. There are some source code control facilities provided with Oracle Developer. Alternatively, you may choose a third-party tool like InterSolv's PVCS. In my experience, source control using the *.fmb* files is the most reliable.

Change management of Designer repository definitions is a future facility. However, there are tools available from other organizations like Oracle consulting, notably ECHO/2000, which provide many useful utilities. However, there are restrictions on purchasing and using these utilities which you should explore prior to choosing them.

Although it is tempting to put a lot of code in the template files, keep these for strictly reusable pieces of code. You will have to maintain these manually. Oracle Designer is not yet equipped to manage the code held in template files. All other code can be attached to the trigger points of a module within the repository. Remember that it is easy to cut and paste such code between modules. Alternatively, try to design reusable module components through the generators. This is where you may see the biggest bang for your buck.

Widgets Case Study: Orders Form

As we were designing the orders form, we realized that it contained a large number of data items. So, we decided to use the tabbed display feature of Forms. Note the restriction that all tabs must be within a single module component, that is, data elements from one base table usage and its lookup table usages. The data view and display view of this definition is shown on the diagrams later.

This feature worked well for displaying the data for the Orders form, but the users did not like it for entering and viewing items in the order. The problem was that it did not allow us to view everything about an item at once. Given this requriement, we decided that spread table display was also inappropriate—the number of data elements to be displayed was too large. The final choice was creating a "single" area in combination with a multi-row display of items. In the module component properties in the Design Editor, we set the *overflow area* property to "*Right*", to achieve this effect.

We also added an unbound item to display the order total. This item was based on a client-side function, because we need to calculate the total with the order items currently on the screen. Rather than including pages of module documentation, we have included a single page excerpt from the module definition. This report is one of the standard repository reports provided together with Oracle Designer.

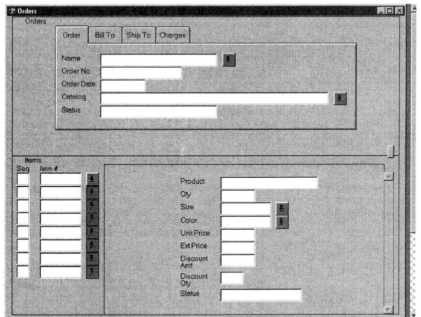

Order Form Layout Illustration

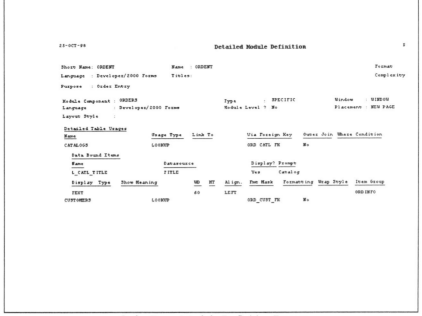

Order Form Module Definition Report

Report Programs

The major part of applications, after interactive screen programs, is reporting. In fact, we generally retrieve data more often than enter it. When developing applications for users who are accustomed to another, older system, you have to take into account that they are likely to demand printed reports for everything. You may have to put a screen on each of their desks to make their typical queries much simpler via interactive forms. But, getting them used to querying on the screen takes time—you are changing their culture! Your best bet is to identify the purposes for which they currently use printed reports and then make sure you supply all of that data on the screen. In the meantime, you still have to develop tedious reports, many of which are rather simplistic. Listings of all clients sorted by name, or grouped by some column, are not exactly stimulating. This is where a good generator for reports proves its mettle.

Rather than reiterate the product manuals, this chapter will describe how to develop the types of reports we discussed in the design phase. You will have to extrapolate from the examples to suit your particular reporting requirements. This chapter is not a tutorial in how to drive a product keystroke by keystroke. In this chapter, we cover the following topics:

- An overview of the tools available for generating reports from an Oracle database. We will examine the types of reports each tool is best suited for.

- Report formatting techniques for SQL*Plus and Oracle Reports. Annotated example code for each of these products illustrates the concepts.

- Generating reports using Oracle Designer generators. We will examine how a Forms module could be turned into a reports as well as the kinds of changes we need to make to its definition.

- Customizing generated reports. We will discuss how generator conventions help.

10.1 Report Development Tools

A report is really just data from the database formatted to look pretty. The SQL language allows us to retrieve data. It is the query language standard with Oracle DBMS. However, standard SQL has few formatting facilities. We cannot, for example, specify page headers. Oracle's implementation adds report formatting facilities to SQL; hence its name, SQL*Plus. SQL*Plus includes page formatting, limited control break processing, and column formatting facilities. With these facilities, you can make even quick and dirty reports look good.

SQL*Plus is particularly suited to writing tabular reports, which we discussed in the design phase. Such reports are a large proportion of typical data processing reports. Typically, you are limited to a single SQL statement per report. Some of these statements become quite complex, especially when you join tables and use subqueries. So, you are not limited to data from a single table in a SQL*Plus report. In fact, with certain types of data, you can also produce a matrix report, though such reports stretch the abilities of the formatting facilities of SQL*Plus.

The SQL *select* statement is the primary means of retrieving data from an Oracle database. We used some of the simpler statements in an earlier chapter for developing forms. In this chapter, we use more complex facilities of SQL, including table joins,

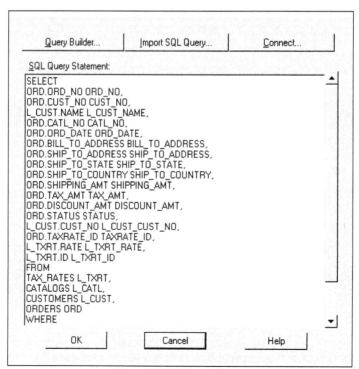

Figure 10-1: Master Query

the *union* operator, *decode* function, dummy columns, and so on. Many of these functions are standard and are extensively covered by textbooks on SQL such as those listed in the bibliography. I annotate the examples in this chapter extensively to clarify the clauses of each SQL statement.

The Oracle Reports product implements a GUI interface. Reports implements a visual interface to defining reports. It is still a utility for developers—I think it is too complicated for end users. It is based on Oracle's new style of utilities with wizards and windows. The primary command menu allows you access to matrices of details for each aspect of a report, such as group control breaks, field formatting, summary definitions, trim text, and so on. Making effective use of these facilities requires you to change your perspective on what a report is made up of. The key concepts you need are the following:

- A report is made up of pages, starting with a title page, then report pages, and ending with a report trailer page. Title and trailer pages are very useful for you to identify who the report is for and whether the report ended successfully.

- Each report page may consist of one or more panels if your report is wider than a physical page. For example, you can print a report which is as wide as two pieces of paper pasted together side by side—each piece of paper

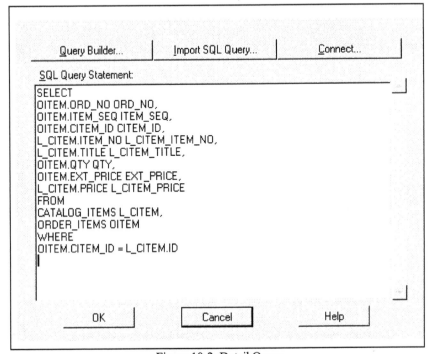

```
Query Builder...        Import SQL Query...        Connect...

SQL Query Statement:

SELECT
OITEM.ORD_NO ORD_NO,
OITEM.ITEM_SEQ ITEM_SEQ,
OITEM.CITEM_ID CITEM_ID,
L_CITEM.ITEM_NO L_CITEM_ITEM_NO,
L_CITEM.TITLE L_CITEM_TITLE,
OITEM.QTY QTY,
OITEM.EXT_PRICE EXT_PRICE,
L_CITEM.PRICE L_CITEM_PRICE
FROM
CATALOG_ITEMS L_CITEM,
ORDER_ITEMS OITEM
WHERE
OITEM.CITEM_ID = L_CITEM.ID

        OK              Cancel              Help
```

Figure 10-2: Detail Query

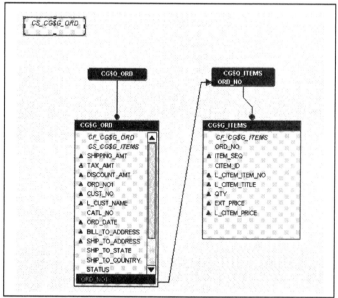

Figure 10-3: Master Detail Data Model in Reports

corresponds to a panel.

- Each report has one or more queries to extract data from the database. Query definition is one of the options on the navigator tree. Each query is a SQL statement. You can connect queries into master detail relationships or into a matrix report. You will need expertise in constructing SQL statements, one potential reason for keeping your end users away from this tool. Figures 10-1 and 10-2 illustrate the two queries necessary for our invoice form report. The customer and order data is linked as the parent and the order items and product data is the child. Figure 10-3 illustrates the data model used by Oracle Reports to represent such a master detail relationship.

- You can define a control break on one or more columns selected in your query. Control breaks are useful for calculating totals, summaries, and so on. For example, in our invoice form report, we need an order total based on *item_price*. So, we define a sum function on this field in the summary option as shown in Figure 10-4.

- Each report has a header, a footer, and a body frame. You can define these to contain custom text such as report name, date of printing, page number, and so on. The body of the report consists of each group and its detail lines.

- Each group also has a header, a footer, and a body frame. Use this header to print summary data before detail lines, or use the footer to print summaries

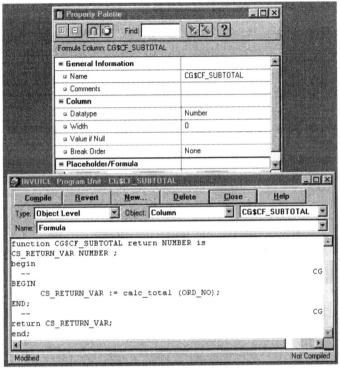

Figure 10-4: Summary Calculation

at the end. For example, print the count of customers in a state using a group header before a detail name list.

- The body frame of the report is the detail data—each row that you extract in the query. This body differs by the type of report you want. For a tabular report, it consists of columns corresponding to those extracted from the database. For an embedded data report, you can write your own wording to make up a form letter with customer names inserted at the appropriate places. In our invoice report example, we intend to use preprinted forms and hence there are no headings in this part of the report definition. In Section 10.7 Embedded Data Reports we illustrate a form letter example.

Reports presents each of these components to you as a hierarchical tree. For example, it presents a list of fields as shown in Figure 10-5. The properties on the right are the different formatting options available to you. Unfortunately, you cannot see the effect of each change, unless you preview the report after each one. I highly recommend frequent preview of your report—to make sure your changes have the desired effect. Remember that you can execute the current report definition at any time. You need not leave any definition screen.

From this description, it should be obvious that you cannot simply sit down with Reports and start developing a report. You need some idea of the layout of your

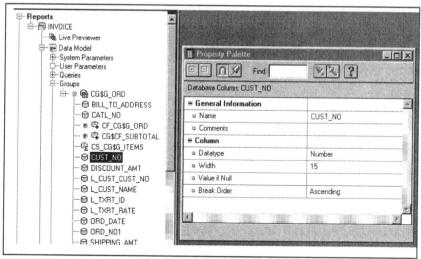

Figure 10-5: Navigator and Field Properties

report before you start. Identify the style of your report: tabular, matrix, preprinted form, or embedded data—the styles we discussed in our earlier chapters on design.

There are several third-party tools for report writing, in addition to the Oracles tools. Typically, these tools work with Oracle as well as other well-known database management systems. They may use the de-facto standard ODBC as the means of connecting to Oracle, a rather slow interface. Many third-party tools offer an interface appropriate to an end user. To present this interface, you will need to populate their data dictionary with business terms for the table and columns names. In addition, you may need to define the foreign key relationships between tables in their dictionary so that they can deduce ways to join tables selected by a user during a query. This may appear to be a lot of work, but it provides a more intuitive interface for end users than accessing cryptically named tables and columns.

10.2 Performance Considerations

The main consideration for making your report run faster is the wording of your SQL statement with respect to the table indexes. From our overview of the tools in Section 10.1, it should be obvious that you cannot get away from SQL in any of the tools, except perhaps ESQR. So, project managers should establish some procedures for reviewing the SQL statements used in each of the performance-critical programs. Although performance is typically less critical in reports, make sure they can complete in the time period for overnight runs. Poorly written reports become resource hogs—slowing down other processing on the same machine. This section provides some tips to keep in mind when writing SQL statements. You can provide *hints* to the optimizer based on these concepts.

- Make sure there is an index on each column used in a join. The index may include other columns from the table, provided that the join column is the first in index sequence.

- At least one of the join columns should have a unique index. This rule is natural if you join along a relationship in the entity-relationship diagram. One of the columns in the join should be a unique identifier (primary key) for its table.

- Explore the use of hash and bitmap indexes. Used appropriately, these indexes can make a dramatic improvement in performance. Typically, though, they are useful only for exact match searches. Bitmap indexes also improve the performance of joins.

- Try the *Explain* facility to determine the order in which it will execute statement clauses. The query optimizer has very definite rules for ordering execution based on table sizes and available indexes. Running *Analyze* to determine table sizes and providing hints to the optimizer may significantly improve execution times.

- Keep the use of *system.dual* to a minimum. Remember that each reference to this table is a database access. In a distributed processing environment, such an access can slow response significantly, unless a local *system.dual* table is available.

- Reduce the use of subqueries in SQL—try joins whenever possible. Oracle's SQL optimizer is tuned for joins, especially when adequate indexes exist. Try your own experiments to see how much of a speed difference there is between subqueries and joins when the tables contain several thousand rows.

- Avoid single table accesses with programmatic joins, unless you have small tables and use memory array facilities, such as SQR provides. The SQL optimizer typically works much faster than any other programming tricks.

The following example illustrates the side effects of poorly written queries. One of my consulting clients was convinced that accessing flat files from a program was much faster than using Oracle. So adamant were they that they were prepared to write off their $250,000 investment in Oracle software. Close examination revealed pages and pages of code scanning Oracle tables one record at a time. They were using the tables as flat files! The programmer was merely substituting SQL statements for record reads and performing all matches in the program. A slight rewrite of the code, to use SQL facilities, not only reduced the code to about one page, but ran quite a bit faster than the C program that worked against the same data in flat files. Such mishaps are common among programmers who have little prior experience with set-oriented query languages and even less training.

10.3 Report Generator

Oracle Designer provides a report generator tool which capitalizes on the detailed data definitions you have already gathered. This generator also uses a module as the basic generatable unit. We introduced modules and module components in Chapter 9 in the context of the Forms generator.

A module in the report generator is a single report. It may be as simple as a *Customer listing* which references a single table, or as complex as a matrix report analyzing *Sales by State*. A report module may contain one or more module components. Each module components consists of a single base table and its lookup tables. We use the same module diagrammer as used for Forms modules. The concepts of customizing with templates, libraries, and application logic are the same when defining report modules. So, we can leverage our knowledge from Forms to Reports. In fact, this is one the main strengths of using the Designer toolset.

The catch is that many of the properties you may see on the property sheets in the Design Editor may not apply to reports modules elements. As a general rule, reports modules are much simpler than Forms modules. They also, in practice, require more customization. This generator provides less control over placement of data elements in the report — which is, unfortunately, a common requirement in most reports.

The report generator supports several commonly used formats of reports: tabular, form style, matrix, labels and embedded data reports. We examine each of these styles with examples of generated reports.

10.4 Tabular Reports

Let us consider a simple report: a list of customers by state. This report involves only the customer table. We would like to start a new page for each new state, and the state name should be printed once at the top of the page. Figure 10-6 shows an annotated SQL*Plus script to produce this report. This type of report is really a remnant of the days of batch systems, where we primarily worked from paper reports. It might be useful for dividing customer calls between many sales staff. But, with an online lookup, such as is possible with a Oracle Forms program, we probably do not need this report.

SQL*Plus is a good tool for developing such simple reports. Its reporting capabilities are ideal for making a quick and dirty report look sufficiently pretty to satisfy most users. However, it is not flexible enough if you try to make the report format exactly as you wanted. It only provides limited formatting capabilities. Note that these annotations should really be comments in the script.

We could use such simple tabular reports for more complex business functions. For example, consider a report showing sales by product, useful for finding our biggest sellers. We can find sales information in the order items table. So, we use the following select statement:

> select product_number, sum(item_price)
> from order_items group by product_number
> order by product_number

The *sum* function allows us to total item values. The *group by* clause ensures that the totals will be for each product number. Obviously, a product name would be more useful to the recipient of this report than product numbers. So we need to use the

REMARK Report To Print Customers by State	
REMARK Application: Sales	
REMARK Author:— Ulka Rodgers	
REMARK Date Created: January 4, 1990	Company Standard Header
REMARK Revision History:	
REMARK Date:——— Revised by:	
set space 3	Space between printed columns
set pagesize 66	
set sqlprompt "	Turn "SQL>" prompt off
set feedback off	Turn "nn records found" message off
set numwidth 5	Default width of numeric columns
set termout off	Don't display output to screen
spool cust	Write output to file "cust.lst"
column customer_number format B999999 -	*6 digits, leading blanks*
— head 'Customer\Number' -	Print "Number" below "Customer"
— justify right	Align values on right edge of column
column name head 'Customer\Name' format a15	
column city head 'City' format a15	Save value of "state" column when
column state new_val st -	it changes in variable "st"
— noprint	Don't print "state" in the select
break on state skip page	Start new page when value of "state"
changes	
*ttitle left '[SQL*Plus]' -*	Page title: left - tool
— center 'Widgets, Inc' -	Center - company
— right 'Page: ' SQL.PNO skip 1 -	Right - page number with variable
SQL.PNO and start a new line	
* center 'Customer Report by State' -*	Title line 2: center - report name
* skip 3 -*	Leave 3 blank lines
— left 'State: ' st skip 3	Title Line 5: Left - Latest value of
"state" from variable "st"	
select customer_number, name, city, state	Retrieve these columns from
from customers order by state, name	customers table and sort
/	Execute statement
spool off	Done writing output to "cust.lst"

Figure 10-6: SQL*Plus Simple Tabular Report

product numbers in the order items table to find their corresponding product names from the product table. The SQL join operation is intended for associating the order items table to the product table. (This, at last, is the practical use of the relationships we drew in entity-relationship diagrams!) The final annotated report is shown in Figure 10-7.

There is no limit on the number of tables you can join in a single SQL statement. However, how fast it executes depends on the wording of the statement. Remember the earlier hints on optimizing statements.

So, writing reports in SQL*Plus is not difficult, if you know the structure of the database. I would hesitate, however, to offer this utility to a non-technical user for ad-hoc reporting, at least without extensive training. There are other reasons for this hesitation. For example, the user may not remember the exact spelling for column and table names. I imagine this is not an uncommon failing. Digging around for dictionary printouts causes a severe decline in my productivity. And, using the *describe table* statement interactively is frustrating because I need to switch back and forth between the editor and interactive SQL*Plus.

10.5 Form Reports

Form reports typically use preprinted forms which come in any number of flavors from checks or customer invoices to year-end payroll tax forms. The tricky part with these reports is the need to align your printing exactly to spaces provided in the preprinted form. Misalignment of the check amount leaves you open to potential fraud. On a less severe case, you lose credibility with your customers when they cannot read your misaligned invoices.

Unfortunately, few DBMS tools provide you with the necessary tools to try alignments repeatedly until you get it right. Instead, you must depend on the print spooling facilities of your operating system. On multi-user systems with remote or shared printers this scheme makes sense. On single-user machines, there is no such spooling facility.

An alternative trick is to create a table that contains a small number of dummy rows, say five or six. The format of this table should match the data for your preprinted form. You could then print these dummy rows repeatedly until your form alignment on the printer is satisfactory. Then, print the report with real data perfectly aligned. In each test print you would only waste a few pages of preprinted forms. If your preprinted forms have a consistent layout, you could use the same alignment test for several different forms.

SQL*Plus has very limited facilities to change the layout of reports. For example, you cannot specify that you would like the customer name printed starting in column 15, except perhaps by concatenating the customer name to a literal of 15 spaces. However, such machinations remove the quick report development benefits of

```
REMARK   Report To Print Sales by Product
REMARK   Application: Sales
REMARK   Author:— Ulka Rodgers
REMARK   Date Created: January 4, 1996
REMARK   Revision History:
REMARK   Date:——— Revised by:
REMARK   Description:
REMARK   Tables: customer
set space 3
set pagesize 66
set sqlprompt "
set feedback off
set numwidth 5
set termout off
spool salesum
column product_number format 0999999 -  6 digits, leading zeros
— head 'Product\Number' justify right
column name head 'Product\Name' format a15
column sales head 'Sales' -              -- Alias for sum(item_price) column
                                         -- assigned in the select statement
— format $99,999,999.99                  -- Leading Dollar Sign, comma separated
                                         -- value up to 99 million
break on report skip 2                   -- At the end of report print 2 blank lines
compute sum of sales on report           -- Grand total of sales at the end of report
ttitle left '[SQL*Plus]' center 'Widgets, Inc' -
right 'Page: ' SQL.PNO skip 1 -
center 'Sales by Product' skip 3
select order_items.product_number,   -- Explicitly state the table for ambiguous columns
   products.product_name,            -- Table name here is good practice
   sum(order_items.item_price) sales -- Total over item_price, call this column
                                     -- "sales" for this statement
from   order_items, products         -- Tables to use in select
where  order_items.product_number = products.product_number
group by order_items.product_number, products.product_name
order by product_name                --      To get totals for each product
/
REMARK Join based on common column - product_number:only take
REMARK rows with matching product numbers
spool off                            --      Done writing output to "salesum.lst"
```

Figure 10-7: SQL*Plus Complex Tabular Report

SQL*Plus. Instead, you need to use a real procedural report generator, like SQR, or in desperation, even the antiquated RPT.

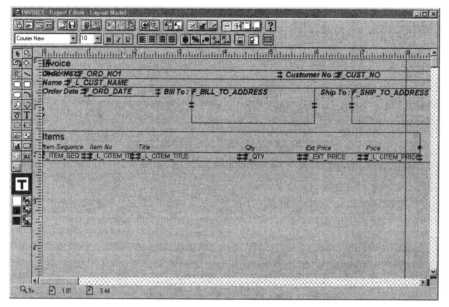

Figure 10-8: Invoice Report Layout

Building form reports in Oracle Reports is not very intuitive. It is more suited to reports where you can make up the layout to fit a mold. Layouts dictated by an outside force such as a preprinted form means you do more up-front work to translate into Reports' development style. Initially you may use wizards to guide your definition, then add to it. Alternatively, use Oracle Designer's generators to give you a headstart in defining your report.

Figure 10-8 illustrates the Reports screen where you edit the layout of the report fields. Notice the ruler displays for easily locating a field position. You will have to measure your layout alignment requirements and test the printout several times.

Remember to use this part after you have verified that the report content is correct. Changing the report content later, that is, the calculations and columns in the report, means that you will have to redo some of the layouts. Figures 10-1 through 10-3 illustrated the queries and total definitions for this same report.

10.6 Matrix Reports

These reports look like a spreadsheet printout. They are very common in financial and management reporting. In our example Widgets sales system, we need a report of customer buying patterns by state. Rather than analyzing the patterns for individual customers, we use products. Thus, the report consists of product as columns across the top, states as rows, and each cell in the matrix shows the number of items sold in this category. The output format for this report is shown in the chapter on application design.

This report could be developed in SQL*Plus, if you hard-code the product category values into the SQL statement as shown below. Notice the use of the *decode* function—one of Oracle's extended facilities. This function matches its first argument (*product_category*) to its second argument (literal value of category). If these two values match, it returns the third argument: if they don't match, it returns the fourth argument. You can repeat the second and third argument pairs with different values, which was not necessary in this example. It would be necessary if our report showed the combined sales for, say, appliances and tools.

```
select state,
    sum(decode (product_category, 1, product_qty, 0)) 'Appliance',
    sum(decode (product_category, 2, product_qty, 0)) 'Clothing',
    sum(decode (product_category, 3, product_qty, 0)) 'Tools'
from order_items oi, orders o, customer c, products p
where oi.order_number— = o.order_number
and  o.order_for_customer = c.customer_number
and  oi.product_number  = p.product_number
group by state, product_category
order by state
```

Imagine if we had to write this report for several dozen categories in SQL*Plus—the result would be an ugly SQL statement. Its performance would be dreadful as it churned its way through megabytes of sales data. Using Oracle Reports or a third-party software like SQR is a good alternative.

In Oracle Reports, we need to write three queries for such a report: one for listing

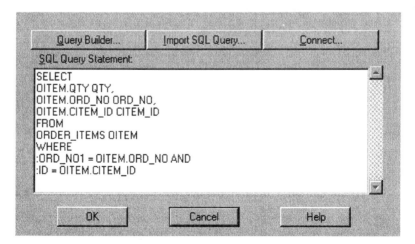

Figure 10-9: Cell Query Window

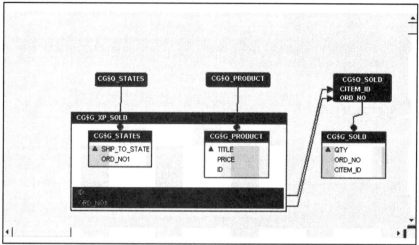

Figure 10-10: Matrix Report Model

states as rows from the states table, one for listing product categories across the page as columns, and one to calculate the value of each cell. Figure 10-9 shows the most complex of these three queries, the cell calculation query. This query is then linked as a child to the other two queries as shown in the report data model.

The data model illustrated in Figure 10-10 shows the cell as the child with two parents. By the way, don't forget to remove the field labels in the module table and column usage properties. Otherwise, your report layout will look like spaghetti. In addition, we would like totals for each category and each state. We use an unbound item for this purpose in the module definition—like in our invoice example. Figure 10-11 illustrates the SQL definition for these totals.

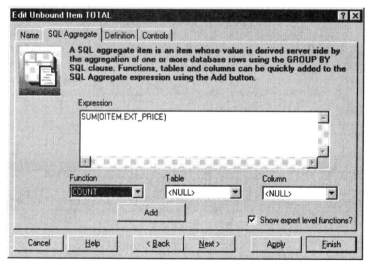

Figure 10-11: Unbound Item for Summary Calculation

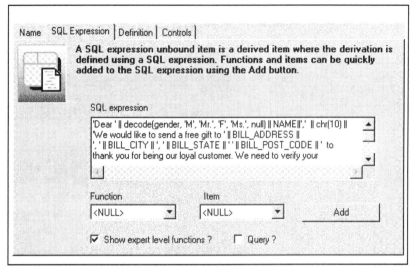

Figure 10-12: Text with Embedded Data

10.7 Embedded Data Reports

These reports have a lot of trim text, also called boilerplate text, with some data embedded into the text. A classic example of such a report is a letter for bulk mailing. Embedding data into such a letter is a similar concept to mail-merge in most word processing programs. Word processors, however, rarely interface with your database to include data.

Figure 10-12 illustrates the text layout screen in Oracle Reports for a form letter. In this example, there are no calculated fields embedded in the text. In Designer, however, we used unbound items to compose the text of the letter, and another unbound item for displaying the address. Using the facilities for defining SQL expressions, we could embed literal text interspersed with data from the database. We could easily have included calculations embedded in the literal text also. For example, we could generate letters to employees showing their performance bonuses, payroll deductions and known tax status. We could also request corrections.

For reports such as this, you could also use the ESQR or SQR products. They support a document procedure for defining boilerplate text and assigning locations for database variables. Then, your *print* statements use these locations rather than line and column positions for each database column. You can even embed printer control strings for font changes and so on.

The difficulty with using report generators in this type of report is the quality of the output. Report generators today have limited publishing features such as font selection, embedding graphics into text, and so on. As I remarked in the earlier design chapter, letters which are obviously computer printed are passe in today's age of desktop publishing. However, there are fancy fonts available these days which mimic handwriting. These together with scanned images of signatures and high quality printing can fool many discerning folks into reading their junk mail.

These features become particularly important when you need to graph the data in your database and print it as part of your bulk mailing report. For example, you might want a graph showing the performance of a mutual fund over several years as part of a prospectus sent to customers. Your data warehouse contains the necessary long term performance data. You have to combine the charting abilities of Oracle Graphics with Reports to obtain your publishing quality report.

If you choose to use your data warehouse as the source of data, make sure it is sufficiently up to date. When charting performance trends, the data can be several days old without significantly affecting the result (except when the stock markets suffer serious drops within a few days as happened in 1998). Individual correspondence data needs to be more up to date.

Outdated data occasionally leads to amusing mistakes. For example, one of my past employers sent me enrollment forms for converting to a new pension investment plan when the company decided to change its pension plans. They delivered these forms to me via overnight courier delivery at considerable expense. The funny part was that this happened three or four months after I had left. They had extracted my name from their database just before my last day to prepare a very nice personalized package. It had taken them nearly three months to produce the high-quality personalized package for mailing to an ex-employee!

10.8 Development Management Issues

Obviously, report generators do not come with built-in debugging facilities. Instead, you have to use the old-fashioned method of putting in *print* statements to find out what's happening. Debugging nonprocedural interfaces such as Oracle Reports are even more difficult. A change in one part of the definition can have unforeseen effects on other parts.

The solution is to test the output after each definition, at least until you gain familiarity with the way these products work. Test the output in Reports after you define the queries, after defining groups, after each field, and so on.

This scenario works well when you have a stable set of table definitions. If your table definitions change frequently, as I noticed in environments where little prior analysis and design was done, you will have to recreate table definitions each time they change for each developer. The alternative method of using a single Oracle user name and password for all developers is almost as bad. You only have one set of table definitions to manage. But, each person must share test data with all others. How can you set up and test extreme case handling and incorrect data handling when your data is constantly blown away by someone else testing their update/delete programs?

Source code management is even more difficult with this fourth-generation development utility. There is no source to manage! Rather, you have some data stored in database tables where you cannot track what was changed, when, and by whom. You could control the generated runtime report definitions. These definitions are in binary format, so make sure your source management package can manage binary files as well. With SQR, you still have traditional source code in a file, and it is therefore easy to incorporate into a source code management system.

Maintenance strategy on reports developed with fourth-generation utilities is rather simple—avoid it! It is usually faster to develop a report from scratch than to attempt to understand what another programmer did. Remember that there is no printed report definition (unless you consider report documentation output to be a report definition). Report definitions are completely nonprocedural with Oracle Reports. If you re-develop a report, remember that you will need to repeat all of the testing done on the original report. This last requirement makes a good case for you to develop automated regression testing for each report. The regression testing package should load data into tables which will cause each of the test cases to occur. Automating the execution of a report is relatively easy in most operating systems.

Interfaces for Server-side Code

In this chapter, we will discuss two ways of writing programs for batch mode processing of data: using PL/SQL and using Oracle's PRO* interfaces. We will use C as the example language; however, similar principles apply whether you use COBOL, Fortran, or any such language. PL/SQL is Oracle's proprietary procedural language. It is a higher-level language than C—incorporating SQL statements together with looping and other structured programming statements.

The third-generation languages supported for interface to Oracle differ based on your hardware and operating system. Pro*C is always available. Avoid using third-generation language interfaces if you can help it! Why? Because the resulting programs are even more difficult to debug and maintain than a fourth-generation program. There are some advantages to using a third-generation language. Programs requiring a large volume of external data or calculations may run faster if written in a third-generation language. Data stored in Oracle is probably processed faster with PL/SQL if you use array processing. Utilities like Oracle Forms, SQL*Plus, and SQL*Loader can also take advantage of array processing facilities.

This chapter covers the following topics:

- PL/SQL facilities for procedural programming and when they are useful. You can use PL/SQL for procedural programming, coding database objects like stored procedures, as well as writing user exits in Oracle Forms.

- Oracle programmatic interfaces including the precompiler interface and function call-based Oracle call interface (OCI).

- Dynamically constructing SQL calls to access the database. This facility allows you to access the database when columns, tables, or retrieval conditions are not known in advance.

11.1 Database Objects

A DBMS manages much more than just data storage. It also enforces integrity constraints—whether declarative or procedural, and procedures to manipulate the data. We need to make the best use of these objects for optimizing the performance in our client-server environments.

In a client-server environment, *where* we process the data can have a significant impact on the performance. If we process the data on the database server and only transport the results, we control the amount of traffic on the network. If we process the data on the client always, we would need to transport much more data across the network. Remember that access across a network is much slower than that to disks local to a machine.

Some of these database objects are declarative, that is, specified as part of the database definition. For example, constraints for defining primary and foreign keys are declarative SQL data definition language statements. Enforcement of more complex constraints, such as business rules, requires procedural programs. We may associate these constraints with database tables as triggers. In Oracle, we commonly use the PL/SQL language to write these programs. Oracle8 and later versions also offer the ability to run external programs coded in languages such as C++.

11.2 Integrity Constraints

There are several kinds of declarative integrity constraints: primary key, unique key, foreign key, and check constraints. In Chapter 7, we discussed primary, unique, and foreign key constraints and how to derive them from an entity-relationship model. The Oracle Designer database design transformer creates definitions for these constraints as part of the model to the schema transformation process. Check constraints allow you to specify simple checks with an algorithm involving one or more columns from the same row in the table. For example, you may check that a column value falls within a range specified by two other columns. Figure 11-1 illustrates a check constraint definition in Oracle Designer. These definitions are included in the DDL generated by the Oracle Designer Server Generator.

You may, of course, create additional constraints to be enforced by Oracle. Realize, however, that Oracle checks for violation of these constraints each time you insert, update, or delete data. In addition, Oracle uses them to determine which parent table to lock whenever a child row is being updated. In an OLTP environment, such locks may seriously affect performance. To avoid the table-level parent lock, you must create an index on the columns in every foreign key constraint.

Sometimes, you may need to replace a declarative referential constraint with a procedural trigger. Remember that Oracle checks the constraint when executing insert, delete or update statements. This means that you must execute these operations on parent and child tables in the appropriate order, and commit the parent row before committing the child row.

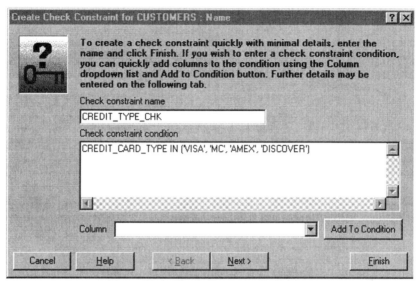

Figure 11-1: Check Constraint Definition

This restriction would require that data loads or bulk updates occur in a particular sequence—a liability in transactions where you are applying pre-validated data to synchronize one database with another. To avoid this restriction, you must remove the declarative constraint and replace it with trigger code that performs the same validation and is deferred until commit. The trigger code executes only at commit time—thus postponing the validation until all appropriate rows have been processed. The only alternative would be to disable constraints prior to the data synchronization and enable them on completion. In a typical application, there may be hundreds of such constraints!

Note that when you create these constraints, the underlying tables and pre-requisite constraints must exist. For example, before creating a foreign key constraint on a child table, the parent table, its primary key constraint, and the child table must all exist. The common way to getting the order correct is to create all tables first, followed by their primary and unique constraints, then create any foreign key constraints. The Oracle Designer Server Generator creates DDL statements in the appropriate order for this reason.

11.3 Database Triggers

Database triggers are code associated with a particular database table. Oracle invokes them when a particular operation occurs on the table. You may specify whether to invoke a trigger each time a particular operation occurs, or on each row affected by an operation. You may restrict the execution of a trigger to occur only on specified operations, for example, only on *insert*. You can also define whether the trigger fires

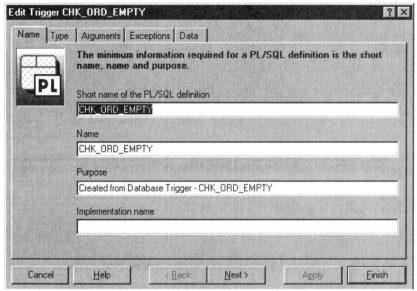

Figure 11-2: Trigger Definition for Implementing a Business Rule

before or after the operation. Figure 11-2 illustrates a business rule implemented using a trigger.

Database triggers may be used to validate data affected by an operation, or to modify data in another table. For example, you may create audit trails of modified data by inserting the old values of each row into an audit trail (or journal) table before executing an *update* operation on a table. Such a trigger should fire once for each row before the *update* operation. Oracle Designer Server Generator will create triggers that implement such audit trails (or journals) including the creation of journal tables. In addition to keeping a copy of the old row values, the generated code can also add information such as a timestamp, user id of the executor, a comment, and so on.

Another use for database triggers is to maintain the integrity of denormalized data. For example, if we stored the extended price (that is, unit price multiplied by quantity) of an ordered item, we would use a trigger to calculate it whenever the unit price or quantity column values were updated. In Oracle Designer, you may code such triggers as individual PL/SQL definitions.

11.4 Stored Procedures, Functions, and Packages

Some business rules require you to process quite a lot of data to provide a simple result. The data may come from one or more tables that must be filtered or joined during processing. For example, to calculate the total amount of an order, we must total all ordered items. Clearly, it is inefficient to transport this data across the network for processing in the client. We may write procedures or functions that perform such tasks and execute them in the database server. Such procedures or functions are stored

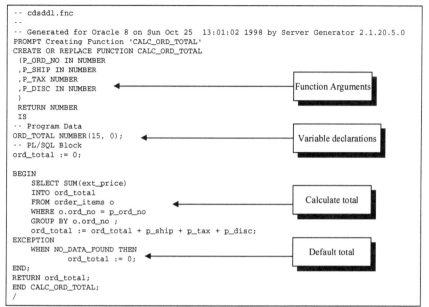

```
-- cdsddl.fnc
--
-- Generated for Oracle 8 on Sun Oct 25  13:01:02 1998 by Server Generator 2.1.20.5.0
PROMPT Creating Function 'CALC_ORD_TOTAL'
CREATE OR REPLACE FUNCTION CALC_ORD_TOTAL
  (P_ORD_NO IN NUMBER
  ,P_SHIP IN NUMBER
  ,P_TAX NUMBER
  ,P_DISC IN NUMBER
  )
  RETURN NUMBER
  IS
-- Program Data
ORD_TOTAL NUMBER(15, 0);
-- PL/SQL Block
ord_total := 0;

BEGIN
    SELECT SUM(ext_price)
    INTO ord_total
    FROM order_items o
    WHERE o.ord_no = p_ord_no
    GROUP BY o.ord_no ;
    ord_total := ord_total + p_ship + p_tax + p_disc;
EXCEPTION
    WHEN NO_DATA_FOUND THEN
        ord_total := 0;
END;
RETURN ord_total;
END CALC_ORD_TOTAL;
/
```

Function Arguments

Variable declarations

Calculate total

Default total

Figure 11-3: Generated Stored Function

in the database. Figure 11-3 illustrates a stored function that calculates order total from an order number specified in its parameter.

Stored procedures and functions must be written in PL/SQL. Oracle8 and later versions support writing them in C++ or Java code. In Oracle Designer, we may create modules that are based on the PL/SQL language. Note that there are no generators for such procedural code. However, we can store the code in the Oracle Designer repository for use by other objects. The Server Generator will create the appropriate DDL from our code.

We can often group related functions and procedures into a package. This approach allows them to share global variables or make certain variables publicly visible to the programs outside the package. They can still protect internal variables from outside programs. In Oracle Designer, we can define packages by creating networks of a parent module, the package, with its component modules.

Another advantage of using the package structure is that we may define more than one procedure or function with the same name but different parameters. For example, we may create two functions called *Validate_Data*: one to validate dates, and another to validate order quantity. Depending on the data type of the parameter, Oracle will execute the appropriate function. This feature, called *overloading*, allows us to process different data types with a seemingly common function. We can simplify the interface presented to the outside programs with this technique.

11.5 Using PL/SQL

PL/SQL is an interpretive, procedural language that allows embedded SQL statements. It is closely integrated with Oracle. The interpreter environment is available with the RDBMS kernel or independently with tools such as Oracle Forms and Reports. You can also execute PL/SQL code using the SQL*Plus interactive interface and embed it in your third-generation language programs. You may develop database objects like stored procedures. Oracle will hold such objects in a precompiled form within the database.

PL/SQL is a structured language. Its code is written in blocks enclosed within *Begin* and *End* statements. You can declare variables using the same data types provided by the RDBMS with a *Declare* statement. In fact, for PL/SQL variables matching database columns, you can specify a *%Type* attribute to determine their data type dynamically at runtime. Then, any changes to the data type will automatically cause a change to the PL/SQL variable data type. No changes to your code will be necessary.

Our sample batch PL/SQL program creates a suggested price list, that is, a catalog and its items for liquidation. Widgets, Inc., will run this procedure in batch mode once a month as they compose their next catalog offerings. The suggested price list will include two types of products: products that had insufficient demand and products that were previously marked down. Insufficient demand is when total ordered quantity is less than half of the quantity remaining in stock. Markdown products are those where the price is less than unit cost plus the 20% profit margin. The first type of product will be marked down by half of their profit margin-based on their lowest price. The second type of product will not be marked down further.

In addition, we need to ensure that a product which was previously marked down and still has insufficient shipment quantities is not marked down again. This is for illustration purposes only. In practice, Widgets, Inc. will probably want to mark down such prices further—to get rid of stock and free up valuable warehouse space for other products. Figure 11-4 illustrates this program written in PL/SQL.

This PL/SQL program contains two sections: the *Declare* section, and the processing section enclosed within *Begin* and *End* statements. The *declare* section contains a variable declaration for *catalog_no* and a cursor declaration for the SQL statement to retrieve products already in liquidation. We use this cursor to control a loop in the processing section.

The processing section starts by obtaining the next available catalog number from the sequence generator *cat_seq*. The *nextval* keyword generates the next value in the sequence. The sequence generator is an Oracle database object. We created this sequence generator as part of the schema definition in Oracle Designer.

The next processing step creates the new catalog entry in the *catalog* table. Details of the catalog are in the *catalog_items* table. Note that we could have used the sequence generator cat_seq with the keyword *currval* rather than declaring and using the *catalog_no* variable.

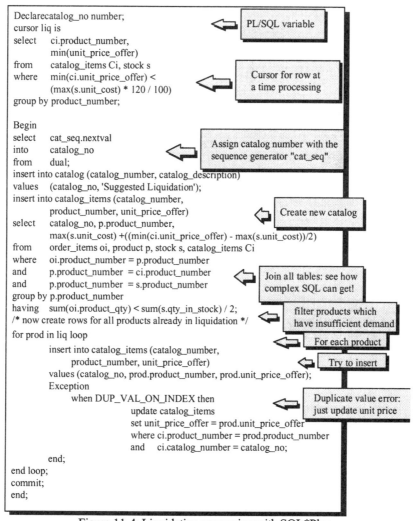

```
Declarecatalog_no number;                          [PL/SQL variable]
cursor liq is
select    ci.product_number,
          min(unit_price_offer)
from      catalog_items Ci, stock s               [Cursor for row at
where     min(ci.unit_price_offer) <              a time processing]
          (max(s.unit_cost) * 120 / 100)
group by product_number;

Begin
select    cat_seq.nextval                         [Assign catalog number with the
into      catalog_no                              sequence generator "cat_seq"]
from      dual;
insert into catalog (catalog_number, catalog_description)
values    (catalog_no, 'Suggested Liquidation');
insert into catalog_items (catalog_number,
          product_number, unit_price_offer)       [Create new catalog]
select    catalog_no, p.product_number,
          max(s.unit_cost) +((min(ci.unit_price_offer) - max(s.unit_cost))/2)
from      order_items oi, product p, stock s, catalog_items Ci
where     oi.product_number = p.product_number
and       p.product_number = ci.product_number    [Join all tables: see how
and       p.product_number = s.product_number     complex SQL can get!]
group by p.product_number
having    sum(oi.product_qty) < sum(s.qty_in_stock) / 2;   [filter products which
/* now create rows for all products already in liquidation */  have insufficient demand]
for prod in liq loop                              [For each product]
          insert into catalog_items (catalog_number,
                    product_number, unit_price_offer)  [Try to insert]
          values (catalog_no, prod.product_number, prod.unit_price_offer);
          Exception
                    when DUP_VAL_ON_INDEX then    [Duplicate value error:
                              update catalog_items  just update unit price]
                              set unit_price_offer = prod.unit_price_offer
                              where ci.product_number = prod.product_number
                              and   ci.catalog_number = catalog_no;
          end;
end loop;
commit;
end;
```

Figure 11-4: Liquidation processing with SQL*Plus

The *select* statement retrieves all products which have insufficient demand and inserts them into the *catalog_items* table, together with the marked down value for each product. This statement illustrates the typical complexity of writing practical SQL statements. Such a statement is almost as difficult to maintain as a three-page program in a third-generation language.

We use a nested block enclosed within *For ... Loop* and *End Loop* statements to include products already in liquidation. It loops once for each row returned by the select statement identified by the cursor *liq*. Here we implicitly declared the row variable, prod, in the *For* statement. This variable represents the current row.

In this block, we use the exception handling facilities of PL/SQL. The philosophy is that most products that are already in liquidation probably do not make our normal 20% profit margin. So, we try to insert liquidation products into *catalog_items* first. If the previous processing inserted a product, this insert will fail with a "*duplicate index value*" error. Note that Oracle will track these unique values only if there is a unique index on the *catalog_number* and *product_number* columns of the *catalog_items* table. The "*duplicate value*" error is caught by the exception handler specified in the *exception* section. In the exception section, the *dup_val_on_index* keyword indicates an error due to a duplicate value. We update the offer price with the previous liquidation price to override the markdown calculated by the previous processing. Figure 11-5 illustrates the use of another keyword, *%Notfound*, which is used with a cursor to detect the end of data. PL/SQL implements several such keywords to make your code more readable. You can also use the *SQLCODE* facility to find the error code when it occurs.

I needed a lot more words to explain what the program does than the program itself. So, you can see that the language is fairly high-level. This program could not be

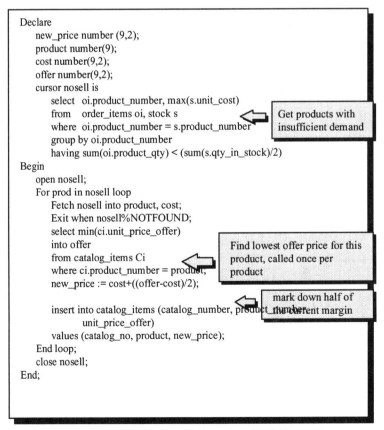

```
Declare
    new_price number (9,2);
    product number(9);
    cost number(9,2);
    offer number(9,2);
    cursor nosell is
        select   oi.product_number, max(s.unit_cost)
        from     order_items oi, stock s          <=  Get products with
        where    oi.product_number = s.product_number   insufficient demand
        group by oi.product_number
        having sum(oi.product_qty) < (sum(s.qty_in_stock)/2)
Begin
    open nosell;
    For prod in nosell loop
        Fetch nosell into product, cost;
        Exit when nosell%NOTFOUND;
        select min(ci.unit_price_offer)
        into offer                            <=  Find lowest offer price for this
        from catalog_items Ci                     product, called once per
        where ci.product_number = product;        product
        new_price := cost+((offer-cost)/2);
                                              <=  mark down half of
                                                  current margin
        insert into catalog_items (catalog_number, product_number,
                unit_price_offer)
        values (catalog_no, product, new_price);
    End loop;
    close nosell;
End;
```

Figure 11-5: Liquidation Catalog Procedural Alternative

written in SQL easily. Even if we could, the result would be an ugly, complex statement which no one would later understand. The complex SQL statement for selecting and inserting products with insufficient demand is a suitable example. Figure 11-5 shows a more maintainable, but procedural, way of achieving the same result.

The PL/SQL interpreter can live with the RDBMS kernel or independently with tools such as Oracle Forms. Figure 11-6 illustrates the relationship among this interpreter, the kernel, and with tools. There are several advantages to running PL/SQL interpreters with the kernel as well as tools. Used with a tool such as Oracle Forms, you can perform complex validation in the client without requiring access to the database. Of course, there are slight modifications to the language in each tool. For example, in Forms, you can reference screen items by preceding their name with a : (colon), and you can also reference system variables maintained by the Forms runtime environment. These facilities are not available when you write PL/SQL that resides in database objects. In SQL*Plus, you can use substitution variables to supply runtime values that are resolved prior to the block of PL/SQL being executed by the server.

You could write triggers in Oracle Forms with PL/SQL code. The PL/SQL interpreter resident with Oracle Forms handles as much of the code as it can, calling the kernel for processing SQL statements only. In a networked environment, this scheme reduces the network traffic by eliminating unnecessary calls to the database tables. However, the results of each SQL statement still cause network traffic. Be careful to avoid fetching unnecessary data over the network. More recent versions of Oracle Forms are much smarter about network traffic. They transport a set of rows for insert

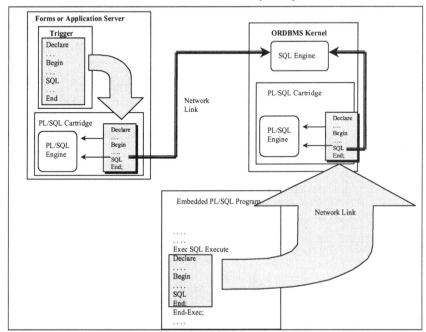

Figure 11-6: PL/SQL, Tools, and Kernel

or update to the database rather than one row at a time. They also retrieve a set of rows and buffer them in the client's memory—also resulting in reduced network traffic.

Using the PL/SQL interpreter resident with the kernel is one way to reduce data traffic over a network. You can execute blocks in the kernel-resident interpreter. Thus, only the final result travels over the network. This scheme is suitable when your procedural code examines several data rows and displays the result of some calculation-based on them to the user. You do not display individual rows, and there is no reason to transfer them to the workstation. Thus, executing the entire block on the database server machine will reduce unnecessary data traffic, albeit at the cost of increased CPU usage on the database server.

You can also execute PL/SQL from SQL*Plus. However, you really don't execute it interactively one statement at a time. You must input a complete PL/SQL block before executing it. You cannot use SQL*Plus extensions such as formatting commands within a PL/SQL block. However, you can mix formatting statements before and after a PL/SQL block. Remember also that commands such as *Break On* and *Compute* work on the result of a query. So you must retrieve the columns on which these commands operate. If you do not want these columns to be printed in the output, use the *Column .. Noprint* command.

11.6 Embedded SQL Interface

The third-generation language interface to Oracle is a lower-level programmers' tool than PL/SQL. This interface allows calls to the Oracle kernel from traditional languages such as C, Fortran, COBOL, and so on. It has been available since the early days of the Oracle RDBMS product, before fourth-generation utilities such as Oracle Forms and PL/SQL were developed.

The initial interface consisted of a library of functions, the Oracle call interface (OCI). You could call these functions and link them into your programs. Within each call, you passed SQL statements that the kernel processed. You had little control over which access path Oracle chose when executing your query. This interface, therefore, provided independence from changes in table and index structures. It was also fairly portable. You can still use this interface with Oracle, although it is quite archaic.

The embedded SQL precompiler interface replaced this function call interface. In this interface, you embed SQL statements into your programs. The precompiler converts embedded SQL statements into calls to the Oracle kernel. You can then compile the resulting code just like any other program in that language on your operating system. Thus, the precompiler converts embedded statements into OCI calls.

Each executable SQL statement starts with the keywords Exec SQL, which trigger the precompiler conversion. You can use any SQL statement in your program. For example, the sample program in Figure 11-7 retrieves the next available catalog number into a C variable called cat_num.

```
/*  Program:liquidate.pc
 *  Author:   Paul Rodgers
 *  Date:     March 9, 1990
 *  Purpose: Compose this months liquidation catalog
 *  Revision History:*/
#include <stdio.h>              ⇐  C Header Files
#include <string.h>
#include <memory.h>
#define  SQL_NOTFOUND    1403  ⇐  Constants: Code for no more data

                                  Forward Declaration: a local function that returns
char *sys_date()  ⇐               pointer to a string containing current date

EXEC SQL BEGIN DECLARE SECTION;   Pro*C Variables:
varchar userid[32];        ⇐      - users' oracle id
varchar passwd[32];               - oracle password
int cat_no;                       - new catalog # to create
int prod_no;                      - product number
float cost_price;                 - unit cost for a product
float cur_price;                  - price from current catalog
float new_price;                  - discounted price
char sql_buff[1024];              - dynamic SQL statement
EXEC SQL END DECLARE SECTION;
#include "/usr/oracle6/c/lib/sqlca.h"  ⇐  Pro*c Header file: must be
                                          AFTER Declare section

/* ------------------------------------------------------ MAIN*/
main(argc, argv)
int argc;
char *argv[];
{                                       - pointers to userid & passwd
char *uid, *pwd; [Printer symbol: ] ⇐  - copy of sqlcode exit status
int  sql_status; [Printer symbol: ]     - pointer into sql_buff
char *sptr; [Printer symbol: ]          - buffer for new catalog name
char cat_name[1024]; [Printer symbol: ]
if (argc != 2)          ⇐  Parse the command line for oracle slash
{                          separated username and password
  printf ("%s: Please supply username and password.\n", argv[0]);
  printf ("\tUsage: %s userid/passwd\n", argv[0]);
  exit(-1);
};
uid = strtok(argv[1], "/");
pwd = strtok(NULL, "/");
strcpy(userid.arr, uid);
strcpy(passwd.arr, pwd);
userid.len = strlen(userid.arr);
passwd.len = strlen(passwd.arr);

userid.arr[userid.len] = 0;  ⇐  Add null terminators, for normal C functions!
passwd.arr[passwd.len] = 0;
EXEC SQL WHENEVER SQLERROR GOTO exit_label;  ⇐  Let Pro*C detect SQL
EXEC SQL WHENEVER NOT FOUND CONTINUE;           errors, we'll check for
                                                NOTFOUND explicitly
EXEC SQL CONNECT :userid                      ⇐  Log on to Oracle, error
IDENTIFIED BY :passwd;                           takes us to exit_label.
printf ("%s: Successfully connected to Oracle.\n", argv[0]);
```

Figure 11-7(a): Liquidation Catalog in Pro*C

Program variables are also called *host* variables. The *Into* clause here is an extension to SQL similar to that in Forms and PL/SQL. You need to indicate to the precompiler which program variables you intend to use in SQL statements. This is done by enclosing the declaration of your variables between the *Exec SQL Begin Declare* and *Exec SQL End Declare* statements. The precompiler remembers the individual addresses of these variables for substitution wherever you refer to them in an embedded statement. You must declare such variables prior to using them in an embedded statement. Look at the example program shown in Figure 11-7.

Oracle cannot handle record-like structures which languages such as C and COBOL offer. So, use simple variables for those associated with a SQL statement. In C, this restriction means no structures, while in COBOL, you must use 01-level field definitions. Record definitions in COBOL cannot be used.

When declaring program variables for use within SQL statements, you must make sure that their data type in the language is suitable for the data type in the Oracle database. Mismatched data types cause incorrect data conversion and difficult-to-find bugs in your program. Oracle has some data types, such as Date, which have no corresponding types in third-generation languages. For example, in the C language, the Oracle Date data type corresponds to a character string. A Numeric data type, on the other hand, can be a C int, short, long, float, double, or a character string,

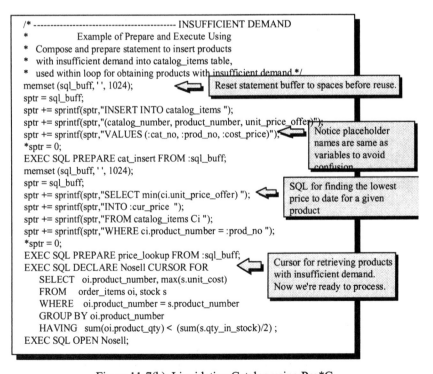

Figure 11-7(b): Liquidation Catalog using Pro*C

depending on the length of the number.

Remember that Oracle can store up to 38 significant decimal digits which can be raised to the power of between -84 to 127. Conversion from Oracle's data types to those of your programming languages raises some interesting portability issues. For example, C, which is one the most portable languages, has different implementations of the data types int, short, and long on different hardware. Thus, a program using an int to hold a nine-digit value may collapse with a core dump when ported to a machine where int is implemented as two bytes. This kind of hardware dependence

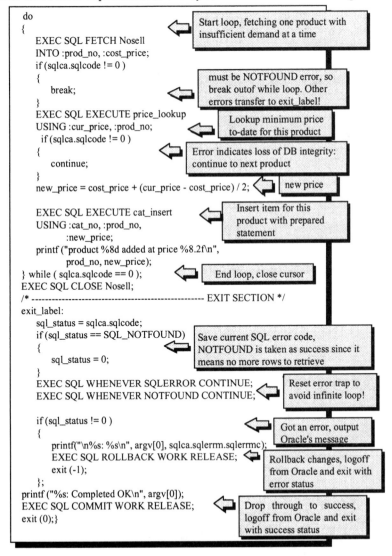

Figure 11-7(c): Liquidation Catalog using Pro*C

makes a third-generation language less portable than PL/SQL. PL/SQL uses the same data types as Oracle. So, there is no data conversion.

A client asked me in panic, one day, why the Oracle server on their network refused connect requests at random. Earlier in the day, they had been working with nary a hitch. After much frantic investigation, a chance remark revealed the culprit. An application running on four PCs was doing its daily download of data from the server to each of the PCs. Unfortunately, the 150 megabytes of data transmitted to each PC concurrently was soaking the network capacity! The connect requests to the Oracle server were getting so many packet collisions that they would time out before the request packet reached the server.

You can make your program more portable by embedding blocks of PL/SQL code where data conversion may potentially cause portability problems. By embedding PL/SQL, you can also reduce network traffic as we discussed in the earlier section. Remember, however, that you cannot mix statements written in your programming language in PL/SQL blocks.

Don't think that I am making a mountain out of a molehill on the subject of reducing network traffic. Networks have a limited throughput capacity and speed. The speed of data transmission on an Ethernet is approximately equivalent to the speed of reading from a slow IBM PC hard disk. Overloading such a network has subtle effects on the response time for everyone using the network.

11.6.1 Cursor Handling

SQL's set-oriented operation is appropriate when you want to retrieve data from one or more tables in the database. An SQL join will typically work faster than will similar code written in a procedural language, if it uses indexes. A program written in a programming language, on the other hand, must retrieve field data prior to attempting a join. When a join involves several tables, or the retrieval conditions are complex, you might choose to write procedural code. Procedural code, in such cases, may be slightly slower than equivalent SQL. But, a well-written procedural program is much easier to understand and maintain.

For procedural handling of data, we need to convert from set orientation to record-at-a-time orientation. Cursors are mechanisms for such conversion. A cursor is always associated with a SQL statement. It points to a row in the data resulting from

```
char *sys_date()
{
    static char *d = "APR-01-1997";
    return(d);
}
```

Dummy function, supposed to return today's date: Note static variable so we can safely return it without causing core dump!

Figure 11-7(d): Liquidation Catalog using Pro*C

executing the statement. You can think of it as pointing to the current record in a file containing the results of the SQL statement. Of course, there is no such physical file in Oracle, only a conceptual one.

The cursor concept exists in all of the Oracle tools. However, you have explicit control in creating and using cursors in PL/SQL and the third-generation languages. In Figures 11-4 we saw examples of using cursor handling in PL/SQL. Figure 11-7 illustrates how we can use cursors in a third-generation programming language.

When you declare and open a cursor, Oracle allocates an area of memory in your program to hold information about it. This area is called a context area. It contains information about the cursor and addresses of appropriate program variables. The SQL statement and its parsed version are held in a shared part of the system global area. The parsed SQL statement is shared between all of the clients that are currently executing it. It is phased out on a first-in-first-out basis. Associated with the cursor are data buffers into which Oracle stores data retrieved by using the SQL statement. The maximum number of cursors in a program is therefore limited by two factors: the amount of memory available to the program, which is an operating system limit, and the number of open cursors allowed in the *init.ora* file.

Every SQL statement requires a cursor. When your program does not explicitly declare a cursor, Oracle creates an implicit cursor on your behalf. This is how Forms, SQL*Plus, and other utilities obtain implicit cursors. Forms obtains a cursor for each screen block, since these correspond to tables in the database—hence the infamous "Maximum cursors exceeded" error messages occurring in forms that refer to a large number of tables. An SQL statement which returns a single row result does not require an explicit cursor. In our example program, the *select* statement for retrieving the next available catalog number results in exactly one row. Oracle assigns an implicit cursor to such a statement.

Statements which return multiple result rows in a third-generation language program must use an explicitly declared cursor. Then, you can fetch the results one row at a time and process them. Alternatively, you can use Oracle's array processing features to fetch several rows at a time. In this case, declare each program variable associated with the result as an array. Since C treats character strings as arrays, you need two-dimensional arrays.

Your program will have to loop through the array and process individual rows in the array. So, your code will be a little more complex than when you fetch one row at a time. Programs which use array processing reduce the number of accesses to the database, hence improving performance. Network traffic is in bursts rather than a steady stream of one row at a time. For interactive programs, short reads result in better user response times. In particular, batch reporting programs benefit from using arrays.

11.6.2 Dynamic SQL

So far, we have only discussed embedded statements, which are constant. But, how do we handle cases where they are not fixed but changed at runtime depending on user actions? For example, suppose a program composed a statement based on user input such as table names, column values, and so on. These are cases suitable for dynamically composed SQL statements in a third-generation program.

The simplest case is where the statement does not retrieve any data. An example is deleting rows from a user-named table based on a user-supplied condition. Other examples are creating or dropping tables, updating tables, changing access privileges for users on particular tables, and so on. In fact, you do not use any program variables with such statements. However, user input is essential before the statement is completely defined.

In the simplest case, you must first declare a string variable so that the precompiler knows its address. Then, compose the statement including items supplied at runtime. The string variable contains the completed statement as a character string in your program. We could execute the statement from a program string variable with the *Exec SQL Execute Immediate* statement. Our sample program in Figure 11-7(b) illustrates this concept.

If you need to specify program variables in a SQL statement where you will place a new value each time the statement is executed, you need another technique. You must prepare the composed statement and then execute it. These are both embedded SQL statements prefixed with *Exec SQL* keywords. The statement may contain a placeholder which the program replaces at runtime with a value in a program variable. The *Prepare* statement allows you to specify which variable the placeholder should be replaced with. For example, consider a catalog purge program which deletes catalogs and catalog items older than a date specified at runtime.

We compose the SQL statements for this purge in two string variables as follows:

```
items_stmt = "Delete from catalog_items
        where catalog_number in
        (select catalog_number from catalog
        where catalog_end_date < :pdate)"
cat_string = "Delete from catalog
        where catalog_end_date < :pdate"
```

pdate in these statements is just a placeholder. You will obtain the date value by prompting the user into a program variable called *purge_date*. The *purge_date* variable replaces the placeholder *pdate* in the *execute* statements. The corresponding *prepare* and *execute* statements are

```
EXEC SQL PREPARE items_stmt FROM :items_string;
EXEC SQL PREPARE cat_stmt FROM :cat_string;
EXEC SQL EXECUTE items_stmt USING :purge_date;
EXEC SQL EXECUTE cat_stmt USING :purge_date;
EXEC SQL COMMIT;
```

In this method, you only need to prepare the statement once. You can execute it multiple times in a session, each time with a different value in the program variable. The *commit* statement actually writes the changes to the database. Up to executing this statement, we could undo our deletes with a rollback statement. We could have written our trivial example in SQL*Plus using its *&variable* (ampersand followed by a variable name) facility. In fact, SQL*Plus will do the same sequence of prepare and execute that we illustrated.

Both of the foregoing techniques work when you are manipulating data in the database without retrieving it. When retrieving data, you cannot know in advance whether the search conditions specified at runtime will retrieve exactly one row or more than one row. So, you have to resort to using cursor-handling statements. Thus, you must declare a cursor for the prepared statement, open it, and then fetch rows one at a time. When the program finishes processing all rows, you can close the cursor. For example, prior to purging catalogs, you might want to review their descriptions and the number of printed copies remaining in stock.

The following SQL statements illustrate the sequence of retrieving:

```
cat_string = "SELECT catalog_number, catalog_desc, qty_in_stock from
              catalog where catalog_end_date < :pdate";
EXEC SQL PREPARE cat_stmt FROM :cat_string;
EXEC SQL DECLARE cat_cursor CURSOR FOR cat_stmt;
EXEC SQL OPEN cat_cursor USING :purge_date;
Start looping
       EXEC SQL FETCH cat_cursor INTO :cat_no, :desc, :qty;
       display catalog details to user...
Loop until no more rows
EXEC SQL CLOSE cat_cursor;
```

Remember that every program variable (prefixed by a : (colon)) used in this code must be declared within the *Begin Declare* and *End Declare* statements so the precompiler knows their addresses. The *Prepare* statement simply names the statement, *cat_stmt*—the statement name is not a program variable. Similarly, *cat_cursor* is just a name for the cursor so you can refer to it in the program, for example, in the *open* statement—it is not a program variable.

This technique is the most common form of dynamic SQL execution. You must use the cursor method with *open*, *fetch*, and *close* whenever you retrieve more than a single row. The cursor method is essential whether or not you use dynamic SQL to supply the program variable in an *open* statement with a *using* clause.

Occasionally, you may need to determine the select columns or tables at runtime. This need arises very rarely—typically only when you are building generic tools such as Oracle Form Builder utility or SQL*Plus. Some developers really believe they needed the fully dynamic SQL technique. In most cases, we found that a little standardization in the way you use tables may remove this perceived need. By the way, such a modification to design also saves several months of programming, because fully dynamic SQL development is not lightly undertaken.

Fully dynamic SQL is very complicated, and should not be attempted unless you have an in-house guru in structures and levels of indirect addressing in your high-level language. For example, in C, it is not sufficient to understand how to declare structures and reference their elements. You will also need to understand how to manipulate the pointer to which these structure elements point—at least a double indirection as part of a structure. In addition, you must be able to cast pointers to variables of one type into a pointer of another type without losing track of the type of data you are really dealing with when you dereference the pointer.

Fully dynamic SQL requires the program to set up a structure defined in the SQL data area (SQLDA). In all other forms of dynamic SQL, Oracle allocates and populates this structure.

To populate the structure, the program needs to figure out the data types for each variable in the select list at runtime. Once the data type is known, the program must dynamically allocate memory space to hold the data and use the addresses and lengths of these variables to populate the SQLDA structure. Then, you need to use the *describe bind variables* statement with this structure to indicate to Oracle where it should look for the variables associated in the statement.

Writing fully dynamic SQL is not easy. In fact, I see little need for it in an application development environment. It is an essential utility, however, for developers of new tools to interface to Oracle. For example, someone building an integrated forms development or report development tool may need to use this technique. I would advise application developers to stay away from it, if they value their sanity, or delivery deadlines!

11.7 Development Management Issues

Each of the facilities discussed in this chapter is just like writing a program in any programming language. You must write the code in a source code file with your favorite editor, compile it, and then test it.

Unfortunately, there are no debugging utilities to help your programming efforts. The PL/SQL facility is even more difficult since you have no idea of how far your program got before failing. You must resort to the primitive ways of interspersing *print* statements throughout your program to track its progress. I would suggest that you write your programs in small blocks and test each block individually. Then, pull all the blocks together to form your final PL/SQL program and test again.

Debugging utilities for your third-generation programming language are not going to help you either. Remember that the precompiler translates each embedded SQL statement into several OCI functions. The generated code resembles spaghetti more closely than your nicely structured code. Although the precompiler retains the original embedded statements as comments, trying to follow the logic of the generated code is not easy. Of course, the generated code is very consistent—for example, each *select* statement transforms into a similar set of calls. However, only a veteran of debugging precompiler code can see the similarities. In addition, some debugging tools, such as sdb on UNIX, do not like working without access to source code for every function call. It is unlikely that most developers have source code for Oracle's function libraries.

Estimating the development effort for PRO*Oracle programs is very similar to any other third-generation programming effort. Take into account the debugging difficulties prior to estimating. So, although there will be fewer lines of code to write, debugging and testing will be rather more complex. Development with PL/SQL is easier since you do not have to worry about data type conversions. In addition, it is a structured language which encourages you to write better code. However, don't try to use it like a third-generation language. Packed fields which require decoding, or bit manipulation, will only get you frustrated. Remember that Oracle is not a file manager where you can designate a field to be a composition of several values. Used as the relational database manager that it is, Oracle will make your development simpler and easier to maintain.

There are differences between the libraries provided by each version of Oracle. In the best case, you will have to merely recompile your code when migrating from one version to another. If you use UNIX facilities such as make, the product supplies files for make with the demo programs which will account for the different libraries. If, however, you use simple command files, you will have to change them when you migrate.

I advise you to set up a separate environment for a new version if you are migrating from an older version. Although most of the internal differences between these versions may be transparent to programmers, the only way to be sure is to test it. This means you will need to at least double the disk capacity needed for the software. Each version requires a significant amount of storage just for software. Then, worry about space for your test database under the new version.

Making Systems Perform

As mentioned earlier, performance is built into the application from the design stage. Retrofitting applications for high performance is very difficult. So, keep the techniques discussed here in the back of your mind as you write programs. These techniques apply regardless of the specific development tool. When building applications requiring fast performance, refer to them frequently. You will soon get into the habit of writing optimal database access code.

The first place to start for improving performance is your application. Review table design and physical implementation, indexes, and then the SQL code. Once you are certain that you have done all you can, investigate other avenues of improvement. These avenues include changing the size of buffers in the shared memory area and changing the timing of background processes.

This chapter describes how Oracle processes application code. We will discuss tools for determining access paths and the rules which Oracle uses to determine them. You cannot ignore the impact of multiple users sharing the database. So, we examine the important contents of the shared system global area.

- How Oracle processes SQL statements. We will discuss the rules used to choose an access path, tools such as Explain for discovering this path, and what to do to alter Oracle's choices.

- Using monitoring facilities to determine bottlenecks. Then, we examine ways of reducing these bottlenecks.

- In this process, we describe several important parameters from the *init.ora* file and their impact on Oracle's behavior. Some of these parameters affect the usage of shared memory. Others affect the behavior of background processes.

12.1 How Oracle Chooses Access Paths

When an application passes a SQL statement to the kernel for processing, the kernel parses it. Then, the SQL optimizer uses a set of rules to determine which available indexes it can use to execute the statement. There are two forms of optimizer: cost-based and rule-based. The rule-based optimizer was prevalent in earlier version of Oracle7. Table 12-1 lists this set of rules. Oracle 7.3 and later versions recommend the cost-based optimizer. Although this optimizer bases its judgement on the *cost* of a particular table access, you can provide *hints* in your SQL statements to alter its choices. The cost-based optimizer uses table sizing and distribution information. But it can only do so effectively if you have recently run the analyze utility. This utility records table size and data distribution information. Run it often, perhaps as part of your regular backup cycle, to keep the statistics up to date.

Indexes improve performance when you retrieve a small proportion of rows from a table, typically 25% or less. The purpose of an index is to reduce the number of key values compared before finding acceptable rows. An index contains only key values and pointers to data blocks. So, more key values fit into one block than the number of

Rank	*where* Clause Condition Type
1	ROWID = constant
2	Unique indexed column = constant
3	Entire unique concatenated index = constant
4	Entire cluster key = corresponding cluster key in another table in the same cluster
5	Entire cluster key = constant
6	Entire non-unique concatenated index = constant
7	Non-unique indexed column = constant
8	Entire concatenated index = lower bound
9	Most leading column in concatenated index specified
10	Unique indexed column BETWEEN low value AND high value, or Unique indexed column LIKE '...%' (bounded range) with at least three or four leading characters for best effect.
11	Non-unique indexed column BETWEEN low value AND high value, or Non-unique indexed column LIKE '...%' (bounded range)
12	Unique indexed column or constant (unbounded range)
13	Nonunique indexed column or constant (unbounded range)
14	Sort/Merge (used on joins only)
15	MAX or MIN of single indexed column
16	ORDER BY entire index
17	Full table scan
18	Unindexed column = constant, or Column IS NULL, or Column LIKE '%...%'

Table 12-1: Some Rules for the SQL Optimizer

Column	Format	Description
Statement_id	Char(30)	Optional identifier.
Timestamp	date	Date and time when statement was analyzed.
Remarks	Char(80)	Your comments, optional.
Operation	Char(30)	Action to perform at this node of the tree.
Options	Char(30)	Amplification of the action, such as type of index scan, etc.
Object_node	Char(30)	The name of the network database node that owns the object.
Object_Owner	Char(30)	The user name that owns the object.
Object_Name	Char(30)	Name of table, view, index, etc.
Object_Type	Char(30)	Amplification of object, such as Unique for indexes.
Object_Instance	Number	A number identifying the sequence of the object in the from clause, assigned from left to right.
Search_Columns	Number	The number of leading columns searching an index. Useful when used in conjunction with a concatenated index.
Id	Number	A unique number assigned to this action in the tree. (Corresponds to a preorder traversal.)
Parent_id	Number	Id of this node's parent action. For a root node, this column is null.
Position	Number	Order of this child within its parent.
Other	Long	Other useful information about the source, if any. For example, the *select* statement to a remote node in a distributed query, etc.

Table 12-2: Plan Table Columns

data rows in a block. Thus, using an index for a small proportion of rows also reduces the amount of I/O necessary. The optimizer prefers unique indexes since it knows that a lookup for an exact match in a unique index yields exactly one row.

As a rule of thumb, when you retrieve a large proportion of rows from a table, a full table scan is faster. This is because the search discards fewer rows than it accepts, and Oracle must retrieve data for the accepted rows. The discarded rows probably share storage blocks with accepted rows. Thus, Oracle will need to do very little extra I/O to scan them and does not need to do any I/O to read the index.

An exception to this rule of thumb is the bitmap index feature available in Oracle8 and Oracle7 version 7.3. A bitmap index is blindingly fast for exact match retrievals of a large proportion of rows. It uses bits to represent presence of a value from a small set of potential values. It is fast because it can use bit manipulation logic in memory to determine which rows match the requirement. Bitmap indexes are also fast for performing table joins—another form of an exact match on a large number of rows.

A B*Tree index on a small table increases the amount of I/O necessary for retrieving data. For example, if a table has 50 rows each containing an average of 100 bytes, the entire table fits in three Oracle blocks of 2 K bytes each. Based on your query, Oracle probably reads all of these three blocks anyway. If it uses an index, it reads at least one extra block to read and scan the index. Good examples of such tables are reference data tables which typically hold a code column and a column for the corresponding description. When estimating the number of blocks a table requires, use average sizes for character columns. Oracle stores character data as variable length without any trailing spaces. Remember that you need a unique index on a column if you want to enforce unique values in that column. In such instances, use the index suppression techniques described below to force a full table scan on these small tables.

In the absence of table statistics, the cost based optimizer reverts to using rules. The rule based optimizer parses from right to left, that is, from the end of the statement toward its beginning. It formulates the set of actions necessary to process the statement. It then uses the rules and their order of precedence to rank each action to decide the action to process first, then the second action, and so on. You can help it to choose the most optimal access path by rewording your statement. It then constructs a

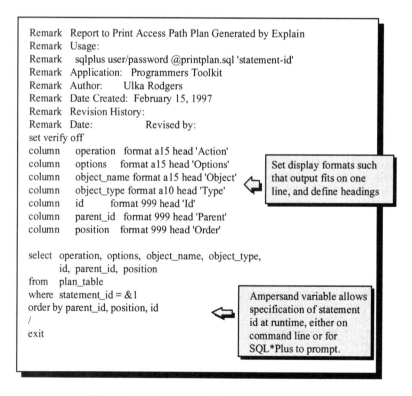

Figure 12-1: Report to Print Execution Plan

tree structure of each action it must process to execute the statement. You can find this tree structure using the *Explain plan* utility.

12.2 Unearthing the Optimizer's Plan

The Explain utility consists of a new SQL statement and a table, usually called *plan_table*, which contains the execution plan. Create this table before using the *Explain* statement. Table 12-2 describes some of the columns in this table. The syntax for the *Explain* statement is

> *Explain plan [set statement_id = '<your constant>']*
> *[into <plan_table_name>]*
> *for*
> *<statement for which you need the execution plan>*

Explain stores output for all statements in the same table, so assign a statement id for each statement to differentiate between them. The default name for the table is plan_table, but you may create it under another name. If you choose another name, you must specify the *into* clause listing the table name.

You can use normal SQL statements to retrieve the execution plan from the plan table. Figure 12-1 illustrates a simple SQL*Plus report that I find useful. Notice that this report only retrieves columns that are of particular interest. Alternatively, you could use Oracle's *Connect by ... Start with* extensions to SQL to print the tree structure. You can even draw a tree structure from the output of this report.

Oracle executes the statement starting from the bottom left of the tree, that is, the child with position 1 at the lowest level. Thus, it executes the lowest-level node first, then proceeds to its parent at the next higher level. To get the best performance, your aim is to reduce the number of rows it has to process as it moves higher in the tree.

The rule-based optimizer does not know how many rows exist in each of the tables or views. Neither does the cost-based optimizer if you did not *analyze* your tables. So, it uses the order in which you list objects in the *from* clause, using the last object (the right-most) as the starting point. Figure 12-2 illustrates the execution plan for a simple join between the *customers* and *orders* tables , as well as the corresponding tree. Notice that the optimizer plans to do a full table scan on the *orders* table, that is, read every row in the table. The nested loops action means that for every row in the orders table, it will look up the corresponding row in customers table. The index action states that it will use the unique index, *cust_idx_1*, for the lookup.

One of the first actions you should look for is an index action. This will indicate whether the optimizer is using any indexes. Then, decide whether the chosen index is the best one for the query, based on your knowledge of the data. In this example, there is a unique index on the *customer_number* column of *customers* and a non-unique index on the *order_for_customer* column of *orders*. Suppose we knew that there were

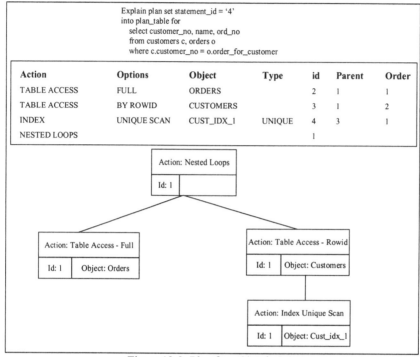

Explain plan set statement_id = '4'
into plan_table for
    select customer_no, name, ord_no
    from customers c, orders o
    where c.customer_no = o.order_for_customer

Action	Options	Object	Type	id	Parent	Order
TABLE ACCESS	FULL	ORDERS		2	1	1
TABLE ACCESS	BY ROWID	CUSTOMERS		3	1	2
INDEX	UNIQUE SCAN	CUST_IDX_1	UNIQUE	4	3	1
NESTED LOOPS				1		

Figure 12-2: Plan for a Simple Join

fewer rows in customers than orders. We could then provide a hint to the optimizer to cause a full table scan on customers instead. Figure 12-3 illustrates the result of such rewording.

Another way of disabling the use of an index is to modify the indexed column in some way within the *where* clause condition. The optimizer will not use an index if you modify the corresponding column. Use a harmless function, such as NVL, to modify a column. On character columns, concatenate a space using the || (vertical bars) symbol. On numeric columns, add a 0 (zero).

Conditions which test for IS NULL or IS NOT NULL suppress the use of an index. To enable the use of the index, replace the IS NOT NULL condition by a test against an unlikely low value. For example, to find all orders which have a *ship_to_customer* value—that is, where *ship_to_customer* is not null, use

> *where ship_to_customer > 0*

As a general rule, any condition involving a not equals comparison suppresses the use of indexes. Oracle transforms inequality conditions involving a not such that it can use an index. For example, a not > (not greater than) comparison translates into <= (less than or equal to) comparison. Remember that you might inadvertently suppress an

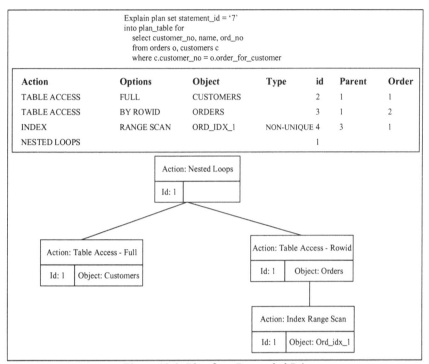

Figure 12-3: Plan for a Reworded Join

index using one of the foregoing techniques. A good habit is to review each statement as soon as you write it to remove all potential cases which may degrade response. Suppress indexes with caution and only after determining the need from Explain output. The next section suggests some rules of thumb for good and bad habits.

If the statement accesses only indexed columns from a table, and there are where conditions involving those columns, the optimizer resolves the query using only the index. In such cases, it does not read row data at all. Where the optimizer has a choice of indexes with no clear preference, it chooses unique indexes over non-unique ones. There is a limit to the number of indexes the optimizer can effectively use. After the maximum number of indexes, it will use row data for further filtering.

The rule based optimizer is sensitive to the order of clauses in the SQL statement. The order of conditions in the *where* clause also determine the order of executing actions. The optimal order depends on whether you use OR or AND logical operators. When you use ORs, the optimizer performs actions similar to a union—that is, one statement execution for the first clause and another for the second clause, filtering the result of the first clause. Thus, you should place the most restrictive condition first. When you use ANDs, place the most restrictive clause last. So that based on the optimizer's parse order, it will be executed first. A rule of thumb is: when using ANDs the most restrictive where clause should be last; when using ORs, place the most restrictive clause first. These rules are superseded by the cost based optimizer—it may rearrange the clauses as it considers fit. It may, if appropriate, convert a subquery to its equivalent join.

Sometimes, Oracle creates a temporary segment to store intermediate results before performing the next action. Creation and cleanup of these segments is a time-consuming process. For example, Oracle needs a temporary segment when you use a subquery with an IN operator to store the results of the subquery. You can avoid this overhead by using joins. Other cases requiring temporary segments are with *order by*, *Distinct*, *Group by*, and any set operators like *union*, *minus*, and *intersect*. Joins where no indexed columns occur are also good candidates for requiring temporary segments. If the optimizer finds an index in the appropriate order, it will try to use it rather than using temporary segments. You can use *Explain* output to determine whether it is planning to use this index. Oracle may use temporary segments when a query produces a lot of output. In such cases, even a union all or minus clauses are quite fast.

12.3 Do's and Don'ts of SQL

Here is a list of the characteristics of virtuous SQL code. Use this list whenever writing SQL to ensure good performance. However, remember the previous discussion of the reasons for these items. They are only guidelines and not for blind faith. Just remember, if you are in doubt, try two ways of writing the statement and compare the execution plan for both.

1. Use joins in preference to subqueries.

2. Create indexes on join columns, except on small tables. Refer to our earlier discussion of what constitutes a small table and the exceptions to this strategy.

3. Define unique indexes wherever applicable, and create the indexed column as NOT NULL.

4. List tables in a *from* clause in largest table to smallest table order if you are using the rule-based optimizer. The cost-based optimizer is less sensitive to table placement.

5. State *where* clause conditions using positive operators rather than using NOT.

6. If your query involves exact matches on columns in large tables, explore the use of hashing or bitmap indexes. These can make a dramatic improvement in performance, but apply only in limited cases.

7. Creating and dropping indexes is faster when processing large tables than unindexed accesses that cause a full table scan of the large table, unless of course you want to process large portions of the table. When

processing bulk loads or updates, drop the index first to speed processing then re-create it on completion. The only exception is a unique index necessary to enforce unique values.

8. Use array processing to speed data retrieval. Most Oracle tools implement array processing, but third-party tools might not. SQL*Plus provides the *set arraysize* option for this purpose. You may need to tune some init.ora parameters to make sure you have enough space in the system global area.

The following list contains the sins of writing poor SQL. However, you may ignore them (at your peril) if fast performance is not important.

1. Don't use subqueries if you can avoid them. Try to use joins, or create tables for temporary use. Oracle's internal temporary segments have no indexes. If you create your own temporary table, you may create an index on it.

2. Don't allow NULLs in columns—use a zero or space, except where meaningful. Testing for nulls suppresses indexes, resulting in poor performance.

3. Avoid using operators like OR, UNION, MINUS, and INTERSECT, except when there is no other way. These cause processing similar to subqueries and tend to be slow. An exception is when a table is partitioned and distributed in Oracle8.

4. Don't use a function on a column within a *where* clause condition. These cause suppression of the index and may result in a slower full table scan.

5. If a condition applies at row level, don't use the *Having* clause for it. Use the *where* clause instead to filter out unwanted rows early.

6. Avoid reparsing of SQL statements that are executed repeatedly within one program. Utilities such as Forms and precompiler products provide settings that allow you to control reparsing. Between multiple users running the same application, Oracle manages sharing of parsed SQL statements.

As a general rule, using PL/SQL cursor based loops is slower than performing the same task in a single SQL statement. There are some cases when the slower cursor loops are preferable. One example is in a long running update transaction. While the update is in progress, all updated rows are locked. This hogs resources as well as preventing other transactions access to the locked rows. In an OLTP environment, this may cause performance delays. Implementing such a transaction using a cursor loop allows us to embed periodic commits to release locked rows.

12.4 How Oracle Manages Database Access

In this section, we examine how Oracle processes use the system global area (SGA) and the parameters that control its use. These techniques affect the behavior of the entire system, so only DBAs should use them. Consider carefully the effect on all applications sharing the database before changing these parameters.

The SGA contains buffers (also called caches) shared between all users of a database. Parameters which control the sizes of these buffers are in the *init.ora* file. There is one *init.ora* file for each instance. The instance reads these parameters at database startup time only. So, if you change any parameter in this file, you have to shut down and startup the database before they will take effect. There are some parameters that may be changed on line using the server manager utilities. There are *init.ora* parameters that control other aspects of running the database, such as names of databases, control, and log files. Most of them are self-explanatory. We will focus on parameters which relate to performance improvement.

In Chapter 8, we discussed the top areas that get you the biggest and quickest improvement in performance. The discussions in this chapter are really not needed for many databases. However, if you have an intense OLTP application or one that supports a large number of users, you may need to tune the database further. You are probably running close to the limits of your platform. Remember that it is often easier and cheaper to buy bigger or faster hardware than lengthy investigations into performance. Performance tuning experts are few and expensive.

The SGA uses shared memory on most operating systems. When you increase the size of a cache in the SGA, the size of shared memory needed increases. On some systems, this may require reconfiguration of the operating system or relinking Oracle executables. In addition, make sure that you have sufficient real memory available to avoid swapping or paging which can negate effects of increasing buffer sizes.

The default installation of an Oracle database creates SGA configurations that is too small for anything but the smallest databases. Even the *Large* SGA configuration is only a 30MB area. This is too small for the database environments these days. We routinely use SGA sizes of 100MB for intense applications. So be prepared to reconfigure the default *init.ora* parameters.

Oracle provides several dynamic performance tables, which are owned by the sys user name. They are really virtual tables and occupy no space in the database. Their names typically have a prefix of V$. Some of the views on these tables are the basis of the monitor facility discussed in the next section. Some of these tables contain performance statistics useful to us. In particular, we will examine V$Rowcache and the V$WAITSTAT tables during the discussion that follows.

You can purchase many third-party tools to monitor the performance of the database. They all access these dynamic performance tables. Use one of these tools for your investigation, unless you are a glutton for punishment. This section reviews the use of some of these tables, but I prefer to see graphical representation of the data.

There are three main sets of caches in the SGA: shared pool, data, and redo. A user's back-end server (dedicated or shared) process first searches these buffers for the required data. If found in the buffers, the server process uses that data. Otherwise, it retrieves the data from disk and allocates space in SGA buffers to hold it. So, all users share the data in the SGA caches.

12.4.1 Shared Pool

The shared pool contains the dictionary cache and shared and parsed SQL statements.

12.4.2 Dictionary Cache

The dictionary cache contains information from Oracle's database dictionary. For example, it contains database table and column information, user access security information, and so on. There is one *init.ora* parameter to control buffers for each type of information. Each dictionary cache-related parameter starts with the prefix DC_. For example, parameter DC_COLUMNS controls the size of the cache for column descriptions; DC_TABLES controls the size of the cache holding descriptions of tables, views, clusters, and so on.

A rule of thumb is that the size of these caches should be large enough to hold all of the information that your application accesses at one time. You can use the Monitor Statistics User display to determine whether the cache is large enough. In addition, you can examine the SYS.V$ROWCACHE table to determine the effectiveness of the cache. We examine these in more detail in Section 12.5.2 Investigating Dictionary Cache I/O.

12.4.3 SQL Cache

This area holds SQL statements in their raw and parsed form. It is also used for shared PL/SQL from any database object such as stored procedures or client programs such as a Forms program. These buffers are freed on a least recently used basis. You may also pin an object into this area to ensure its availability. Remember though that pinning reduces the available space in the cache.

12.4.4 Data (Buffer) Cache

This set of buffers holds application database data, index, cluster, and rollback (undo) information for transactions in progress. Buffers for rollback information are grouped logically as rollback segments. You can control their allocation size with appropriate storage parameters in the *Create Rollback Segment* statement. Each buffer is the same size as an Oracle block, typically 2K or 8K if you expanded the block size. These buffers account for the largest portion of the SGA.

The main purpose of these buffers is to reduce the amount of physical I/O necessary for servicing user requests. Thus, the rule of thumb is to define as many data buffers as you have real memory. Increase the value of the init.ora parameter

DB_BLOCK_BUFFERS. Be conscious, however, that at some point, increasing buffers will not improve performance. You can determine this point from the cache hit ratio statistics shown on the Monitor I/O display. In addition, you can use the X$KCBRBH table to determine the number of extra blocks to allocate for performance gains. The X$KCBCBH table statistics help in determining whether you could reduce the cache size without affecting performance. The V$WAITSTAT table helps you in determining whether user processes wait for an excessive number of times with the current buffer configuration.

12.4.5 Redo Log Cache

These buffers are a circular area from which the Log Writer (LGWR) process obtains redo log file entries. A user's Oracle shadow process writes into these buffers when committing a transaction.

The important statistic to look for is the redo log space wait item in the Monitor Statistics Redo facility. If this item has a value of greater than zero, then you need to increase the buffer size using the *init.ora* parameter LOG_BUFFER.

12.4.6 Latches

Latches are locks of a short duration on resources in the SGA. Oracle uses these to control concurrent access to structures in the SGA. UNIX semaphores are the common mechanism for implementing latches. Some examples of SGA resources controlled with latches are cache buffers, redo buffers, sequences, and locks.

Suppose our Oracle shadow process wants to obtain some cache buffer space. It first obtains a latch on the cache buffers list. This list is organized in a least recently used order. The latch prevents other processes from changing the structure of this list, causing them to wait until our process releases the latch. Our process then determines which cache buffer blocks it can use, reorganizes the cache buffers list so that the chosen blocks are at the end of the list, and then releases the latch.

In the meantime, other Oracle processes may choose to wait for the latch held by our process. The length of wait time depends on Oracle's implementation for your operating system. When their wait time expires, they may choose to retry and the wait cycle begins again. Processes may choose to time out either at the first attempt to obtain a latch or after retrying several times.

12.4.7 Locks

Oracle utilities refer to locks as enqueues. These work in a similar manner to latches, except that they control concurrent access to database resources. Examples of resources requiring locks are database objects (TM), redo log buffers (RT), data dictionary objects (TD), temporary segments (TS), and transaction on an active process's row (TX). Oracle implements several types of locks:

- **Share:** More than one process may obtain this type of lock on the same resource. You will frequently see them on dictionary objects, since while a process executes any SQL statement, Oracle prevents others from altering the structure of that object.

- **Exclusive:** Only one process may hold a lock of this type at a time on a resource. Such locks on dictionary objects mean the process is executing a DDL statement such as create, alter, drop, and so on. Seen on transaction resource, it means that the row is exclusively available to that process.

- **Row Share:** This type of lock is like share lock, but on a row within a database object. Processes typically use these when accessing a table without the intention of updating the locked row.

- **Row Exclusive:** This type of lock is similar to an exclusive lock, but on a row within a database object. Processes typically use these when updating, deleting, or inserting a row.

- **Share Row Exclusive:** This type of a lock is a combination of a share lock on the database object with a row exclusive lock on a specific row within it.

Oracle uses its own structures in the SGA to implement locking. Thus, a process trying to obtain a lock must first latch these structures before manipulating them. A process holds several latches and locks at a specific time. For example, a Forms application querying data from a single table may hold:

- A share lock on the dictionary definition of the table (TD).

- A row exclusive lock on the database table.

- Several row share locks, one for each row already viewed on the screen.

- A row exclusive lock on the row currently displayed on the screen. It obtains this lock as soon as the user types into one of the fields starting an update transaction. Before the user types into a field, only a Row Share lock is held. Changing from one type of lock to another is called lock conversion.

- A latch on the lock structure for a very short duration while it converts a row share lock to a row exclusive lock.

Locks held for longer than momentarily can lead to performance issues in heavily used OLTP applications. Locks use up database resources. They also prevent other users form updating locked rows, forcing their transactions to wait until locks are released. In addition to row locks, Oracle also uses constraint indexes in applying locks. For example, when updating a row in a child table, Oracle also locks the corresponding parent entry using the index on the foreign key. In the absence of this index, however, Oracle locks the parent table. This table level lock may cause delays in processing updates to the parent table. So, make sure your database design includes indexes on every foreign key column.

12.5 Finding Bottlenecks

Oracle provides a monitor facility as part of the Enterprise Manager utility for you to watch database activity. This utility groups types of activities logically, allowing you to display one group at a time. It counts how often each type of activity in a group occurs through an interval specified by cycle time and displays them on your screen each interval. Table 12-3 describes activity groups. The continuous display and counting imposes quite an overhead on your system, so use it sparingly. Choose a longer cycle interval to reduce the impact of monitoring.

You can discover most of the bottlenecks causing performance degradation in your system using this utility. Use it as the next logical step after improving the application SQL statements. The counts displayed with this utility change depending on which programs are running. So, the ideal time for using it is during peak activity when performance degradation is at its worst.

Make sure your users know each of the periods when you plan to monitor, particularly since they will notice an additional performance degradation during their busiest periods. Most of them will appreciate your attention to their needs and forgive the intrusions.

Discovering specific causes of performance degradation requires repeated monitoring sessions with lots of think time in between. The steps to use iteratively are

1. Formulate a hypothesis about the cause of degradation.

2. Determine which programs are active when degradation occurs.

3. Choose the best time period for monitoring based on when these programs run.

4. Determine which database activities to monitor to verify the hypothesis.

5. Guesstimate the count values you expect for these activities to verify your hypothesis, based on your knowledge of the active programs, and write them down beforehand!

6. Select the activity groups from the monitor facility and which processes they apply to.

7. Monitor these displays for a period comparing actual count values to those you expected. Turn the spool option on to log the actual values in a file so that you can examine them at your leisure.

8. Determine which *init.ora* parameters you need to modify to improve performance. Some causes of degradation may require other work such as redefining tables with appropriate storage parameters.

9. Estimate the new values and apply them to your database. Remember that you have to shut down and restart your database for the new values of the *init.ora* parameters to take effect.

10. Monitor displays again at the appropriate time to verify the effects of the change.

Group	Class	Description
File I/O		One row for each operating system file assigned to the database. Useful if you use multiple physical disks. If you know the physical disk on which each file resides, you can determine the load on that physical disk.
I/O		This displays a histogram of logical and physical reads and writes performed by each active process. This display helps determine whether you need to increase buffer caches. You can choose a range of processes to limit your display.
Latch		Displays latches currently held for each SGA resource.
Lock		Displays locks currently held, type of lock, and the id of the resource on which lock is held.
Process		Displays one row per active process. Each user may have more than one process listed here. Shadow processes for Net8 may not have corresponding system process id.
Rollback		One row per rollback segment listing its size, actions, and I/O rates.
Statistics		Several screens displaying runtime statistics on rates of use per second and performance. These are divided into classes. You may choose to display a particular class or display all classes of statistics. In each case, values displayed are current, average, maximum, minimum, and cumulative total since screen display started
Statistics	User	Activities performed by user processes, all or selected processes.
Statistics	Enqueue	Rates of locking activity, all or selected processes.
Statistics	Cache	Activity on cache buffers, all or selected processes.
Statistics	Redo	Activity on redo buffers, all or selected processes.
Table		Lists tables currently accessed and which Oracle process is using each table.
User		Summary information about a process together with the most recently executed SQL statement.

Table 11-3: Monitor Display Groups

Tuning performance is very much an art, even though the above steps imply an engineering approach. The art is in deciding which count values to consider too high, that is, indicating a cause of performance degradation. So, expect to spend some time just monitoring together with the relationships described here before forming a hypothesis. Don't be discouraged when some of your hypotheses do not bear out. Just form another hypothesis and try again. Expect to get radically wrong results on your first try. But remember, write down what you expect to happen first. Then investigate. This approach will let you know immediately if you are on the right track or not, i.e. looking at the right parameters.

If users of a specific program experience sluggish performance, choose to monitor those processes initially. However, you may need to monitor others to determine if their activities affect the program under consideration. We discuss the circumstances for including other processes later.

In the following sections, we examine two areas which encompass the commonly occurring causes of performance degradation: I/O and multi-user contention. Beyond these, you need expert help, since the tuning you might perform has complex interdependencies. The primary area to attack is I/O. It accounts for most performance degradation you will ever see.

In each area, we discuss possible causes, how to verify if they are the culprits, and what to do to reduce their effect on performance. We show some sample monitor displays so you know what the screens look like. Producing appropriate count values in these examples is very difficult, so don't pay much attention to the actual counts.

12.5.1 Finding and Reducing I/O Bottlenecks

I/O occurs due to several different activities:

- User's server processes retrieving data from disk into the SGA.

- Oracle calling itself (recursive calls) to service a request by a user's shadow process.

- DBWR writing data from the SGA to disk.

- LGWR writing redo buffers from the SGA into the redo log files on disk.

The first two activities are interrelated. A recursive call may be to retrieve dictionary information into the SGA, or to allocate additional extents for a table if an insert or update is in progress. Use the Monitor Statistics display to discover whether too many recursive calls are occurring. The values shown for recursive calls on this display are in rates per second.

Immediately after database startup, the rate for recursive calls will be high while Oracle fills the empty dictionary caches. After users have been active for a while, the rate should reduce. Ideally the rate should be zero. Since there are two possible reasons for high rates of recursive calls, you need further investigation.

12.5.2 Investigating Dictionary Cache I/O

The SYS.V$ROWCACHE virtual table reflects data dictionary activity since database startup. It has one row for each dictionary cache, listing the total number of requests for dictionary information (GETS), the number of requests that were not satisfied from the cache (GETMISSES), the number of entries in that cache (COUNT), and the number of entries that are used (USAGE).

If COUNT and USAGE values are equal, look at the GETMISSES value. A high value in GETMISSES indicates recursive calls for retrieving dictionary information. You should minimize these calls by increasing the size of the corresponding dictionary cache. The Parameter column of the V$ROWCACHE table lists the *init.ora* parameter corresponding to the cache.

As a rule of thumb, oversize the cache by at least 50 percent. But if memory is a scarce resource, then explore wasted SGA space. If USAGE value is significantly less than COUNT, then you may be wasting SGA memory space that is useful for other caches. Decrease the corresponding *init.ora* parameter. Aim for COUNT values a little greater than USAGE values.

12.5.3 Investigating I/O Due to Fragmentation

If recursive call rates are still high after this tuning, their cause is probably dynamic allocation of additional extents for tables. Your database may be fragmented or chained; that is, your tables may be made up of a lot of extents which result in noncontiguous sets of blocks. Oracle reads each contiguous set in a single multiblock read. A single read is much more efficient than several reads, one for each extent.

If you discover fragmentation, reorganize your tables using storage parameters as described in Chapter 8. Aim for a single extent to hold all data for small and moderate size table, thus obtaining contiguous blocks. For large tables measured in gigabytes, single extents are impractical. In these cases choose an extent size that is a large multiple of the block size. For example, for a block size of 8K, an extent size of 1 or 2 megabytes is typical.

Fragmentation can potentially create unusable blocks of free space. Oracle will attempt to consolidate these blocks as needed, a time consuming process. One trick to avoiding this occurrence is to assign identical extent sizes to all tables within a tablespace. Then, free space will always be of a usable size.

The reorganization of storage parameters takes effect when you export tables, drop them, re-create them with new storage parameters, and then import back table data.

12.5.4 Investigating Buffer Cache I/O

Use the Monitor I/O display for this purpose. Check the hit ratio to determine the proportion of reads where the data was found in the SGA cache buffers. The maximum possible value is 1, which indicates that data was already in the SGA for every read. A highly-tuned system will have hit ratios of 0.8 or higher. Lower values indicate that you could improve performance.

There are several possibilities for the cause of low cache hit ratios. The program may be performing unnecessary I/O or there may be an insufficient number of data cache buffers. Another less likely reason may be that the DBWR is not cleaning out cache buffers fast enough.

12.5.5 Investigating Unnecessary I/O

From the Monitor I/O display you can determine which process performs the I/O. Use the Monitor Process display to discover which program causes it. Also, use the Monitor User display to discover the most recent SQL statement that caused it. This procedure is difficult because more than one SQL statement from the program may be the culprit. Repeat the monitor displays several times to find the culprits. Use the Explain facility to determine if you can improve these statements.

12.5.6 Finding the Optimal Increase to Data Cache

After exploring the above avenues of improvement, consider increasing the data cache buffer size. You can confirm the need by examining the values for *free buffer inspected*, *free buffer requested*, *free buffer scans*, and *free buffer waits* in the Monitor Statistics Cache display. If you see high rates-per-second values in free buffer scans and free buffer waits activities, then there are insufficient buffers. If free buffer inspected rates are high also, you may have DBWR problems.

By increasing the *init.ora* parameter DB_BLOCK_BUFFERS, you increase the size of the data cache. If you can afford lots of memory, I suggest you simply guess the size and increase it. If you have a large number of users, or are short on capital expenditure budget, use the X$KCBRBH virtual table. You must enable the collection of these statistics by setting the *init.ora* parameter *DB_Block_LRU_Extended_Statistics* to a little more than the number of additional cache buffers you might consider. The number of additional buffers you may consider depends on whether you have sufficient real memory available. For example, to consider an additional 100 buffers, set *DB_Block_LRU_Extended_Statistics* to 120. This will result in 120 rows in the X$KCBRBH table, one row for each additional buffer.

The X$KCBRBH table contains two columns: Indx, which indicates the potential number, less 1, of additional cache buffers, and Count, which indicates the number of additional hits you would obtain. For example, the lowest value in the Indx column is 0, the next lowest value is 1, and so on. The best way is to consider incremental cache buffers in groups, say 50 buffers at a time. In this case, use the following SQL statement to group data into 50 buffer ranges:

```
Select   (50*Trunc(Indx/50)+1) || ' to ' ||
                50*(Trunc(Indx/50)+1) Range,
                sum(count) Expected_Hits
From            sys.X$KCBRBH
Group by        Trunc(Indx/50)
```

The Range column in the result indicates the maximum number of buffers you might add to get the number of hits in the EXPECTED HITS column. Choose the number of buffers which provide a good trade-off between available memory and cache hit ratios.

Don't forget to use the operating system analysis tools to see if swapping or paging occurs. If so you need even more memory to bring swapping under control first. Then, you might use this procedure to find out how much more memory you need to buy.

12.5.7 Distributing Disk I/O

Once you have reduced disk I/O as much as possible, consider further gains by using multiple physical disks. This may allow I/O in parallel through disk striping, if your operating system provides such facilities. If you distribute your database so that parts of it reside on different disks, parallel I/O reduces the overall time required to read and write to disks. We discussed methods for distributing the database across disks in Chapter 8.

To determine the proportion of I/O to each disk, use the Monitor File I/O display. The important activities are rates per second for read and write requests and the batch size blocks per write. If these disks contain files used by non-Oracle applications, use the operating system facilities to determine I/O distribution.

If you cannot use disk striping, you may have to manually distribute I/O between disks.To manually balance Oracle I/O between disks, you can store tables accessed together on separate disks, store tables and their indexes on separate disks, and store redo log files and database files on separate disks. If heavy concurrent access is necessary for any large table, divide it over one or more disks. To do such striping, you need several files, distributed across disks. Assign all files to one tablespace which will hold the table to be striped. When creating the table, make sure the storage parameters specify extent sizes which are a little smaller than file sizes. Remember to reserve the entire tablespace for this table.

12.5.8 Investigating DBWR Efficiency

DBWR is the only process that writes to the physical database files and thus imposes a significant overhead whenever it works. Maintaining optimal DBWR efficiency is a fine balance between the frequency of waking it and the number of buffers it writes each time. On some platforms, you may set up multiple DBWR processes.

DBWR batches several blocks into a single write whenever possible to reduce I/O. It wakes up periodically to clean out the data cache, attempting to maintain an optimal number of free data cache buffers. Each time it wakes, DBWR writes out twice the number of buffers specified in the *init.ora* parameter, DB_BLOCK_WRITE_BATCH.

A server process, which cannot find a free data cache buffer may wake DBWR to do its job. Frequent signals from the shadow process to DBWR result in high values for free buffer waits and DBWR free needed on the Monitor Statistics Cache display. You should increase the data cache size, if you can, before paying attention to these values. Check the value of the *init.ora* parameter DB_BLOCK_MAX_SCAN_CNT to ensure that it is set to the default value for your operating system.

While searching the free buffer list, if the shadow process finds a certain proportion of modified blocks, it wakes DBWR to write buffers to disk. This proportion is one-half of the value of the *init.ora* parameter DB_BLOCK_WRITE_BATCH. To reduce the frequency of waking DBWR, increase the value of this parameter. However, increasing this value is only beneficial if your operating system provides the ability to write blocks to different disks in parallel or to write adjacent blocks in a single I/O. In many systems, this is dependent on the disk controller used.

DBWR also wakes up whenever a checkpoint occurs requiring DBWR and LGWR to synchronize database and redo log files. A checkpoint occurs whenever LGWR switches to a new redo log file, and each time LOG_CHECKPOINT_INTERVAL number of blocks are written to the redo log file. The DBWR checkpoints activity on Monitor Statistics Cache display shows the number of checkpoints since database startup. You can increase the value in LOG_CHECKPOINT_INTERVAL to reduce checkpoint frequency. However, each checkpoint will then cause a larger number of buffers for DBWR to write. Also, recovering from the last checkpoint will take longer to complete.

12.5.9 Investigating LGWR Efficiency

LGWR's effect on performance is an issue only in applications with high transaction rates. Use the Monitor Statistics Redo display to verify the value of the redo log space wait activity. A nonzero value for this activity indicates that processes wait for space in the buffer. In this case, increase the value of the *init.ora* parameter LOG_BUFFER, which specifies buffer space in bytes.

12.6 Finding and Reducing Multi-user Contention

Multi-user contention occurs when more than one user's server Oracle process accesses a resource at the same time. Latches control the sharing of resources in the SGA and locks (enqueues) control sharing of database resources. The most important of these two is locks. Applications usually control the type of locks necessary in their code.

On multiple CPU systems, more than one process can access some resources in the SGA at the same time. On such systems, Oracle allows multiple latches for these resources. Such resources include redo copy latches and free lists for data cache buffers.

12.6.1 Data Cache Buffers Contention

Contention for cache occurs when processes try to obtain either data or rollback buffers. Oracle uses rollback buffers to hold changed data for rollback and read consistency purposes. Use the Monitor Statistics Cache display to determine whether your systems suffer contention for these buffers. The important activities are consistent gets, db block gets, and buffer busy waits. The ratio of buffer busy waits to the sum of the other two indicates the proportion of requests that had to wait. If this ratio is more than 10% or 15%, you need to determine whether most of the contention is for rollback buffers or for data buffers.

The V$WAITSTAT virtual table contains information on the class of blocks requested and contention since database startup. We are interested in undo segment, undo block, and data block classes. The operation of interest is buffer busy waits. Other operations and classes do not help us in this tuning. The best way to retrieve information from this table is using the following query

```
Select  class, sum(count) Total_Waits
From    sys.V$Waitstat
Where   operation = 'buffer busy waits'
and—class in ('undo segment header', 'undo block', 'data block')
Group by class;
```

Large values in the TOTAL_WAITS column for *undo segment header* or *undo block* indicates that you have insufficient rollback segment buffers. In this case, add more rollback segment buffers using the *Create Rollback Segment* statement. A general rule of thumb is four rollback segments for each set of 16 concurrent transactions. Remember that concurrent users may not be performing concurrent transactions, but this is a good starting point for your estimate.

Large values in the TOTAL_WAITS column for data block class indicate insufficient free lists for data blocks. There is one free list per table containing a list of blocks which have sufficient free space for inserting new rows. This type of contention is likely if several processes are inserting rows into the same table concurrently. Each process must access a free list for that table. Contention indicates that there are fewer free lists than processes trying to insert. Use the Monitor Table display to help determine which tables need extra free lists.

The *init.ora* parameter FREE_LIST_PROC specifies the number of free lists to maintain for each table. The ideal value for this parameter is the number of concurrent processes requiring access to the same table with a maximum value of 32. For the new values of init.ora parameters to take effect, you must shut down and restart the database. This parameter only affects tables created since changing its value. So, to affect existing tables, you may need to recreate them.

12.6.2 Latch Contention

Use the Monitor Latch display to determine which latches, if any, may be the cause of performance degradation. Although this display shows several different types of latches, you can control only a few. On most single CPU systems, you may not have the choice of controlling any. Also, Oracle uses operating system facilities, such as semaphores on UNIX, to implement latches. So, increasing their number may require reconfiguring your operating system.

Typically, if the timeouts value for a latch is more than 10% or 15% of the total value, your system is suffering because of latch contention.

12.6.3 Redo Allocation Latch Contention

Most processes obtain the Redo Allocation Latch and immediately copy the redo entries into the SGA. There is only one latch of this type. The *init.ora* parameter LOG_SMALL_ENTRY_MAX_SIZE controls the maximum redo entry size that a process can copy immediately. Redo entry sizes larger than this must obtain a Log Copy Latch—they can only obtain the redo log buffer on the Allocation Latch.

12.6.4 Redo Copy Latch Contention

Single CPU systems have only one Redo Copy Latch; multiple CPU systems can have one Redo Copy Latch per CPU. The *init.ora* parameter LOG_SIMULTANEOUS_COPIES defines the number of Redo Copy Latches on multiple CPU systems. You may define up to twice the number of such latches as there are CPUs with beneficial effects.

Another method for multiple CPU systems is to force prebuilding of more log entries prior to processes requesting the latch. This method reduces the length of time a process holds a latch by reducing the number of redo entry pieces to copy into the SGA. The *init.ora* parameter LOG_ENTRY_PREBUILD_THRESHOLD defines the maximum size of redo entries that may be pre-built. Increasing this value causes more redo entries to be prebuilt. However, this will increase the memory requirements for each process.

12.7 Development Management Issues

The good and bad habits for SQL should be pinned on every Oracle programmer's wall. Although they should follow these habits whenever they write SQL, I find that most programmers do not initially. So, code reviews for the performance-critical portions of applications are essential. In addition, you need to follow them for the rest of the programs as well—especially in a multi-user environment. As we saw in this chapter, a poorly written program can affect well-written programs by causing contention or unnecessary I/O.

DBAs and application programmers must work closely together when investigating performance issues. Ideally, both types of staff will work on the project together; they will even have offices close to each other. If both groups know enough about Oracle's internal structures and the application, they can combine their ideas. In practice, I these groups in separate corporate reporting hierarchies. Such environments require a formal staff assignment to the project. DBAs and programming staff are often spread over a wide area. This may be a reason why initial programming overlooks performance issues. During system testing, or worse, even later, you have to initiate a performance retrofitting project. You can avoid such a belated reactive approach by including an experienced DBA from the start of the project.

Oracle provides many choices for improving performance. However, the principal gains in my experience come from good table design, well-written SQL, use of indexes, and increasing data cache buffers. Ultimately, the more real memory you can devote to the SGA, the better Oracle programs perform.

Part

4

Data Warehouses, Distributed Systems, and the World Wide Web

We have learned a great deal about applications in the past few years. The funny thing is we have not discarded much. In earlier parts, we discussed the new techniques and models that help us build better quality systems. They covered primarily our operational systems. In this part, we discuss unconventional systems.

Businesses have come to rely on information for setting strategies. To support these sophisticated needs, we have learned to collect and integrate historical data. The unique needs of this environment require us to build data warehouses or data marts to consolidate our operational data. The process of designing these databases is quite different from our operational systems and deserves separate discussion.

Users are on the move. As businesses globalize, we need to support the needs of users around the world. Current communications technologies just cannot keep up with the traffic demands of client-server systems. We need to distribute our data and processing so that users have the speed of local access while sharing data with their global offices. We discuss the challenges posed by these needs in a separate chapter.

Client-server systems require a high cost infrastructure. To work around the issues of upgrading to souped-up PCs on every desk, we may consider using Internet browser technology. The thin client supported by this alternative reduces infrastructure cost per user. The approach implemented by Oracle and other vendors reduces administrative headaches of deploying client server systems. However, the user interface in this environment is really different from other client-server tools.

Data Warehouse

We need a data warehouse to accumulate historical data for trend analysis. Businesses depend on monitoring the trends of various metrics, such as revenues, sales, costs,— to gauge the progress toward achieving their goals. We also need a warehouse to consolidate and integrate data that is otherwise divided among many separate operational systems. Keeping history in each operational system impacts its performance but provides only a portion of the benefit of a consolidated warehouse.

In the 1980's, we saw this need for trend analysis materialize in the form of executive information systems (EIS). EIS systems needed historical data far beyond that provided by operational systems. Their primary characteristic was trend analysis. A secondary characteristic was that the queries were not nearly as repetitive as IS staff would have liked. So, we saw a proliferation of ad-hoc query tools aimed at the savvy executive. Early in the 1990's, the characteristics typical of decision support databases were formalized and called a data warehouse. In this chapter we cover

- Data models for a data warehouse are different from OLTP data models. We discuss how to extend data models to rise to this challenge.

- A methodology for developing a data warehouse including ways to specify the rules for loading data from the source system into the target warehouse.

- Meta data for a data warehouse. We discuss the kinds of rules that we need to capture about our data such as transformation rules, source to target mapping rules, historical business rules, validation rules, and conflict resolution rules.

- The impact of database facilities such as bitmap indexes and parallel processing in a data warehouse.

13.1 Overview of a Data Warehouse

A data warehouse is a corporate repository of information over time. Its concept is fundamentally different from operational systems, that is, systems that support the day-to-day operation of your business. The purpose of a data warehouse is to support the analysis of data to forecast trends, discover unplanned patterns, and so on. In this sense, they are a little different from *executive information systems* (EIS) which target specific predetermined analysis. The EIS functionality is a subset of that supported by a data warehouse.

Operational systems are concerned with recording and processing transactions conducted by the business. For example, the Widgets operational systems include order entry, inventory management, shipping, receiving, and so on. Operational systems usually contain only current transactions. For example, they may contain open orders or recent shipments. If any corrections are necessary to our transactions, ideally we make them in the operational systems.

Sometimes, operational systems also include some reporting facilities that allow us to view effects of the transactions over time. For example, we may record customer account balances that we update whenever they place an order or send us a payment. Such reporting facilities are called *operational data stores*. It is possible to update data in an operational data store if it provides update access, although such updates are not ideal as they create inconsistent data.

A data warehouse contains data only for reading. Figure 13-1 illustrates the conceptual relationship between operational systems, operational data stores, data marts, and data warehouses. Users cannot update any data in a warehouse. All of this data is obtained from one or more operational systems. A warehouse also accumulates data over time. So, we might gather the historical record of our interactions with a customer in a warehouse. For example, we may hold all orders placed by our customers along with their status such as complete, canceled, shipped, paid, and so on. Later in this chapter, we will discuss how to model history using our data modeling conventions. A data warehouse can serve the needs of many user constituencies. For example, the Widgets warehouse may serve sales management, the business planners in forecasting revenues, the marketing staff in analyzing demographic trends, the purchasing staff in analyzing purchasing patterns, and so on.

A *data mart* is a warehouse that focuses on the needs of just one user constituency. It may not contain all of the data for a business, or even data used by other parts of the business. For example, a sales-oriented data mart would not contain data about shipping and returns. Data marts may be *independent*—that is, populated from source operational systems. A *dependent* data mart is populated from a data warehouse—that is, it contains a subset of the data warehouse data.

When designing a clinical trials data warehouse, we created dependent data marts from a central data warehouse by extracting subsets of the data. This approach allowed us to meet performance requirements while adhering to the data integration

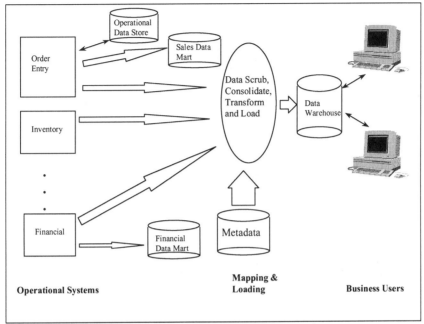

Figure 13-1: ODS, Data Mart, and Data Warehouse

rules. Independent data marts allow you to bypass the political issues relating to standard terminology necessary in a data warehouse. Because data marts contain a subset of the data warehouse data, we can get good performance without a significant investment in resources.

Data in a data warehouse typically comes from one or more operational systems. Figure 13-1 also illustrates the typical process of getting data into a data warehouse from operational systems. If you followed the ideal approach of developing a systems strategy prior to developing your operational systems, you probably have integrated data between the different operational systems. However, remember that operational systems are commonly fragmented because they are developed piecemeal without the benefit of an overall strategic model. So, we may have overlapping or duplicate data between systems. We need to consolidate this data before loading it into the warehouse. We also need to resolve any discrepancies between matching data from separate operational systems.

The data warehouse development process is a little different from the traditional system development approach. Superficially, we have an analysis phase, a design phase, a development phase, and then a production rollout phase. There the similarity ends. The analysis phase actually consists of

- Determining the user community and their known analytical requirements. These requirements consist of the kinds of trend analysis they would like to perform, the kinds of calculations they use in their known requirements, and business rules and policies that govern these analyses. We will discuss these items in Section 13.3 Meta data for a Warehouse.

- Modifying the normalized data (or object) model to reflect historical data gathering, discussed in Section 13.2.3 Modeling History.

- Modifying the business rules model to reflect historical changes. Rules are effective for specific periods of time and with business objective changes. We discuss some examples of changes in Section 13.2.5 Historical Business Rules.

- Examining the operational systems to determine the source of required data. This process is also called data mapping. We may need to perform some transformation or derivation on the source data before it meets the target requirements. The data map, together with the transformation rules, is called meta data. We will discuss this in Section 13.3 Meta data for a Warehouse.

The design phase of a warehouse refines the meta data and data models to derive a data warehouse schema model, also known as a star schema. A simple star schema consists of a fact table, such as sales, surrounded by related *dimension* tables, such as sales region, sales person, product, and so on. Dimension tables are typically the criteria used for filtering facts during data analysis, or are the axes in a trend analysis. They often correspond to reference tables in one or more operational systems.

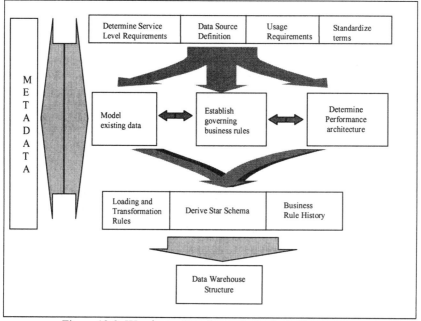

Figure 13-2: Warehouse Requirements Analysis Components

During the design phase, we also develop specifications for the data loading process as illustrated in Figure 13-2. We define how to extract the data from the source system, the transformations to be applied, and how to load it into the data warehouse. We define the initial data load process as well as the on-going data update process. We identify the tools, languages, and platforms on which this process will take place. In this phase, we may pilot a portion of the data warehouse to determine if our tool and platform choices will work in practice.

The development phase of a data warehouse consists of coding the data loading programs and creating the data warehouse database environment. Performance is a critical issue during this phase since we are loading large volumes of data. Repeating a data load is a time-consuming process! Initial data loads often involve significant manual intervention since we expect to do it just once. We would test these programs piecemeal as well in a concerted end-to-end test.

The implementation phase of the data warehouse begins with loading initial data. This often takes a significant amount of time since we may load several years' worth of data. We also begin the periodic warehouse data update process. How often we update depends on how current we need the data warehouse to be. For trend analyses, we rarely need up-to-the minute data updates. There are other factors that determine the frequency of updates that we discuss in Section 13.5.1 Data Scrubbing and Loading.

13.2 Analyzing Requirements

"But we can't predict what they [users] will do with this data. We just want to give the data to them!"

This is a frequent excuse for not analyzing requirements. The truth is the users do know *some* of the analysis they would like to perform. If our data warehouse does not support at least these needs adequately, the project will be a failure!

Data warehouses often end up as data landfills. If their performance is inadequate due to poorly organized data, the warehouse simply becomes a black hole, absorbing data without providing any service. People stop using it as it gets more and more difficult to find what they are looking for. To prevent this fate for your warehouse, a good requirements analysis is essential. How is analysis for a warehouse different from analysis for an operational system? Can we use the same techniques that we described in earlier chapters? The answer to these questions is yes, but with a change in our focus. Figure 13-2 illustrates some of the components of data warehouse requirements definition.

13.2.1 How to Gather Requirements

A data warehouse aims to support inquiries about trends or history. When we analyze requirements for a warehouse, we focus on understanding the objects of the business rather than the transactions conducted by the business. So, our questions focus on the events that relate to the business objects rather than the processes that respond to these events. We focus on the information represented by these events rather than how to collect and process that information. Of course, good data modelers have been doing this all along. The additional challenge with a warehouse is representing history.

One example of our event-based focus is customers and orders. An order may be placed, backordered, shipped, partially shipped, paid, in dispute, and so on. A customer may be a prospect, an approved customer, or an inactive customer. Notice that our state transition diagrams or life history techniques are invaluable in understanding events. One difference here is that our primary interest is in what information was known as a result of an event occurring rather than what triggered the event, which process responded to it, or even which business rule was enforced. If you used these techniques during the analysis of the underlying operational system, you may have enhanced the model as discussed later.

You may use any of the information gathering methods discussed in earlier chapters. The only technique that is transaction oriented—and hence inappropriate for analyzing data warehouse requirements—is the *UseCase* analysis technique. However, the preparation necessary for UseCases includes useful elements such as event determination. UseCases focus on the detailed interaction involved *within* transactions. The focus of data warehouse requirements gathering is events and related information *across* transactions.

Note that your preparation for interviews is different. Prior to the interviews, we need some background on the measurements used by the user community in their work. For example, regional sales directors monitor sales over a period of time within their regions. They may compare the sales volume and revenue to the same period, previous year, past three months, or other similar comparison variable. We can use these variables as initial guides to prepare for our information gathering. Our homework prior to the interview is to obtain information about such reports used by our target user community.

The questions that we might prepare before the interview will also be different. Here are some examples:

- What kinds of analysis do you need to support your work and decision-making? Do you have examples of these from your current method of preparing it?

- Can you define the [business term such as *"region"*]? How many of these does the company have? Is this term standard between all departments or divisions?

- In the sales analysis report, you currently use sales volume and total revenue figures. Are there other summaries that you would like to have available?

- Do you also need drill-down data? If the cost for drill down data for your needs were $20,000.00 (that is, relatively high) would it still be worthwhile?

- How many years of historical data do you need for comparison purposes? At what cost? Use some high dollar amount to gauge their interest in history if it goes beyond a couple of years. Some businesses, such as insurance, mortgage, or lease financing, have inherently long cycles. So, they will need to keep many years of history. But other business, such as telephone service or mail order, may be volatile and history beyond one or two years is of little use because of the drastic changes in the market.

- What data elements should we keep a history for? Not all changes to data over time are of interest to the users of a data warehouse. For example, in a mail order business, maintaining history of customer address changes is really not useful for any business analysis; however, changes to orders are! In a clinical trials data warehouse, any change to any data is of interest for the purposes of audit reporting to the US Food and Drug Administration.

- We know the following major events in the life cycle of a [reference entity—such as customer]. Are there other events that we missed? What information relating to any of these events is useful to you? Where do you obtain it from today?

- Were there any significant changes in business operations during the required history period? What kinds of rules changed? Try to use real examples to start them off, such as *"Our commission structure changed last year. Were there other changes in our operations during the history period?"*

Document the findings rigorously. As a first step, write them as declarative sentences that express a rule about the data. For example, *"Sales analysis compares year over year data"* or *"Revenue growth analysis compares total and average yearly revenue for the previous ten years."* Some rules may express mathematical calculation. For example, *"Sales volumes are total units sold over the specified period."* You may express them as mathematical formulae if that is more convenient.

These requirements are quite likely to change over time. We are really not planning to develop reports based on them. We will, however, extract from them the kinds of calculations our users expect to perform and the data needed for performing these calculations. In constructing our meta data definitions, as discussed in a later section, we will make sure we can obtain as a minimum this required data from the operational systems.

You may find some terms that are inconsistently defined. It is actually quite important to pin down the differences. Poor definitions of differences could make your warehouse usable to very few people. For example, the term *"domestic"* to a salesperson might mean the states in the mainland USA, but to a regulatory service person, it includes all fifty states in USA including Hawaii! So, if you simply assume the coverage defined by one or the other party, your pre-calculated summaries would be useful only to one. Standardizing terminology is one of the greatest challenges of a data warehouse. If you are unable to standardize, you may be better off developing departmental data marts, not a data warehouse!

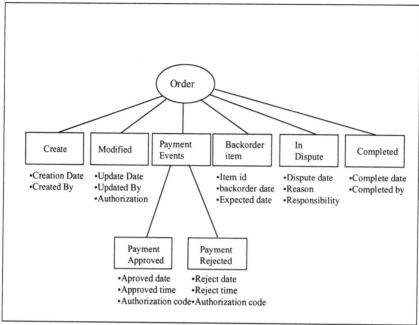

Figure 13-3: Life History of ORDER

Don't forget to estimate the load that the warehouse must support. As a minimum, estimate which groups of users would use the data warehouse. Then, estimate how many users within each group might access the warehouse and how often they would do so. These estimates are essential for sizing the warehouse. Realize that many of the queries that run aginst a warehouse process large amounts of data. However, users do lose patience quickly with long-running queries. So, you should determine the threshold of patience with the known queries as part of your analysis effort. Our design will consider these requirements when forming the warehouse strategy.

13.2.2 Techniques for Analyzing Requirements

Many of the modeling techniques we described in earlier chapters are useful as starting points for a data warehouse. The most important techniques represent data structures either as an object model or an entity-relationship model. Remember that data is the heart of a data warehouse. If you already have one of these models, you have a head start. Otherwise, your first step is to develop a data model based on operational data. You can then modify the model to reflect history of the data elements of interest as described in a later section.

Another modeling technique that is useful is object type or entity life history. This technique allows us to determine the states of each major reference object type that are of interest to the target users. Figure 13-3 illustrates the life history of Orders. In Oracle Designer, we can use the repository object navigator to record events. We can use *Domains* to record the possible statuses of a particular entity. However, we cannot really represent the life history or a state transition model.

The additional information to the life history includes the data elements associated with the status of the entity. In our Order life history example, we need to record the date of each status, the person responsible for the transaction that changed the status, and so on. We obtain these elements from our requirements gathering process. For example, suppose our users indicate that they analyze the intervals for status transition to measure the company's service quality. To support this requirement, we must capture the date of each status in our model. In the warehouse, design may later pre-calculate the intervals for status transition. Suppose our users require statistics on products that are backordered. We must make sure that we capture this status in the warehouse.

The real challenge of a data warehouse is that we can only gather the requirements for known analyses. Users may change their minds later, or devise new analyses after the data warehouse is operational. If the data needed for supporting the analyses is not in a usable format in the data warehouse, we may have to restructure some of the derived data in the warehouse from detailed transactions.

Change in a data warehouse is frequent. For example, suppose we package several component products into a packaged product. After our warehouse is operational, users would like to obtain statistics on sales of some of the components packaged in a new way. We would need to derive these statistics from the breakdown of the previously packaged product. Our operational transactions are not likely to contain

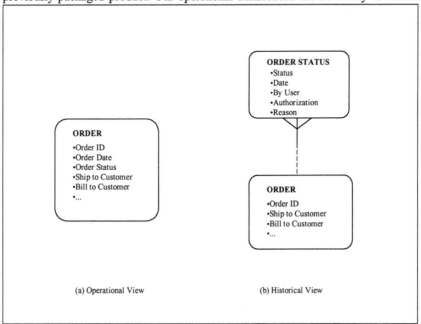

Figure 13-4: History of an Attribute of ORDER

this information as they record transactions only on the package! Expect to support such care and feeding of the warehouse on an ongoing basis.

13.2.3 Modeling History

A data warehouse accumulates data over time. This collection of history significantly impacts the structure of our data model. For example, an operational system's data model might store the current status of an Order. To keep the history of all statuses of orders, we need a separate entity in an ERD, or an embedded object type in our object model. Figure 13-4 illustrates the operational and historical view of Orders.

Realize that keeping history is different from keeping an audit trail or a journal of modifications. Audit trails make data access complex, even though you can extract the required trend information from them. Complex data access often leads to performance degradation. More importantly, we would have a hard task teaching users to extract the information from audit trails using off-the-shelf tools.

13.2.4 Historical Data

There are many instances where keeping history of an element alters its underlying data (or object) model. The most common kinds of elements on which we keep history are attributes, relationships, and entities.

Figure 13-4 illustrates the structural change that we need to keep history of an attribute. In this example, we need to keep the history of the attribute *status*—that is, maintain a list of statuses achieved by an order. With each status we need to record additional information such as when the status was attained, who authorized it, and other appropriate information. Since each order will have several statuses associated with it, we need to normalize it into a separate entity as shown in our entity relationship diagram. If we were using an object model, we would represent this new set of attributes as an embedded *collection attribute* or embedded class.

When we keep history of a relationship, we alter its cardinality—for example, we turn a one-to-many relationship into a many-to-many relationship. Figure 13-5 illustrates the example of keeping a history of suppliers for a particular product. The rule in the operational system is that we only have one supplier for a product at a time. However, we may switch suppliers over time for that product. So, from an historical perspective, we may have multiple suppliers for a product. Of course, we would want a record of the start and end dates of the period when we used a particular supplier, and perhaps a reason for terminating the relationship. The result is a separate entity to represent the product-supplier relationship with its appropriate attributes. In an object model, we would represent this as an embedded class within the definition of the Product class. However, the normalization principles applied here created the new entity, *product supplier*.

Sometimes, we need to keep history of an entity itself. For example, suppose a customer may have one or more accounts with our company. Our operational system

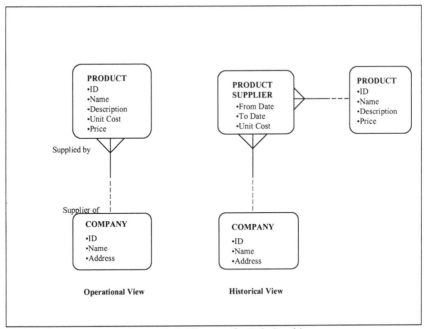

Figure 13-5: History of a Relationship

may only require active accounts. Closed accounts may be relegated to history. To model this requirement, we need to add start and end dates to the Account entity. You might define a convention of adding *effective date / termination date* attributes to every entity for which we must maintain history. Some older operational systems maintained this kind of history in their database. However, it unnecessarily complicated retrieval of current data and served only a few users. One of my clients, a guides and directory publisher, was able to halve the development time of several operational systems by separating historical data into a data warehouse. Much of the savings was due to a simpler data schema design resulting in straightforward access.

The most challenging type of history is structural changes such as organization hierarchy or product components. In this type, the data model itself does not change. Consider, as an example, a common scheme where we combine one or more products into a package for sale. We can track the date we started offering the package and the date we discontinued it by simply adding *effective date* and *termination date* attributes. However, we may later package the same components into a new package for sale with different prices. We need the ability to maintain the information on the individual components of each package as well as the package itself. Trend analysis in such a situation will require additional work during data load or on demand.

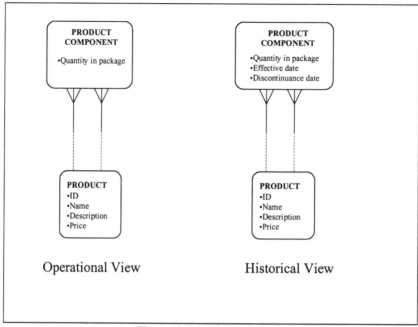

Figure 13-6: Package Contents

13.2.5 Historical Business Rules

Business rules are statements of a constraint or a fact that govern the way a business operates. They may, of course, change based on the kinds of behavior a business wishes to encourage. For example, if a business decides to promote Product A instead of Product B because of its higher margin, it may increase the commissions on Product A and lower them on Product B. The business may alter its product structure or mix to promote one product over another.

All of these changes lead to additional requirements of the data warehouse. We must capture the duration for which a particular rule was in effect. We must also associate it with the data elements that are affected by it. Some rules may be expressed in the data model itself, while others may be declarative statements associated with certain data.

In our earlier example of a packaged product, the model itself expressed the rule about the contents of the package. Figure 13-6 illustrates this model. While the business continues to offer a package, the sales data for the package is useful for trend analysis. However, when a new package is designed made up of some or all of the same components of the current package, we have no history data for its sales trend.

Our data warehouse users may wish to construct a forecast of the trends for the new package. For example, they may analyze the sales trend of all packages that contain one or more of the component products in the new package. They would like the sales data for the package trickled down to its component products. Then, they would like to analyze the trends for a product regardless of which package it was included in. To facilitate such analysis, we must associate with the package structure model, the business rule that trends of a component product may be derived from trends of its parent package. We should explicitly state this rule in the meta data for this warehouse and make it accessible for business users to browse.

Another example of a requirement is that business users wish to analyze sales of *similar* products. To satisfy this requirement, we will need an additional structure to categorize products that indicate *similar* kinds of products. The rule expressed here is that certain products may be categorized as being *similar* to others. Figure 13-6 illustrates this categorization. Our challenge is to get all of the user constituencies to agree on when two products are similar and belong in one category. We must also find someone to *own* the categorization process so that they are responsible for categorizing products at source.

Another example is products where the name is recycled for different underlying reasons. A notorious example is the Ford car name Thunderbird. This name was used with several physically different cars over a period of several years. Recycling of popular names is a common marketing practice to gain the advantage of brand recognition. With each different underlying product with the same name, the warehouse must indicate when the product began under the name and when it was discontinued. If there was an overlapping period between the name being discontinued for one product and reused for another, we need to separate associated data to avoid confusion. When users select such a product by name, it must be clear to them which underlying product they chose.

You may find many such instances of data warehouse analysis where you need data not provided by an existing operational system. Some projects find themselves developing update screens into the warehouse to allow users to add such information. However, exercise extreme caution—data warehouses are not updateable for a good reason. Users may inadvertently modify irrecoverable historical data! Or they may unintentionally alter a business rule. A better approach is to modify the operational system to capture the required data—then, process it through the standard data loading process.

Some rules may be expressed as declarative statements rather than as part of the data model. One example is the rule that "*The business offers 3% commission for the sale of a product.*" Another example is "*Commission is paid after collecting payment from the customer.* "Experts such as Ronald Ross have developed graphical notation for expressing such rules, but I find the statements work well with business users. We must record the *effective* and *termination date*s for each rule, if known. Rules for handling discount structures are often too complex to represent with just data models.

The challenge with associating a history of rules with data is that we may not know the rules that are no longer in effect. Whether it is worth delving into history for them is dependent on the time available for such research and its value to the users of the warehouse. It may be worthwhile providing tools to the business users that allow them to express and associate rules with data. If the rules affect the transformation of legacy data, you will hear about it as soon as you provide incorrectly processed data. This is a compelling reason for piloting your data transformation as early as possible.

13.3 Meta data for a Warehouse

Meta data is data about data. Meta data in a warehouse is a record of all of the information that we have discussed so far about the data elements stored in it. Meta data for a warehouse is useful to technical and business users if it is organized and presented properly. It is essential for the continuing support and enhancement of the warehouse.

Meta data can be categorized into three groups: physical, transformational, and informational. Physical meta data describes how data is stored physically in the database; for example, the names of the tables, columns, formats, and so on. The data described includes the source system and target data warehouse. Transformational meta data describes how data from source systems is manipulated prior to loading it into the target data warehouse. From this meta data, you can determine where any data element in the warehouse comes from and the derivation rules applied to it before storing it in the warehouse. Informational meta data provides business users with information about the content of data in the warehouse. It provides information like the meaning of an element, who *owns* it, its context, and availability.

13.3.1 Physical Meta data

Physical meta data comes from both the storage definitions for the source systems and the physical implementation design for the data warehouse. If your source systems are based on a DBMS product like Oracle, the definitions can be extracted from the DBMS data dictionary. The ideal case is where you used a product like Oracle Designer for analysis, design, and implementation of the source system. In this case, you already have the physical meta data and more. For flat-file based source systems, you may have to load record definitions into the meta data definition. If you are using Oracle Designer for storing the meta data, you need to write some utilities using the Oracle Designer API for loading the definitions. The target warehouse meta data is the design for the warehouse described in a later section.

As part of the physical meta data description, you need to keep at least the following information:

- Application system name.

- Responsible party, that is, the IT group and user organization that owns the application with contact information.

- Name of each file, record type, or table in the application.

- Organization of the file, e.g., VSAM, Relational, and so on.

- Access Security restrictions, if any.

- Data elements and their formats.

- Primary keys for accessing records or rows.

- References to data elements in other files or tables such as foreign key constraints.

- Data element editing rules applied by the source application.

- Description of the insert and update transactions that add new records or update existing ones.

- Description of the delete transaction so that we can record a termination date in the data warehouse.

We need descriptions of the transactions so that we can design a data extraction interface. In most warehouses, it is impractical to reload all of the source data from scratch each time. Reloading is extremely time-consuming and inefficient. The ideal is to only load data that has changed since the previous load cycle. So, we aim to apply transactions incrementally.

You need to document data obtained from external sources as well as from in-house systems. You may have to negotiate with the data supplier to obtain incremental update transactions. Make a particular note if such transactions are not available. Your on-going periodic updates to the data warehouse may be different from the initial data load. We will discuss these issues in more detail as part of the data loading section.

Physical meta data is very technically-oriented. It is usually defined and maintained by IT staff based on requirements gathered from warehouse users. Business users get involved in selecting the data elements from the source system that will be used to load data into the warehouse.

13.3.2 Transformational Meta Data

Transformational meta data describes how to transform source data before storing it in the target warehouse. It consists of rules on validation, cleansing, derivation, summarization, and matching conditions. Many of these rules cross application boundaries. For example, if two applications each hold data about customers, we need to consolidate it into a single view of customer in the data warehouse. We will apply these rules for the initial data loading and for the on-going periodic updates to the warehouse. These transformations are the bulk of our requirement specification. There are several categories of transformations applied to the data to be loaded into a warehouse:

- **Mapping**: A mapping rule specifies the correspondence between one or more source elements to a single data warehouse element. The rule may include conditions for choosing one source over another, and methods for resolving overlapping information contained in multiple source applications.

- **Filtering**: These rules specify the criteria used on each data source to subset or filter information selected for loading into the warehouse. For example, we may exclude data from an external source used by an in-house source application, but which we plan to load directly into the warehouse.

- **Transactional**: We need to transform transactions from our operational systems into status-based data in our data warehouse. For example, we may get an *insert* transaction from our customer management system. We would transform this into customer data with the status of *created*, and the creation date. Combining these rules with the appropriate mapping rules may raise some challenging situations. For example, we may get an *insert* transaction on a customer from one source application where that customer already exists in another source application!

- **Simple derivation**: These rules perform some calculation on one or more source data elements to create the contents of a target warehouse element. These rules typically populate data elements in the warehouse which have no single corresponding element in any source system. They are simple in the sense that they usually take individual data elements rather than operate on sets of rows. An example of a simple derivation is calculating a patient's age from their date of birth and date of administering treatment.

- **Summarization**: These rules, a special case of derivation, involve calculations performed on sets of data records or rows. An example of summarization is average order quantity for a product over a specified period of time, such as average daily order quantity. These rules are dependent on one or more dimensions of the warehouse.

Transformational meta data is defined jointly by IT staff and business users. Business users take responsibility for the algorithms and mapping. IT staff usually translate the algorithms into technical specifications and implement them. IT staff also discover any conflicts or exception conditions in data and work with the business users to resolve them.

Transformation rules are probably the most difficult to define. The reason is that business users cannot always visualize the information they will need in the warehouse.

My strategy for dealing with this difficulty is to set up an iterative implementation environment. In this environment, we define phased delivery of the warehouse where each phase is a distinct deliverable that results in a usable, albeit incomplete, warehouse. The phases may be based on incorporating one source application's data per phase, or source data *owned* by a particular user organization. Each phase builds on the results of the previous phase. The key to this strategy is to have an overall design of the warehouse and then iterate on defining the meta data and designing the data loading processes.

13.3.3 Informational Meta Data

This kind of meta data supports data analysis activities of the warehouse users. It builds on the rules in the transformational meta data. It provides business-oriented information about data such as

- When was this data last updated from the source?

- Where did this data element actually originate? This information is about the result of applying a mapping rule to a particular data element, not the mapping rule itself.

- What does this data element mean? The description here is business-oriented rather than the technical definition supplied in physical meta data.

- How was this data element calculated? Again, the information is about the actual calculations and conditions applied to a particular element, not what the transformation rule defines.

This kind of meta data is partly held in the warehouse and partly in the meta data repository. For example, we might keep *last update date* for each of the fact table rows in the warehouse. The description of elements in that fact table, however, would be in the meta data repository. Depending on the warehouse query tools selected, some of these descriptions might also be in the repository that supports the tool. For example, the BusinessObjects product contains a *Universe* definition which consists of physical warehouse data elements and their business-oriented meanings. The Impromptu product similarly has a catalog definition as does the Forest and Trees product. We will describe the capabilities of such tools later in this chapter.

Informational meta data is the responsibility of the warehouse users. It ought to be maintained by them with some assistance from IT staff. In reality, business users delegate this task to analysts who have gained a significant knowledge of the business through their requirements definition work.

13.4 Data Warehouse Design

Some of the activities described as part of analyzing requirements are critical for the data warehouse design. For example, we need the historical data models before design can commence. However, we need not complete the definition of all meta data before starting the design. I am not offering you an excuse to abandon the difficult task of meta data definition—merely suggesting that you can overlap these tasks to some extent. This section discusses approaches to structuring your project. Regardless of the approach you choose, an overall model of the warehouse, and an implementation schema based on it, are essential.

13.4.1 Project Strategy

There are two basic approaches to building warehouses: an all-or-nothing approach and an iterative implementation approach. The all-or-nothing approach requires that you design the warehouse and implement all of it together. This means that you will designate a *D-Day* when the entire warehouse will be operational with all data from all source systems. The iterative implementation approach consists of designing the warehouse, but implementing it in phases. Figure 13-7 illustrates the high-level task plan for both of these approaches.

The all-or-nothing approach is appropriate when you have a set of well-integrated source applications. The integration should have eliminated overlapping data stored in multiple applications. Instead, their common data should be shared between them. They should have clearly defined data stewardship and applications that support the responsibility. In such an environment, you probably already have existing data models for these integrated applications. You probably also have the physical meta data for the source systems.

Your tasks, then, consist of modifying the models to incorporate storage of historical data followed by definition of the meta data. Mapping from source to warehouse elements is straightforward because the underlying source systems are well-integrated. You will need to gather requirements for transactional, derivation, and summarization rules. You may design the dimensions and fact data of the warehouse. Design of the

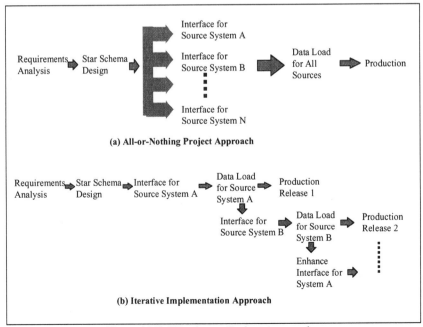

Figure 13-7: Warehouse Project Approaches

data loading should be simpler as little cleansing should be necessary.

You may develop the data loading processes in parallel by subject areas or by reference entities. For example, you might commission several development teams, each assigned to developing the data load procedures for one subject in the warehouse. Implementation consists of executing the initial data load procedures before making the warehouse publicly available. Of course, if any of the rules yield an incorrect result, from the users' perspective, you may need to repeat the data loading process.

In practice, few companies have such a well-integrated architecture. Applications are developed without a strategic model or plan for the portfolio. They are developed as funding for a specific need becomes available. Overlapping and conflicting data is not uncommon. Rarely are there data integrity constraints imposed between applications. As a result, the all-or-nothing approach becomes too unwieldy in these environments.

Meta data in such environments is quite convoluted. Mapping of any overlapping data turns into a series of conditional processing. It must be followed by inevitable manual review of the data by users who can detect erroneous results. These users must describe how to correct the source or the mapping rules to produce the correct result. One of the projects I was involved in actually spent several months in this iterative cycle of defining a mapping rule, developing the data load process, reviewing the results, and modifying the mapping rule. This was in a company with only eight years of legacy data. Imagine the difficulty in companies that have longer legacies or that have data spread across many applications!

At another client, the spaghetti of data copied and transformed in legacy decision support applications was so involved that none of the IT staff could pinpoint the data source system. Of course, this client had a few systems that dated back to the early 1970's! They also had the greatest need for consolidated data that could give them a true picture of trends. Their legacy reporting systems could only provide data that could not be reconciled between reports from separate systems.

The iterative approach of tackling one source system at a time generally yields a more manageable project plan. The initial data loads are easier and more quickly completed. Thus you can show real deliverables in a fairly short time-frame. These data loads also yield a usable warehouse—it just may not contain all of the required data. Each subsequent source system make data loading more complex. However, you can tackle the conditions of each system with a smaller group of respective users.

Notice that the summarization rules need not be defined or developed until the base data is loaded. However, to make the warehouse usable, you may choose to define them as each source system's data is incorporated.

You can, of course, parallel several development and implementation activities. There is nothing that restricts you from taking on more than one source system at a time. The constraint is your resource availability. However, remember that the larger the

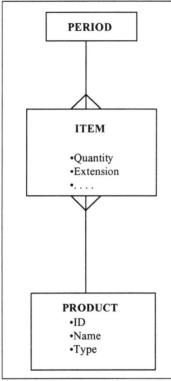

Figure 13-8: Widgets Star Schema

implementation team, the more communication issues you must address. Invariably some portion of the time must be spent in communicating issues between teams.

The iterative approach allows you to pilot the usage pattern of the warehouse in stages. You get a better estimate of the actual size of the warehouse as it grows. You can monitor the performance and address any tuning needs along the way. With an all-or-nothing approach, you must tackle performance tuning as part of the warehouse design. Any unanticipated usage patterns that cause performance degradation must be addressed on a production database.

13.4.2 Design Components

There are two distinct parts to designing the warehouse: the schema design and the data loading. Designing the schema consists of determining the fact table and dimensions for analysis—that is, designing the *star schema*. Data load design consists of determining the sequence and dependencies between the meta data rules for the initial data and also the incremental updates to the warehouse.

A star schema is so named because it models a fact table surrounded by the potential analysis dimensions. Figure 13-8 illustrates a portion of the schema for the Widgets data warehouse. A fact table in a star schema is the table that contains data values used for trend analysis. For example, the fact table in Figure 13-8 is the sales data table. A simple warehouse has just one fact table, but it is not uncommon to have multiple fact tables that are related to common dimensions.

Dimensions are categories used to classify the data in the fact table. For example, Widgets sales can be classified by geographic region, product category, time period, and so on. Determining the dimensions is a critical part of designing the warehouse because they represent the criteria used for data analysis. If we miss a dimension, we may restrict the usefulness of the warehouse. You can think of dimensions as lookup lists or as the axes on trend charts.

Many dimensions are simple lists. Others have a complex organization of their own, leading to models that are sometimes called *spider* or *snowflake* schemas. Figure 13-9 illustrates a larger portion of the Widgets warehouse schema including some complex structures. In this example, Widgets packages several products together as a single offering. One product may be packaged into many offerings. The sales fact table must provide data about the individual products as well as the packaged offerings.

Similarly, regions are grouped in several ways depending on the kind of trend analysis needed. For example, the basic unit of region is the city specified in the mailing address. We may group cities into a county, or a state, or a political district, and so on. The groups may contain overlapping regions.

Note that the schema does not include customer as a dimension—only customer type. Although it is possible to keep detailed data in the warehouse, information about individual customers adds little to the trend analysis required by Widgets staff. So, the warehouse summarizesthe data based on the demographics as the dimensions. This approach makes sense if your detail data is voluminous and used very rarely. For example, one of my warehouse projects involved 300 million detail records per month. Keeping these in the data warehouse is a massive commitment of resources with little return on investment. The biggest bang for the buck was the data summarized by dimensions. Beware of completely discarding that detail data. Future analysis requirements may uncover some dimension not included in your design. You may have to dig into the detail data to find them.

Designing the data load processes is like designing bulk update processes. You extract data from the operational systems and load it into the warehouse, with some transformations applied along the way. There are two designs—one for the initial data

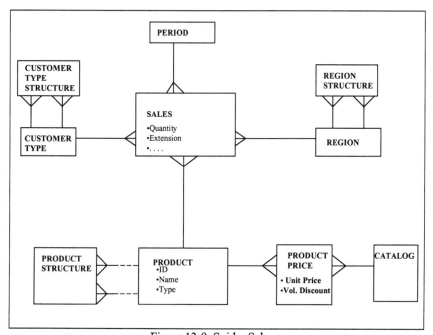

Figure 13-9: Spider Schema

load and another for the ongoing replenishment of the warehouse. The difference between these two is the kind of data formats they obtain from the source system.

The initial data load must load all data from the operational systems, including any historical data in older systems. Often the historical data is in a different format from the current operational system—it was not converted when replacing the older system. There may be data integrity problems in the historical data that were eliminated in the newer operational system. The resulting bad data must be cleaned up prior to loading it into the warehouse. When the cost of this cleansing was high, some of my clients chose to discard the bad data. In their opinion, the loss of a portion of the data did not significantly skew the trend analysis—that was their major purpose of the warehouse.

An important consideration when designing the data load processes is to share the enforcement of rules between the initial data load and the ongoing replenishment processes. It is important to identify the rules that apply in both contexts. These rules must be applied uniformly to avoid discrepancies between the initial data and ongoing replenishment.

The actual design of the process is dependent on the tools you plan to use for your warehouse. If you plan to use a data scrubbing and transformation tool, you may merely need to articulate the rules to the appropriate tool. The tool may simply perform the transfer or may generate code to do so. If you plan to use a generic database, you need detailed specification of the batch process that will perform the data loading.

Don't forget that you'll also need to design the operational procedures to go hand-in-hand with your data load program design. These procedures should include the design for modifications to be captured from your operational systems incrementally, the backup of these files, definition of the time period when the replenishment process should begin, and so on.

13.4.3 Object-Oriented, Relational, or Multi-Dimensional?

One of the most frequently asked questions is what kind of database is needed for implementing a warehouse? The market offers three kinds of technologies: object DBMS, relational DBMS, and proprietary multi-dimensional DBMS. Although you could use any of these technologies, each places its own restrictions.

Object DBMS require the least external change for storing historical data. The internal structure of an Object type changes as we discussed in an earlier section. However, its methods need not change. The drawback is that you must have a method defined on the object types to produce summarized or derived data. Another drawback is that the model creates a bias in the way users would view the data. New perspectives are harder because of reduced flexibility of the structure. Overall, I suggest that you consider other technologies before using an object DBMS for your warehouse needs.

Relational DBMSs are the most flexible of these three technologies. However, bear in mind that a data warehouse does not (and should not) subscribe to the normalization principle of relational design. So, your design will be highly denormalized. This is not a requirement imposed by any commercial RDBMS product, so there is no restriction on implementing the warehouse. The key criteria, then, is performance. Most RDBMSs have implemented significant features to enhance performance in the warehouse environment. For example, they can use multiple CPUs to perform parallel operations like data loading and updating, index building, querying, and so on. Their query optimizers are also enhanced to consider the drastic size differences between fact and dimension tables. In these environments, you will need to custom build your data loading processes and management of your meta data. There are also a large number of third-party query, analysis, and reporting tools to access the data in these products.

Multi-dimensional databases are designed specifically for the data warehouse environment. Their strength is handling meta data and the data transformation process. They provide toolsets to derive data elements and create summaries. However, they are proprietary tools and they limit your choices for query and access tools. They are also not as well established in handling really large volumes of data as relational DBMSs. So, if your warehouse promises to be really large or is likely to grow rapidly, benchmark these tools before choosing one.

13.5 Data Warehouse Implementation

When you implement your warehouse, there is a lengthy stage when you prepare the database. Depending on the industry you are in, you may need to load many years' worth of data. This loading is an inherent part of the project, unlike normal OLTP projects. In an OLTP project, we might hand off the database setup and loading to a DBA. In a warehouse project, getting the data loaded *is* the implementation stage of the project.

Implementing a warehouse requires many of the skills of a database administrator. But, these skills are a little different from those of a production database administrator. The kinds of database physical design considerations that apply to a warehouse are different from those applicable to an operational system database. We will discuss some of these physical layout issues in Section 0 The warehouse batch update process is normally a much more extensive operation. It is usually run at an idle time (e.g., weekends), often when the database is unavailable for other users. Although this batch may run unattended, it is still largely a manual process. It is monitored by a human who makes the decision about when to bring the database back to normal operation.

Performance Tuning Technologies.

Part of the implementation is also to select one or more query tools appropriate to the aniticipated work of the warehouse users. These tools should include tabular and charting utilities commonly used. You may have to massage the database structure to present easily understood views of the data. These views may be in the database or the reporting tool's repository. We will discuss some ways to construct business views in Section 0 Warehouse Access Tools.

13.5.1 Data Scrubbing and Loading

Your initial data load may have a loose deadline for completion. However, the on-going replenishment has a limited window for completion—limited by the service level requirements of the warehouse. For example, if you plan on transferring daily updates to a warehouse that needs to be available 16 hours daily, you only have eight hours to complete all replenishment. You may have to share this time window with other administrative work such as software and hardware upgrades, data reorganization, and so on.

Many organizations begin their warehouse project with the misconception that they will reload the warehouse each period. Even some of the early multi-dimensional data warehouse databases require such reloading. Before you make such plans, estimate the time needed for reloading. One of my clients found that monthly reloading of their warehouse would take three weeks—they had 300 million transactions per month to process and 24 months of history! Albeit, we could reduce that time with parallel processing technology. We could reduce it even more dramatically by processing only new transactions since the previous replenishment.

One of the biggest implementation decisions you need to make is whether you will use the database facilities to perform the data scrubbing and loading work. The decision depends on a number of factors:

- **Volume of the data to be loaded**: If you need to load large volumes of data, consider the relative speed of performing the task in the source environment. Database management systems impose some overheads that may slow down their data load processing performance. Many products now provide fast loading paths, such as Oracle's DirectPath option of SQL*Loader. However, these loaders cannot perform data validation or scrubbing work.

- **Source of the data:** If your data already resides in a database like Oracle, you can use the database facilities for data manipulation. If the data is in flat files, you have a choice: process before loading or load and then manipulate. The trade-off is between the ease of RDBMS data manipulation language vs. the speed of execution in a third-generation language outside the database.

- **Environment:** If you choose a packaged warehousing product to do the data loading, you may be forced to use its scripting language or its generated code. If you choose a generic database management product, you have the choices discussed earlier.

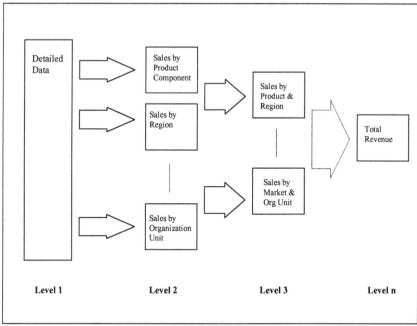

Figure 13-8: Sample Drill-down Summary Levels

- **Complexity of transformation:** You may need to store information about mapping one form of data to another for use by the transformation process. In one of my projects, we had to store the key values used by the external data provider against our internal primary keys. The map was not always one-to-one either. Such information is easier to store and manipulate in a database.

- **Transfer medium:** Consider the method planned for transferring the data to the warehouse platform. For example, would you use a LAN/WAN to transfer it, or tape, or CD-ROM? If you have to move large volumes of data, you may exceed or seriously hog the capacity of your existing network. Tape or CD-ROM may require physical transportation from one machine to another, but they provide localized access and use of high-speed channels. In addition, you also get a backup of the data.

These choices apply also to any reformatting or consolidation of data. If you are unsure about estimating the time, pilot a representative portion of the data load process.

You may pre-calculate some of the summary data in your warehouse to improve query performance. This is not strictly necessary as many query and reporting tools can summarize data as part of producing a report. However, consider the amount of data to be used for generating the summaries. You may avoid much user frustration if you can predict the commonly used summaries and pre-calculate them in the database. If you choose a multi-dimensional database product, summarization is part of the data load process. Figure 13-10 illustrates one approach to creating summary levels to support *drill-down* queries performed by many users. You also get levels of summaries when you calculate a summary for each level of organization hierarchy or product structure.

The warehouse batch update process is normally a much more extensive operation. It is usually run at an idle time (e.g., weekends), often when the database is unavailable for other users. Although this batch may run unattended, it is still largely a manual process. It is monitored by a human who makes the decision about when to bring the database back to normal operation.

13.5.2 Performance Tuning Technologies

The tuning issues discussed here are based on implementing your warehouse using Oracle. Multi-dimensional databases share some of these elements, such as disk I/O distribution, but their implementation parameters are different.

The basic goal of physical design is the same for a warehouse as for an operational system database—to optimize performance. To plan this, you need to study four main components of how the application will map into a physical disk structure: the traffic pattern, index usage, storage parameters, and tablespaces.

Warehouses typically have a few long-running complex queries at any one time, interspersed with frantic batch load-and-update jobs. This presents the DBA with a completely different set of problems to the typical OLTP scenario where the DBA's tuning is usually aimed at minimizing response time during lots of contending short transactions that update the database.

Since warehouse traffic is mostly queries, there is not much chance of lock contention. However the length of the queries means that Oracle's read consistency model uses huge amounts of rollback segment space. A good rule of thumb is that your rollback segment tablespace should be about 50-100% the size of your largest table if you have about 4-8 rollback segments.

Most warehouse users use some ad-hoc query tool as their primary interface. These tools translate users' point-and-click query definitions into database queries. They often generate complex queries which can defeat the Oracle optimizer. The DBA needs to stay alert for the *query from hell*—this is where an interactive monitoring tool is invaluable.

A warehouse needs to have lots of indexes —on almost every column that ever turns up in a *where* clause. So, you should plan for lots of space for indexes, for example, 2-3 times the space for data is normal. Large number of indexes does not impact performance perceived by users significantly since most of their traffic is not updates. It affects the performance of data load and replenishment processes, however. In an OLTP environment, we would drop indexes before updating and then rebuild them after updates are complete. This practice falls apart in a warehouse environment because of the very large tables, for example, tables that have tens of millions of rows. It can easily take hours to recreate a set of indexes on one of these tables.

Parallel processing of updates and index creation does help if you are using Oracle8. You can add more CPUs to speed up these tasks. Remember, however, that there is a point of diminishing return when adding CPUs. Monitor the state of your machine. If it is not CPU-bound, adding more processors is not going to help.

A warehouse usually has a few big objects that are tuned by hand. Since the warehouse continually grows, one objective is to ensure that you never get an allocation failure during a massive load or a complex query because you cannot afford the time to do it again. Another conflicting objective is to minimize the amount of unused disk space allocated to database objects.

Oracle provides many types of indexes that may help improve performance for specific queries. The normal index is a binary tree index. This type of index is good for range matches or pattern-based filtering. It also works best when your query selects 20% or less of the data from a table. In warehouse queries, it is common to select large portions of a table. Others types are good for exact match queries. For example, queries that use exact matches may benefit from hash indexes. Table joins benefit from bitmap indexes provided that your query is selecting large portions of data from the table.

Another characteristic of data warehouse queries is that they join very small (relatively speaking) dimension tables to very large fact tables. The Oracle optimizer recognizes this pattern and processes these queries in a different way than a normal table join. This method, called star query optimization, joins the dimension tables before joining them to the fact table. Even if the dimension table join results in a cartesian product, the resulting table is still smaller than if we used the fact table in a join. Many multi-dimensional databases use this kind of optimization.

13.5.3 Warehouse Access Tools

In a data warehouse most queries are really batch jobs. The user submits a complex long-running query and does not expect an answer for many minutes, or even hours. Even short queries are measured in "human-time" vs. "real-time"; we measure response time in tens of seconds or minutes rather than fractions of a second.

This pattern lends itself to the use of batch queues, usually implemented on top of OS facilities or with some sort of spooler. The only vital requirement is an easy way for anyone to check the status of all the available queues and where their jobs are in those queues.

The rule of thumb here is to add queues until the OS slows down, then subtract one. If possible, make sure that there is a high-priority queue for short jobs which aborts a job if it uses more than a few minutes of CPU time.

13.5.4 Security

Ad-hoc tools used in the warehouse environment mean that the DBA cannot rely on an application to provide security. It must be built into the database. Database security is often implemented using roles. Thus, the security is part of the database and works even for new ad-hoc tools the users may acquire later. Since a warehouse typically has fewer users (or at least fewer Oracle accounts), user management is not a great burden to the DBA. Many warehouse designs simply have a fixed set of Oracle accounts or roles established at application installation time and maintained manually.

Updates in a warehouse are normally a privileged (read DBA) task. They are usually carried out by a batch operation outside of normal processing hours. An application-specific account is usually set up to handle most of this work, with a limited set of people having access. All other users have only read access.

Warehouse applications rarely need extensive audit trails since updating is a batch process. It is common to track database connect time and possibly user quotas in order to get some sort of bill-back information.

13.5.5 Disaster Recovery

Disaster recovery is not nearly as big an issue as you might think. A warehouse usually contains mostly historical or derived data with updates applied periodically. Smaller warehouses often do a complete reload each period—for example, weekly or monthly. In this scenario, disaster recovery can be as simple as recreating the database on a new machine and re-running the reload process. The main limitation for reloading data is load speed. This issue will need to be addressed when designing the batch process anyway. Currently, the fastest way is to use SQL*Loader with the direct path option from a set of flat files

The strategy for a larger warehouse may be to take a full backup intermittently together with incremental upload transactions. Really large warehouses are often too large for a full cold backup to complete in the available time window. You might take online backups safely, however, since there is little, if any, update activity outside the replenishment window. A warm standby machine and a tape autoloader are often the cheapest insurance—and you can use the machine for development to boot.

Recovery time is proportional to the size of the warehouse. However, you can design for a longer recovery time requirement, provided that you do not lose any data. Warehouse users are typically much higher level analytical staff and are intolerant of being required to repeat work because of a failed recovery. Fortunately, their work is usually on a much longer term schedule; a delay of a few hours is rarely critical as long as sufficient warning is given.

Distributed Systems

Oracle is capable of running in a networked environment with the database running on one or more independent machines. These machines may be on a single LAN or spread across the world linked with WANs. These potential scenarios require a little more analysis. The purpose is to explore the impact of networked configurations. It provides the basis for choosing one configuration over another, although our judgment (and our users'!) is the final selector.

Some applications lend themselves to distributed databases. Distributing the database allows us to use the mips at the each server machine. Distributed databases give us flexibility for better local customization while retaining central consolidation. In our analysis, we have to collect information which will allow us to weigh these options. In this chapter, we discuss analysis which you can do up-front to decide whether a distributed solution is feasible and then how to implement it. In particular, we address the following topics:

- The advantages and disadvantages of distributed databases, within the context of which applications are suitable for this approach.

- Important areas for investigation, including geographic locations, functional logistics, and business units. We examine techniques for determining whether your data is suitable for partitioning.

- The performance costs of distributed databases. We discuss ways of estimating network traffic volume and throughput to determine the feasibility of distributing.

14.1 Overview of Distributed Systems

The advantages of running in a client-server environment are obvious. All users have their own machines over which they have complete control. Any work done on an individual's machine does not affect anyone else. For data sharing, we install Oracle on a server machine shared by users on the network. Forms, Reports, and other programs would run on individual machines with the database server processes on the server machine. This scenario still uses a single shared database. However, networks have a limit on their transmission capacity. So, we analyze the transaction which causes data transmission over the network.

The single database server scenario works well when all users are local to the server, that is, a LAN configuration. But, what if the department is actually spread geographically over long distances? Some users will be remote. We could connect their individual machines to the departmental server machine via a WAN. But the speed of data transmission goes down as distance increases. For better performance, these remote users may need their own local database server. So, we need to partition the database such that each remote location gets its own server, and all servers synchronize data between them.

Let's consider another scenario. Suppose that more than one department wants to share data while retaining their departmental databases. Traditionally, this scenario was an argument for a single large machine located centrally. Oracle's networking capabilities offer nontraditional solutions. We need to consider a database that is logically a single database but is distributed over several physical machines. We need to analyze the natural partitions of our data for feasibility of such an installation.

There are many other reasons for partitioning data over several physical machines. For example, we might implement applications with local variations if we distribute the database. We could use cheaper, smaller hardware for such configurations rather than the traditional large central mainframe. We reduce perceived bureaucracy of the IS group if we work in smaller groups that are closer to the users and their machines—like mini IS groups. In fact, small super-powered PCs have managed great feats of data manipulation with the right design.

The overriding consideration in all distributed architectures is the bandwidth of the network used to connect the pieces. Although the processing capabilities of machines have doubled many-fold, as has storage capacity, network speeds are far behind in their throughput. This disparity is even more noticeable in long-distance WANs. Bandwidth issues apply to LANs as well as WANs. Dial-up connections are a special case of a WAN with very slow speeds. We will examine store and forward techniques for bypassing these speed restrictions.

Global distribution of data raised language issues. We examine differences in application behavior due to different character sets. These issues are important when you mix 7 bit and 8 bit character sets, and even more so when you mix languages that use multi byte character sets. Oracle offers some tools for handling national languages which can be applied to local installations. However, you have to cater for multiple languages in your applications too.

14.2 Data Distribution Analysis

The basic analysis components we need are geographic information, traffic analysis for networks, and database partitioning. Note that the Designer/2000 repository support the recording of most of this information.

14.2.1 Business Units and Logistics

We recorded each of the company business units in the strategy phase. These units were not only logical groups, such as accounting, but also geographic locations, such as manufacturing plants. Noting the geographic distribution of company personnel is necessary for our analysis of distributed systems.

It is easy to identify geographic locations as business units. But, how should we handle a location where multiple logical groups exist? For example, consider a printing company. Each printing plant in this company has its own accounting group, sales group, and so on. There are company-wide policies on how the sales group functions; but, there are local or industry based variations. Should we treat each such group as a separate business unit? Yes and no! There are two ways to tackle this situation: As business units or through mapping business units to locations.

We might define each group in a particular location as a business unit when there are major variations in their business practices. The main reason is that each sales group in a remote location is potentially a system. Another reason is that with local systems and IS group, we can be responsive to local needs. Each location could have its own local system while sharing common data with sales groups in other locations.

The matrix approach of mapping business units to locations is appropriate when the variations between groups are small. One way to determine the variations is to compare the business rules. I find it useful to model the business rules with one group and then using them as the basis for the next group. This approach allows us to determine the variations and also verify the rules.

14.2.2 Geographic Groups as Business Units

With local systems, we could implement minor variations in applications to satisfy localized needs without affecting the rest of the company. Before we can do so, however, we need to define what data is strictly local and what data is a company-wide resource. Here is one way of determining this.

You need a definition of each local group as a business unit. You also need a complete definition of functions or processes, and the data entities used by those functions. Then, we construct matrices, using the Matrix Diagrammer, for business units against each of the functions and data entities.

Our matrix shows not only that a unit performs a given function, but also how often. For example, if there is a local order entry group in each location, a business unit, we show the number of orders entered per hour (or per day, whichever is meaningful) for that unit. In addition, we note how many people do the function in each location. Thus, we can determine the average transaction rate per person per hour in each location. From our function-to-entity matrix, we can derive the size of that function as a transaction. Then, we can calculate the amount of data that has to travel over the network.

We also need to map business rules to each group in a similar way to functions. We may find that some rules are not used by some groups. We may also find rules that are only applied by certain local groups. If we used the functions to record business rules then we can use the matrix facilities to record the mapping.

14.2.3 Geographic Groups Mapped to Locations

We can record just logical groups as business units regardless of their distribution over different locations. We then record all of the physical locations. A map between these two models then provides us with the cross reference: about groups located at various physical locations. The cell in this matrix contains volume information such as the number of people performing a function at a location. Another fact we may record is the head or managerial person of the group at that location.

In this scenario mapping business rules against a group is not appropriate. Instead we map business rules against the location. In this approach, the rules that apply to a particular group are a little more difficult to record. So, make sure that you have fewer variations between locations when you choose this approach.

14.2.4 Volume and Traffic Analysis

We record entity volume information in the Designer/2000 repository. Unfortunately, this information is on an annual basis. For distributed database analysis, we need volumes by location. Designer/2000 lets us record these volumes using the matrix diagrammer facility. A key to making the matrix diagram useful is to select a unit of time consistently. If you choose volumes per hour, stick to this unit of time throughout your analysis, unless of course, the time unit is not meaningful. Figure 14-1 shows a sample matrix of function vs. business unit. In this example, we mapped each location of the business unit as a unit in its own right.

The business unit vs. function matrix shows the frequencies of each function at that location. This, together with the number of users at the location, helps us determine the traffic. We use a function vs. entity matrix to determine how many rows of an entity the function uses. We also record the specific attributes used by the function, not just the entity.

Business Function	Sales, Timbuctoo	Purchasing, Timbuctoo	Accounting, Timbuctoo	Warehousing, Timbuctoo	Sales, U.K	Purchasing, U.K.
Support Customer	15 / Hour				20 / Hour	
Receive Order	100 / Hour				35 / Hour	
Accept Returns			1 / Hour	1 / Hour		
Accept Delivery			1 / Hour	1 / Hour		
Fill Backorders				100 / Hour		
Pick, Pack, and Ship				100 / Hour		
Prepare Catalogs		2 / Month				10 / Month

Figure 14-1: Volume-Frequency Analysis Matrix

Network traffic can be estimated for each function using the following formula:

$$Transmission\ size = sum\quad (frequency\ of\ function$$
$$*\ (\ number\ of\ rows\ of\ each\ entity\ used$$
$$*\ sum\ (\ size\ of\ attributes\ used\ )\ )$$
$$+\ message\ overhead\ )$$

The overhead for a message depends on the type of networking software used.

14.2.5 Data Partitioning

We could divide the data in many ways. Relational theory says that we can partition any relation by columns or by rows. Assuming that each of our entities becomes a table, what types of relational operations will we need? The concern here is for distributed database operations. Each time we access a physically remote database, we suffer from the speed restrictions of a network. This restriction is almost acceptable on LANs, but on WANs it is significantly slower. We also should be wary of loading the network to its capacity, which will further degrade response times. Remember, users are not aware that they make a remote access when they perform a certain function.

The types of operations we need to avoid are those that cause a lot of data transmitted over the network. For example, joins of two or more tables, where some of the tables are remote, will cause the data from the remote tables (yes, all of it!) to be transmitted over the network. So, partitioning tables by columns where columns, on separate machines are accessed together, is not very good. Figure 14-2 illustrates a vertical partition. We can identify the best partitioning by columns from our function-entity

Catalog Items (United States)				Catalog Items (Europe)			
Catalog #	Item #	Product #	Unit Price Offer	Catalog #	Item #	Product #	Unit Price Offer
970901	10-234-1	12354	49.99	970901	10-234-1	12354	35.45
970901	10-234-2	12356	12.59	970901	10-234-2	12356	9.99
970901	10-444-5	23455	34.25	970901	10-444-5	23455	29.99
970901	10-543-6	44321	99.89	970901	10-543-6	44321	59.78

Figure 14-2: A Vertical Partition

matrix. Similarly, a horizontal partition of a table—that is, by rows—where we union the two separate partitions, is also a poor choice.

Horizontal partitions, on the other hand, allow us to divide the data rather more logically. For example, we could divide customers by geographic region. Each local sales group in a location contains only those customers who are in the designated territory. Figure 14-3 illustrates a horizontal partition. The logical view of the customer table will be the union of all separate tables, but each location primarily uses their local piece only. We can identify such types of access from our function-entity matrix as well as the frequencies defined in our business unit-to-function matrix.

When we cannot partition data such that most of the access is to the locally stored portions, we need to consider other choices. A potential choice is to replicate data from headquarters' central system to each local system. For example, we might replicate the entire customer table at each location. There are obvious data integrity problems with this approach. How do we update the replicated local copies, and how do we keep them synchronized? Replication is an ideal solution for data that is updated very infrequently. For example, price sheets that are updated a few times per year are a good candidate. Otherwise, we need to warn our designers to build data integrity mechanisms for replication.

Customers (United States)

Customer #	Customer Name	Company	Address	State	Zip Code

Customers (Europe)

Customer #	Customer Name	Company	Address	Country	Post Code

Figure 14-3: A Horizontal Partition

Another issue we identify for designers is when the system should update the replicated data. Ideally, updates should be done at the same time to all remote systems so that they are all in sync. However, even with technical support staff in each location, we face potential technical difficulties. For example, what should we do when one of the remote systems is down due to a local power failure?

By the way, individual system outage is a much larger issue. If some of our programs access a remote system for some validation, a system outage makes that program unusable. You need to consider this issue when choosing data for remote access. Consider the business requirements when making a decision. A noncritical function can suffer outages so long as critical business functions carry on. Also, your transition plan needs to define procedures in case of such outages.

14.3 Formulating a Distribution Strategy

14.3.1 When to Distribute Data?

Although a central database has been the common way to go, more and more companies are looking for ways to use cheaper technology by distributing data. Centralized databases make database administration easier than distributed databases. However, such close control also fosters bureaucracy, which makes users' lives difficult. Central databases require large, expensive machines simply to support the large number of users who need to access the data. Requirements for interactive access compounds the horsepower requirements.

Distributed databases allow you to use cheaper technology such as smaller machines on a network. Advances in hardware have greatly increased the horsepower and storage capabilities of such small machines. In addition, they have opened doors to making some local autonomy possible. Users can take ownership of their data and applications, since they are closely involved in their inception and maintenance.

The key to successful distributed systems is reducing the amount of access necessary to remote systems. A majority of the data required by a set of users should reside on their local machine. Occasional access to other, remote machines is possible with the network speeds available today. Remember that WANs are slower and more expensive than LANs because of the distances involved.

The scenario in which distributed databases make the most sense is when departments of a company are geographically distributed. Typically, in such cases, business responsibilities are also distributed to allow local decision-making. Headquarters provides guidance on policy issues, one of which could be data requirements. Figure 14-4 illustrates a schematic of this scenario.

Each department could have its own system, either a database server with a network of PC workstations, or a single machine with dumb terminals. Networks are a LAN, with a bridge to a WAN to connect to the central headquarters machine. Most of the data necessary to the department resides on the local system. Occasionally, access to

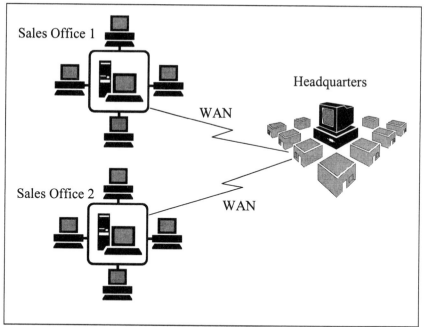

Figure 14-4: A Good Scenario for a Distributed Database

the central database may be necessary to obtain data supplied by other departments or locations.

The central database, on the other hand, needs access to data from each of the departmental databases. Typically, this data is only required in a summary form. Nitty-gritty details are of little interest to corporate headquarters. In fact, up-to-the-minute information is unnecessary at the central location. So, an old-fashioned batch daily upload can suffice.

14.3.2 Network Issues

There are many types of networks and even more ways to combine them. I do not intend to discuss the theory underlying each of these types, or the hardware bridges and routers necessary to combine them. I will merely introduce their properties as they apply to our discussion. Details of networks are vital to communications administrators, but of little importance to developers of Oracle-based applications. Figure 14-5 illustrates a high-level view of the components of a network system as it relates to Oracle products. This diagram bears almost no resemblance to OSI layers which depict network interaction at a much more detailed level.

The hardware connection level, the network type, and the network software are closely tied together. For example, to use Ethernet on an AT&T 3B machine, you must buy the add-on cards for the machine and the software from AT&T, though you

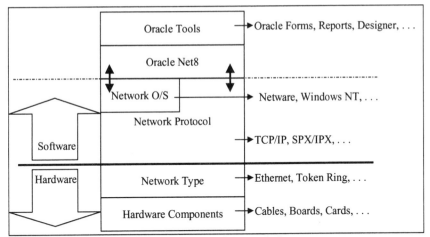

Figure 14-5: Overview of Network Components

may use cabling materials from your cable installer. In the PC world, there is a little more flexibility as vendors support each other's hardware cards.

The protocol on your network depends heavily on your choice of software. For example, vendors like DEC have their own protocol, DECnet, which runs on Ethernet, though you could also run TCP/IP on Ethernet. Whether the different protocols will coexist on a single wire depends on the software. Some Ethernet software implementations will not coexist. Among Ethernet protocols, TCP/IP is a widely used standard. It is also the standard for Internet access.

In addition to the interdependencies between hardware, protocols, and network software, you have to worry about SQL*Net support for your choice. Since there are many implementations of network protocols, Oracle can support only a few. Be very careful in checking the hardware and software supported by Oracle's SQL*Net for your hardware platforms.

When configuring networks, keep in mind that you can connect different types of networks to each other via hardware or software packages. There are many hardware boxes for connecting two networks, called gateways, bridges, routers, and combinations of these. The differences between their operation is too much detail for our purposes here. So, I will use the term "*bridge*" interchangeably for all of them.

Figure 14-6 illustrates a configuration of three different types of networks bridged together. These bridges convert data packets on the network from one protocol to another. They can also determine whether a network packet needs to be passed to the other network, or if the packet is for a node on the local network. Thus, some bridges can filter packets such that they convert and pass through only those destined for the other side of the bridge.

Each type of network has its own throughput and capacity limits. For example, a standard IBM token ring network can theoretically work at 4 megabits per second, while Ethernet can theoretically work at 100 megabits per second. Realize, however, that these figures include the overhead for each packet added by the network management software. Each packet must contain information about where it originated, where it is going, and error checking data. Thus, the maximum actual data throughput on the network is typically about 75% of the network bandwidth.

Beware of judging network throughput based on such theoretical figures. In practice, the number of nodes on the network and the traffic volume determines the actual speed. An Ethernet with a large number of nodes and high volume of network traffic will reduce throughput to 50% of network capacity in most cases.

The typical services provided by networking software, such as Novell's Netware and DECnet, are the ability to share files stored on a server, printers, and other devices. The machines that support such services have multitasking operating systems. In some cases, the operating system is multi-user as well, for example, the DEC OpenVMS, Microsoft NT, or UNIX operating systems. MS-DOS, unfortunately, is a single-user, single-tasking operating system. For this reason, vendors such as Novell, Banyan, and 3Com supply their own multitasking operating systems for supporting network servers on PCs.

Remember that an Oracle database is not a set of shared files. It requires a multitasking operating system to act as a database server. We describe the Oracle server architecture in the next section. So, on Novell and 3Com networks, Oracle servers must run on a machine separate from the network server. Windows NT is a multitasking system and Oracle can run under it. Note that Personal Oracle can run on single-user operating systems like Windows 97. But, it does not support distributed access as the Oracle Workgroup Server running on Windows NT can.

14.3.3 Where Does Net8 Fit?

Application programs, such as Oracle Forms applications, specify how to connect to the Oracle database server over the network each time a user starts up the application. This specification is called the *connect* or *host* string. The database string specifies which Net8 driver to use, the name of the network node which is the database server, and which database instance to connect to on that server. For example, to run SQL*Plus with a database string to connect using the TCP/IP driver to a network node called ACCT which runs the database with the Oracle SID (system id) HQ, you might type

sqlplus user/password@T:ACCT:HQ

In this example, the driver *T* specifies TCP/IP. There are other drivers, one for each type of connection. In fact, even front-end interfaces running local to the database use a local driver such as *P*—a pipe driver under UNIX. This type of string is much too

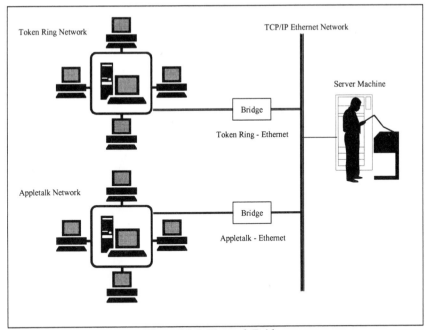

Figure 14-6: Network Bridges

complicated for an average user. Your application must hide it, so that remote connection is transparent to the user. You can define an alias for the database using the configuration tools provided by Oracle. Then, your application must create synonyms for each database object that provide a simple, meaningful name that translates to the remote database object.

If you run a database locally on each workstation, as well as on the shared server machine, you can create aliases or database links. Aliases are just one way of giving a meaningful name to the cryptic database string. Thus, you might substitute the alias "*accounting*" for our example database string. If your environment is fairly stable, that is, node names and addresses rarely change, you could consider hard-coding the database string into your programs. In general, aliases or database links are preferable.

Realize that a theoretical 10-megabit throughput is very slow compared to the throughput speeds of today's disks. The practical throughput from networks is comparable to that of a CD-ROM drive on a typical PC, and it is shared between many users. So, the less data transmitted over the network, the faster our response time will be. With an asynchronous dial-up interface, speed is even more important. Don't forget that one workstation using the network for a large-volume data transmission affects everyone else connected to that network. The network is, in every sense, a shared resource which you should avoid abusing.

Application developers need to become very conscious of every database interaction. Each interaction causes network traffic. Thus, scrutinize carefully each trigger in Forms that uses a *select ... from dual* to see if you could perform the same task locally. Although using DUAL is very convenient for the programmer, the statement must be transmitted over the network, processed by the Oracle kernel, and the result passed back to the workstation. This transmission back and forth results in a slower response than when using a local database. These network traffic issues were one of the driving forces behind implementing PL/SQL in Forms. The procedural capabilities of PL/SQL eliminate the need for unnecessary database access over the network.

An advantage of using PL/SQL at the database server end is that you can send the entire query once across the network and retrieve the end result. You do not need to retrieve intermediate results for further processing. This option is possible with tools such as SQL*Plus, PRO*C, and other programmatic interface products. Intermediate results in a multiple-step process can generate a significant volume of unnecessary network traffic. Performing most of the work on the database server machine increases its load. So, don't expect to support a large number of users on a 386 machine—even one with a high clock rate.

Data from lookup tables is the culprit of unnecessary network traffic, since the values are included in almost every row retrieved. If this data changes only rarely, you should store it locally on the workstation. With Forms, this would mean that you would need a small database locally on each workstation. This can be an expensive option, since beefed-up hardware configurations for workstations become necessary just to run Oracle locally. Many third-party products, such as SQR, offer in-memory arrays which are useful for local storage without requiring copies of Oracle for each workstation. Just load these arrays once at the start of your program and use them repeatedly throughout.

Another way to reduce network traffic is to use Oracle's array facilities. When retrieving a large number of rows, transmitting one row at a time results in a lot of network packets. Instead, obtaining a set of rows at a time reduces the volume of packets transmitted over the network. Remember, however, to only retrieve the columns needed. There is a limit on the maximum size of network packets. So, retrieving an array of rows, where each row is quite large, will not reduce the volume.

Once you start thinking in terms of where the programs will execute, you need to become fussy about portability issues. Forms applications are fairly portable, even to the Macintosh environment. Use of Microsoft-specific components like OCX and VBX in forms layout, C user exits, and HOST calls to the operating system can make your application almost impossible to port.

Watch for differences in Oracle versions supported for the workstation platforms. If all of your workstations are MS Windows PCs of the same ilk, there is no problem. However, if your workstations are a mixed bag—SUNs, VAXen, MS Windows 3.1, MS Windows 95, or MS Windows NT PCs—you will probably have to use the oldest version, the one common on your platforms. Remember that newer versions of software can usually run programs developed with older versions, not vice versa. This also leads to update lags since you need to wait months after a new version *ships* before it is available on all of your platforms.

Distributed queries in Oracle use the database link facilities. A database link is a predefined access path to another database. You can create a database link while connected to one database using the following SQL*Plus command:

> *CREATE DATABASE LINK chicago*
>
> *CONNECT TO user IDENTIFIED BY password USING database string;*

This command is one of Oracle's extensions to the SQL language. Once you define this link, you can refer to any accessible table on the remote database by simply specifying the link name after the table name. For example, suppose one of our remote database tables is *product*; we can retrieve data from it with

> *SELECT * FROM PRODUCT@chicago;*

A database link restricts your access according to the security privileges granted to the user and password specified in the *create database link* statement. A database link is only available to its creator user id. A DBA can make a database link available to all users by using the keyword PUBLIC in the *Create* statement. Public database links should typically use restricted user names on the remote database, to prevent undesirable updates. It is common to use a user name which has only *select* privilege. Otherwise, all of the careful security controls you place on each local database may be bypassed.

There are a few limits on such remote access. For example, you cannot retrieve a column with data type long (maximum size 1GB) from a remote database. Remember that all of the results of your query on remote database tables get transmitted over the network. So, be very careful in the types of queries you perform.

14.4 Distributed Database Design

The basic design requirement for a good distributed database is that a large proportion of the database accesses should be to the local database. However, it is not always easy to partition our data in such a way. There are two elementary partitioning strategies, horizontal and vertical. Before we discuss these strategies in more detail, review the database design we developed in the earlier parts of this book. The discussion of data partitioning uses these preliminary table definitions as the basis.

A horizontal partition is dividing a table into sets of rows based on some column in that table. Thus, we might divide the customer table into North American customers and European customers. The complete corporate view of customers is the union of the two sets. In the case of Widgets, Inc., this partitioning works quite well. After all, customers do not move between North America and Europe very frequently.

Customer buying analysis, similarly, is likely to be continent-specific. However, if Widgets, Inc., wanted statistics on buying patterns across continents, it would have to consolidate the data at the corporate level. Since this process is infrequent, say, once every six months, copying all of that data from the local to the corporate level is reasonable.

A vertical partition divides a table by its columns. For example, the catalog items table might contain pricing for both North America and Europe in separate columns. (This table is worth denormalizing since we are not likely to open new warehouse locations frequently.) We could partition the table into the parts for North American prices and parts for European prices. We have to duplicate some of the columns, such as catalog number and product number. Again, once we create a catalog—that is, print and mail it to our customers—we really cannot change it! So, catalog number and product number are static, and data duplication is okay. A similar vertical partition of the customer table, however, would require frequent joins between the local and remote tables.

Lookup tables, as we noted in an earlier section, are good candidates for storing in the local database. However, lookup tables do change, albeit not very frequently. At Widgets, Inc., some of these tables will contain information specific to the continent anyway. For example, a lookup table for state codes in North America could be country codes in the European system. We are not particularly worried about such tables of local significance. Other tables, such as the product table, are more critical.

One alternative is to use Oracle's snapshots and replication features discussed in later sections. If these are too complex and you are looking for a simple, yet effective update strategy, consider another alternative. We could use Oracle's auditing facilities to track updates and insertions into such critical tables. Oracle's auditing facilities can be set to record only specific types of access. Their real purpose is to track who is attempting to violate security or doing suspicious work. However, we are not interested in who made the change, only the fact that a row in a critical table changed. We would use the following statement to track changes to the product table:

```
AUDIT INSERT, UPDATE ON product WHENEVER SUCCESSFUL;
```

Don't forget to turn auditing on in the *init.ora* parameter AUDIT_TRAIL. We only care about successful attempts to change this table. If the user rolls back a change, the table does not change. Then, we could set up a batch process, say, nightly, to query the AUDIT_TRAIL table to discover whether the table changed, and take appropriate actions to update all databases which locally store this table. Since we do not add many new products or change existing ones very frequently, a nightly batch update should be sufficient.

Turning auditing on usually causes significant overhead, affecting the performance of the database. I do not recommend general system-wide auditing due to the performance and disk overheads. However, limited auditing such as that described above should impose very little overhead. It offers a nice solution for tracking changes to replicated data in the case of distributed databases.

Notice that all of my suggestions for distributed database use infrequent access to the remote database. Your analysis for distributed systems should aim for a similar setup. The advantage is that you are not dependent on the remote system being up all the time. If you suffer communications difficulties, which are not uncommon, each local database can continue operation autonomously. Remember that Oracle provides only a local database dictionary. It does not replicate dictionary information or provide transaction updates and recovery across the distributed databases. So, if the remote system goes down due to some mishap, our setup does not cause the entire company to grind to a standstill.

14.4.1 Implementation Rules of Thumb

Here are some rules which I have collected over time. They will guide you when developing distributed access systems. Remember that these rules are based on today's technology. As network bandwidth and speed increase, you will have to adjust the figures appropriately.

- Calculate transaction size using the formula explained earlier. Divide it by network bandwidth to get an answer for the number of bytes per second; double this result to allow for the request to be transmitted. Add an overhead of 2–3 seconds for the database server turnaround. This is the minimum response time you can expect on your network.

- For example, assume an 56kb connection with Net8. This means our network bandwidth is aproximately 7,000 bytes per second. Assuming our transaction size is 1000 bytes, we take 0.15 seconds to transport it (1000 / 7000=0.15). Double it and add 600 milliseconds for satellite roundtrip transmission resulting in an estimated speed of 0.306 seconds—a slow response time compared to 80 milliseconds access time of a hard disk!

- From the above calculation, figure out an optimum transaction size that will result in an acceptable response time. Use the *arraysize* tuning facility for the Forms, SQL*Plus, and PRO*programs to reduce the number of bytes retrieved at one time. Thus, the actual transaction size may be larger, but users will see more frequent displays of data retrieved. So, the perceived response time will be much more acceptable.

- WANs are slower than LANs. Even at the speed of light on fiber optic connections, expect an extra 1- to 2-second delay just for transport. So, don't even think of systems operating at subsecond response times in such scenarios.

- Use facilities of Forms 2.1 and later that reduce network traffic. For example, Forms can batch insert, update, and delete actions on a multi-row block so that multiple rows are transmitted together.

14.4.2 Heterogeneous Environments

Heterogeneous environments can be categorized into three types, to make this discussion easier:

- Different hardware and operating systems all running the Oracle database management system and tools. This environment is where Oracle is at its best. Oracle runs on almost every hardware platform and operating system. Programs developed in its GUI tools are highly portable between these environments. The only exceptions are when one platform is a character-based terminal environment rather than a windowing environment like MS Windows. The behavior of Forms applications changes between these environments. Programs written in third-generation languages, or user exits, are very vulnerable to porting difficulties. Beware of different versions of each product on each of the platforms. The large range of platforms supported by Oracle means that there is a significant time lag between new versions becoming available and their port to each platform.

- Different database packages and tools on one hardware platform. In this environment, you may have some applications written in Visual Basic using Microsoft Access files, as well as Oracle-based applications on an NT platform. Another example is DB2 on IBM machines. Oracle is making significant progress in supporting such environments. The Gateway series of products allow Oracle tools to use DB2 as the database on IBM MVS systems. A flavor of Oracle Gateway is also available for accessing flat files on IBM and VAX VMS systems, Sybase and other relational databases. Oracle supports ODBC access to its database and allows its tools to use ODBC to access any database that also supports it. Oracle will probably add more products in the future.

  Gateway products aim to provide transparent access to a non-Oracle database. If the database supports SQL access, they will pass through the SQL statements from the application. For non-SQL databases, the gateway translates SQL into the access language appropriate to the database. In all cases, the gateway translates SQL that refers to Oracle's data dictionary objects to access their equivalent objects in the non-Oracle database. An important feature is the *two-phase commit* supported by Oracle for distributed databases. Gateways for many non-Oracle support this feature by ensuring that a transaction either commits on all instances or is rolled back in all instances that participate in the transaction.

- Different national languages, regardless of hardware or software platforms. As we develop multinational applications, handling multiple languages becomes an essential requirement. Even though programming is always done in English based-languages, the end user should see screens, reports, and data in the appropriate language. What's more, they ought to see error messages in their language of choice as well.

Based on your language and character set choice, Oracle uses a set of message files containing all messages to the user that the DBMS might display. There is a message file for the kernel and one for each of the utilities such as Forms. Note that this choice applies to the entire system or individual user session.

You can set the language individually for each user of a utility. For example, one of your users might use forms developed in French, while another uses forms developed in German on the same database. Obviously, each one's workstation must support the appropriate language. They will each see Forms interaction messages in their chosen language, although all ORDBMS messages will be in the installation language. So, if the language specified in *init.ora* is French, the user working in German will see all ORA-nnnn messages in French. Realize, however, that the Oracle kernel will treat the data they enter as one character set.

The implications of national language support are far-reaching. A normal numeric sort, such as used for ASCII character sorting, is insufficient. In fact, it will produce incorrect ordering of results. Oracle also allows you to specify sorting in the national language, via a parameter in the *init.ora* file. An Oracle internal date converted to character format will yield day and month names in the language of choice. There are extensions to the SQL language for handling national language.

- *Convert:* This function allows you to convert character data from one source language to another destination language character set. This function merely converts a character from one character set representation to another. It does not convert the language itself.

- *Replace:* This function allows you to define a replacement character for a particular character in the specified string. This function is useful to handle cases where a character set does not include a code representing the appropriate upper- or lower-case equivalent of the character. For example, if the accented e (é) in French does not have the upper-case equivalent in your character set, you could specify a replacement by the normal upper-case E as an acceptable alternative.

Both of these functions must be used in your application. The replacements and conversions do not occur on a permanent basis in the database.

Note that comparisons for < (less than) and > (greater than) on character strings are still done using their numeric values. So, such comparisons may yield unexpected results. I recommend that you avoid inequality comparisons on characters strings entirely. Use the LIKE predicate or equality comparisons wherever possible. Remember that similar unexpected results occur between two machines using ASCII and EBCDIC character sets, respectively.

In all of these cases, handling cultural differences is left up to the designer. For example, salutations are not uncommon in the United Kingdom. A prefix of Sir to the name John Smith results in unexpected ordering. You will have to separate such prefixes and suffixes into separate columns. The problem yields amusing results in non-European languages. For example, Arabic names are often prefixed by EL as an honorific. If some names have this prefix and others don't, the ordered results are again unexpected.

Such differences between data are critical in a distributed database environment. Queries involving remote tables containing data in a different character set can completely mess up your query results. Remember that sorting done on your current North American character-set based database will yield completely different results from the same sort performed on a remote French character-based database. Be prepared to make users understand these limitations, but first, take the time to understand them yourself.

14.5 Data Distribution

Physical distribution of data is a consideration whenever the volume of data is large enough to warrant it. Ideally, the logical view is still the consolidated view. While this may help performance, distribution of data raises other issues. Some examples of issues include:

- **Security**: Oracle does not allow grants and access privileges to be defined for remote objects. For example, if the customer table is on instance B, a user on instance A may not be explicitly granted access to it. If you need to specify access security, you may have to build access controls in the application, create views based on each remote object and control access to the views, or duplicate user accounts and access rights on the local and remote instances.

- **Declarative integrity constraints**: Oracle does not allow integrity constraints such as foreign key constraints to span instances. A table with a foreign key reference to a remote table must enforce integrity with table triggers.

- **Data integrity**: When we create multiple copies of data from one or more tables, we need to maintain integrity of data dependent on those tables. Thus, we need to update tables as a set based on integrity constraints. This requirement makes design and administration of a distributed database very complex.

- **Sequence generators**: A sequence generator provides the next available number in sequence. However, if tables or partitions are divided across instances, we could not use just one sequence generator for local and remote databases. We may have to designate a range of numbers to each instance and create instance-specific sequence generators. The resulting consequence is that we may not get consecutive numbers. Not a good strategy for a critical area such as a *check number*.

Distributed data is a fact of today's global databases. It is important to design the strategy for distribution with a full understanding of its consequences. The following discussion provides an overview of the available choices. However, I would highly recommend obtaining expert advice before attempting an implementation.

14.5.1 Partitioned Tables

Oracle8 allows you to store tables partitioned just the way we discussed in Section 14.2.5 Data Partitioning. We may store each partition on a separate instance of Oracle, or store two or more partitions in one instance. Each partition may have its own index. Partitions are transparent to a user issuing a query statement. The user is only aware of the logical table.

Partitioning is based on values of a particular column. Good choices are columns that have values based on a limited set of possibilities. A rule of thumb is, in Designer, a column that might belong to a domain with allowable value sets. Each partition may contain rows with a single value for that column or a range of values. You may add partitions without drastic rearrangement of data. However, changing the base criteria of a partition will require significant data manipulation.

There are a couple of advantages to partitioned tables. The primary benefit is that the query optimizer is aware of partitions. It will attempt to satisfy the needs of a query closest to its storage. Suppose, for example, that we partition based on the *state* column and store each partition in a separate instance of Oracle. A query relating to just "New York" state will be satisfied from just one partition. A query relating to several states will concatenate the partitions to satisfy the query. Note that although the concatenate is like performing a *union* in SQL, the optimizer still uses indexes to resolve the result.

Another benefit of partitioning tables is that storage management is easier. Partitions can be treated as if they are separate tables for determining their storage and growth requirements. So, capacity planning and sizing exercises are a little easier.

The drawback of partitions is that if you decide to change the reference column on which partitioning is based, major reorganization of data becomes necessary. Since the initial incentive for partitioning a table is the large volume of data, reorganization is no trivial task.

14.5.2 Data Snapshots

Snapshots are a read-only copy of data stored in a remote database. This facility requires that you designate one Oracle instance as the master. Snapshots consist of copies of data from this master instance. Data in a snapshot may not be updated. Updates must be performed on the master copy and propagated to all snapshots.

Oracle can manage the creation and periodic refreshing of data in a snapshot. Refresh cycles may be as short as minutes or span days depending on your needs. Keep in mind that refreshing a snapshot adds to the overhead and may affect performance.

You can define snapshots using familiar SQL syntax specifying the selection criteria on each table to be included. You may copy the entire table or a portion of it by specifying a *where* clause. You also specify refresh parameters—that is, how often the snapshot should be refreshed. A simple condition does not affect the speed with which the snapshot is refreshed. A complex condition, however, may cause the entire table to be transported to the snapshot site and then filtered to satisfy the *where* condition.

14.5.3 Data Replication

Snapshots are the basic form of replication, that is, read-only copies of master data. You can also set up more advanced forms of replication where updates may be applied to any copy of the data. The marketing buzz word for this is *update anywhere* replication.

Administration of a replicated database is hairy to put mildly. Since updates may occur on any copy, Oracle must synchronize the data on all copies without impacting performance significantly. Using a simple two-phase commit approach is not always practical because of the potentially unacceptable delays while each copy is updated. Oracle implements a deferred update approach. So the update on a copy completes as soon as it is committed on the local copy of data. Background processes and database triggers track the update transaction, and periodically forward it to a designated master. The designated master then propagates the changes to all other copies. You may manually force a synchronization by overriding the periodic refresh.

Designating a single master is dangerous because it is a potential single point of failure. Advanced replication allows us to designate multiple masters. The architecture of Oracle's advanced replication allows for continued operation even if one or more database instances are offline. However, such operation means that data conflicts are possible. For example, two instances of a piece of data may be updated independently and thus end up with different values. Which value should be kept and which one overridden? Oracle provides strategies for conflict resolution when the same data element updated in more than one copy has different values.

Replication is complex topic and deserves discussion in greater depth that is possible in this chapter. My intention here is to provide an overview of the possibilities so that you may consider the choices for application design.

14.6 Development Management Issues

Central database administration in a distributed database environment is quite a nightmare. Oracle facilities allow you to monitor a running database remotely. Most operating systems with networking support allow you to log into a remote machine over the network. However, these facilities assume that the system is up and running. What can you do if the remote system crashes or the communications link is down? How can you perform a backup which requires mounting a tape?

There are many operating system specific tools to administer machines on a LAN. However, few administrative tools exist for WAN management. Resign yourself to maintaining some technical experts at each geographic location of a distributed database. You can then support these personnel from a central pool of experts. The remote staff can also perform simple development tasks such as custom reports for local use.

The key benefit to users of distributed database systems is the local control it makes possible. You can sweeten the deal by allowing some customization of the application at a local level. After all, if the data design remains constant, your central consolidation processes will continue to run.

Don't be afraid that this will lead to the chaotic setup we are used to today—where every department chooses its own tools and builds its own database design. If you focus on controlling the data design, you can allow local variations in presenting data without compromising business objectives. This is where enterprise wide models support your work. Remember to set standards for naming conventions—otherwise you will create communications barriers between technical staff in different locations.

If all applications, with or without local variations, are developed by a central pool of resources, you will need strict source management controls. Be sure to enforce formal application release procedures so you have master copies of all programs actually in production. Ad-hoc methods of program enhancements and release, common in a central database environment, if used in a distributed environment spell disaster.

Application portability is more critical in a distributed environment since you can no longer assume a single hardware and operating system platform. The beauty of a distributed environment is that you can use the best option for hardware and operating system available for the site. So, pay particular attention to enhancing portability of all designs.

There are several advantages to managing the implementation of a distributed system. Instead of getting all of your users trained and ready for the new system before cutover, you can phase your cutover by each location. You could even persuade one site to become a beta test site. If you can publicize the importance of such pilot testing throughout the company, they will be proud to be part of the effort, despite all the ensuing difficulties. Thus, you will be able to test your software in a production environment without risking a major company-wide disaster.

You can schedule user training one site at a time. Be sure to allow sufficient "*oops*" recovery time between the scheduled training and implementation at each site. Expect a few mishaps at each location—"*oops*" recovery time gives you a chance to handle them before your next deadline. The responsiveness you can show with such planning is sure to win user support. Winning their support is important if they are to assume ownership and commit themselves to making it successful.

The World Wide Web

The vast popularity of the World Wide Web means that we cannot ignore this environment. In fact, we may leverage it to reduce some of our costs. For example, we may utilize the user interface provided by Internet for our internal applications. However, this user interface may be quite different from our normal GUI tools. We have to modify our expectations based on its capabilities. In this chapter, we will cover

- The characteristics of an Internet and intranet environment, including what these terms mean. We will discuss the issues of the tools available for development in this environment.

- How to assess which applications, or portions of applications, are suitable for this environment.

- What additional information must we capture during analysis to support our design?

- The infrastructure implications of implementing a web application, including the kinds of gateway choices available.

- Security issues, since web applications differ from traditional client-server applications.

- Development tools for developing these applications require some thought, as any choice today will probably be obsolete tomorrow.

- Development management issues including enhancements and error correction.

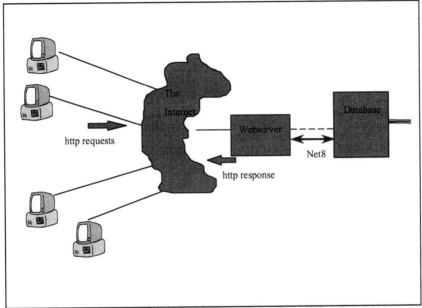

Figure 15-1: The HTTP Request Servicing Process

15.1 The Internet, the Intranet and the Extranet

The World Wide Web is a collection of computer nodes connected to a communications network backbone. The backbone is managed by a consortium of multinational companies. The computer nodes are owned by companies or Internet service providers (ISP) who pay a fee to the consortium for a connection. Any company can gain access to the net by registering a domain on their own computer that has been connected to the net, or by obtaining hosting services from an Internet service provider. This network is called the *Internet* because it is independent of any one company. In fact, it is global—spanning geographic and political boundaries.

The Internet service providers provide individuals with access to the Internet via dial-up connections. With this access, individuals can access any domain on the Internet regardless of the physical location of the domain server computer. We use browser software, such as the Microsoft Internet Explorer or Netscape Navigator, to view the pages posted on a domain. Figure 15-1 illustrates the process of accessing a domain and the page transmitted in response.

This process basically requires a gateway, a network, and a client browser. So, we can use the process over a private network as well as the Internet. The private network, in this context, is often referred to as an intranet—that is, a network within a company. An extranet is the ability to use applications designed for private networks using the public access capabilities of the Internet. Extranet applications demonstrate the

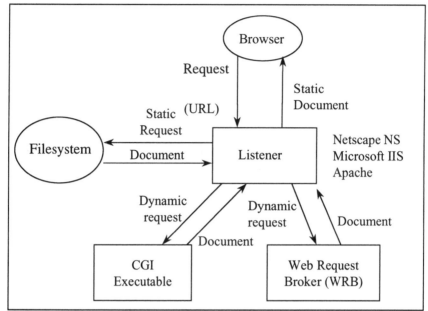

Figure 15-2: Web Server Processing Concepts

security and confidentiality characteristics of an intranet application. Electronic data exchange between two corporations is an example of an extranet application.

There is of course a difference in performance. For access through the public Internet, performance depends on the traffic generated by unpredictable accesses. In a private network, the traffic is just company applications. We have some measure of control—at least we can monitor traffic and upgrade the infrastructure as needed. On the public Internet, we can only control the speed of our own connection to the Internet; the rest we share with the world!

There is much confusion caused by the terminology used in this environment At least some of this confusion is due to the rapid change of technology, and some is attributable to the rapid change in product names. Oracle's web products have evolved through the first four generations of technology in the short space of two or three years—and as many corresponding name changes. Figure 15-2 illustrates how the different components interact with each other to process a URL request. Notice the terminology difference between Oracle's Listener process and servers of its rivals. Microsoft's IIS and Netscape's NS are analogous to this Listener. Oracle's Application Server also includes the Web Request Broker, which is necessary for generating dynamic HTML documents. Microsoft's equivalent product to the WRB is the ActiveServer.

There are many tools to design and build web pages—that is, write the HTML code that displays a web page. You can even embed Java or JavaScript procedures as applets in a page to perform some task. The browser executes the applet code in the

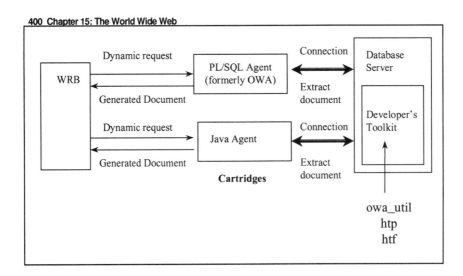

Figure 15-3: Application Server Architecture

client machine. It is common to use applets to perform display tasks that HTML cannot perform, such as scrolling banner text. These pages, however, are static. Each change must be manually applied to the page, either by modifying the HTML directly, or by using the original web page editing tool.

Static pages work for information that changes infrequently. However, to display data that changes frequently, such as in an order entry application, using statically designed pages is too cumbersome. Most often, such data comes from a database like Oracle. So, we need a way of dynamically generating HTML with data embedded in the page. To implement this approach, we need two tools: an HTML generator and a database access engine. There are two kinds of tools available that implement this approach— embedded database access tools and dynamic HTML generators.

Embedded database access tools consist of HTML template pages with embedded calls to retrieve data from the database and place it in the page definition. Many products with this style of access retrieve each data element embedded in the page with separate individual statements. Dynamic HTML generators construct the entire page containing HTML and literal data retrieved from the database. Oracle's Application Server and Microsoft's ActiveServer are examples of this approach. These products do not begin with a template. Both approaches are flexible, but the embedded access approach may be inefficient in some page designs; for example, in a page where HTML and database access is heavily interspersed. If data retrieved from the database is in one or two large blocks in the page, there is no appreciable difference in the efficiency between the approaches.

The WRB is capable of performing additional tasks. Figure 15-3 illustrates some of the internal workings of the WRB. This figure illustrates how some more of the buzzwords, like cartridge, fit into the web architecture. You may develop your own application as a cartridge for deployment in this environment. In fact, some third-party product vendors are opting for this approach.

Database access in a web environment is a little different than in a typical desktop environment. Once a page is delivered to the client browser, its connection to the database is no longer maintained. This is because there is no means of predicting whether there will be any further interaction. However, the webserver itself needs to maintain a persistent connection to the database. Otherwise, it would need to make a separate connection to the database for each page—resulting in performance inefficiency. In fact, very early releases of Oracle's webserver worked this way and had unacceptable performance under a heavy load.

The HTML page delivered to the browser is stateless—that is, it does not contain any information about the state of the user's interaction with the database. Contrast this to interaction in a desktop Forms application. The form remembers the previous action taken by the user—the action that resulted in its current state. The form can also remember such global information as the username used for connecting, the previous menu, or specific data values, provided you program it appropriately. The HTML page cannot remember the username or global data values unless you explicitly embed them in the page. Embedding them in the page leaves them open to viewing by the user. Browsers allow you to view the HTML source for the currently displayed page!

This style of persistent connection by the webserver means that the user does not have to explicitly logon to the database. Instead, all users access the database via the webserver's account on the database. Thus, the account used by the webserver may have access to all of the database objects needed by the application. If your application permits inserts, updates, or deletion of data, the webserver's account must permit appropriate access to the objects. This approach works well for applications where we do not know the user in advance. For example, in a publicly available ordering application, we cannot insist that the person placing the order must first be authorized to use the order application—making its use inconvenient. We are likely to lose potential customers by such insistence. The more convenient we make our site, the more likely customers are to use it and to return.

An alternative to this single account approach is to use the Oracle Application Server's security features. These features require each user to have a corresponding database account. This database account may have appropriate access to the database tables based on the authorized activities of the user. Such users must go through a login procedure before access to the application is granted. This approach is appropriate for an extranet application—where company users (not public users) access a private application via the Internet.

15.2 Formulating a WWW Strategy

Most companies already have home pages advertising their capabilities. This approach is, however, akin to printing an advertising brochure. Most of the capabilities of a web site remain unexplored in these companies. Before you rebuild all of your applications to be web-enabled, make sure you put into place a sensible strategy for your business. You need to understand the capabilities and restrictions that we discussed in earlier sections. Not all applications are appropriate for the web.

Keep in mind the characteristics of the Internet surfing public. They consider the Internet as a *free* resource, or *almost* free. They are rarely willing to pay a fee to view your site. So, you must provide a compelling reason for them to subscribe to your service. However, there are many areas where you can exploit the web to support the business and, in some cases, reduce your costs. Here are some ideas for using the web:

- Many companies make viewing access free and recoup their costs through advertising revenues. If your web offering is on some topic of interest that would attract people to visit your site, advertising is an option for you. Some examples of such areas are news, library catalogs, area guides, travel services, and so on.

- If you sell products to individuals, you may wish to offer the same service through a web site. This is a good option to consider for any company in the retail business. Our Widgets case study is an example. In fact, you may reduce customer support efforts by providing more detailed information on the web than you can over the telephone. For example, electronic product sellers could provide technical specifications as part of the catalog, or at the very least, point the viewing public to the manufacturer's site through a link.

- Realize that you are not expanding the market through this offering. You are merely exploiting another way to reach your customers. You may gain some savings in reduced data entry costs. However, don't count on this happening to eliminate your telephone order entry completely.

- You may use the Internet to improve communications with your customers and vendors. For example, if you provide information to a vendor on a periodic basis via a printed report or fax, consider sending the information via e-mail or file transfer. This option is worth considering for a company that sells data as its product. I can't wait for the day when my banks and investment brokers send me information electronically instead of drowning me with paper!

- If you support customers by sending them software or patches, consider the Internet as a medium of transport. For example, you could set up download sites accessed via a login id provided to customers who signed up for maintenance. You can even consider enhancing your software so that the downloads could be automated and authorized via a dialog with the user.

- Some industry gurus are predicting a drastic change in the software licensing styles attributable to the Internet. They predict that instead of paying for features and modules of the software that you don't need to use, you would pay for only those parts that you need. The way you would obtain the portions that you need would be to download them as and when you need them.

It should be clear that you need to experiment with using the web for new offerings that are not part of your normal business. For example, a stock information company may offer stock quotes on the web to anyone, even though their traditional style is to only service customers with accounts. In some instances, the business may need to change their perception of how their interaction with customers works. For example, a real estate company traditionally uses advertising as a bait to get customers into their office. The advertised properties may in fact be unavailable. They may use a web-based home advertising approach to actually narrow down a customer's search. In this case, instead of the typical bait, they would advertise homes that are really available.

As with any new technology, tread with care into this environment. However, the best way to learn what works on the Internet is to try quick experiments. Then plan to make rapid changes to the offerings based on your observations. For example, Widgets may begin by simply offering an interface for viewing order status when the customer specifies their name and order number. Then, they may progress to providing an online guide to the products in their catalogs, complete with detailed specifications that are excluded from a printed catalog. The next phase may be to offer an abbreviated online catalog and allow viewers to place orders online. You need to formulate a similar phased strategy for your company.

A strategy for public access is necessary, but you also need a strategy for using the web for access by company staff. We discussed earlier the kinds of applications that are suitable for web-based access. Choose your strategy based on this guideline.

There are two choices of the kinds of tools you may use to implement web applications. One option is to develop your application in native mode—that is, using Oracle's webserver, CGI gateway, or a similar webserver product. The second option is to use a full-fledged forms tool like Oracle Forms or a similar third-party product. Many of these products now operate without any modification in both the desktop and the web browser environments.

Figure 15-4 illustrates Oracle's Developer Server approach, which allows you to run an Oracle Forms executable from a browser with minimal modifications. Keep in mind that Forms was architected for a client-server environment. So, the resource requirements of application server are likely to be quite hefty. You need to make sure that you use appropriate estimates of the application user population to calculate the configuration of the machine which will run the Developer Server. Future versions of this product may be re-architected to reduce the resource requirements. You also have the option of using multiple machines to run the Developer Server. Oracle provides some basic load balancing tools which are likely to improve in future versions.

With Oracle's tools, you have two architectural choices: one based on Developer and the other based on the native webserver. Which option you choose depends on several criteria:

- The native mode tends to have a more intuitive interface and is suitable for applications where training users in the peculiarities of the Forms interface is not practical. For example, an application provided for use by the general public should aim for no training requirements.

- Presenting a complex application in the native mode is rather more challenging because of the limitations of HTML. For example, this interface requires several separate navigation pages before you obtain the page to update. So, you might consider using the Forms approach which provides better control over the presentation. Of course, you can minimize potential confusion with good design techniques such as providing appropriate context information.

- The Forms interface on the web works in exactly the same manner as it does on the desktop. For example, you must press the Query button *before* entering the query criteria and then press it again to execute the query. Users need training to use this interface. So, this option is suitable for deployment to company staff.

- If you already have an application developed with Forms, the Application Server option is easy to implement. It requires minimal effort. However, most of the processing in this approach is handled by the *Developer Server*. Benchmark the target user load with this tool to determine the processing power you will need to adequately support your application. Make sure the cost of the configuration is within the bounds of your budget before choosing this option.

- There are a few restrictions on the features of Forms when running with Developer Server. These restrictions revolve around network traffic. When running in a client-server environment, Forms executes primarily on the

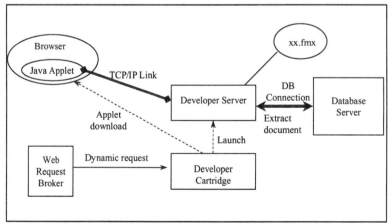

Figure 15-4: Developer Server Approach

client PC. In a web environment, the Forms applet only performs basic user interface tasks. It interacts with the Developer Server for all other Forms actions. For example, the applet performs cursor movements between items. However, for every item, it passes control to the server to perform triggers and basic validation actions. This approach generates significant network traffic—much more than in a client-server environment. The Developer Server does not support mouse events to reduce the potential for even greater network traffic—potentially for each mouse movement! There are other restrictions as well. As the applet gets more sophisticated, some of these restrictions may disappear.

A strategic issue here is whether you should use a single tool to provide web and desktop interfaces. If you choose to use different tools, keep in mind that you need staff training in each tool. The larger variety of tools you use to implement applications, the larger your skill set requirements for maintaining them. There are also some short term considerations. Using leading-edge tools means that you will train your staff in the new tools and techniques. There are few outside resources available to provide experienced insights. Hiring experienced people, as employees or contractors, is a challenge. Be sensitive also to the fact that training your staff in these desirable skills makes them more marketable. Keeping them after they gain some experience is also a challenge. After a time, the staff you train may move on unless they have a good reason for staying. So, plan on at least two generations of training. Put into place an effective succession plan for the skilled technical staff.

The support needs in this environment are a little different from the client-server environment. The burden of supporting users in a client-server environment falls upon the application development and support personnel. If a user cannot execute a program, they call the support person for that application. In the web environment, the burden of support shifts to the desktop support personnel similar to the support for other desktop software like word processors. Browsers and web access software are considered standard desktop software.

15.3 Suitability Analysis

Before you attempt to rebuild all of your applications to run on the web, make sure you understand the environment. Not all applications are suitable for deployment via the web to the general public. Before you begin planning public environment applications, you need to understand some of the restrictions posed by the environment. Note that these issues apply to applications developed on Oracle's webserver. Deploying an application based on Oracle Forms is not practical without significant user training. The primary issues for webserver based applications are:

- **Access security:** Does the application require user authentication? If it does, how will users enroll? How will you communicate the authorization to them? Remember that Internet users consider it to be essentially free! So, charging them to obtain user authorization may not be practical. It may also turn away potential users.

- **Data security:** Does the application transmit sensitive or confidential data that must be secured? If so, you must design in the process of securing this data. There are mechanisms available in the browsers today to provide such security

- **Kinds of interaction:** Because of the disconnected nature of web pages, you need to design your application to minimize database interaction. Consider the option of restricting database-driven validation to page level—just like we did in the 3270 block mode environments. Some kinds of interaction, for example, field-by-field interaction with the database, are not possible in HTML. So, to provide that level of interaction you will have to develop applets that maintain a persistent connection to the database. Remember, however, that applications that require significant interaction result in a heavy load on the webserver and network.

- **Flow of control:** Bookmarks can bypass the designed sequence of page access. Does your application need to enforce a certain flow, for example, to authenticate a user before permitting any other actions? You will need to design your application so that bookmarks cannot result in unexpected entry to parts of your application. So, either hide the navigation within the application, or embed checks in every page that ensure the desired flow of control.

- **Verifiability of data:** Can you depend on the data provided by the public through a web interface? The web interface provides highly automated data entry—performed by people who know nothing about your business rules and have no training. You may need tests performed by a representative group of public users. Alternatively, you can plan for extra reviews after the initial release of the software. Don't anticipate savings in staff time until you get over the initial review and enhancement efforts.

- **Training requirements:** You cannot hope to train all the people who will use your web based application. Your application will be available to the entire world as soon as you roll it out. You have little choice about controlled introduction as you would within your company.

- **Concurrent access issues:** Webserver-based applications have to use a messaging style of interaction. So, once a page is delivered, the database cannot keep a memory of its data—it certainly cannot lock the data as it would for a normal client-server application. Instead, this interface implements an optimistic locking approach. This approach assumes that most transactions do not conflict with each other. The few conflicts that do occur can be resolved by rolling back one or the other. Make sure your application conforms to this model of concurrency. A high conflict ratio will just lead to frequent error messages, resulting in frustrated users.

One kind of application suitable for this interface is a query application. Since this does not update any data in the database, there is little opportunity for concurrency conflict. This is the reason why order status inquiry is a good place for Widgets to begin their introduction to the Web. Another good candidate is product query to get more details than a printed catalog can provide. In this application, Widgets plans to track the products queried to understand the distribution of interest in their product line. However, this tracking merely requires inserts into a table without causing a concurrency conflict.

Another kind of application suitable for this interface is a casual data entry application that requires no updates. These applications primarily insert new data and so should lead to few concurrency conflicts. Widgets' order entry is a good candidate, provided that we update stock quantities only after an order is complete.

The right application should be simple to present even if it has a lot of data elements. The interface is then intuitive and easy to follow. Choose your applications carefully.

15.4 Running a Webserver Application

The webserver consists of a listener and several sets of database packages, called the *owa, htp, and htf* utilities. The listener receives an http request, a URL, and translates it into its component parts as follows:

URL*: http://etrans:80/widgets/plsql/ordstat$.startup*

http:, the protocol.

Groupr, the machine identifier.

:9000, the listener port.

Widgets, the Database Access Descriptor (DAD).

Plsql, the PL/SQL cartridge.

Ordstat, the module name.

---

http: the protocol, *hypertext transfer protocol*. If you use a Secure Socket Link (SSL) encrypted link, this phrase will be *https*.

etrans: The *machine identifier* is the name of the machine on which the webserver is running. In an Internet environment, this will be a domain name such as *www.etransitions.com.*

80: The listener port. Normally you use the defaults: 80 for http and 443 for https. If you use default listener ports, you may omit this phrase.

widgets: The *database access descriptor* is simply an Oracle account with the ability to run the webserver packages, the module package, and has access to the application tables. You can have any number of database access descriptors for an application and they can all share a common listener. When you grant table access to the DAD account, just remember that this will be a publicly accessible account.

plsql: The PL/SQL cartridge. There are different cartridges available with Webserver. Earlier releases, such as webserver 2.1, called this cartridge *owa*. The PL/SQL cartridge was the first one available with the earliest release. Also available are Java and, in later releases, C++ cartridges. Each cartridge contains the necessary procedures to process the module code.

ordstat$: The package name, which is really the name of a Designer module. *startup* is a procedure that is part of this package. The Designer generators, by convention, always generate a *startup* procedure for each module.

You should provide a user-friendly way of accessing such a cryptic URL—for example by setting up a visually appealing menu page with links.

15.5 Web Application Concepts

A web application delivers pages consisting of HTML, JavaScript functions and applets to the browser. It may contain literal text, bitmap pictures, fields for input, and other GUI components. The browser downloads one page at a time and displays all of its components. The applets may produce display effects that are not supported by HTML, or perform validation on data typed into the input fields.

The application pages follow a predictable pattern based on the operations to be performed. A query application presents a page for entering the query criteria,

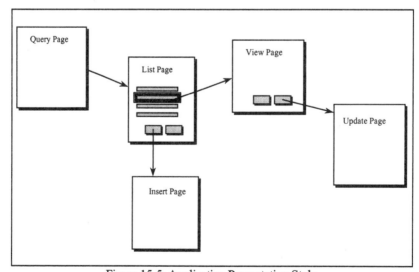

Figure 15-5: Application Presentation Style

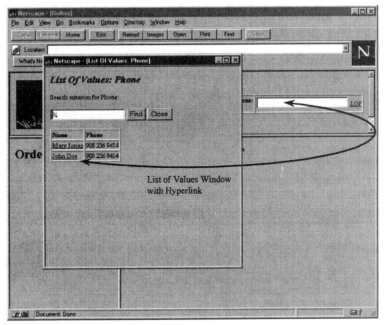

Figure 15-6: LOV page Illustration

followed by a list of the records that meet the criteria. Each record in the list is a link to a page displaying the details in the record. Figure 15-5 illustrates the style of these pages. These displays need not be on separate pages—we can place them all in separate frames on one page. However, we cannot always be sure that the browser supports frames, some of the older versions do not. We will examine how the Designer webserver generator supports this presentation style later.

Applications that only allow inserting need a simpler style—just an entry form page with fields for input. Simple field validation could be performed with some applets in the browser, if it is capable of it. Remember, however, that most validation may only be performed when the user clicks on the *submit* button. Lists based on database data, such as referential integrity checks on foreign key fields, could be through LOV (list of values) pages. Figure 15-6 illustrates an LOV page.

An update operation needs to combine query and insert functionality. In fact, it is common to provide a button on the details page to invoke the update page. Figure 15-7 illustrates the navigation sequence for an update operation highlighted in the page hierarchy.

Choose the components of each page with care. Judicious use of graphics make the page visually appealing, but don't cram it. Each graphic image increases the size of the page and hence lengthens the time for downloading it. Here are some tips for composing a page:

- Keep graphics to a minimum size.

- If you include images, be consistent in their placement on the page.

- Compress any bitmaps. Remember the resolution on the screen is not nearly as good as on a printed page.

- Place all the important context information at the top of the page so that it is the first thing visible to the user. Other information may be placed further down the page and may be accessible by scrolling downwards.

- Use reasonably large font to make reading easier. Small fonts may fit more text on the screen, but they are hard on the eyes.

- Keep text short and to the point. Long discourses should be made available in a downloadable format or on another page via a link.

- Design data field layouts with a small monitor in mind.

- Try displaying the page on a typical small monitor to make sure the important components of the page are included in the displayed window.

15.6 Implementing Security

There are several challenges when considering security in your web-based application. In an earlier chapter we discussed the three A's of security:

- **Authentication**: How do we know that you really are who you claim to be?

- **Access Control**: Once we know you, how do we make sure you are only allowed to do the appropriate tasks?

- **Audit Trail**: Once you perform a task, how do we keep a record of what you did and when?

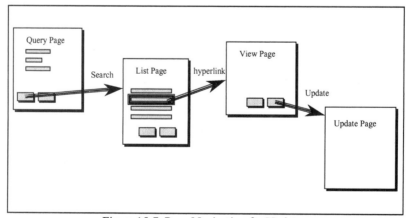

Figure 15-7: Page Navigation for Updates

Lets review some of the issues we mentioned earlier, before we discuss some of the implementation options.

15.6.1 Authentication

Authentication is only needed for applications that require prior authorization, such as those that deal with confidential company data or require a subscription. Most public access applications do not require authentication. You may instead offer registration for the purposes of obtaining contact information without enforcing access restrictions. Registration is also good for remembering *user preferences* or *favorites*, a common hit with the public since it lets them get to the point faster.

If you have an application that requires user-level authentication, you may use the facilities provided by the webserver. Webserver version 3.0 and later offer the ability to authenticate users at three levels of strength: basic authentication (weak), digest authentication (stronger), and database authentication (strongest). The web server manages basic and digest authentication using its own user repository. Digest authentication encrypts the password in the repository and during the login process, but basic authentication does not. In both cases, you would create only one application schema in the database and let webserver manage the authentication.

Database authentication is based on Oracle user accounts. It requires an account for each user who may access the application. The application must grant appropriate database access to the application tables and roles to each user account. This facility offers the strongest authentication because you would use the strong access controls already provided by the database.

In all of these cases, we can only provide one level of access—we cannot control the access from the application. For example, to provide read-only access from sources other than our application and allow the user to update using the application, we cannot use these authentication approaches. The application must implement a custom authentication approach.

In this approach, all users connecting via the web application use one Oracle user account—the one set up as the *database access descriptor*. We do not depend on using Oracle's login and password for authentication. We need to design a user tracking subsystem so that we can track authorized users and the type of access permitted. We need to store the password encrypted or otherwise protected from normal viewing.

For applications where custom authentication is important, make sure you prevent bypassing security through the use of bookmarks for pages beyond the login page. User's can place a browser's bookmark on any page within your application, if the URL is visible. Then, in another session, using this bookmark would access the application without going through a login authentication first.

There are a couple of alternatives for preventing the user from bypassing login: check for the user on every page or hide the navigation. To check the user on every page, we need to remember that the user logged in, say, assign them a session identifier. Then, on every page, we must verify that the user submitting the page did previously log in successfully, within a reasonable timeframe. Normally, we have no reliable means of knowing when a user closes out a session or abandons it.

We also need to carry the context information, such as the session identifier, from one page to another. We can embed such context information in hidden fields. However, these hidden fields are visible through the browser's *view document source* utility. Another method is to bury a cookie in the page containing the hidden information.

An alternative to user verification is to simply hide the navigation, so that placing bookmarks in the middle of the application is not possible. We can use the database to hide navigation information. Remember that every page URL in the webserver is the name of a procedure. So, we could design a navigation table that lets us decide the next page to display to the user. Then, the generated HTML pages could simply reference the navigation procedure for any page navigation.

15.6.2 Data Access Security

Together with user authentication, we may want to control access to data depending on the user's role. This requirement is typical for an application designed for company staff. Applications designed for public access may require fewer restrictions. The only control you may wish to apply may be to protect confidential corporate information. In our Widgets example, we may not want public access to product cost information, just its sales price.

Remember that all users connecting via the web application use one oracle user account—the one set up as the *database access descriptor*. This account should have access to perform all of the actions permitted to any user of the application. So, we really cannot use database controls for data access. However, there are two options for implementing data security: separate the DAD for each role, or build controls within the application.

If we can determine the user roles to be supported by the application, we can set up separate DADs for each role. This approach is practical if we have only a few roles. A large number of roles makes it difficult to administer. We need clearly defined access controls for each role. Designer provides facilities for us to record the access restrictions needed for each group of users. For each application table, we may record whether create, retrieve, update, or delete access is permitted to each group of users. Then each corresponding DAD account can be assigned the role granting the appropriate access.

Application controlled access depends on embedding access restrictions in the procedures that generate or process a page. In this case, we need to develop code that prevents unauthorized access. All of the code that generates or processes pages is in database objects, such as stored procedures, functions, or packages. An alternative is to create database triggers on the tables that prevent unauthorized access.

All such code could be stored in a common project library. Then we could use the application logic facility of Designer to incorporate them into our applications. Since we would need to incorporate calls to access control code in every module, another approach would be to modify the appropriate underlying *wsgl* packages to call it. We only need to modify *wsgl* packages once. Good programming habits can reduce *wsgl* modifications to a few calls to project library procedures.

15.6.3 Data Security

Data over the Internet can potentially be intercepted and misused. So, you need to protect any confidential data that is transmitted between the browser and webserver. Browsers provide a mechanism called *secure socket link*, SSL. This protocol encrypts transmitted data to protect it. You can invoke this from the server end, or from the client, by specifying *https* as the protocol in the URL.

This encryption is based on a certificate issued by a third-party such as Verisign. Most browsers support such certification and require no further installation. Although you may implement your own certification process, you would then have to implement its support in each user's browser—defeating the purpose of easy deployment. Publicly supported certificates do not require any deployment to individual browser installations.

15.7 Webserver Generator

Designer provides a code generator for the Oracle Application Server. This generator uses a library of PL/SQL code, the *wsgl* packages, together with generated module-specific code to provide the interface. The module definitions follow a similar pattern to those for a Forms or Reports module.

There are some important differences, however. Forms programs impose their underlying data-driven user interface model. The user interface of a web application does not have a data driven model. Instead, the interface model is driven by the messaging style of this environment. So, we have a model that is based on interactions: query, record list, view form, insert form, and update form.

For a successful design, you need to use this model to determine the layout and content of each type of form. Before you define a module in the Designer repository, sketch out the contents of each form. Determine the columns you would like to query, columns that ought to appear in the record list, and columns that should be included in the insert or update form.

Your next step is to determine if your design for each form can be satisfied through the module component architecture imposed by Designer. Remember that a module component is a single base table with its associated lookup tables. In Section 15.7.8 Adapting to the Business View, we discuss how to handle cases where a single base table is insufficient.

The appropriate layout for a page depends on a number of factors: the capabilities of the target browser, the target size of display screen, anticipated download speed, and so on. For example, whether you should use frames depends on whether you can mandate a minimum browser capability to support frames. Applications designed for public use may need to target the lowest common capabilities. Intranet applications, on the other hand, may mandate a frames-capable browser. You can create a template for the generator to use with or without frames based on these decisions.

The amount and size of graphics on the page should be tempered with an understanding of the download speeds available to the typical user. When in doubt, test in a realistic environment. Size the fields and images to accommodate the typical screen size of your users.

You need to set standards on the color scheme and font styles to be used by your applications. Remember the characteristics of your audience when making these decisions. Can they easily read the 10-point font that you display on a screen? Is blue on black easier to read than black on pale grey? Is the use of so much red really necessary? Good web developers get advice from graphic artists on these issues. I highly recommend including such skills on your web development team.

15.7.1 Defining a Webserver Module

You can use the module data diagram to build the module definition for the webserver generator. This process is similar to defining a forms or reports module. There are some key differences in the impact of certain properties, however.

The module is made up of module components, each of which is based on a base table. You need to specify the operations allowed by the module on the base table: insert, update, delete, or query. Similarly, you also need to specify the columns to be included for the base table, with their corresponding operations. In addition, you may specify whether a column is to be displayed. Keep in mind that any displayed column with a *query* usage will appear on the query form, a displayed column with an insert usage will appear on the insert form, and so on. A column is only displayed on the *record list* page if you set the *context* usage flag. Columns with the *context* usage set will also appear as header above the detail record on a view page.

Included in the module component are any lookup tables, for which the base table contains foreign key columns. You may specify display or query operations on columns from these tables. Insert, update, and delete operations are not allowed on lookup tables. If you need this ability, we discuss an effective approach in Section 15.7.8 Adapting to the Business View.

Base tables in module components may be related to each other in a hierarchical fashion, for example *customers* to *orders* to *order items*. You can also design navigation hyperlinks between them by setting a preference. The webserver generator will generate navigation links from one to the other, as illustrated in Figure 15-8. The operations specified on the columns of the tables in each component determine the kinds of pages generated, such as query, list, view, and so on. Each module

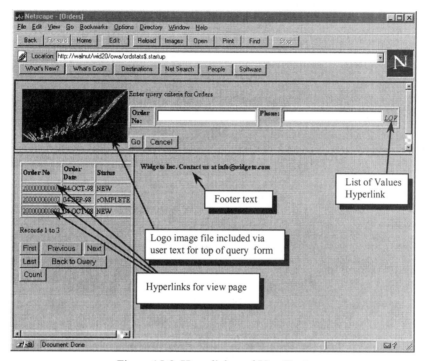

Figure 15-8: Hyperlinks and User Text

component will be on a separate page, unless you set the *placement* property of each module component to *same window*.

The generator may display the record list for a child module component on the view page of the parent provided there is no *query* operation on the child. In this case, a query page is not needed for the child component. If a query page is needed for the child, you will get a hyperlink for the child on the parent's view page. Figure 15-9 illustrates the parent view page with the child's record list placed on one page.

There are many other column properties that you need to specify, other than allowed operations. Some of the key properties include the label for the item on the screen, width, height, display data type, and so on. These are propagated initially from the column properties, but you may change them within the module.

15.7.2 Layout Control

An important point to remember about layout in this environment is that HTML provides limited facilities. Another point is that, ultimately, the browser chooses how to interpret the layout commands. For example, it may wrap fields onto the next line depending on the actual space available in the window at runtime. Interpretations vary

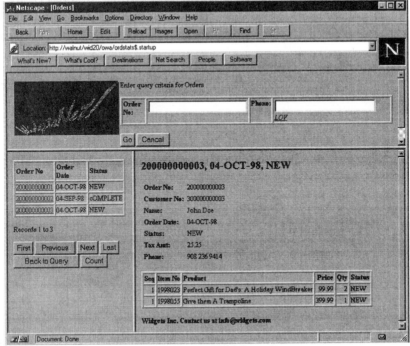

Figure 15-9: Parent-Child Query Layout

quite a bit between different browsers. So, try to restrict your layout expectations to the technology available on your users' desktops.

You can add layout components at various points in a page. For example, you can add standard header and footer text throughout the application as shown in Figure 15-7. You can add text or HTML commands at text control points in each page. There are control points at the top and bottom of each page. For example, we added the Widgets logo image to the top of the query form, aligned left, by adding the following text:

```
htf.img('/ows-img/widlogo.jpg', 'LEFT', 'WidgetsLogo')
```

The first parameter, '/ows-img/widlogo.jpg', specifies the location of the image file relative to the configured directory in the web listener. Remember that the image file must be accessible to the webserver at runtime. Pay particular attention that references like this are configured in your production webserver instance prior to rollout. Also, make sure that image files are copied to the appropriate directory as part of your software release, especially if the webserver and Oracle database are set up on separate machines.

```
<HTML>
<FRAMESET ROWS = "20%, *">
  <FRAME NAME=HDR1">
  <FRAMESET COLS="30%,*">
    <FRAME NAME="LST2">
    <FRAME NAME="DET3">
  </FRAMESET>
</FRAMESET>
</HTML>
```

Figure 15-10: Template for 3 Frames

You can define frames for page layout in a template. The frame layout is specified using HTML commands. So, you can use your favorite page layout tool to design the frames. Figure 15-10 illustrates the frames used for the Widgets order status inquiry program. You specify the name of the template file in a preference. Each kind of form can be mapped into a frame by specifying the frame name, such as HDR1 or LST2, in the appropriate preference. There are preferences for mapping a query, record list, view form, insert form, and so on.

The generator also provides preferences to control the style of each kind of page. These are specified as a template containing HTML *style* commands. You may name a style template for each appropriate kind of form, that is, query, list, view, and so on. These styles control the colors and fonts used in that page, and override the choices configured by the user on their browser.

15.7.3 Generated Web Server Code

The webserver generator produces PL/SQL code in packages that may be installed on the database access descriptor account. The webserver translates a URL into the specific package and procedure that service the URL. When executed, these procedures produce HTML code together with Java applets that are passed to the requesting browser.

The generated module initial procedure is typically called the *ModuleName$.startup*. This procedure then calls other modules to produce the HTML code for the first page. The generated code contains many levels of PL/SQL:

Table API

Module Component API

Module code

Application logic code defined at each of the above levels.

These are conceptually hierarchically organized, although the lower-level table API is shared between modules. Module component API for reusable modules is also shared between modules incorporating the reusable module component.

15.7.4 Table API

For each table, the API is a PL/SQL package containing procedures that perform CRUD operations. As a minimum, the API package contains *ins, upd, slct,* and *del* procedures. In addition, there are procedures for additional processing:

- To validate any allowable values on columns in that table.

- To validate any *arc* processing.

- To process any denormalizations.

All processing is based on definitions in the repository. These API procedures provide an ideal place to incorporate code that helps prevent the violation of business rules. Table API procedures are called from the code generated at the module component or module level.

The generator also produces trigger code for *before* and *after* events on each table. These events are anchors for your custom code. For example, you can associate custom code at the beginning of a *before insert row* event. This code will be incorporated into the trigger associated with *before insert row*. There are anchors for each combination of *before* and *after* events at the *statement* and *row* level.

15.7.5 Module Component API

One package, typically called *ModuleName$ComponentName,* is generated for each module component as part of the module code. This package contains code to perform each action possible in that component. Some of the procedures in the module component package *ordstats$order* in *order inquiry* are shown in Table 15-1.

This is not an exhaustive list. The actual procedures generated depend on the actions

Name	Description
ActionQuery	Code to process the query form user input
FormQuery	Code to produce HTML for the query form
QueryHits	Code to count the number of rows in the result of the query
FormView	Code to produce the HTML for viewing fields in the module component
QueryList	Code to produce the HTML for the record list resulting from executing the query
Cust_no_listofvalues	Code to process the list of values on the customer number field

Table 15-1: Procedures in a module component package

possible in the module component. The package may also contain code to create JavaScript applets that perform a particular task, such as display alerts.

Module components also provide event-based anchors to associate custom code. For example, you can associate custom code to be executed *before query* or *after query*.

15.7.6 Module Code

The module code is a package typically called *ModuleName$*. It contains code for the *startup* procedure where the URL request begins. It also includes the *about* page processing and header processing code. The startup procedure calls the module component startup to initiate the building of the HTML page. The rest of the work of composing the HTML page is performed by the module component code.

15.7.7 Customizing Generated Code

The generator provides several control points (events) where you can specify custom code. You can choose whether the code is executed on the client side or server side by selecting an appropriate event. Events are organized hierarchically based on the element hierarchy in the Designer repository. For example, events are defined at the item level, the table level, the module component level, and the module level.

Item-level events, such as *OnClick* and *OnBlur*, are client-side events supported by JavaScript. You may specify JavaScript code on such events. Events may also be defined at the table or module component level. These events provide control before and after a database access. For example, prequery and postquery events allow you to specify custom code executed before and after the retrieval of a row for display. Server-side events must be written in PL/SQL up to Oracle version 8. Oracle8i supports Java for server-side events.

15.7.8 Adapting to the Business View

The data presented by a module component is typically displayed one table at a time, including any descriptors related via foreign keys. This may not be appropriate to your users' needs for the tasks they must perform. For example, at Widgets, a majority of the queries to customer service ask for the status of a particular item in an order. Customer service representatives would find it easier if they could query based on an item within an order, but obtain a display of the order and other items included in that order. The customer may not know the order number, so our query must be based on the phone number and item number. These columns are not in directly-related tables.

In order to meet such needs, you can base a module component on a view which contains appropriate columns. We would then need to create custom API for this module component that supports the module-level calls. We also need to map any data manipulation actions from this module component to the appropriate underlying tables. For example, the module component code may make a call to a non-existent *ins* procedure in the package for the view. We can manually write such API procedures to process the call and apply the appropriate action to the tables underlying the view. This process is similar to the Oracle8 *instead of* triggers.

This manually written API is also an appropriate place to enforce business rules. If we implement business rules as database server-based procedures and functions, calling them from PL/SQL code is simple. Remember that some business rules need to be implemented at the trigger level and should be incorporated as application logic for the table API.

Designing views to meet business needs is not a trivial task. Defining the business interaction as well as the system responses is invaluable in determining the appropriate views.

There is a significant advantage to using view-based definition. Once defined, we can separate user interface development from business logic coding. User interface development may proceed through Designer. Business logic coding consists of procedures that translate the insert, update, and delete API calls to the underlying table API calls. You can also incorporate calls to business rules procedures as part of this translation. Developers who develop this need traditional programming skills—in coding PL/SQL; they need know nothing about Designer.

15.8 Development and Rollout Issues

A significant requirement for a web-based application is the service level. If your application serves the public, it must be available round the clock—not only because an individual user may access it any hour of day or night, but that user may be located anywhere in the world, literally! At the very least, it must be available 20 hours each day for coverage in a large continent like North America. Design your application to minimize downtime. You may also need to boost your operations to provide this level of service.

This interface provides us with a powerful concept: a common environment for users inside and outside a company. Here are some advantages of the web environment:

- The common use of browser software means that many computer-aware users already have training in its use. Thus, we should need less training in the interface. Of course, we will still have to train them to understand the business rules implemented in the software, which should be more meaningful for the in-house users anyway.

- The interface software, the browser and HTML, are common on desktop systems. They are on par with word processors or spreadsheets in their widespread use. So, assistance with navigation and problems become the domain of desktop software support. Thus, we reduce our application support load.

- The browser software has a small footprint compared to typical client forms tools like Oracle Forms, Powerbuilder, or SQL*Windows. So, we don't need souped-up PCs on the desktop.

- In a webserver environment, the code is mostly objects in the database together with a few HTML pages. So, code control issues are similar to those for procedural code. We do not need to control binary files as well as source files.

- Since all of the code lives in the database, distribution is much simpler than in a client-server environment. We simply install the code in the production database to make it available worldwide. We do have to make the database unavailable during installation. Thus, we have the ease of software distribution possible in the traditional mainframe environment. Note that with Oracle8 replication features, we could even distribute code on auto-pilot by replicating the code.

There are a few downsides to this scenario. The largest impact by far is the fast-paced change in technology. Expect this technology to change radically every six to eight months. Even if you plan to stay one generation behind, rather than at the bleeding edge, you will need to make one or two releases each year. The pace of change means that your staff are constantly on a learning curve. So, adjust your project estimates accordingly. Foster a learning organization if only because you cannot afford the expense of deadwood.

We have already discussed the difficulties of establishing user and access security. Browsers and webservers are implementing many facilities to simplify the challenges of implementing security. Plan your projects to take advantage of these new developments as they are implemented.

The Internet environment is unpredictable. There are no volumes or statistics available to help you size the hardware needed for your application. The best approach is to monitor continuously to determine the accesses (hits) on the site and the load you need to handle.

CASE Study: Order Status Inquiry

Our plan for deploying to the web called for a two-phase development effort. In the first phase, we would simply provide an order status inquiry application. This would be publicly accessible. Throughout the chapter, we illustrated various parts of this program. In the actual public version, there were a couple of changes.

An important change was that the phone number criteria for the query form was inappropriate. Considering its public access, this would constitute a privacy violation, especially if it displayed the name and billing or shipping address of the customer. It would be even worse if we provided an LOV on the phone. However, for internal use by customer service representatives, we needed this query criteria. So, we decided to provide two separate query programs: one for public use and one for internal use.

Designer provides module copy facilities for just such situations. We copied the *internal use* inquiry module and modified it for the *public use* module. Expect such proliferation of the number of modules during design and implementation in this fashion.

The public use module provides two query criteria: order number and customer number. There are no LOVs. The business rule was: *if you cannot remember your order number or your customer number, you should call a Widgets customer service representative.* Another approach to the privacy problem would be to require customers to first register to obtain a personal identification number (PIN). Then, the application could authenticate the user prior to displaying confidential information. This is a common approach, implemented by many companies with a good web presence.

Rather than illustrate pages of PL/SQL code resulting from the generator, here are just the specifications of the procedures generated. Of course the code varies between versions of the generator, but the concepts in this chapter apply overall.

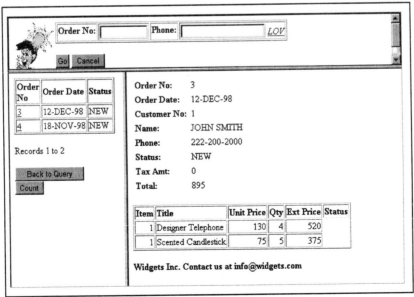

Figure 15-11: Order Status Inquiry

```
-- Package specification for Order Status Inquiry
PROMPT
PROMPT Package ordstats$...
SET SCAN OFF
create or replace package ordstats$ is
   procedure Startup;
   procedure FirstPage(Z_DIRECT_CALL in boolean);
   procedure ShowAbout;
   procedure TemplateHeader(Z_DIRECT_CALL in boolean,
                            Z_TEMPLATE_ID in number);
end;
PROMPT
PROMPT Package ordstats$worders...
SET SCAN OFF
create or replace package ordstats$worders is
   procedure Startup(
            Z_DIRECT_CALL in boolean default false,
            Z_CHK in varchar2 default null);
   procedure ActionQuery(
            P_ORD_NO in varchar2 default null,
            P_L_CUST_PHONE in varchar2 default null,
             Z_DIRECT_CALL in boolean default false,
            Z_ACTION in varchar2 default null,
            Z_CHK in varchar2 default null);
   procedure TextFrame(Z_HEADER in varchar2 default null,
                       Z_FIRST  in varchar2 default null,
                       Z_TEXT   in varchar2 default null,
                       Z_FOOTER in varchar2 default null);
   procedure FormQuery(Z_DIRECT_CALL in boolean default false,
            Z_CHK in varchar2 default null);
   procedure QueryView(
            P_ORD_NO in varchar2 default null,
            Z_POST_DML in boolean default false,
```

```
                Z_FORM_STATUS in number default WSGL.FORM_STATUS_OK,
              Z_DIRECT_CALL in boolean default false,
              Z_CHK in varchar2 default null);
procedure QueryList(
              P_ORD_NO in varchar2 default null,
              P_L_CUST_PHONE in varchar2 default null,
              Z_START in varchar2 default null,
              Z_ACTION in varchar2 default null,
              Z_DIRECT_CALL in boolean default false,
              Z_CHK in varchar2 default null);
   procedure QueryFirst(
              P_ORD_NO in varchar2 default null,
              P_L_CUST_PHONE in varchar2 default null,
              Z_ACTION in varchar2 default null,
              Z_DIRECT_CALL in boolean default false,
              Z_CHK in varchar2 default null);
   function QueryHits(
             P_ORD_NO in varchar2 default null,
             P_L_CUST_PHONE in varchar2 default null) return
number;
   procedure l_cust_phone_listofvalues(
              Z_FILTER in varchar2,
              Z_MODE in varchar2,
              Z_CALLER_URL in varchar2,
              Z_ISSUE_WAIT in varchar2 default null);
end;
PROMPT
PROMPT Package ordstats$items...


SET SCAN OFF
create or replace package ordstats$items is
   procedure Startup(
              P_ORD_NO in varchar2,
              Z_DIRECT_CALL in boolean default false,
              Z_CHK in varchar2 default null);
```

```
    procedure QueryList(
            P_ORD_NO in varchar2 default null,

            Z_START in varchar2 default null,

            Z_ACTION in varchar2 default null,

            Z_DIRECT_CALL in boolean default false,

            Z_CHK in varchar2 default null);

    function QueryHits(
            P_ORD_NO in varchar2 default null) return number;

end;
```

Appendix: Recommended Standards

When using Oracle products, setting some standards and conventions in your organization will save you a lot of headache. There are many significant benefits of standards:

- New staff can come up to speed quickly since they won't need explanation of every nitty-gritty detail.

- Improved communication via the use of well-defined terminology. When you say pick-list, another person will not visualize a pop-up window if your standards do not define it to be so.

- Better use of CASE tools—they are only as good as your use of them. If you use cryptic naming with no explanations, your staff will have difficulty no matter how good the CASE tool is.

Naming Conventions

Object	Convention
Entity	The name used most commonly in business, singular noun. Use synonyms to relate all other business names.Define alias as a two- or three-character string so that foreign key column names derived by CASE*Dictionary will be short but still indicate the source entity.
Attribute	The name used most commonly in business.
Function Label	Abbreviations of the function represented while you are developing the function hierarchy. In the earlier edition of this book, I suggested hierarchical labeling such as 1.1, 1.2, 1.2.1. Hierarchical labeling a good once your functional model is stable. Otherwise, you may spend unnecessary amounts of time relabeling whenever you reorganize the hierarchy.
Function	The name most representative of the activity. Use active verbs such as **Accept, Distribute, Ship,** etc. Keep function descriptions short — typically less than 10 words. Avoid ambiguous names such as **process**.

Object	Convention
Process Label	Same as Function label.
Process	Same as Function.
Data Store Label	Sequential numbering prefixed with the letter D. Sequence is top to bottom, left to right starting from the top-level data flow diagram, for example, **D1, D2, D3,** etc.
Data Store	Use the name most representative of the data in the store, a business term where possible, for example, **Product Stock, Customer List,** etc.
Data Flow Name	Representative of the data in the flow. Use the business name where possible, for example, **Customer Order, Return Authorization,** etc. Keep it short — typically less than five words.
Module Name	Noun form of the function or process represented. For example, **accept customer order** process becomes **Order_Entry** module. Keep module names short, as they may become file names for forms, reports, PRO* programs, etc.
Application Name	Representative of a logical group of activities—typically performed by one department or user group within a department.
Table Name	Same name as the entity it represents, except use plural, for example, **Products** as the table representing the entity **Product**.When denormalizing two or more entities into a single table, use each of their names separated by an underscore.
Column Name	Same name as the attribute it represents, prefixed by a two- or three-character prefix. The prefix allows you to easily identify which table the column belongs in.Where a foreign key column name is derived from the relationship, Oracle Designer uses the entity alias in the derived column name.
Database File Name	dbs<SID>.ora in V7 and V8, dbs<SID>.dbf in V6, dbs<SID>.dbs in V5. Keep the filename to a maximum of eight characters and file extension to three characters for portability. Add a sequence number for each additional file.
Redo Log File Name	log<SID><nn>.log. nn is a number indicating the sequence of the file within the set of Redo Log files. Same rules as Database File Name for portability.
Before Image File	In V5 only, bi<SID>.dbs. Same rules as Database File Name

Object	Convention
Name	for portability.
Control File Name	In V6 only, cntrl<SID><nn>.dbf, where nn indicates the copy of the control file. Thus, when you have 3 copies of the control file, the file names will have 1, 2, and 3 as the values for nn. Same rules as Database File Name for portability.
Init Parameter File Name	init<SID>.ora in both V5 and V6. Same rules as Database File Name for portability.

Bibliography

Abbey and Corey, **Oracle8: A Beginner's Guide**, Oracle Press. This newly updated version of the Beginners Guide offers an excellent introduction to the database and its critical products.

Abbey, Abramson, Corey and Taub, **Oracle8 Data Warehousing,** Oracle Press. A step-by-step tactical guide that addresses the full scope of Oracle8's data warehousing capabilities.

Anderson and Wendelken, **Oracle Designer/2000 Handbook,** Addison-Wesley Publishing. This book has information about the repository API that you will find nowhere else, written in a style that actually makes the book enjoyable to read.

Anstey, David A., **High Performance Oracle8 Object-Oriented Design,** Written by a data modeler for data modelers, this book explores in-depth the object/relational model.

Aronoff, Loney, and Sonawalla, **Oracle8 Advanced Tuning and Administration**, These 3 authors collectively are the most knowledgeable people I know on the subject of tuning. Oracle Press.

Barker, Richard, **CASE*Method-Entity Relationship Modelling,** Addison-Wesley Publishing. The definitive guide to Oracle's conventions for entity relationship.

Billings and Tower, **Rapid Application Development with Oracle Designer/2000: A Workshop Approach,** Addison-Wesley Publishing. This book is a detailed self-paced tutorial on not only learning the concepts of application development, but also on the intricacies of using the tool itself.

Bisland, Ralph B. Jr., **Database Management Developing Application Systems Using Oracle**, Englewood Cliffs, NJ: Prentice Hall, 1989. An academic approach to learning relational database theory and practice with examples based on Oracle tools. The extensive coverage of SQL for novices is one of the best I have seen. Although this book refers to UFI, the Oracle Version 4 precursor to SQL*Plus, all of these facilities still exist.

Blaha, Michael and Premerlani, William, **Object-Oriented Modeling and Design for Database Applications,** Prentice Hall. This book is a follow-on to the authors' highly successful work - Object-Oriented Modeling and Design. It extends the work they have done on OMT (**Object Modeling Technique**) to actual use with real database applications.

Booch, Grady, **Object-Oriented Analysis and Design with Applications**, 2nd Edition, Addison-Wesley. In this new edition, improved methods for object development and a new unified notation are introduced. Booch discusses essential concepts, explains the method and shows successful applications in a variety of fields.

Booch, Grady, **Object Solutions: Managing the Object-Oriented Project**, Addison-Wesley. Booch draws on his many years of OO software engineering and explains how to apply OO technology to systems development. His pragmatic advice reinforces with rules of thumb and recommended practices.

British Computer Society, **The Computer Journal: Special Issue Databases**, Vol. 31, No. 2 (April 1988). Research papers on database languages, expert systems, and object-oriented and distributed databases.

Burleson, Don, **High-Performance Oracle Data Warehousing,** Coriolis. Complete life cycle of a data warehouse project from selecting the team through final cutover.

Celko, Joe, **Joe Celko's SQL for Smarties,** Morgan Kaufmann Publishers. In this easy to read book, you may find solutions for your practical SQL application problems.

Chen, P. P., **The Entity-Relationship Model: Toward a Unified View of Data**, ACM Transactions on Database Systems, 1976.

Codd, E. F., **A Relational Model of Data for Large Shared Data Banks**, CACM 13, No. 6 (June 1970). Reprinted in CACM 26, No. 1 (January 1983). The first proposed ideas of the relational model.

Codd, E. F., **Extending the Relational Database Model to Capture More Meaning**, ACM Transactions on Database Systems, December 1979. Extended relational model called RM/T.

Codd, E. F., **Relational Database: A Practical Foundation for Productivity**, CACM 25, No. 2 (February 1982). Paper presented by Codd on the occasion of his receiving the 1981 ACM Turing Award.

Cronin, Daniel J., **Mastering Oracle**. Indianapolis, IN: Hayden Books, 1989. Good coverage of the development process after the analysis is complete. This book is a little light on Oracle's CASE products and their use in real life. It has extensive coverage of the programming tools, SQL*Plus, SQL*Forms, and SQL*Report Writer with worked examples. Its tutorial style makes it difficult to locate specific coding examples.

Date, C. J., **An Introduction to Database Systems**, Vol. II, Reading, MA: Addison-Wesley, 1984. Advanced topics in database theory; very heavy reading for professionals.

Date, C. J., **A Guide to DB2 Reading**, MA: Addison-Wesley, 1985. Good coverage of IBM's DB2 product.

Dodge and Gorman, **Oracle8 Data Warehousing,** John Wiley & Sons. A solid resource for anyone planning an Oracle data warehouse.

Fowler, Martin, **Analysis Patterns: Reusable Object Models**, Addison-Wesley. This book provides a catalogue of patterns in a wide variety of domains such as trading, measurement, accounting and organizational relationships.

Fowler and Scott, **UML Distilled**, Addison-Wesley. Various modeling techniques associated with UML are profiled: use cases, CRC cards, design By contract, dynamic classification, interfaces and abstract classes.

Fowler and Stanwick, **The GUI Style Guide**, AP Professional. The books that reaches beyond the "what" of GUI design to get to the "why."

Gane, Chris, **Computer Aided Software Engineering: The Methodologies, the Products, the Future. New York**: Rapid Systems Development 1988

Gane, Chris, and Trish Sarson, **Structured Systems Analysis: Tools & Techniques** (Improved System Technologies, 1980). Saint Louis: McDonnell-Douglas Corporation, 1981–1985.

Graziano, Silverstein and Inmon, **The Data Model Resource Book**, John Wiley. This book provides a set of standard data models that can quickly be adapted to any development project.

Hay, David C., **Data Model Patterns: Conventions of Thought,** Dorset House. Dave is a master of entity modeling and brings the benefit of years of experience and insight in the form of generic models.

Hickman & Longman, **CASE*Method-Business Interviewing,** Addison-Wesley Publishing. A key component to any software development project is the extraction of business functional requirements from the user community.

Hobuss, James J., **Building Oracle Web Sites,** Prentice Hall, CD-ROM. This is the first book to discuss building websites using Oracle8 as the data repository. It serves as a complete introduction to both the Web and Oracle.

Inmon W. H., **Building the Data Warehouse**, 2nd Edition, John Wiley & Sons. The book that started the data warehouse buzzword.

Inmon, W. H., **Oracle Building High Performance On-Line Systems**. QED Information Sciences, 1989.

ISO-ANSI, Working Draft of Database Language SQL2, June 1988.

Kent, W., **A Simple Guide to Five Normal Forms in Relational Database Theory**, CACM 26, No. 2 (February 1983).

Kimball, Ralph, **The Data Warehouse Toolkit,** John Wiley & Sons. Using many real-life case studies, Ralph Kimball provides clear-cut guidelines on how to model data and design warehouses to support multi-dimensional decision support systems.

Loney, Kevin, **Oracle8 DBA Handbook,** This newly revised edition is the standard for DBAs. Oracle Press.

Lulushi, Albert, **Developing Oracle Forms Applications**, Prentice Hall. This is an excellent book, by a working developer.Lulushi, Albert, **Inside Oracle Designer/2000**, Prentice Hall. This book is for release 2.0! The CD-ROM has a number of application systems that can be loaded into Designer/2000 as well as a number of Screen-Cam movies to illustrate various components of the software.

Martin, James, **Recommended Diagramming Standards for Analysts and Programmers: A Basis for Automation**. Englewood Cliffs, NJ: Prentice Hall, 1987.

Microsoft Corporation, **The Windows Interface Guidelines for Software Design**, Microsoft Corporation. If you need a reference book that answers the questions of what Microsoft recommends, then this is the book for you.

ODTUG Conference Proceedings. Papers in these proceedings are an excellent source of expert advice.

O'Neil, Schrader, Dakin et al.,, **Oracle Data Warehousing Unleashed,** SAMS Publishing. Expert authors share their stories of implementations demonstrate the potential pitfalls and traps.

Rodgers, Ulka, **UNIX Database Management Systems**. Englewood Cliffs, NJ: Prentice Hall, 1990.

Ross, Ronald G., **The Business Rule Book, 2nd Edition**, Database Research Group, Inc. This book introduces the **Ross Method**—a graphic technique for expressing business rules and practices in a rigorous fashion. A little tedious at times, but great as a reference.

Sobell, Mark G., **A Practical Guide to UNIX System V**. Benjamin/Cummings, 1985.

Stonebreaker and Moore, **Object-Relational DBMSs the Next Great Wave**, 2nd Edition, Morgan Kaufmann Publishers. The author and founder of the object-relational DBMS Illustra, discusses why O-RDBMSs will become the dominant database technology of the future.

Yazdani and Wong, **Data Warehousing with Oracle, an Administrator's Handbook,** Prentice Hall. The authors completed several large-scale data warehouse projects with Oracle 7.3 and share their experience here.

Yourdon, Edward, **Modern Structured Analysis**, Englewood Cliffs, NJ: Prentice Hall, 1989. The authoritative book on Yourdon's structured methodology; includes additional material on real-time systems, prototyping, and data modeling which did not exist the older publications such as the Gane and Sarson book.

Index